Crafting a Collection

The Cultural Contexts and
Poetic Practice of the *Huajian ji* 花間集
(Collection from Among the Flowers)

Harvard East Asian Monographs 263

Crafting a Collection

The Cultural Contexts and
Poetic Practice of the *Huajian ji* 花間集
(Collection from Among the Flowers)

Anna M. Shields

Published by the Harvard University Asia Center
Distributed by Harvard University Press
Cambridge, Massachusetts, and London 2006

© 2006 by the President and Fellows of Harvard College

Printed in the United States of America

The Harvard University Asia Center publishes a monograph series and, in coordination with the Fairbank Center for East Asian Research, the Korea Institute, the Reischauer Institute of Japanese Studies, and other faculties and institutes, administers research projects designed to further scholarly understanding of China, Japan, Vietnam, Korea, and other Asian countries. The Center also sponsors projects addressing multidisciplinary and regional issues in Asia.

Library of Congress Cataloging-in-Publication Data

Shields, Anna M., 1966–

    Crafting a collection : the cultural contexts and poetic practice of the Huajian ji : collection from among the flowers / Anna M. Shields.

        p. cm. – (Harvard East Asian monographs ; 263)

    Includes bibliographical references and index.

    ISBN 0-674-02142-8 (cl : alk. paper)

    1. Ci (Chinese poetry)--History and criticism. 2. Chinese poetry--Tang dynasty, 618-907--History and criticism. 3. Chinese poetry--Five dynasties and the Ten kingdoms, 907-979--History and criticism. I. Title: Cultural contexts and poetic practice of the Huajian ji : collection from among the flowers. II. Hua jian ji. III. Title. IV. Series.

    PL2341.S56 2006

    895.1'1308--dc22

2006000334

Index by Jake Kawatski

∞ Printed on acid-free paper

Last figure below indicates year of this printing
16 15 14 13 12 11 10 09 08 07 06

To my parents

Nicholas L. Shields, Jr., and

Johanna Nicol Shields

Acknowledgments

The making of this book stretches back more than a decade, reaches across many states and a few continents, and owes much to other people. Throughout the research and writing, I have been fortunate enough to be sustained by advisors, fellow scholars, institutions, and good friends. At Harvard University, where I studied Chinese poetry with Professor Stephen Owen, I found a tireless mentor who has helped me often in the years since I left Cambridge. My debt to him is huge, and I am happy to acknowledge it here. At Indiana University, where I completed my doctoral degree with Professor Stephen R. Bokenkamp, I found yet another extraordinary mentor. He used his own broad learning to widen my perspective on medieval China; his intellectual interests enriched mine, and his unflagging support kept me on course through the years. I thank him for these things and much more. I have often said that I had the best dissertation committee one could possibly imagine, and it is true. The work that Professors Bokenkamp, Peter Lindenbaum, Lynn Struve, and Yingjin Zhang committed to the dissertation made its transformation to a book conceivable, and I thank them once again for their critical readings and encouragement. I would also like to thank Professor Robert Eno of Indiana University, whose scholarly rigor and patience were important models for me.

In the several years I spent teaching at different universities, I learned a great deal from colleagues who read chapters, listened to presentations, and gave me comments that influenced this work. While at the University of Maryland, I benefited from discussions with traditional China scholars; Jonathan Chaves, Philip Kafalas, Tobie Meyer-Fong, and Stuart Sargent were especially helpful. From my year spent as a visiting professor at the University of Michigan, I wish to thank William Baxter, Shuen-fu Lin, Donald R. Lopez, Jr., David Rolston, and Robert Sharf for their advice and comments. At the University of Arizona, I have been lucky to have colleagues willing to exchange chapters and ideas; I would like to thank Todd Brown, Noel Pinnington, and my former colleague Roel Sterckx, now at Cambridge University, for their intellectual companionship and their responses to a version of Chapter 1.

An earlier version of Chapter 3 appeared as "Gathering the 'Flowers' of Poetry and Song: Anthologies in Tang and Shu," in *T'ang Studies* 15–16 (1997–1998), and I thank *T'ang Studies* for permission to republish the material in its present form. When the book manuscript was completed, two scholars paid me the great favor of reading all of it: I am grateful to Daniel Bryant and Paul W. Kroll for their careful work on my behalf. Many thanks also to Michael A. Fuller, who read both the dissertation and the later book chapters and gave me precise, helpful suggestions. Anthony DeBlasi, Franciscus Verellen, and Sophie Volpp also read and commented on individual chapters, and I appreciate their timely comments. I would also like to acknowledge the funding from the Provost's Author Support Fund at the University of Arizona for assistance in completing the index for the book. Finally, I am very grateful to the two readers for the Harvard University Asia Center, who offered suggestions and corrections on a wide range of issues in the book and improved it enormously. The errors and infelicities that remain are of course mine.

Closer to home, I am glad that my boys—Tommy, Michael, and Jack Hegarty—were able to put up with their mother's late nights at the office and her occasional preoccupation with things other than themselves. And I thank my husband, Stephen Hegarty, a *zhiyin* 知音 in every sense. The evenings we have spent listening to songs and talking about what and how they mean shaped this book in many ways; his support and love made the whole thing possible. Finally, I dedicate this book to my parents, in gratitude: to my father, Nicholas L. Shields, Jr., who let me keep my nose in a book and taught me never to be afraid of hard work; and to my mother, Johanna Nicol Shields, who all her life has shown me the struggles and rewards of being a wife, mother, and scholar. I owe them more than I can say.

A.M.S.

Contents

Tables xiii

Abbreviations xv

Introduction 1

Part I Cultural Contexts

1 A Matter of Taste: Tang Culture and Song Lyrics (*quzi ci*) 17

2 Poets in their Place: Court and Culture in Tenth-Century Shu 66

3 Gathering the "Flowers" of Poetry and Song: Anthologies in Tang and Shu 119

Part II Poetic Practice

4 From Imitation to Innovation: The Poetic Craft of the *Huajian ji* 161

5 Gender in the *Huajian ji* Song Lyrics: Style, Subject, and Voice 220

6 Divine Beauties: Apparitions of
   "Goddesses" in the *Huajian ji* 278

Conclusion 345

Reference Matter

Bibliography 365

Index 381

Tables

1	*Huajian ji* poets from the Former or Latter Shu	108
2	Titles given to all 18 poets in the *Huajian ji* and their Tang ranks, if known	113
3	*Huajian ji* poets with lyrics to "Pusa man"	187
4	*Huajian ji* poets with lyrics to "Jiu quanzi"	231
5	*Huajian ji* poets with lyrics to "Huanxi sha"	244
6	*Huajian ji* poets with lyrics to "Lin jiang xian"	295
7	*Huajian ji* poets with lyrics to "Nü guanzi"	317

Abbreviations

Unless otherwise noted, the edition of the *Huajian ji* used throughout the text is Li Yi, ed., *Huajian ji zhushi* (Chengdu: Sichuan wenyi chubanshe, 1986).

HJJZS	*Huajian ji zhushi* 花間集注釋
JTS	*Jiu Tang shu* 舊唐書
QTS	*Quan Tang shi* 全唐詩
QTW	*Quan Tang wen* 全唐文
QTWDC	*Quan Tang Wudai ci* 全唐五代詞
QTWDCSZ	*Quan Tang Wudai ci shizhu* 全唐五代詞釋注
SGCQ	*Shiguo chunqiu* 十國春秋
WX	*Wen xuan* 文選
XTS	*Xin Tang shu* 新唐書
ZZTJ	*Zizhi tongjian* 資治通鑒

Crafting a Collection

The Cultural Contexts and
Poetic Practice of the *Huajian ji* 花間集
(Collection from Among the Flowers)

Introduction

In the year 940, at the court of the kingdom of Shu, a group of literati compiled an anthology of song lyrics written by ninth- and tenth-century poets. One Shu poet who was included in the anthology, Ouyang Jiong 歐陽炯 (896–971), was asked to compose a preface and to give a title to the collection: he entitled the work *Huajian ji* 花間集 (The collection from among the flowers). The *Huajian ji* is the earliest extant collection of song lyrics—which Ouyang calls *quzi ci* 曲子詞, lyrics to tunes—by literati poets, and by the standards of poetry collections of the Tang dynasty, it was also quite large, containing 500 lyrics by eighteen poets, most of whom had lived in Shu. In the history of the genre that came to be called *ci* 詞, or simply "lyrics," the *Huajian ji* has long been regarded as the founding collection. In his preface to the *Huajian ji*, Ouyang Jiong explicitly praised the elegance of the Shu court and its courtiers, and suggested that a courtly setting was the perfect climate for the composition and performance of song lyrics, a claim no poet before him had made. The song lyrics of the collection had been composed to popular melodies from the entertainment world of the ninth and tenth centuries. But unlike literati or popular lyrics that are extant in other texts before the *Huajian ji*, the *Huajian ji* song lyrics take romantic love as their sole, all-absorbing topic. The Shu taste for romantic song is thus reflected in the collection's title: the "flowers" in the title point not only to the real flowers of spring so common in the scenes of the song lyrics but also to the beautiful women whose faces and voices appear throughout the collection.

One of Ouyang Jiong's lyrics captures well the style and sensibility of the work as a whole.

To the tune "He ming chao" 賀明朝
(Congratulating the enlightened court)
Ouyang Jiong

I remember that after we saw each other among the flowers,	憶昔花間相見後
I could only toss him with my fragile hand	只憑纖手
a red bean love-token.	暗拋紅豆
In front of others I couldn't find a way	人前不解
to artfully tell the things in my heart—	巧傳心事
how since we've parted, it's been the same—	別來依舊
spurned forever one spring morning.	辜負春晝
On my deep blue gauze robes, dense gilt stitching—	碧羅衣上蹙金繡
I gaze at pair on pair of mandarin ducks-and-drakes	睹對對鴛鴦
pointlessly soaked and stained by traces of tears.	空悒淚痕透
I imagine my lovely complexion won't last for long.	想韶顏非久
For him, in the end,	終是爲伊
I can only waste away in secret.[1]	只憑偷瘦

Ouyang Jiong's phrase "among the flowers" occurs in both of his lyrics to the tune "He ming chao" in the *Huajian ji* and likely inspired the title. This lyric explores ideas we find throughout the collection. By revealing his female speaker's weeping over the loss of her own beauty, Ouyang Jiong frames and comments on her desirability; although the speaker laments her inability to "artfully tell," *qiao chuan* 巧傳, her own love, the poet communicates her feelings clearly to the listeners and readers of the song lyrics. This

---

1. *HJJZS*, 221.

exploitation of the ironies of performed literature—the tension between the perceptions of the speaker and those of the listening and reading audience—is but one example of the sophisticated literary craft that the *Huajian ji* writers brought to the composition of song lyrics. In his preface, Ouyang Jiong boasts of the talents of the Shu court poets who followed certain Tang predecessors in composing song lyrics, and he suggests that the skillful use of "artifice," *qiao* 巧, was their trademark; in their intense focus on beauty and the artful expression of feeling, the song lyrics of the *Huajian ji* substantiate his claims.

In this book, I explore the cultural contexts of the compilation of the *Huajian ji* and the poetics of its song lyrics, and I argue that the two are tightly linked. The *Huajian ji* has traditionally been studied as the precursor to the lyrics of the Song dynasty or in terms of what it contributed to the later formal and stylistic development of the genre. In the eyes of readers of the Ming and Qing dynasties, the *Huajian ji* lost its relevance after the work of the great *ci* poets of the Song; although it continued to be read in late imperial China, it was generally perceived as an "immature" formulation of the genre. In the hands of modern readers, the anthology has rarely been examined *as an anthology*; instead, scholars have more often focused on the works of individual poets—most commonly the late Tang poets Wen Tingyun and Wei Zhuang—and their respective contributions to the genre. I suggest that these perspectives obscure the significance of the anthology in several key ways. By evaluating the *Huajian ji* only in terms of its contributions to a later "model" of the genre of *ci*—wherever one wishes to locate that model in Chinese literary history—we unnecessarily limit ourselves to a single literary form, and we risk overlooking the broader influence of Tang culture on the *Huajian ji*. Second, by ignoring the unique cultural context of the Shu kingdom in which the anthology was compiled, and in which many of its song lyrics were written, we misunderstand the conception of song lyrics, *quzi ci*, that the Shu poets held and practiced. Most notably, without acknowledging the influence of court culture on the creation of the anthology, we cannot understand the significance of imitation and convention in the *Huajian ji* song lyrics.

I intend to reorient our perspective on the *Huajian ji* by studying the anthology from a series of historical and literary perspectives. In the first half of the book (Chapters 1 through 3), I examine the song lyrics of the anthology as an outgrowth of certain Tang literary and cultural trends; as a cultural artifact that reveals important social and political features of tenth-century Shu; and as a defense of a collection of *quzi ci* as elite literature. In the second half of the book (Chapters 4 through 6), I examine the poetic grounds of the anthology in order to demonstrate its coherence as a statement of a genre. This is, therefore, an exploration both of the cultural practice of writing songs in ninth- and tenth-century China and of the song lyrics of the *Huajian ji* as a product of that practice. By illuminating the historical and literary contexts of the anthology, I hope to situate the *Huajian ji* within some larger problematics of Chinese literary history, particularly the development of romantic literature and the influence of cultural forces on the emergence of genres.

Collections are critical to the formation of literary genres in most cultures, but they are especially important for understanding Chinese literary genres, in part due to the relative scarcity of broad discussions of genre in the Chinese literary tradition. In the early medieval period, texts such as Lu Ji's 陸機 "Wen fu" 文賦 (Rhapsody on literature) and Liu Xie's 劉勰 *Wenxin diaolong* 文心雕龍 (The literary [or patterned] mind and the carving of dragons) explored the internal modal coherence of genres in a theoretical manner, and yet their influence was not widely felt before late imperial times.[2] In the same period as the *Wenxin diaolong*, however, the genre anthology *Wen xuan* 文選 (Selections of refined literature) was compiled at the Liang court, and its models shaped the development of its constituent genres for centuries afterward. In the Tang, we see the emergence of poetry manuals and many discussions of individual genres aimed at refining or reforming literary practice, but little comparative discussion of genres. Collections, and the prefaces to those collections, were frequently used by medieval Chinese writers to explore problems of classification of genres and the qualities inherent to unique forms. As Pauline Yu has

---

2. See Owen, *Readings in Chinese Literary Thought*, 134, 210ff.

noted, the medieval Chinese literary tradition contains a wide range of approaches to collecting, from canon-making and culturally normative approaches to individualistic and curatorial efforts. Many medieval collections shared the goal of valorization, the preservation of the "best of a kind."[3] Anthologies that were designed to establish literary and cultural paradigms, such as the *Wen xuan*, often manifested their ambitions quite plainly; other collections with lesser claims often protested in the guise of humility that they had no motive other than pleasure.[4]

In studying anthologies of single or mixed genres, it is important to remember the roles that different literary genres played in medieval social and political life. In the case of a canonical work like the *Wen xuan*, the genres selected for preservation were meant to stand as models of appropriate elite literary expression, the basic components of the literati repertoire. Due to the expansion and reform of the examination system in the Tang, such models became all-important in literati education and professional life. However, when literary genres emerged from a socially marginal quarter, as song lyrics did, or represented non-canonical subject matter, such as the amatory verse collected in the sixth-century anthology *Yutai xinyong* 玉臺新詠 (New songs for the Jade Terrace), collections of works from those genres often had to be cautiously defended. Such anthologies demand extra scrutiny because their selections, exclusions, arrangement, prefaces, and colophons often provide information about period literary tastes in the absence of other discussion of the new forms. Whether their contents were orthodox or heterodox, all literary collections articulated models for others to follow, reject, or challenge. Anthologies are therefore valuable to our understanding of literary history, to the reconstruction of the dynamics of literary change, and to mapping the dimensions of literary genres over time.

---

3. Yu, "Poems in Their Place: Collections and Canons in Early Chinese Literature," 167–68, 171.
4. For a comparison of the ambitions of the *Wen xuan* and its contemporary, the *Yutai xinyong*, see Knechtges, "Culling the Weeds and Selecting Prime Blossoms," 200–241.

My exploration of the song lyrics of the *Huajian ji* as both a cultural practice and a literary genre redirects the study of the genre of *ci* toward its historical formation. In the past few decades, a number of scholars have taken this historical turn in the study of genres.[5] In an influential essay, Hans Robert Jauss formulated the phrase "horizon of expectations" (*horizon d'attente*) to describe how readers and writers respond to the continually changing shape of the codes of a genre through literary history, arguing that the historical study of genres was essential to understanding the causes for these transformations.[6] Jauss's emphasis on the historicization of genres provides a needed complement to the synchronic study of forms. Although his own work focuses primarily on form, Tzvetan Todorov's definition of genre—"the codification of discursive properties"—also highlights the need to study both the historical process of codification and the formal properties of individual genres.[7] From a rather different disciplinary perspective, the sociologist Pierre Bourdieu has illuminated the importance of genres in the formation of cultural hierarchies of taste and value. The *Huajian ji* lends itself particularly well to both diachronic and synchronic approaches, because it was the first collection to claim song lyrics as an elite literary genre and was thus both a transformative moment in literary history and a defining collection for the genre. As we will see,

---

5. Genre study and theory has become an active field of literary study, particularly since the 1970s, with a wide variety of research perspectives. In my understanding of the development of generic codes and forms, the works that have most influenced my thinking are Guillén, *Literature as System: Essays Toward the Theory of Literary History*; Todorov, *Les genres du discours*; and Fowler, *Kinds of Literature: An Introduction to the Theory of Genres and Modes*. For the historicization of genres, I have found most useful Genette and Todorov, eds., *Théorie des genres*; Lewalski, ed., *Renaissance Genres: Essays on Theory, History, and Interpretation*; and Pierre Bourdieu, *The Field of Cultural Production*.

6. Hans Robert Jauss, "Littérature médiévale et théorie des genres," in Genette and Todorov, 56–57.

7. Todorov, *Les genres du discours*, 49. In emphasizing the need for both kinds of study, Todorov argues that "genres are the meeting-place between general poetics and event-based literary history; as such, they constitute a privileged object that may well deserve to be the principal figure in literary studies" (52).

studying the cultural contexts in which this claim was made is essential for understanding the poetics of the song lyrics themselves.

The *Huajian ji* provides evidence that song lyrics had become integrated into elite culture in the tenth-century kingdom of Shu. In Chapter 1, I reexamine the evidence for the literati composition of song lyrics, by which I mean *quzi ci*, in Tang culture. In my reading of the historical and literary evidence, I argue that song lyrics were one piece of a critical trend of the mid- and late Tang: the flourishing of a culture of romance between literati and courtesans in the ninth century. The culture of romance can be perceived in a variety of mid- and late Tang literary genres, including song lyrics; Tang romantic poetry deeply influenced the treatment of romantic love in song lyrics of the Tang and later periods. But in terms of their cultural or literary weight in the Tang, *quzi ci* were a negligible part of elite literature more broadly considered. The practices of performing and listening to songs occurred at all levels of Tang society, from massive imperial entertainments featuring thousands of performers to the solo performances of winehouse singing girls. Although literati did occasionally compose song lyrics in the Tang, historical records suggest that songwriting was strongly associated with the world of popular entertainment. Outside of mere personal interest, there were few incentives for poets to compose song lyrics; at the same time, the association of song lyrics with the entertainment quarters likely strengthened the negative effect on a would-be official's career. This social stigma may have affected Tang poets' desire to circulate or preserve song lyrics outside their immediate circle of friends and thus may be responsible for the small number of lyrics by literati that we have today—a few hundred lyrics from the three hundred years of the Tang dynasty. The claim made in the *Huajian ji* preface that the work represents elite culture is thus radically different from statements or descriptions of *quzi ci* in the Tang and represents a true innovation of the Shu anthology. Supporting that claim is historical evidence from both the Former and Latter Shu courts indicating that song lyrics were indeed a central piece of tenth-century Shu culture.

The poets found in the *Huajian ji* include a few late Tang poets, one tenth-century poet not associated with Shu, and thirteen poets who had been active in Shu during the tenth century, most of whom had held official positions in the Former or Latter Shu regimes. In Chapter 2, I investigate the place of these poets by exploring the social and political contexts for song lyrics at the courts of the Former and Latter Shu. The preface to the *Huajian ji* offers the anthology as proof of the refinement of their Chengdu court, a successor to the elegant courts of the Southern Dynasties. The appearance of this work from a regional, peripheral court is noteworthy in medieval Chinese cultural history, since it occurs in a period in which the traditional relationship between the center and the periphery had been completely disrupted. The tenth-century flourishing of new "centers" in the old periphery affected almost every feature of Chinese culture, society, and politics. The centripetal forces that scattered Tang literati across the Chinese mainland brought the influence of Tang culture to the courts of the new "Ten Kingdoms" as well as the successive regimes of the "Five Dynasties," and yet different regions absorbed—and transformed—those influences differently. Due in part to its geographical isolation, and in part to its preexisting wealth, the region of Shu enjoyed almost unparalleled independence and prosperity, which strongly influenced the social and political environment of the Shu courts.

The preface and the contents of the *Huajian ji* give us a glimpse of the social and political changes in Shu and their influence on Shu culture. When we examine the records of Former and Latter Shu officials, it becomes clear that the literati of Shu were a remarkably heterogeneous group and that the officials whose lyrics are collected in the *Huajian ji* reflect the larger patterns taking place in Chengdu. This social diversity is echoed by a surprising range of cultural activity in Shu. Although traditional historians have generally dismissed Shu culture as decadent and hedonistic, a closer evaluation of the range of artistic activity in Shu—which included instrumental music, songs, and painting, as well as orthodox types of literary composition—suggests something more complex. The historical records for the two Shu kingdoms of the tenth century, despite their lacunae and silences, reveal music and song to have been central cultural activities both before and after 940, the date of the *Huajian ji*. Despite historians' criticism of the pleasure-centered atmosphere of the Latter Shu—the era when the *Huajian ji* was compiled—the evidence also shows that the Latter Shu ruler Meng Chang 孟昶 (r. 934–65) oversaw the revival and reconstruction of key elements of traditional literati culture in Chengdu, namely the examination system, the engraving of the Classics and the printing of the *Wen xuan*, and the formation of a Hanlin academy. Similar efforts to sustain the culture of the Tang can be found in other tenth-century kingdoms, most importantly in southeastern China. What is noteworthy about Shu is that its rulers enthusiastically sponsored its "decadent" musical entertainments alongside more orthodox literary and political pursuits, suggesting a rather broad definition of *wen* 文, culture, in this independent regional center.

In reviewing the extant records of Shu history, we discover that the *Huajian ji* was only one literary work among many from the period, although most have not survived. One important text that did survive was a 1,000-poem collection of Tang poetry, the *Caidiao ji* 才調集 (Collection of the tunes of the talents), which was compiled by an official at the court of the Latter Shu, Wei Hu 韋縠. In Chapter 3, I examine the Shu approaches to anthology-making in the context of some Tang precedents for poetry anthologies. In the preface of the late Tang and Former Shu poet Wei Zhuang 韋莊 to his collection *You xuan ji* 又玄集 (Collection of the ever-more mysterious), as in the preface of the Shu literatus Wei Hu to the *Caidiao ji*, and the preface to the *Huajian ji*, we discover a similar approach to poetry collection, valuing the discriminating taste of the individual connoisseur and the coterie in selecting the "best" texts. In the Chinese poetic tradition, the compilation of a poetry anthology was a culturally weighty project; the model of Confucius's collection of the *Classic of Odes*, whether or not it was explicitly acknowledged by collectors, stood at the beginning of the tradition and influenced the rhetoric of prefaces throughout the history of poetry collections in imperial China. However, the few anthology prefaces extant from the final century of the Tang dynasty articulate a growing variety of literary values and indicate a broader range in the kinds of poems selected.

Though Wei Zhuang's *You xuan ji* looks backward to Tang poets, its aesthetic judgments also influenced Shu literary tastes. Although their prefaces suggest similar collecting strategies, the differences between the *You xuan ji* and the *Caidiao ji* demonstrate the results that individual discrimination could produce: where Wei Zhuang's 300-poem anthology is modest and unsurprising, and includes many poems familiar from earlier anthologies and appraisals of Tang poetry, Wei Hu's anthology focuses almost exclusively on romance and parting. In the preface to the *Huajian ji*, Ouyang Jiong presents a quite different version of the anthology of taste: he praises the lyrics and the poets of the *Huajian ji* as elegant products of Shu court culture. His defense of song lyrics as a cultural activity is unusual in Chinese literary history, but it is a provocative and clever move in the advocacy of a suspect literary practice.

Traditional and modern readers have long recognized that the *Huajian ji* has a singular style. Fewer scholars have acknowledged that the *Huajian ji* as a whole represents a coherent statement of a literary genre in terms of both style and form. I study the *Huajian ji*'s conception of song lyrics as a genre in the three chapters of the second half of the book. In its conceptual integrity, the *Huajian ji* draws upon the full range of meanings of the Chinese term *ti* 體: "form," "style," and (in some medieval discussions of literature) "genre." The anthology's song lyrics take the form of metrical structures attached to specific tunes. As noted above, the central concern of the *Huajian ji* is romantic love. The style of the collection occupies a fairly narrow range between highly "poetic" description and somewhat looser, more vernacular expression, but these styles are employed toward a single end: the depiction of romantic vignettes. In the preface, the poet Ouyang Jiong argues for the use of artifice, *qiao*, in the craft, *gong* 工, of making art that can rival the natural in beauty. This emphasis on artifice and craft is everywhere visible, in the structure and language of the *Huajian ji* song lyrics, in the overall construction of the collection, and in the arrangement of lyrics within an individual poet's works. In particular, the Shu poets' use of imitation and borrowing—whether at the level of rhetorical structure, the construction of individual lines, or the use of phrases and words—is central to the collection. The Shu poets' interest in imitation and craft as shared literary values emerges from the court culture in which they composed and performed song lyrics. The poets' attention to and consciousness of performance can be seen throughout the anthology; it specifically informs my reading strategy, which is to read song lyrics in tune title sets. We know from descriptions of song lyric performances in the ninth and tenth centuries that performers would sing a series of lyrics to a single tune; my analytical approach thus reproduces tenth-century performance practice. The strategy of reading song lyrics in tune title sets demonstrates the literary craft of the collection by revealing the central themes and subjectivities available to the Shu poets whose work makes up the majority of the anthology. At the same time, reading across the works of different poets exposes the importance of imitation throughout the collection. At the same time, this reading strategy also opens up intratextual dialogues and meanings that could have been produced in performance, by allowing lyrics of different poets to speak to one another.

The song lyrics of Wen Tingyun have long been acknowledged as a critical stylistic influence on the *Huajian ji* as a whole, and in Chapter 4, I examine some of his most influential lyrics in the collection—those to "Pusa man" 菩薩蠻 (Bodhisattva barbarian)—as well as lyrics by other *Huajian ji* poets to the same tune. The juxtaposition of various poets' lyrics to this important tune reveals not only how Shu poets imitated Wen Tingyun's influential model but also how they sought to avoid the limitations imposed by his stylistic extremes. Wen Tingyun's style in "Pusa man" is syntactically and imagistically dense, a compression of centuries of conventional figures and techniques; Wen combines an exploration of the older medieval "palace style" with a new attention to the unrevealing surfaces of beautiful objects. The Shu poets' adoption of Wen as a model appears in their construction of romantic scenes and their attention to beautiful women as objects within ornate settings; and yet we see them moving away from the most opaque expressions of his style to focus instead on the creation of mood in song lyrics. As the metrical forms of the many tune titles in the collection demonstrate, the two-stanza, often heterometric verse forms composed to late Tang and Shu tunes allowed poets to experiment with the construction of a scene on the level of stanza and line. In all three chapters of the second half, my reading of tune title sets focuses on the Shu poets' use of imitation and their innovations in the use of song lyric forms.

In Chapter 5, I explore the different approaches to the representation of male and female lovers in the "romantic story" of the collection. Here, the ambitions of literati poets of song lyrics become more evident. The dense, descriptive style of Wen Tingyun is largely reserved for depictions of abandoned boudoir women, and the Shu poets who adopted Wen's style followed his lead in representing these women as silent, or silenced by their condition. But this typically voyeuristic perspective is not the only approach to scenes of romantic distress in the collection. There is a significant minority of song lyrics that can be read as first-person expressions of longing or sorrow, and a large number of those—perhaps as many as a hundred lyrics—can be read in a male first-person voice. The gendered representation of subjectivity in the *Huajian ji* song lyrics has often been overlooked because of the predominance of the third-person descriptive view of the female subject. However, I argue that the minority male perspective is critical to our understanding of the poetics of the collection, because it sheds light on the *Huajian ji* poets' appropriation of techniques from *shi*, specifically the use of the "authentic" first-person voice that is traditionally read as a male voice. In this chapter, I explore the complex relationship of style, voice, and gender in the lyrics to two tunes, "Jiu quanzi" (Wine springs) and "Huanxi sha" (Sands of [silk-]washing streams), which are also two of the most important tune titles of the collection. The creation of an alternative male voice in song lyrics is a development that is usually located in the lyrics of the Southern Tang poet Li Yu, and yet it is already present, and significant, in the lyrics of the *Huajian ji*. In the Northern Song, poets used the male voice to transform the genre. Its presence in the *Huajian ji*—that is, from the inception of song lyrics as a genre—shows that late Tang and Shu poets perceived the male voice as an alternative perspective to the feminine, descriptive depictions of romance.

In Chapter 6 I consider a subset of lyrics in the *Huajian ji* that engage the ancient tradition of depicting male mortals' encounters with goddesses, focusing on lyrics to the tunes "Lin jiang xian" (Transcendent by the river) and "Nü guanzi" (The Daoist nun).

Edward Schafer and Suzanne Cahill have examined these lyrics in order to argue for the centrality of Daoist practices and concepts to the song lyrics in these two tune title sets. However, I argue that we cannot understand the use of "Daoism" in the *Huajian ji* without placing such lyrics in the context of the entire anthology. The court of the Former Shu had a particularly strong relationship with Daoism, and there is much evidence for the prominence of Daoist religious persons and practices in Chengdu throughout the tenth century. Thus, the historical evidence of the Shu court explains at least the presence of Daoist language in the *Huajian ji*, a feature of the collection's song lyrics that does not continue to be widely influential in the Song. Yet there is a distinct range of uses of Daoist imagery and goddess narratives in the lyrics of the *Huajian ji*, and it is important to make nuanced discriminations within that range. We cannot categorize all song lyrics that use allusions to Daoist figures or practices as fundamentally "Daoist," but neither should we dismiss such usages as entirely secularized transformations of religious language. The use of a goddess-encounter narrative has the potential to problematize relations between male and female lovers, because, in the medieval Chinese tradition, the goddess has the power to come and go as she chooses. She is thus not only the desired object but also potentially the ultimate arbiter of the romance. In this chapter I argue that only a few of the poets who worked in this tradition exploited its potential as a counter-voice to the tradition of mortal romances in which men played the decisive role. Furthermore, in the lyrics that use the imagery of Daoist ritual, most prominently those to "Nü guanzi," very few poets are able to employ the language of Daoism in a manner distinct from the mundane romantic scenes of other lyrics. What we see in the *Huajian ji*'s use of Daoist language is, on the one hand, the influence of Daoism as a cultural presence at the Shu courts and, on the other hand, the tenth-century extension of a Tang literary trend. This trend did not become prominent in the history of the genre, but the presence of "goddesses" in the collection adds a new dimension to the *Huajian ji* representation of romance.

The literary complexity of the *Huajian ji*, as demonstrated by its formal innovations and experimentation with conventions and subject matter, represents powerful evidence for the anthology as a realization of a new literary genre. Ouyang Jiong argues in his preface that the Shu collection and its poets continue the work of poets of *yuefu* and song lyrics from the Southern Dynasties and the Tang, and from the perspective of literature as a social phenomenon, one can certainly see the lineage of medieval court literature being sustained in the wealthy and independent kingdom of tenth-century Shu. From the perspective of literary history, however, Ouyang Jiong's defense of song lyrics as an elite practice cannot fully disguise the important turn that the *Huajian ji* marks in the development of Chinese poetry; certainly, generations of readers after the *Huajian ji* saw it as a pivotal collection. By reconsidering the cultural and literary contexts of the anthology, I hope not only to show its links to the Tang literary past but also to demonstrate the specific and deliberate ways in which it articulated a future model for the *ci* genre.

PART I

Cultural Contexts

ONE

A Matter of Taste

Tang Culture and Song Lyrics (*quzi ci*)

In the last years of the Tang emperor Wenzong's 文宗 reign (827-40), the poets Bai Juyi 白居易 (772-846) and Liu Yuxi 劉禹錫 (772-842) each wrote a series of twelve lyrics to the tune (*quzi* 曲子) "Yangliu zhi" 楊柳枝 (The willow branch). In the first lyrics of these matching series, the two men praise the originality of their own compositions.

"Yangliu zhi" (1st of 12)
Bai Juyi

Everyone's singing the "Six Toughies" and the "Water Tunes"—	六幺水調家家唱
Everywhere they play "White Snow" and "Plum Blossom," too.	白雪梅花處處吹

| Ancient songs and worn-out tunes—stop listening to them! | 古歌舊曲君休聽 |
| Just listen to my newly arranged "Willow Branch."[1] | 聽取新翻楊柳枝 |

"Yangliu zhi" (1st of 12)
Liu Yuxi

North of the border, Qiang flutes blow the "Plum Blossom" tune;	塞北梅花羌笛吹
"Huainan cassias" are in the lyrics of Xiaoshan.[2]	淮南桂樹小山詞
But I beg you not to play tunes of ages gone by—	請君莫奏前朝曲
Listen to them sing my newly arranged "Willow Branch."[3]	聽唱新翻楊柳枝

Bai and Liu both claim that their "newly arranged," *xinfan* 新翻, lyrics to the stylish tune "Willow Branch" are fresh, much more suited to the times than are the songs of "ages gone by." The poets' open boasting about their talents at composing song lyrics—known in the Tang as *quzi ci* 曲子詞, or lyrics composed to a *quzi*, tune, with a fixed tune title[4]—makes these texts unusual in the body of extant Tang lyrics, most of which do not call attention to their own composition. It also seems likely that the two men wrote new music

---

1. "Six Toughies" ("Liu ao" 六幺) and "Water Melodies" ("Shuidiao" 水調) were the names of two tunes popular in the mid-Tang; both survived past the Song. "White Snow" as a tune title can be traced to the Warring States era. *QTWDCSZ*, 184.

2. The "Plum Blossom" tune was attributed to an Eastern Jin poet; "Huainan cassias" refer to the cassia trees in the first line of the "Summoning the Recluse," a lyric attributed to a poet styled Xiaoshan at the Western Han court of Liu An, Prince of Huainan. *QTWDCSZ*, 158.

3. Ibid., 158.

4. I should note here that I deliberately exclude meter from my definition of Tang *quzi ci*, in contrast to Ren Bantang, in his important work on Tang poetic forms set to music, *Tang sheng shi*. Ren argues for the existence of a distinct Tang poetic practice known as *sheng shi*, "musicalized poetry"—isometric poems to which are affixed tune titles. In his definition, quatrains composed to "Yangliu zhi" are thus considered *shengshi*, not *quzi ci*. My argument, explained fully in the final part of this chapter, is that since we know that the practice of designating *quzi ci* as such by the use of a tune title predates the use of heterometric verse for *quzi ci*, we should not rely on heterometric verse to define the practice of *quzi ci* in the Tang.

for their lyrics, a feat that would make their compositions even more novel.⁵ In the rest of their "Yangliu zhi" lyrics, they are not as self-promoting, playing instead with the many metaphorical uses of willows, willow branches, and famous willow-planted sites. Since willows were traditionally snapped at partings, as a pun on the resemblance between *liu* 柳, "willow," and the word "to stay," *liu* 留, poets often incorporated beautiful, willow-like women parting from their lovers in their quatrains to "Yangliu zhi."⁶

Some decades after Bai Juyi's and Liu Yuxi's songwriting episode, the poet Xue Neng 薛能 (ca. 817–d. after 880) wrote a preface to his own set of "Yangliu zhi" songs, lamenting the very popularity of the tune and its contents. He defended his efforts to sound original among the poetasters of his day:

> This tune circulates everywhere, and many people make lyrics for it. Literary men and exam candidates brag about their skill, such that every willow frond becomes a dancer's waist, and every leaf a made-up brow. When they all come out like that, it becomes too familiar. But since I am especially good at poetic regulation and am not fond of following others, I'm always seeking out difficult and new things, vowing to avoid the common way. Although [those of lesser talent] don't intend to break the rules, how can those of us who truly understand music not adhere to them?⁷

Xue Neng's preface tells us that he and other literary men and exam candidates (*wenren caizi* 文人才子) were still writing lyrics to the

---

5. This is the conclusion of Ren Bantang in *Jiaofang ji jianding*, 76, which is supported by Wang, *Sui Tang Wudai yanyue zayan geci yanjiu*, 88. The Tang anecdotal text *Ben shi shi* (True stories of poems) relates a story in which Bai composes new lyrics for "Yangliu zhi" for his singing girl Pansu, but it does not refer to the music. Guo Maoqian briefly discusses the incident in *Yuefu shiji* 81.1142.

6. The last line of Liu's final lyric in the series refers to yet another song, the "Zhu zhi" (Bamboo branch) tune, to which Liu famously composed eleven lyrics and a preface. *QTWDCSZ*, 164.

7. *QTS* 561.6518. Also included in *QTWDCSZ*, 389. Later in his series of "Yangliu zhi" lyrics, Xue appended a note to one lyric that mocks and criticizes Liu and Bai, saying that their songs had "obscure" (*pi* 僻) language and a poor understanding of melody (400). In turn, the Song scholar Hong Mai, in his *Rongzhai suibi*, dismissed Xue Neng's own lyrics for their shallowness. Hong Mai's comments are cited in Shi, *Tang Wudai ci jishi huiping*, 286–87.

"Yangliu zhi" tune in the late ninth century (Xue dates his compositions to 877). According to Xue, most poets were still using the same figures for willow-as-woman found throughout the lyrics by Bai and Liu; in the late Tang, lyrics to "Yangliu zhi" apparently remained within narrow topical boundaries that were set in part by the title itself, in part by the practice of the literati. It seems that composing lyrics to this tune had become yet another element of literati competition and bragging rights.[8] Xue Neng also composed "new music," *xin sheng* 新聲, for his lyrics,[9] lending credence to his claim to be both one who truly understood music and a highly skilled poet. An activity that appears as an episode of friendly play between Bai and Liu in the 830s seems both more competitive and more commonplace from the perspective of Xue Neng a few decades later. And yet the extant Tang lyrics to "Yangliu zhi" do not corroborate Xue Neng's remarks about the tune's popularity; before the 24 quatrains of Bai and Liu, there are only 5 extant quatrains preserved with the title "Yangliu zhi," and 59 from the remaining decades of the Tang, including Xue's own set of 19.[10]

The "Yangliu zhi" lyrics by Bai Juyi and Liu Yuxi and the preface by Xue Neng give us tantalizing glimpses of Tang poets engaged in writing song lyrics and praising their own compositions, but such evidence is rare among Tang texts. For scholars of the genre that came to be called *ci* in the Song dynasty, explaining the relationship

---

8. With his 19 extant "Yangliu zhi" songs and his 3 lyrics to the tune "Shi zhi ci" (Pomegranate branch lyrics), Xue Neng ranks fourth behind Liu Yuxi (47 lyrics), Bai Juyi (38 lyrics), and the late Tang poet Sikong Tu (23 lyrics) in the number of lyrics by Tang literati outside those whose work is collected in the *Huajian ji*. This ranking excludes the poet Yi Jing, for reasons I address below. *QTWDC*.

9. Also noted in *Yuefu shiji* 81.1143.

10. This count and all subsequent references to extant lyrics are based on the lyrics collected in *QTWDC* and *QTWDCSZ*. It excludes the ten lyrics to "Yangliu zhi" by the Tang poets Huangfu Song and Wen Tingyun that were included in the *Huajian ji*, for reasons I explain below. Murakami Tetsumi has argued that the formal equivalence of "Yangliu zhi" lyrics to the regulated *jueju* should disqualify "Yangliu zhi" lyrics from being considered as *ci* (Murakami, "Yōryūji shikō"). Since I follow the definition of the editors of the *QTWDC*, which includes all texts composed to a tune title for which we have external documentation, I include them here in my discussion of *quzi ci*.

between the small and disparate body of Tang literati *quzi ci* and the coherent collection of *quzi ci* found in the *Huajian ji* is a long-standing problem. In what follows, I offer a new perspective on Tang song lyrics by shifting the discussion of ninth- and tenth-century *quzi ci* from the grounds of genre development—the context in which the *Huajian ji* has traditionally been assessed—to that of cultural and literary history. In order to understand the achievement of the *Huajian ji* in Chinese literature, we must first acknowledge the significant discontinuities in the record of song lyric development and consider the implications of those discontinuities. In 940, Ouyang Jiong, the poet who wrote the preface to the *Huajian ji*—a collection of no fewer than 500 literati *quzi ci*—claimed that he and his fellow poets from Shu were following in the path of Tang poets, specifically mentioning the High Tang poet Li Bai 李白 (701–62?) and the late Tang poet Wen Tingyun 溫庭筠 (ca. 812–ca. 866), whose work is included in the anthology.[11] The 500 *Huajian ji* lyrics constitute a collection that is sizable even by the standards of the few extant period collections of Tang poetry,[12] and it is the earliest extant collection of literati *quzi ci*, though it is possible that it was not the first. When we seek the Tang precedents for the *Huajian ji*, however, we find some troublesome evidentiary problems. Why is it that we have a preponderance of evidence of Tang musical entertainment and the performance of *quzi* at all levels of Tang society, and yet we have relatively few lyrics (a few hundred) as evidence of Tang literati interest in composing *quzi ci*? The lyrics collected in the *Huajian ji* exhibit significant formal and topical differences with other extant lyrics from the Tang. Were the

---

11. Whether or not the song lyrics attributed to Li Bai were actually composed by him is a question that has long been debated, but it is significant that Ouyang Jiong believes that he was a composer of *quzi ci*. For the problem of Li Bai's authorship, see note 80 to this chapter.

12. The two largest extant poetry anthologies from the Tang, the *Yulan shi* and the *You xuan ji*, contain, respectively, 286 poems (out of an original 310) and 300 poems. There are extant references and prefaces to collections that may have been larger, such as Gu Tao's *Tangshi leixuan*, discussed in Chapter 3, which collected 1,232 poems. The High Tang anthology that is now extant only in fragments, *Yutai houyong*, originally was said to have collected 670 poems.

Huajian ji poets—including the Tang poets represented in the anthology—composing lyrics differently from other Tang poets whose work was not in the *Huajian ji*? Or are we simply facing a problem of transmission, of Tang texts that were not preserved? These questions of composition and preservation cannot be completely answered with the available evidence for Tang *quzi ci*, but we can find more satisfying—if still partial—answers by looking beyond the boundaries of genre history.

In this chapter, I contextualize the practice of composing *quzi ci* in Tang musical entertainment and the "culture of romance" of ninth-century literati in order to integrate *quzi ci* into a broader picture of Tang elite culture. In my discussion of romantic literature from the ninth century, I focus on a few key conventions of romantic verse that also appear in the *Huajian ji* lyrics, as a means of filiating the *Huajian ji* to its most influential medieval literary antecedents. Finally, I reexamine the extant data for Tang literati *quzi ci*. Most importantly, I disaggregate the *Huajian ji* song lyrics of Tang date from a consideration of Tang *quzi ci*, in order to demonstrate the quite different conclusions that can be drawn from sets of song lyrics that include or do not include the lyrics of the *Huajian ji*. In reorienting my study of the *Huajian ji* toward the Tang rather than the Song, I hope to counter the tendency found in many genre histories to assess the early genre in light of the "mature" version, and to seek in the early practice only the seeds of what flowered later. The tenth-century *Huajian ji* presents *quzi ci* as a literary form, but also presents the composition of *quzi ci* as a cultural practice of Shu court society. Both claims appear surprising against the Tang cultural and literary background, in which *quzi ci* existed merely as one form of musical entertainment, and a negligible literary interest among Tang elites.

In its claims and its contents, the *Huajian ji* signals a fundamental change—not just the outcome of gradual development—in the literati practice of composing lyrics to *quzi*. Other scholars have noted that the *Huajian ji* was the first collection to defend *quzi ci* as an acceptable form of literati writing, but scholars have only recently begun to examine the social implications of writing song lyrics in Tang culture, implications that the *Huajian ji* preface attempts to disguise.[13] In the Tang, *quzi ci* were a component of entertainment culture, and literati poets who wrote lyrics to *quzi* revealed themselves to be willing and interested participants in that world. Through its praise of *quzi ci* as a Shu court activity, the preface of the *Huajian ji* suggests an apparent shift in the social propriety of composing song lyrics from the ninth to the tenth century. In contrast to the many topics found in other Tang literati *quzi ci*, the poets of the *Huajian ji* depict romance—romantic relations between men and women—as their central concern, linking a single topic to a single literary form with a consistency almost unprecedented in Chinese literary anthologies. Moreover, the poets of the *Huajian ji* overwhelmingly chose heterometric, two-stanza forms for their lyrics (or chose tunes that demanded two-stanza lyrics), in contrast to the isometric, single-stanza forms found in the majority of extant Tang literati lyrics not collected in the *Huajian ji*. The song lyrics of the *Huajian ji* thus represent a fully conceptualized literary genre in that they are topically and thematically consistent, sharing the topic of romantic love across lyrics to different tune titles, and they are formally coherent, revealing a relatively narrow set of rhetorical strategies, stanza structures, and verse forms that were linked to fixed tunes. As I demonstrate in later chapters, the clarity of the *Huajian ji* conception of song lyrics results in part from the Shu editors' selections and arrangement, in part from the Shu poets' imitative practice. By seeing the *quzi ci* of the *Huajian ji* against the background of late Tang cultural history, we can reconnect the anthology to its Tang precedents and reveal the ways in which the Shu poets went beyond them.

Tang Musical Entertainment and Quzi ci

We have a great deal of Tang evidence for the popularity among literati of singing songs of various sorts, hearing performed songs, and turning poems into songs. Documents such as the monographs

---

13. See, for example, Yang, *Tang Wudai ci shi*, 102–3; Wu, *Tang Song ci tonglun*, 283. For an examination of this claim in the context of the history of collections of lyrics, see Yu, "Song Lyrics and the Canon," 73–79.

on music in the *Jiu Tang shu* and the *Xin Tang shu*, the discussions of music in texts such as the ninth-century *Yuefu zalu* 樂府雜錄 (Miscellaneous records of "Music Bureau" verse) and similar anecdotal sources, descriptions of singing found in stories and poems, and of course the trove of song lyrics found at Dunhuang all contribute to a picture of the complexity and vitality of Tang sung music at all social levels.[14] However, if we focus on the Tang literati *quzi ci* that are specifically preserved as such—as a set of lines of poetry (minimally characterized by at least rhyme, and often some tonal balancing) attached to a tune title for which there is at least one external corroborating record—we discover that the evidence for Tang literati interest in this single practice is both fragmentary and spread unevenly over the course of the dynasty. For the literary historian, the challenge is to sort through the many labels that were variously and inconsistently attached to texts that were, or could be, sung.[15] If the literati practice had died out in the chaos following the

---

14. Some of the most important Tang-era textual sources for music are Du You's chapter on music from the *Tong dian*, the chapter on ritual and music of the *Xin Tang shu*, and Duan Anjie's *Yuefu zalu*, among others. Among the many works on Tang music from the past century, the studies that have been most useful for this chapter are: Kishibe, *Tōdai ongaku no rekishiteki kenkyū—gakuseihen*; Shi, *Ci yu yinyue guanxi yanjiu*; Picken, "T'ang Music and Musical Instruments"; Picken, ed., *Music from the T'ang Court*, 5 vols.; Gimm, *Das Yueh-fu Tsa-lu des Tuan An-chieh: Studien zur Geschichte von Musik, Schauspiel und Tanz in der T'ang-Dynastie*; Ren, *Tang sheng shi*; Wang, *Sui Tang Wudai yanyue zayan geci yanjiu*. A recent reference work has compiled passages from standard histories that deal with Sui and Tang music: Ji, ed., *Sui Tang Wudai yinyue shiliao*.

15. Other scholars have made this point at least implicitly. In the introduction to *Sōshi kenkyū: Tō Godai Hoku Sō hen*, Murakami Tetsumi discusses the changing referents of the word in the Tang and Five Dynasties. Murakami, *Sōshi kenkyū: Tō Godai Hoku Sō hen*, 7–20. In his study of the development of song lyrics in the Tang and Song, the scholar Yang Haiming also raises the question of whether or not there is a coherent group of texts that can be called *ci* in the Tang; however, he emphasizes the content of lyrics over their formal features and thus steps away from the problem of whether or not *ci* had a distinct formal identity in the Tang. Yang, *Tang Song ci shi*, 71–72. Most recently, Wang Kunwu argues that scholars should keep in mind the primacy of *music* in the Tang and should use the term *quzi ci* and not the later term *ci* for the Tang practice; the widespread use of the term *ci* in the Song dynasty, to Wang, is a strong indication that the words had become more important than music to poets by that time (16–17).

fall of the Tang—if song lyrics had not gone on to become one of the most important literary genres of the Song dynasty—it would be easy to dismiss Tang literati *quzi ci* as a minor and indeed trivial poetic form on the grounds of numbers and of content. However, in the decades after the fall of the Tang, we find more extant song lyrics being composed and circulated by literati in Shu, by the *Huajian ji* poets, and later in the Southern Tang, by the poets Li Jing 李璟 (916–61), Li Yu 李煜 (937–78), and Feng Yansi 馮延巳 (903–60). The bibliographical evidence from the tenth-century kingdoms is very partial—we have many more titles than we have extant texts—but it is sufficient to show us that *quzi ci* were at least preserved more consistently in the tenth century by literati poets.

The practice of composing lyrics to *quzi* was by no means a socially neutral activity among Tang literati. Many scholars have noted that the melodies, the *quzi,* were a part of the tradition of "banquet music," *yanyue* 燕樂 (a term that came to include *suyue* 俗樂, "common music," and *huyue* 胡樂, "foreign music" [specifically that of Central Asia]) ranging from the Sui through the Tang. This ancestry meant that they were forever associated with entertainment, whether of the expensive imperial court variety or the cheaper winehouse brand.[16] Furthermore, the court performers of banquet music were mostly women entertainers—singers, dancers, and instrumentalists—who performed at nonritual court functions. Outside of courtly or elite household settings, these *quzi* were also commonly performed by women in the entertainment

---

16. Wang Kunwu traces the important sites of *quzi* composition, performance, and circulation. Although the most famous among these sites were the court musical institutions—which included performers, instrumentalists, and composers—anecdotal evidence, along with the Dunhuang tunes, points to the widespread popularity of *quzi* among entertainers outside the court (18–23, 59–60). Marsha Wagner, in *The Lotus Boat: The Origins of Chinese Tz'u Poetry in T'ang Popular Culture,* argues, as her title suggests, that popular song antedates literati song. Yang Haiming also emphasizes popular musicians as the originators of lyrics to *quzi,* in "Lun Tang Wudai ci," *Tang Song ci lun gao,* 86–87. Wang, however, suggests that the question of "origins" is ultimately unanswerable given the state of the Sui and Tang evidence; moreover, he argues that the privileging of "popular" over "literati" music or vice versa obstructs a better understanding of the two as mutually influential throughout the Tang (82–83).

districts of Chang'an, Luoyang, Yangzhou, and other major provincial capitals, appearing wherever there were women to sing and men to be entertained.[17] Thus, not only were there no strong political or literary incentives for literati poets to take up the practice of writing lyrics to *quzi*—they could neither prepare one for examinations nor advance one's reputation as a prospective official—but they could even bring the charge of frivolity down on poets who chose to write them.[18] And indeed, the Tang poets for whom we have the most lyrics to *quzi*—men such as Bai Juyi, Liu Yuxi, Xue Neng, Wen Tingyun—were also known for writing about or consorting with entertainment girls. Although many Tang poets created songs in other forms, such as *yuefu*, or put their *shi* poetry to music, the extant evidence suggests that not many Tang poets (109 poets over the course of 300 years) chose to dabble in writing lyrics to *quzi*.[19] Moreover, for the majority of these poets we have only one or two lyrics extant, a fact that forestalls broad conclusions about literati tastes in lyrics.[20] The potential stigma attached to *quzi ci* obviously raises the question of transmission and circulation, a problem that I examine at the end of this chapter.

---

17. Kishibe, I, 90–98. Wang, *Sui Tang Wudai yanyue*, 72–77.

18. Tang Guizhang and Pan Junzhao noted this as an important factor that affected the preservation of lyrics in the Tang in "Lun ci di qiyuan," 25–26. Shuen-fu Lin has also discussed the reputation of banquet music in "The Formation of a Distinct Generic Identity for Tz'u," 12–13. See Palandri, *Yuan Zhen*, 69–70, for a discussion of the late Tang criticism of the poetry of Yuan Zhen and Bai Juyi, associated with the "Yuanhe [reign period] style" 元和體. However, the late Tang criticism of Bai Juyi and other poets associated with him is aimed not at the poets' *quzi* lyrics specifically but at the general content of their poetry from the Yuanhe period. There is little evidence that *quzi* were singled out from among other songwriting practices as particularly nefarious, but their association with the entertainment quarters would surely have amplified the danger they posed to the reputations of prospective officials.

19. Ren, *Tang shengshi*, lays out the range of songwriting practices available to literati in the Tang in his definition of *shengshi* as a distinct poetic and musical practice (vol. 1, 1–10, and 341–46).

20. *QTWDC* collects the lyrics of 109 individual Tang poets, excluding Wen Tingyun, Huangfu Song, Li Bai, and Yi Jing. Among these 109, 84 poets are represented by two or fewer lyrics.

Even if the evidence of literati composition of song lyrics is scarce, standard histories of the Tang, as well as other texts, provide evidence that Tang elites, from the emperor down to local officials, spent a great deal of money and time on musical entertainment. Perhaps the single most important of these evidentiary texts is the High Tang record of the imperial music instruction, the *Jiaofang ji* 教坊記 (Record of the imperial instruction quarter), which was composed by Cui Lingqin 崔令欽, a literatus at the court of Tang Xuanzong (r. 712–56).[21] The *Jiaofang ji* and other texts on music and entertainment, such as the chapters on music in the official Tang histories, provide descriptions of the divisions of performers at the imperial court, the kinds of music that were sung, and the titles of officials, performers, and songs. A few even note that, at various moments in the Tang, performers of banquet music numbered in the thousands.[22] Although the numbers and kinds of musicians in imperial employ varied—falling sharply after the An Lushan Rebellion, when the *jiaofang* was disbanded, and rising again during the reigns of a few late Tang emperors—their performances at court must have strongly influenced musical tastes among elites in Chang'an and Luoyang.[23] Performers of the imperial court popularized songs, instruments, and dances that would have been shared with the smaller troupes of entertainers attached to provincial po-

---

21. Tang Xuanzong supposedly established the *jiaofang* to train musicians specifically in *suyue*, preserving the distinction between musical performance as entertainment and music as part of ritual. Cited in Wang, *Sui Tang Wudai yanyue*, 20.

22. Wang (*Sui Tang Wudai yanyue*, 18–22) cites these discussions of the imperial divisions of musicians and their specializations. *Xin Tang shu* says that when the Tang was at its height, there were "several tens of thousands" of people in the imperial court who could be counted as musicians, *yinyue ren* 音樂人, which included all varieties of instrumentalists, singers, and the many apprentices attached to the various offices. *XTS* 22.477.

23. For example, *Xin Tang shu* notes that at the beginning of the Dazhong 大中 era (847–60) of Tang Xuanzong 宣宗, there were over 5,000 musicians at the imperial court, 1,500 of whom were specialists in *suyue*. Xuanzong was very fond of music, and he himself "composed new tunes" (*di zhi xinqu* 帝制新曲), to which beautifully dressed women would sing and dance. *XTS* 22.478.

litical establishments and private elite families.²⁴ In addition, music performed for elites would also have been shaped by many different social and ethnic influences, given that the imperial court music institutions recruited performers from the entertainment quarters and absorbed music of both popular and foreign origins.²⁵ The Tang saw what Lawrence Picken has described as an "ongoing secularization of music," a diffusion of elite music outward from court functions to the smallest of winehouses, to the point where clear boundaries among ritual, popular, and foreign music were no longer distinguishable.²⁶

The more scholars have learned about Tang popular culture, the more they have reconsidered their interpretation of the early history of song lyrics. The discovery of hundreds of lyrics at Dunhuang early in the twentieth century irrevocably reoriented scholars' views of their production in Tang culture generally. Despite the problems with dating many of the lyrics in the Dunhuang corpus, their discovery has provoked scholars to abandon the older "top-down" approach to the history of song lyrics, which placed the sole focus on literati compositions²⁷ The oldest explanation of the

---

24. Robert des Rotours describes the kinds of women who would commonly form part of the entertainment troupes attached to the households of elite families outside the imperial court, in *Courtisanes chinoises à la fin des Tang*, 12–14. Such troupes could range in size, from dozens to as many as 100 women. The provincial establishments of military governors (*jiedu shi* 節都使) and prefects (*cishi* 刺使) also kept troupes of female performers (known as "official entertainers," *guanji* 官妓), whose quarters were known as the *yueying* 樂營, "music garrisons." For discussion of these women and their lives, see Rotours and also Gao, *Tang dai funü*, 64.

25. Evidence for the adoption of popular and foreign music is found throughout the chapters on music in the standard histories. In the early Tang, music from different regional sources was kept distinct in different divisions, but from the High Tang on, there was apparently a greater blending of influences, from the importation of new instruments to the use of foreign singers. *XTS* 22.476–77.

26. Picken, "T'ang Music and Musical Instruments," 77.

27. Many scholars have studied the Dunhuang corpus of song lyrics since its discovery, but before the 1970s, the dispersal of the texts in libraries around the world made close examination of the texts difficult for most scholars. The recent explosion of Dunhuang studies, made possible in part by the wider reproduction and dissemination of texts held in different locations, will surely yield results for the study of song lyrics as well. Ren Bantang, in the essays of his *Dunhuang qu*

emergence of song lyrics originated with Song literati, who argued that Tang poets began the practice of composing song lyrics by interpolating *shi* verse forms with extra words, forming the "long-and-short-lines," *changduan ju* 長短句, that Song poets saw as the formal hallmark of song lyrics. This view, perhaps most influentially argued in the past century by Hu Shi, was held by many scholars as late as the 1970s.[28] Today, greater familiarity with and appreciation for the Dunhuang texts and the popular culture they record has generally led scholars to believe that popular musicians and songwriters were the first to begin writing lyrics to new tunes in the Tang, and that literati poets took up the practice rather later; there is, however, no single argument for the dating of the origins of the practice that receives universal support. However, the Dunhuang evidence does not fundamentally alter the picture of Tang literati interest in composing lyrics to *quzi*. Instead, it offers a "popular" complement to the *Huajian ji*, more proof that ninth- and tenth-century people of all sorts liked to write, perform, and

---

chutan (1954) and *Dunhuang qu jiaolu* (1955), as well as in the later, larger, annotated edition of Dunhuang song lyrics, *Dunhuang geci zongbian*, proposed a corpus of 545 texts to be regarded as song lyrics. He divided this corpus into three large groups: *putong zaqu* "common miscellaneous songs," a group that includes the *quzi* we have been discussing; *lianzhang*, "linked verse," which consists of songs of three types (*chongju lianzhang*, "doubled-line linked verse"; *dingge lianzhang*, "linked verse of fixed structure"; and *changpian dingge lianzhang*, "long linked verses of fixed structures"); and *daqu*, or "great suites." In *Dunhuang qu chutan*, Ren argued that 248 pieces can be dated, but among these only a few dozen can be dated to the Tang. Rao Zongyi's work—in the volume published with Paul Demiéville (*Airs de Touen-houang: Textes à chanter des VIIIe–Xe siècles*), and in *Ci ji kao*—dates lyrics individually, but does not generalize about the dating of the corpus as a whole. Ren has dated the Dunhuang collection of *quzi ci* entitled *Yunyao ji* to before 922 (*Dunhuang qu chutan*, 204).

28. Hu Shi's theories, which largely summarized older positions on the development of song lyrics, were articulated in his essay "Ci de qiyuan," 詞的起源. A number of scholars in China and the West began to reexamine this theory in light of the Dunhuang evidence. One important early article was Chen, "The Rise of the Tz'u, Reconsidered." Murakami's 1974 reexamination of the emergence of song lyrics raises the issue of social class in their composition and transmission. *Sōshi kenykyū: Tō Godai Hoku Sō hen*, 83–87. As I argue in the second half of this chapter, one necessary step toward rethinking the development of song lyrics is to uncouple the use of heterometric verse from the question of the genre's first appearance.

listen to these *quzi*. Particularly given the difficulty of dating the Dunhuang songs, we cannot turn to them to answer questions about literati interest in composing *quzi ci*. Given that *quzi ci* had such a strong association with musical entertainment and female entertainers, we should instead look for shifts in Tang culture that might have made composing song lyrics an appealing pastime for elite poets.

The Tang "Culture of Romance"

In the *quzi ci* of the *Huajian ji*, the chief topic is romantic love between men and women. The most common depiction of the romance revolves around a silent, abandoned, and sorrowful woman in her boudoir, but we occasionally hear the voices of such women, or the voices of their male lovers, recounting their experiences. The *Huajian ji* lyrics constantly draw our attention to the delicate construction of the scenes and, from the carefully selected images, their prevailing moods. These are snapshots of romance. Two examples of lyrics to the tune "Genglouzi" 更樓子 (The water clock) show the melancholy of lovers' separation coloring every detail.

"Genglouzi" (2nd of 6)
Wen Tingyun

The starry dipper dims,	星斗稀
bells and drums cease.	鐘鼓歇
Beyond the shades, dawn orioles and a waning moon.	簾外曉鶯殘月
Dew on the orchids is heavy,	蘭露重
willows are blown aside in the wind.	柳風斜
A courtyard filled with piles of fallen blossoms.	滿庭堆落花
Above in the empty chamber,	虛閣上
she leans from the balustrade to gaze.	倚欄望
Just like last year's melancholy!	還似去年惆悵
Spring at its close,	春欲暮
longings without end.	思無窮
Old pleasures seem as if in dream.[29]	舊歡如夢中

---

29. *HJJZS*, 18.

"Genglouzi" (1st of 1)
Wei Zhuang

Sounds of bell and drum are chilly,	鐘鼓寒
the high chamber darkened.	樓閣暝
Moon shines on an old paulownia by the gilded well.	月照古桐金井
The deep courtyard closed up,	深院閉
its little veranda empty.	小庭空
On fallen blossoms, fragrant dew reddens.	落花香露紅
Misty willows seem heavy,	煙柳重
spring fogs fine.	春霧薄
The lamp is put out by the high chamber's small window.[30]	燈背小窗高閣
Idly, she leans in the doorway,	閑倚戶
secretly soaking her robes with tears.	暗沾衣
She waits for her man, but her man doesn't return.[31]	待郎郎不歸

As I will explain in later chapters, the stylistic and rhetorical similarities between the two lyrics are not at all coincidental. What I would note here, however, is the importance of the common romantic situation—the separation of lovers—to our understanding of the imagery and actions of the lyrics. Our understanding of "what happens" in these brief texts is shaped first by the conventional images for solitude and the passage of time: the bells and drums, the dew, and the fading moonlight all signal the arrival of dawn; the "fallen blossoms" of both first stanzas immediately suggest beautiful abandoned women waiting at the end of spring. In both lyrics the fact of lovers' separation is made clear by the figure who leans from her chamber, repeating a familiar pose ("just like last year's melancholy!") and weeping over ongoing separation ("she waits for her man, but her man doesn't return"). The anonymity of the women in

---

30. Most editions of the text have *shui* 水 instead of *xiao* 小, but Li Yi notes that *xiao* occurs at least once as a variant, and I translate the line thusly. Although Li Yi cites a usage of *shui chuang* from a poem by Bai Juyi, the phrase *xiao chuang*, "small window," occurs eight separate times in the collection (and *shui chuang*, other than this instance, does not appear at all), and seems more likely in context. *HJJZS*, 106.

31. Ibid.

both lyrics in no way blocks our perception of their emotions or circumstances; instead, one could argue that the generic quality of these women—their unmarked, anonymous poses and figures—allows the mood of romantic sorrow to dominate the scene.

These romantic vignettes by the poets Wen Tingyun and Wei Zhuang can be linked to mid- and late Tang literati writing, across genres, on the subject of romance—writing that created what Stephen Owen has called the "culture of romance." From contemporary Tang accounts, we know that the entertainment quarters of Chang'an, Luoyang, and major provincial cities were the places where Tang literati most often encountered musical performances and interacted with women performers. Many, if not most, of these women performers were also prostitutes of varying price and attainability.[32] It was in the representation of encounters between "singing girls" and poets that a culture of romance was born. In his essay "Romance," in *The End of the Chinese 'Middle Ages': Essays in Mid-Tang Literary Culture*, Owen argues that "the Mid-Tang saw the rise of a culture of romance, with the representation of individually chosen and socially unauthorized relationships between men and women."[33] It was not, of course, that romance among literati and courtesans was a new phenomenon in the Tang, but rather, as Owen has argued elsewhere, that the ninth century was the period in which "the demimonde achieved an unprecedented level of publicity."[34] Stories, anecdotes, poems, and songs on romantic love appeared in previously unheard of numbers from the beginning of the

---

32. The problem of adequately translating the Chinese term *ji* 妓 into English is intractable. Edward Schafer proposed borrowing the Japanese term *geisha* in an effort to retain the importance of a variety of entertainment skills (singing, dancing, recitation of poetry) in their profession, but I find this term more intrusive than useful. These women were commodities in a market whose definition of "entertainment" ranged from musical to sexual performance. At the high end of this market would be women whose status might best be translated as "courtesan," since their financial resources apparently afforded them some luxury to choose among suitors. The stories of the *Beili zhi* tend to focus on these women—sought out and competed over by literati—rather than women of lesser talent and price.

33. Owen, *End of the Chinese 'Middle Ages,'* 131.

34. Owen, "What did Liuzhi Hear? The 'Yan Terrace Poems' and the Culture of Romance," 83.

A Matter of Taste 33

ninth century through the end of the dynasty. The Tang literati who composed lyrics to *quzi* played a part in this culture of romance: by composing and preserving their lyrics, they revealed themselves as participants in the world of popular song—which is to say the entertainment quarters.³⁵ However, this was not a world entirely defined by relations between men and women; as Paul Rouzer notes, the private sphere so carefully documented in Tang stories of romance also circulated publicly, in "the informal male communities of readers."³⁶ And, as Xue Neng's criticism of other poets' lyrics showed, literati competed in composing song lyrics just as they competed in other cultural pursuits.

Although I draw on the work of Stephen Owen, my use of the term "romance" in this book deserves discussion, because I use it somewhat differently, as a topical category—romantic love—that cuts across genres. At its simplest, the "romance" of mid- and late Tang romantic literature refers to a standard story, whose plot is as follows: a beautiful woman meets a handsome, young, and talented man; they have a brief relationship that may or may not involve promises on his part for future plans; he then abandons her, leaving her with the hope that their relationship is not entirely severed. There are two features of this story that receive the most attention in mid- and late Tang literature: first, the relationship usually ends badly, with regret on both sides. The pain of separation and loss, whether experienced during the romance or after its termination, is a given—as a rule, there are few happy endings in the depictions of romantic love in medieval Chinese literature. Second, this story assumes that the male lover is largely a free agent and that the female lover has little power.³⁷ Although *chuanqi* are the lengthiest explo-

---

35. A number of scholars of song lyrics have discussed the connections between the entertainment quarters and the rise of literati song lyrics over the course of the Tang. See Chang, *Evolution of Chinese Tz'u Poetry*, 12–15; Wagner, *Lotus Boat*, 79–103; Wang *Sui Tang Wudai yanyue*, 72–79; Liu, *Tang Wudai ci de wenhua guanzhao*, 117–20. In this brief discussion, I intend to locate these connections in the literati culture of the ninth century.

36. Rouzer, *Articulated Ladies*, 227.

37. Owen has suggested that, for *chuanqi* tales, the assumption of free choice applies to both partners in the romance, that in fact the "culture of romance de-

rations of romance from the ninth century, the poetry and songs of the period also show an increased attention to the topic of romantic love, and the longstanding subgenres of medieval poetry that concern love are absorbed and transformed by a number of influential poets. Literati song lyrics on romance are but one manifestation of this ninth-century cultural development.

The Tang culture of romance possessed both a site and a discourse. Certainly the most important single text documenting the site is the *Beili zhi* 北里志 (Account of the northern ward), by the late Tang literatus Sun Qi 孫棨 (fl. 880). In its stories of courtesans and the men who pursued them, the *Beili zhi* paints an extraordinarily rich picture of the mingling of men and women in the Pingkang quarter of the capital, Chang'an.[38] Sun Qi not only tells stories about the people involved in these romances but also includes poems, songs, and vital historical details that make this text a valuable guide to the district, its inhabitants, and its folkways. In his analysis of the *Beili zhi*, Paul Rouzer has noted the following:

As is not surprising, this insular world quickly produced a subculture of its own, replete with conventions, customs, and expectations. Most evident in surviving texts is the relationship between the culture of courtesans and that of examination candidates. The latter seem to have placed a particular value on the artistic training of the prostitutes, often preferring the

---

pended on a fiction of continuing free choice" (*End of the Chinese 'Middle Ages,'* 133). I disagree slightly with this reading of the discourse because I believe that in the poetic treatment of romance the assumption of inevitable sorrow is both older and stronger than any other part of the story, and that if the female half of the romantic couple were assumed to have the same freedom as the male half, the relationship would not be so ineluctably bound to fail. The pathos of the figure of the "abandoned woman," whether in narrative or poetry, derives from her inability to change her fate.

38. Two important studies of the *Beili zhi* and its inhabitants are des Rotours, *Courtisanes chinoises á la fin des Tang*, and Ishida, "Chōan no kagi." An earlier translation is Levy, "Record of the Gay Quarters." For a discussion of women performers in Tang society, including the Chang'an courtesans of the *Beili zhi*, see Gao, *Tangdai funü*, 56–74. For one study of the relationship between the development of *ci* and female performers, see Li, *Tang Song ci yu Tang Song geji zhidu*.

company of women who could compose verse or engage in intelligent conversation.[39]

As the *Beili zhi* makes clear, the appeal of courtesans was not merely sexual: literati men sought out and competed for women who were as talented and clever as they were physically beautiful; winning these talented women would obviously reflect well on the literati who succeeded. The text's stories depict competition within and between the sexes: between women for desirable men, between men for desirable women, and between lovers for mastery of their relationships. Although we know he was himself an habitué, and so perhaps had a motive to paint its society as more lovely than it was, Sun Qi claims to be telling us the truth of the entertainment quarters. Whether or not he polished his stories, the *Beili zhi* gives us important insights into "the mentalities of literati and upper-class Chinese males and . . . the role prostitutes played in this form of instituted sexuality."[40]

Beyond the late ninth-century *Beili zhi*, many other texts from the mid- and late Tang take romantic love as their topic: the *chuanqi* stories of the mid-Tang, some of which are stories of love lost and found; hundreds of poems devoted to singing girls and their liaisons in the collections of Tang poets; and anecdotes in other texts, such as the *Ben shi shi* 本事詩 (Storied poems),[41] that describe encounters between courtesans and literati. The sheer number of such texts attests to the appeal of the topic of romance among mid- and late Tang literati. However, the histories of the various genres greatly influenced their respective representations of romantic love. In contrast to the narrative exploration of the limits of romance (problems of class, money, and familial expectations raised and unfulfilled) found in *chuanqi*, the treatment of romance in Tang poetry tends to be conventional, ahistorical, idealized, and brief. Where mid-Tang *chuanqi* reveal the changing social ambitions and class anxieties of literati men as they negotiated both careers and

---

39. Rouzer, *Articulated Ladies*, 251.
40. Ibid., 252.
41. For a study of this text, see Sanders, *Words Well Put*, 158–278.

marriages, Tang poems on romantic topics rarely venture into such details and remain within a narrow set of inherited conventions. The reasons for the relative conservatism of even ninth-century poetry on romance are complex, and an adequate exploration of them is beyond the scope of this study. However, by briefly surveying romance in medieval poetry, we can identify some key aesthetic and formal features that survived into the Tang and influenced the song lyrics of the late Tang and Five Dynasties/Ten Kingdoms period.

The romantic story I have sketched is, on the one hand, as old as Chinese poetry itself (the love poems of the *Classic of Odes* provide evidence of its age). Yet the literary conventions of mid- and late Tang romantic poetry should rather be traced to the medieval *gongti shi* 宮體詩 (palace-style poetry) and other *yuefu* 樂府 (Music Bureau poems) of the Southern Dynasties, in particular those found in the Liang anthology *Yutai xinyong* 玉臺新詠. Just as writers' choices among large generic categories influenced their explorations of romance in the ninth century, so too did the smaller subgeneric traditions of poetry, distinguished by titles and form, shape portrayals of women, encounters, abandonment, and longing from the Southern Dynasties through the Tang. I do not think that the Southern Dynasties poems on beautiful women, palace ladies, or related topics constitute a coherent discourse on romance such as we can perceive in the mid- and late Tang. However, the distinctness of what David Knechtges has called "amatory verse," as a subset of the larger poetic tradition, is demonstrated by the very existence of the *Yutai xinyong*—an anthology quite different from its much more influential and orthodox contemporary, the *Wen xuan*—as well as by the words of its prefacer, Xu Ling.[42] The amatory verse of the Liang court was part of a culture of connoisseurship and competition among literati, not simply the product of their liaisons with courtesans. Paul Rouzer has explored the importance of craft in late Southern Dynasties palace-style poetry and has suggested that "the author of a palace poem addresses and woos not a lover but instead

---

42. Knechtges, "Culling the Weeds and Selecting Prime Blossoms," 234–35.

his fellow poets in an extended commentary they all observe and seek to capture in language."[43] The assumption of romantic longing in, for example, a poem about a woman lingering in her boudoir on a spring morning, might still be present in the palace-style poetry of the *Yutai xinyong*, but the woman's appearance, not her emotional distress or romantic circumstances, was the focus. As Knechtges and others have noted, there is an essential similarity between the "poems on objects," *yongwu shi* 詠物詩, of the *Yutai xinyong*, and poems on women depicted as objects.[44] Within elite literature, we can say generally that the late Southern Dynasties saw the emergence of categorical representations of women and romance in poetry, and that these representations were often dictated by titles, attached either to specific persons, such as Ban Jieyu or Qin Luofu, or to normative emotional states, such as the sorrow of parting in "Libie nan" 離別難 (The difficulty of parting) or the resentment at having been abandoned in poems of *yuan* 怨, "plaint."

The tastes of the poets of the *Yutai xinyong* came under attack in the early Tang, and attacks on the "palace style" persisted late into imperial Chinese history;[45] in the collections of early Tang poets, we find fewer poems written to the titles found in the *Yutai xinyong*. But the luxury, or hedonism, of the era of Tang Xuanzong may have affected this poetic taste as well as many others. In many collections of High Tang poets, the "palace plaint," *gong yuan* 宮怨, functions as a stock piece of the literati poetic repertoire. In the High Tang palace plaint, form prevails over the title; although palace plaints generally depict a woman who is abandoned, presumably in a palace or tower of some sort, the use of the quatrain (regulated or unregulated, pentametric or heptametric) became far more important to the Tang subgeneric tradition. Although they eschewed the static ornateness of "palace-style" poetry, High Tang poets transferred the light eroticism and femininity of that style to their quatrains. We see in palace quatrains an intersection of two

---

43. Rouzer, *Writing Another's Dream*, 73.
44. Knechtges, "Culling the Weeds and Selecting Prime Blossoms," 237.
45. Ibid., 239.

aesthetic trends in Tang poetry: the interest in mood and the poetics of the quatrain, including qualities such as deftness, lightness, and even wit, were extended to the realm of poems on abandoned women.[46] In palace plaint quatrains, we find poets less bound by specific titles (though the older *yuefu* titles were still sometimes used) and more willing to draw upon a broader set of poetic conventions for women in romantic situations. Examples of the broadening of the range of possibilities in the Tang include variations on the "plaint," *yuan,* such as "Spring Plaint," *chun yuan* 春怨, "Jade Steps Plaint" 玉階怨; variations on "palace," *gong,* such as "Palace Lyrics," *gong ci* 宮詞; and titles that included "feeling" coded as feminine, such as "Boudoir Feelings," *gui qing,* cited above, "Spring Feelings," *chun qing* 春情, and the like. A recent study of Tang palace plaints reveals the breadth of approaches to both female abandonment and "plaints" encompassed by that title category, and also suggests that after the High Tang, the titles of such poems grew even more varied, and the content boundaries between title categories that had perhaps once been clear—for example, between poems on generalized "longing" written to the title "Chang xiang si" and poems on the plights of singing girls—were becoming blurred.[47]

---

46. Although his study ends in the early Tang, Daniel Hsieh, in *The Evolution of Jueju Verse,* traces the formation of these poetic values in *jueju* verse in the early medieval period and sketches the legacy of the tradition for the Tang (229–32). Owen, *The Great Age of Chinese Poetry,* 101–3, discusses the High Tang poet Wang Changling's development of these qualities in his romantic quatrains.

47. Zheng, *Tang dai gongyuan shi yanjiu.* Although he examines many poems from across the Tang and isolates their use of specific images and perspectives, Zheng does not clearly define the category of *gong yuan* in formal terms, although he does argue that "imprisonment in a palace," "abandoned in springtime," and "regret over the loss of beauty" were three key elements of palace lament poetry (1–8). At some points, he seems to suggest that the *gong,* palace imprisonment, is the critical term of the two, but at other moments, the "lament" seems more dominant in his discussion. He examines poems from a wide range of titles in his analysis, including the ones I list here and many others with *yuefu* roots. One earlier influential article is Miao, "Palace-Style Poetry: The Courtly Treatment of Glamour and Love."

The Tang "palace plaint" tradition is a rich topic that needs further study; here I focus on only a few elements that were especially influential to the poetics of the *Huajian ji*.⁴⁸ The quatrain tradition had roots in popular song, particularly stanzaic song, and the many *yuefu* on the topic of romance from the folk tradition show clear links to the song lyrics from Dunhuang.⁴⁹ But the literati song lyrics of the *Huajian ji* show a stronger aesthetic relationship to elite poetry on women and romance, and particularly to Tang palace plaints.⁵⁰ Tang poets constructed their brief scenes on the foundation of the romantic story I have outlined above. Titles could be used to signal the boudoir setting and its abandoned female subject, but Tang poets also exploited the anonymity of the subject to their poetic advantage. As historical or circumstantial markers (mapping the female subject to a known historical figure, for example) became less important in such poems, the skillful deployment of conventional images to create a coherent mood became the chief goal. Direct expression of emotion was rare; evocative description of scene and subject essential. Three High Tang examples of "plaint" poems show us some of the literary values of this form.

"Plaint of the Blue Tower" 青樓怨
Wang Changling 王昌齡

Winds blow through the fragrant curtains, flowers come into the tower,	香幃風動花入樓
while a high tune on a resounding zither slows the evening's sorrow.	高調鳴箏緩夜愁

---

48. Many traditional commentators and modern scholars have noted the links between the quatrain tradition of the Tang and the development of song lyric aesthetics, although the traditional view of the development of the song lyric form, which held that song lyrics developed as literati added words to the *jueju* form to make them fit to popular tunes, has been largely abandoned.

49. See Frankel, "*Yueh-fu* Poetry," 94–98, for an overview of the *Wusheng ge* and *Xiqu ge* subtraditions of *yuefu* in quatrain form, for which the "favorite theme is love."

50. For a brief overview of the Tang palace plaint tradition, including comments on the poetics of the subgenre, see Hu-Sterk, "Les 'poèmes de lamentation du palais' sous les Tang."

Broken-hearted by the barrier mountains, but unable to speak it out— 腸斷關山不解說
faint and dim, the waning moon sinks beneath the bed curtain hooks.[51] 依依殘月下簾鉤

"Spring Plaint" 春怨
Li Bai 李白

The white horse with its gilded bridle is off to east of Liaohai; 白馬金羈遼海東
behind gauzy curtains, in embroidered quilts, one sleeps in spring breezes. 羅帷繡被臥春風
The setting moon sinks to the railing to spy the candle gone out; 落月低軒窺燭盡
flying flowers, coming in through the doors, laugh at the empty bed.[52] 飛花入戶笑床空

"Spring Plaint" 春怨
Liu Fangping 劉方平

The sun sets through the window screen, slowly turning to dusk; 紗窗日落漸黃昏
in the gilded chamber, there's no one to see the tracks of tears. 金屋無人見淚痕
The empty veranda is lonely and still, spring near its end— 寂寞空庭春欲晚
pear blossoms so cover the ground that the gates cannot be opened.[53] 梨花滿地不開門

These three quatrains share the same anonymous, suppressed female subject, the boudoir setting, the seasonal markers of spring, and a hint of emotion, the latter expressed either through music, the

---

51. Wang Changling has two other poems composed, according to the *Tang wen cui*, to the title "Tune of the Blue Tower," *Qinglou qu* 青樓曲. The title is not found in the *Yutai xinyong* nor in the *Yuefu shiji*. Li, ed., *Wang Changling shi jiaozhu*, 144, 166. QTS 143.1445.

52. Li Bai, "Chun yuan," in Wang, ed., *Li Taibai quanji*, 1175. QTS 184.1880.

53. Liu Fangping, "Chun yuan," QTS 251.2840. This poem was preserved in two Tang anthologies, the *Yulan shi* (from ca. 817) and the Shu anthology of Tang poetry, *Caidiao ji*. Fu, *Tang ren xuan Tang shi*, 377, 876.

traces of tears, or a conventional feminine lassitude. The word that links the three, "plaint," *yuan*, is never spoken by the female subjects; instead, the poets allow scenic detail to articulate feeling that the subject is "unable to speak out." Li Bai most cleverly subverts the potential pathos of the scene when he personifies the moon and the flowers, who spy on the abandoned woman and "laugh at the empty bed" while also "blooming," *xiao*. The aesthetic qualities of these quatrains—lightness, delicacy, and a careful, perhaps unexpected, use of conventional images—demonstrate the importance of craft and wit in the subgeneric tradition of palace laments, features that are central to the romantic song lyrics of the *Huajian ji*.

Mid- and late Tang poets continued to write such palace plaints, but they went beyond the formal and topical constraints of the palace lament quatrain to expand the boundaries of poetry on women and romance considerably. Mid-Tang poets such as Bai Juyi and Yuan Zhen became known for their poems describing beautiful courtesans and romantic entanglements;[54] Li Shangyin, whether or not he was actually involved in a series of romantic affairs, certainly wrote about them;[55] writers of *chuanqi* tales sprinkled love poems throughout their narratives; and according to Sun Qi, courtesans and literati in the Northern Ward used poems to swear their love and break it off.[56] Poems that were used in this latter fashion tended to be less descriptive and more expressive, serving as vehicles for lovers' feelings; they thus can be filiated to the anonymous medieval romantic *yuefu*, such as the "Midnight" (*Ziye* 子夜) poems, in which women's voices spoke more frankly of their feelings for and about heartless men. One famous poem of this sort was used by Cui Yingying 崔鶯鶯, in the "Tale of Yingying" 鶯鶯傳 (attributed to Yuan Zhen 元稹), to lure young Zhang to a confrontation:

---

54. I have explored the ways Yuan Zhen attempted to incorporate such poetry into a broad understanding of *wen* in "Defining Experience: The 'Poems of Seductive Allure' (*yanshi*) of the Mid-Tang Poet Yuan Zhen (779–831)."

55. See Owen, "What Did Liuzhi Hear?"

56. Rouzer, *Articulated Ladies* (269–83), discusses the uses of poetry in the *Beili zhi* anecdotes.

I await the moon on the western porch, 待月西廂下
welcoming the breeze, my door half-open. 迎風戶半開
Brushing the wall, shadows of flowers move— 拂牆花影動
perhaps it is my lover who comes.[57] 疑是古人來

Such brief poems (quatrains were the most common form) reveal one lover's feelings about the romance in an anonymous—and sometimes even ungendered—voice, a feature that enables their use in different contexts. In Tang stories and anecdotes, and when shared within the community of literati and courtesan participants, such poems had contextual meaning, and were often left untitled. When collected in a poet's corpus or in anthologies, however, they were given titles (though these were often quite general), and thus, with the passage of generations, became independent of historical actors or situations. The reverse movement was also possible: as in the case of Wen Tingyun, romantic poems or song lyrics could themselves generate stories in later dynasties about the poets themselves. Or, in the case of the above poem spoken by Cui Yingying and embedded within the "Tale of Yingying," the poems could become attached to fictional characters, then detached and preserved as their compositions. This particular poem was titled "Answering Student Zhang" and credited to a woman named Cui Yingying when it was collected by the Shu literatus Wei Hu in the *Caidiao ji*, a 1,000-poem anthology of Tang poetry I examine further in Chapter 3.

Extant Tang literati song lyrics intersect the culture of romance but do not overlap it entirely. Although we see in romantic *quzi ci* the same kinds of conventional approaches to women in boudoirs and lovers' plaints, the topical diversity of extant *quzi ci* demonstrates the fundamental importance of the titles of *quzi* to the lyrics that literati poets composed. Though romance may be a common topic in Tang literati lyrics outside the *Huajian ji*, it is by no means the only one. Rather than sharing a single topic, many Tang lyrics seem instead to follow from their tune titles, with these titles

---

57. As far as I have been able to determine, the Shu-era *Caidiao ji* is the earliest extant text to preserve this poem. Fu, *Tang ren xuan Tang shi xinbian*, 963–64. See also the version in Wang, *Tang ren xiaoshuo yanjiu*, vol. 2, 255.

sometimes even appearing as the first line of a lyric. Many of these tune titles obviously inspired romantic content. Some titles, such as "Yi Qin E" 憶秦娥 (Recalling the beauty of Qin), or "Taohua qu" 桃花曲 (Song of peach blossoms), or "Libie nan" invited the composition of lyrics on beautiful women, women as flowers, and lovers' separation. As we noted above, the lyrics to "Yangliu zhi" cover similar ground. A lyric to "Yangliu zhi" by the late Tang poet Duan Chengshi 段成式 (?–863) shows a typical treatment of the "willow" trope in ninth-century lyrics:

"Yangliu zhi" (4th of 7)
Duan Chengshi

As they open, the tender leaves can't bear the cold;	嫩葉初齊不耐寒
a gentle breeze occasionally brushes them across the jade balustrade.	風和時拂玉闌干
On the day the traveler left and "broke it off,"	征人去日曾攀折
she wept in the rain, wounded by spring, her darkened brows fading.[58]	泣雨傷春翠黛殘

Here we see the images that Xue Neng dismissed in his fellow-poets' "willow" verses: the female figure is sketched by the fragile willow branches in spring, and the arc of their fronds is echoed in the faded, or tear-smudged, brows of her face. The markers of parting are also in place: the branches and the relationship are both "broken off" in the third line, which prompts the abandoned woman to tears that damage her appearance. The conjunction of specific images (willow branches, eyebrows, spring as youth and time of "blossoming") with the treatment of parting can be found in any number of these willow lyrics. The large number of "Yangliu zhi" lyrics within the body of extant literati lyrics demonstrates the importance of romance as a topic of Tang literati *quzi ci*.

Outside the "Yangliu zhi" lyrics in the *Huajian ji*, there are 88 lyrics to "Yangliu zhi" in Tang literati lyrics, the largest number of lyrics to any single tune from the Tang (there are 10 Tang lyrics to the title in the *Huajian ji*). The reason for the popularity of "Yangliu

---

58. QTWDCSZ, 311.

zhi" among literati poets is probably simple: the structure of the lyric is that of a heptametric quatrain, and most of the extant Tang lyrics to the title follow the rules for tonal regulation and rhyme for that poetic form. In other words, composing a lyric to "Yangliu zhi" required the same poetic techniques as the regulated quatrain. The facts that there is only one lyric to the tune in the 545 Dunhuang lyrics and that it is composed in heterometric verse, with no mention of willows, women, parting, or other images associated with literati treatment of "willow branches," indicate that Tang literati paid more attention to the meanings of tune titles when composing than popular lyricists did.[59] This literati attention to tune titles links *quzi ci* to its older medieval counterpart, *yuefu*. By the Tang, the musical settings of early medieval *yuefu* had been lost for centuries; the sole signifier of content or mood for *yuefu* composition was thus the title, which poets assiduously followed in their compositions. At the same time that the tune title provided a set topic, the familiar heptametric quatrain form of "Yangliu zhi" may also have meant that lyrics to the tune were more often preserved in poets' collected works.

Other *quzi* that appear frequently in the body of Tang literati lyrics, such as "Yi Jiangnan" 憶江南 (Remembering the Southland), "Yi Chang'an" 憶長安 (Remembering Chang'an), and "Hao shi guang" 好時光 (Scenes of good times), seemed to have provoked reminiscences of youth spent in beautiful places. Here are two lyrics by Bai Juyi that demonstrate this perspective (a viewpoint that Wei Zhuang, a *Huajian ji* poet, takes up again, as we will see in Chapter 4).

"Yi Jiangnan" (1st of 3)
Bai Juyi

The Southland is fine,	江南好
Its scenery as fresh in my mind as ever:	風景舊曾諳
When the sun rose, river flowers were redder than fire;	日出江花紅勝火
When spring came, river waters were like indigo.	春來江水綠如藍
How can we not remember the Southland?	能不憶江南

---

59. Ren, *Dunhuang geci zongbian*, vol. 1, 515–16.

"Yi Jiangnan" (3rd of 3)

Memories of the Southland—	江南憶
Next I remember Wu palaces.[60]	其次憶吳宮
With a cup of spring "bamboo leaf" Wu wine,	吳酒一杯春竹葉
And the Wu beauties dancing in pairs, like drunken lotuses.	吳娃雙舞醉芙蓉
When will I ever meet them again?[61]	早晚復相逢

Such reminiscences could include youthful liaisons with singing girls, or represent singing girls as part of the beautiful "scenery" of the far-off land. Some *quzi* titles invoked romance only faintly. The extant Tang lyrics to the medieval Daoist tune "Bu xu ci" 步虛詞 (Pacing the void) sometimes, but not always, invoke stories of mortal men's encounters with goddesses. Other tune titles may have referred to the tune's origin—such as the title "Qingping yue" 清平樂 (Qingping music),[62] and the title "Bai xinyue" 拜新月 (Bowing to the moon)[63]—or to the form, such as "Yi qi ling" 一七令 (One-through-seven melody), in which the first line of the lyric contains one word, the second line two words, and so on. A few tune titles reveal their links to other musical or dance pieces, such as "Ta ge ci" 踏歌詞 (Stepping-song lyrics) or "Jian qi ci" 劍器詞 (Sword lyrics), which derived from a longer martial dance suite, "Xihe jianqi" 西河劍器.[64] The diversity of content in literati lyrics stems from the va-

---

60. In the second lyric, Bai speaks of Hangzhou; here, his reference to the Warring State of Wu means Suzhou.

61. *QTWDCSZ*, 180-81. Liu Yuxi also composed two lyrics to this tune (they composed them together), but where Bai follows the topic of the tune, Liu's lyrics focus on their present situation: a meeting late in life in Luoyang. Liu explicitly describes their getting drunk and "reminiscing together over our days of beauty and splendor." Ibid., 156.

62. Ren Bantang, in *Jiaofang ji jianding*, 67, distinguishes between "Qingping yue" and the tune title "Qingping diao," arguing that only the former had a dance that accompanied it. From evidence in the Tang histories, he argues that the title derives from an official title, not from the musical modes of *qing* and *ping*.

63. The title refers to a custom of reverencing the new moon. Ren, *Jiaofang ji jianding*, 99-100.

64. There are eleven lyrics to "Ta ge ci" collected in *QTWDC* and *QTWDCSZ*; of these, the seven earliest lyrics (from the High Tang) describe dancing women, and the four later lyrics by Liu Yuxi are, like his "Zhu zhi" (Bamboo branch) lyrics,

riety of tune titles, but this diversity should be compared to the more varied content we find in Dunhuang lyrics, whose topics include patriotism, military exploits, life on the frontier, reclusion, and Buddhist themes.⁶⁵ In comparison, Tang literati lyrics seem decidedly narrow, emphasizing parting, beautiful women, scenic nostalgia, and occasionally the frontier—stock topics of popular song and of literati imitations of centuries of *yuefu* poetry.

The ninth-century culture of romance thus shaped Tang literati song lyrics in various ways. We know that the melodies called *quzi* were an important part of musical entertainment in elite Tang society. In the lyrics by Bai and Liu, and in the many poems that describe women singers, we have evidence that Tang men listened to such songs and occasionally composed them. The most common sites for performance were the entertainment quarters and parties thrown by literati for their friends and colleagues. Given the context of the entertainment quarters, where romantic love was both a topic and a commodity, it was natural for literati to sometimes write about romance. Moreover, it seems probable that the musical settings of these romantic *quzi* played some role in their contents. These tunes surely featured modes, instruments, and tempi that were associated with sorrow. We can reconstruct some of the musical associations of the tunes—such as the association of the *pipa* with singing girls, the association of the vertical flute with the music of Central Asia, the association of drum songs and suites with martial themes, or the association of certain modes, such as the *shang* 商,

---

about the folk customs of a province in which he was posted. *QTWDCSZ*, 6, 40, 45, 176–78. There are three literati lyrics by the mid-Tang poet Yao He to "Jian qi ci" that describe the movements of the dance; it is also described by Du Fu in a preface to a poem about viewing a performance of the dance. See Ren, *Jiaofang ji jianding*, 105; *QTWDCSZ*, 230–32.

65. Ren (*Dunhuang qu chutan*, 276) divides the topics of the 545 Dunhuang lyrics into 20 categories, of which 6 are the most prominent. Of Ren's 20 categories, 5 concern women or romance ("plaintive longing" *yuansi* 怨思, "love" *aiqing* 愛情, "boudoir feelings" *guiqing*, "parting" *bieli*, and "singing girls' feelings" *jiqing* 伎情), for a total of 94 lyrics of 545. However, among the other topical categories, the 298 lyrics concerning Buddhism outnumber all the rest of the lyrics combined.

with melancholy[66]—but the musical settings of most individual *quzi* will likely remain hidden to us.[67]

Though the poetry, stories, and anecdotal texts from the ninth century demonstrate the fascination of romance to the literati, *quzi ci* were clearly not the most important literary vehicle for the exploration of the theme. Paul Rouzer has suggested that the literati preference for poetry over songs in the romantic exchanges of Tang *chuanqi* points to the continuing ideological importance of poetry within the male literati community.[68] It may also indicate the lesser status of song lyrics as a literary form in the Tang. But how well does our extant body of literati lyrics reflect Tang practice? If, despite the enthusiasm of Bai Juyi and Liu Yuxi, the composition of song lyrics was a trivial pastime among even ninth-century literati, would poets have commonly preserved their lyrics? Would they preserve them in their collections as song lyrics (poetic texts attached to a tune title), or did they perhaps preserve them under different titles or forms? If we are to understand the motives that lay behind the Shu poets' preservation of the song lyrics in the *Huajian ji*, we must first consider the issues of definition, preservation, and transmission of *quzi ci* in the Tang.

---

66. For a reconstruction of one such "melancholy" tune, see Picken, ed., "Piece: 'A Jade Tree's Rear-Court Blossom' *Gyokuju gotei-ka Yushu houting-hua*," in *Music from the Tang Court*, vol. 3, 1–19. See also the reconstruction of the *quzi* "He manzi" (the translation is uncertain; according to Bai Juyi, He Manzi was the name of a female singer), vol. 4, 10–21. Bai Juyi himself said of the song, "from beginning [to end] it is a pathetic tune" (11). There are five lyrics to "He manzi" in the *HJJ*, and four in the Dunhuang texts. The Dunhuang lyrics concern travel on the frontier and do have an element of homesickness; the *HJJ* lyrics are indeed melancholy, but not more so than other lyrics. More interesting than Bai Juyi's comment on mood, however, are his remarks on structure. Bai states that the tune has "four lines and eight repeats," which would mean that quatrains would fit the tune; but the lyrics to the tune in the *HJJ* have six lines per stanza, and contain two stanzas (except for the lyric by Mao Wenxi, which has only one). This may signal that the tune found in the *HJJ* was not the same as the mid-Tang tune.

67. For one attempt to reconstruct musical modes for specific tune titles in the Tang and Song, see Qiu, *Yanyue tanwei*, 93–98.

68. Rouzer, *Articulated Ladies*, 265, n21.

Song Lyrics in the Tang: Problems of Definition

Genre histories, by their very nature, seek clear patterns of cause and effect in the literary record, and genre histories of the song lyric are no exception. Too often, however, arguments for gradual, steady "development" in fact mask lacunae or discontinuities in the literary record that could force us to reassess our models of generic change. The Tang record of song lyric development contains many such lacunae, and although many of these can be ascribed to the loss of texts over the centuries, some require reexamination. In the early period of a genre's development, even descriptive texts are scarce; prescriptive texts (those that attempt to rationalize formal rules and topical propriety) generally appear much later, often coinciding with or immediately following the genre's moment of greatest popularity. The scarcity of descriptions of Tang literati composition of *quzi ci* makes it difficult to understand the changes in *quzi ci* across different contexts or periods. Reconstructions of the genre's early development thus depend heavily on the evidence of lyrics themselves and the fragmentary historical evidence for their composition or performance. Lyrics can tell us a great deal, of course—they embody formal tendencies and topical preferences among types of poets, as we saw in the texts by Bai Juyi, Liu Yuxi, and Xue Neng—but they tend to be silent about their own origins.

For purposes of clarity, we first have to acknowledge that identifying a text as a *ci* from the Tang is anachronistic. In the Song, the formal definition of *ci* went beyond the simple definition of *quzi ci* we are using here: "lyrics composed to tunes identified by a fixed tune title." Unlike Tang *quzi ci*, the Song conception of *ci* included a fixed metric structure that usually employed heterometric verse. However, as should be clear from the lyrics we have examined above, heterometric verse was not a requirement for lyrics composed to songs in the Tang, and in fact may have been avoided by literati poets before the mid-Tang. As I have noted, for this discussion I am setting aside the problem of verse form and basing the identification of a poetic text as a *quzi ci* solely on its use of a known tune title. Ideally, one would rely only on Tang materials to identify a text as a *quzi ci*, but many texts are only so labeled through their later compilation and classification in the hands of Song, Ming, and Qing readers. Therefore, in examining the development of Tang *quzi ci*, we must wrestle with evidentiary problems, the first of which is establishing the number of extant texts to be considered *quzi ci*, and the second of which is dating the literati preference for heterometric verse—a formal feature that became critical to the genre. The issue of the distribution of lyrics across the length of the Tang dynasty is important but problematic, since all conclusions based on extant evidence are undermined by the possibility of other lyrics or collections that did not survive. The pattern traced by the extant song lyrics—very few of High Tang origin, more from the mid-Tang (post-Rebellion to 820), and then the majority from the late Tang—suggests a sudden rise in both literati and popular interest in the late Tang, but there may be other valid explanations for this skewed distribution of lyrics. The revolution in song lyric scholarship since the publication of the Dunhuang discoveries should serve as a cautionary reminder about the dangers of basing arguments only on currently extant texts, and yet accurately describing the rise of song lyrics in the Tang requires that we pay attention to current dating and distribution of texts, insofar as those can be known.

The question of the number of *quzi ci* from the Tang bears on the issue of formal changes in the composition of song lyrics from the ninth to the tenth century, most importantly the shift from isometric to heterometric verse and the use of two-stanza songforms. Although there were many different poetic forms in the mid- and late Tang, the song lyrics of Tang literati poets *not* collected in the *Huajian ji* show an overwhelming preference for isometric verse, or lines of equal length of five or seven characters, the standard meters of *shi* poetry. However, the Tang poets whose work is collected in the *Huajian ji*—Wen Tingyun, Huangfu Song, and Wei Zhuang—preferred heterometric verse, or lines of varying length. The formal shift from writing song lyrics in lines of even length to lines of uneven length might seem a trivial one to those outside the tradition, and yet heterometric verse went on to become one of the most prized features of the *ci* genre, forever distinguishing it from its isometric *shi* counterparts. Heterometric verse was not itself a new formal development in the Tang—it can be seen even in the *Shi jing* 詩經, and many medieval poets since the Han had used heterometric verse exclusively in the composition of *yuefu*—but by the Tang, isometric verse was the norm for poetry. Literati poets who used heterometric verse for song lyrics in the Tang and Five Dynasties / Ten Kingdoms changed the path of the genre irrevocably. Since very few Tang accounts of the use of the "long-and-short line," *changduan ju,* are extant, any conclusions must be speculative, but the significance of the shift in verse forms mandates some speculation.

In the Tang, songs could be created in many different ways, and in a variety of forms, but only one subset of those songwriting practices, Tang *quzi ci,* developed into the genre known as *ci.*[69] No matter what their position on the origins of *quzi ci,* scholars agree that there are critical differences in form and content between extant Tang lyrics outside the *Huajian ji* and those collected in the *Huajian ji* itself. Explaining these differences is the task of genre historians; yet current explanations tend to skirt some problems in the evidence. In his work *Tang sheng shi* (Musicalized poetry in the Tang), the scholar Ren Bantang examined evidence from Tang poetry, Tang music manuals, and tune title lists in order to demonstrate the existence of many different song practices in the Tang, including a distinct subset of song called *sheng shi* (musicalized [isometric] poetry)—isometric verse that was put to preexisting tunes. Tang song practices included setting poems to old tunes, composing new music for old poems, writing new words to old tunes, and composing both words and tune together. Any kind of song could employ either isometric or heterometric verse. With respect to the literati practice of *sheng shi,* Ren Bantang argued that it antedated and then coincided with the practice of composing heterometric lyrics to tune titles, but that literati strongly preferred isometric verse through the end of the Tang. Ren's analysis, which includes

---

69. Wang, *Sui Tang Wudai yanyue,* 7, provides a useful chart of the development of song practices on the popular and literati levels. However, he considers only the forms in which music was primary, not the practice of taking poems and putting them to music.

comparing lyrics written to the same tune titles in different eras, makes clear that extant Tang literati poetry contains more isometric verse forms for song throughout the eighth and even the ninth centuries.[70] Ren excludes the metrical characteristics of a text from its definition as a song-text: he argues that only the tune title should be considered as a formal marker of a text that accompanied a specific melody (we cannot say such texts were "composed to" a melody, since we cannot determine authorial intention unless it is specified in a preface).[71] However, Ren argues for the separation of Tang song texts into the categories of *sheng shi* and *quzi ci*.

The strategy of relying on tune titles to identify texts as *quzi ci* raises critical problems due to the instability of titling practices and the overlap of *quzi ci* with another well-established Tang poetic genre, *yuefu* poetry. Of all Tang poetic genres, *yuefu* was surely the most protean, to the point where it should perhaps not be regarded as a genre in the Tang, but rather as a poetic mode that took many different shapes over the course of the dynasty. Based on the songs and literati poetic imitations of songs from the Han and period of division, Tang *yuefu* appeared in many different lengths and metric forms. In the work of Tang poets, one finds isometric poems written to old *yuefu* titles, heterometric poems written to old *yuefu* titles, isometric poems written to new "*yuefu*-like" titles (three-word titles including a final word that was usually a term for "song," such as *qu* 曲, *yin* 引, and *xing* 行), heterometric verse written on clearly defined "new topics" (the *xinti yuefu* 新題樂府 of Bai Juyi, Li Shen, and Yuan Zhen), and texts of both isometric and heterometric verse that are elsewhere identified as *quzi ci* but are included by the Song literatus Guo Maoqian 郭茂倩 in his influential twelfth-century anthology *Yuefu shiji* 樂府詩集 (Collection of Music Bureau poetry) under various rubrics, most often in the *jindai quci* 近代曲辭 (lyrics

---

70. Ren, *Tang sheng shi*, 1–10, for definition of *sheng shi*; 341–46 for a summary of the differences between *sheng shi* and song lyrics; 371–72 for a comparison of Tang tunes that have both isometric and heterometric lyrics from the Tang and Five Dynasties / Ten Kingdoms period. Of the 37 tunes, three have lyrics in both forms from the Tang.

71. See Wang, *Sui Tang Wudai yanyue*, 62–65, for a summary of the criteria for identifying song lyrics.

to recent tunes) section. With respect to meter, rhyme, and tonal balancing, we find every possible variation in Tang *yuefu*, from completely regulated quatrains written to old *yuefu* titles, to unregulated, deliberately "archaic" (*gu* 古) pieces. In Tang texts on music, writers also sometimes used the term *yuefu* for both the musical piece and the words performed to it, or for what we would now identify either as a *quzi*, tune, or as a *quzi ci*, lyrics to a tune. Our modern identification of a poetic text as a song-text relies upon the manner in which the text was titled and preserved. But there are also *quzi* titles that obviously overlap with *yuefu* titles, such as the title "Chang xiang si"—which exists both as an old *yuefu* title and as the title of one of the *quzi* listed in the *Jiaofang ji*—or the *yuefu* title "Zhe yangliu" and the *quzi* title "Yangliu zhi," both of which appear attached to heptametric quatrains.[72] In addition to similar titles, there is overlap in content—for example between a text written to old *yuefu* titles on the sorrow of parting and *quzi* lyrics that take parting as their subject—cautioning us against drawing overly sharp distinctions between the two types of text.

Given this range of continuity between texts preserved as *yuefu* and those preserved as *quzi ci*, I do not think that we can argue that poets perceived distinct generic boundaries between the two kinds of *texts* in the Tang. But what about the relationship of text and music? This is more troublesome. We know very little about the musicalization of *yuefu* in the Tang, particularly in the ninth century, the era from which we have the most extant *quzi ci*; though it

---

72. In the case of "Yangliu zhi," however, we have two different metrical forms for the same title in the *Huajian ji*. In his discussion of the existence of different metrical forms for the same tune title in the Tang and between the Tang and Five Dynasties / Ten Kingdoms period, Ren argues that the music for the Tang tunes, as recorded in music manuals, *yuepu* 樂譜, was lost or changed in the collapse of the dynasty. He argues that one form could have "evolved" into another by adding words, in all but a few cases (Ren, *Tang sheng shi*, 368–72). Wang takes up this problem again and argues that the cases for which the relationship between isometric and heterometric forms is unclear may stem from their association with song-suites (*daqu* 大曲), new tunes composed during the Tang, or from the existence of different tunes for song and for dance (87–92). A possibility that neither considers seriously is that the tunes to which later heterometric lyrics were composed were new, but composed to the old titles.

is generally assumed that *yuefu* had become a nonmusical genre by the ninth century, the mid-Tang "new *yuefu*" may have been put to music and have circulated both as song and recited verse—Bai Juyi claimed that he wrote them in a manner that would allow them to be easily set to music.[73] In the absence of clear evidence about the musicalization of specific *yuefu*, we can only rely on extratextual evidence to identify a *quzi ci* as having had an accompanying melody. In the end, although we are trying to determine the extent of a particular musical-literary practice—the composition of lyrics to tunes—we ultimately must depend on textual evidence that may obscure the practice. With respect to this textual evidence, the number of texts bearing the titles of *quzi ci* rises over the course of the ninth century, whereas, with a few exceptions, we do not see a similar increase in the number of texts composed to older *yuefu* titles in the collections of late Tang poets.[74]

In the comprehensive anthology of Tang and Five Dynasties/Ten Kingdoms song lyrics, the 1986 *Quan Tang Wudai ci*, the scholars Zhang Zhang and Huang Yu use the following criteria for defining a text as a song lyric (they use the term *ci*) from the Tang: the use of a tune title for the title of the text, and the appearance of that text in at least one other collection of song lyrics or *cihua* (comments on song lyrics) text. They quite explicitly acknowledge the difficulty of making firm identifications among very similar kinds of texts in the Tang, and the potential misidentifications resulting from using later texts for their definitions.[75] Although I take issue with some of their inclusions, I would note that from one perspective this collection represents the minimum number of extant texts that may have been considered *quzi ci* in the Tang. To reiterate the point made above, including a Tang text in a collection of "*ci*" such as the *Quan Tang Wudai ci* means relying upon dis-

---

73. See his comments on his *xin yuefu* in the preface to the series of 20; *Bai Juyi ji jianjiao* 3.136.

74. There is a significant increase in mid-Tang poets' use of *yuefu* titles and *yuefu*-like titles, but that interest does not seem to continue in the work of late Tang poets. One important exception to the late Tang pattern is Wen Tingyun, who was of course the single most influential poet of the *Huajian ji*.

75. *QTWDC*, 3-4.

tinctions made after the end of the dynasty, when the form had taken on greater definition. The risks here run both ways: one may overlook texts that were sung to tunes whose titles did not survive the Tang or were not recorded in any extant Tang historical work; or, one may include texts that perhaps were not originally composed for or set to the melody referred to by the tune title, but were only later put to music and given the tune title.

Many scholars of song lyrics argue for a "gradual" or "slow" development of the song lyric, stretching from the High Tang through the end of the dynasty.[76] As noted above, the evidence for the presence of performed *quzi* at all levels of Tang culture is considerable; and yet the evidence of literati interest in composing song lyrics contains many puzzles. A closer analysis of the body of Tang literati *quzi ci* does not support the common argument for "gradual" development of song lyrics; to see this, however, we must discriminate among kinds of song lyrics in the evidence to be considered. Despite the *Quan Tang Wudai ci* editors' laudable desire to be comprehensive, I do not think we have 1,000 Tang literati *quzi ci*—the number of lyrics compiled by Zhang and Huang—with which to establish *quzi ci* as a coherent Tang literati genre. This number misleadingly includes lyrics that are either undatable or external to mainstream literati practice. The most important such

---

76. See, for example, Chang (*Evolution of Chinese Tz'u Poetry*, 26), who refers to Wen Tingyun as the turning point in the evolution of formal conventions for song lyrics: "after 850 the *tz'u* genre slowly acquired its independent structural principles, departing from the *chueh-chü* conventions"; Wagner (*Lotus Boat*, 106) notes: "By the mid-Tang literati imitations of popular *tz'u* had become a widespread vogue," and "it is clear that the *ch'ang-tuan-tz'u* with lines of unequal length did not suddenly spring to life after 850, but rather, this development was the culmination of a long, gradual process" (119). See also Chang's statement that "behind the impression of a separation of the poetic styles represented by Wen T'ing-yun and Wei Chuang, there lies a slow current of synthesis gradually realized in the *tz'u* poetry of the Five Dynasties." However, the extant Tang lyrics do not support an argument for "synthesis"—instead, what the *HJJ* lyrics reveal, when juxtaposed against other lyrics from the period, is the singularity of Wen's work. Similar statements are found in arguments about the early or High Tang development of lyrics; since there is little evidence that can support detailed conclusions about this early period, scholars simply assume gradual development. For another example, see Tang and Pan, "Lun ci de qiyuan," 22–23.

cases are the 154 lyrics attributed to or grouped under the name of the ninth-century Daoist Lü Yan, and the 500 lyrics by one Yi Jing to the tune "Wang Jiangnan" (Gazing at the Southland) that describe various military strategies—a kind of *Art of War* in song. As the editors to the *Quan Tang Wudai ci shizhu* make clear in their introductions and annotation, the lyrics attributed to Lü Yan (later venerated as the immortal Lü Dongbin) display enough inconsistency to suggest that they come from different hands. Moreover, the historical figure of Lü Yan is tentatively dated to the tenth century, born at the end of the Tang.[77] The lyrics grouped under the name Yi Jing were tentatively attributed to a Tang-era writer in the Song bibliography *Junzhai dushu houzhi*, which cites the Song imperial bibliography, *Chongwen zongmu*; one late imperial edition of the lyrics attributes the works to the Tang literatus Li Jian.[78] This attribution is not only weak but seems unlikely, given that we have no other extant lyrics to the tune "Wang Jiangnan" from the Tang. Furthermore, these 500 lyrics are composed in heterometric verse, and their content—military strategy—is completely at odds with the topic announced in the tune title. Both of these features point to a late date of composition for the Yi Jing lyrics.[79] Thus, I suggest that these two groups of lyrics, even in the unlikely case that they are of late Tang date, would lie far outside mainstream literati practice and therefore demand exclusion from this discussion. Of the Tang lyrics remaining after the exclusion of Lü Yan and Yi Jing, we should also exclude the 18 lyrics attributed to the High Tang poet Li Bai, an attribution that has been persuasively contested by a number of

---

77. For a summary of the evidence for Lü Dongbin's existence as a historical figure, see Katz, *Images of the Immortal: The Cult of Lü Dongbin at the Palace of Eternal Joy*, 52–54. See also Baldrian-Hussein, "Lü Tung-pin in Northern Sung Literature."

78. *QTWDCSZ*, 450.

79. For a careful examination of the issues surrounding the 500 military "Wang Jiangnan" lyrics, see Wang Zhaopeng, *Tang Song ci shi lun*, 215–34. Wang considers the Li Jian attribution, questioned since the Ming, to be false and furthermore argues that the lyrics can be no earlier than the very late Tang and are more likely of tenth-century origin, with some of them being composed perhaps as late as the eleventh century.

scholars.[80] If we use the *Quan Tang Wudai ci* as our base text, the exclusion of these three poets' lyrics leaves us with 441 *quzi ci* by known Tang literati authors. This by no means represents the thousands of poetic texts from the Tang that are preserved with some marker of song in the title, but only texts for which we have external evidence of their having a fixed tune to which the lyrics were or could be performed.

When we examine the distribution of these 441 lyrics across the course of the dynasty and, even more importantly, disaggregate the *Huajian ji* from the Tang literati lyrics not collected in the anthology, we discover some important imbalances in the evidence. First, the bulk of the literati lyrics—approximately two-thirds of the 441— come from the ninth century (an estimate that must remain rough, given the difficulty of dating the majority of lyrics to the lives of individual poets). Thus, the evidence shows a large rise in the number of song lyrics in the mid- and late Tang. Second, among the 441 Tang literati lyrics, 78 of those lyrics, 12 by Huangfu Song and 66 by Wen Tingyun, were collected in the *Huajian ji*.[81] If we remove the Tang-era *Huajian ji* lyrics from the 441 Tang literati lyrics, we are left with only 363 literati *quzi ci* from the eighth and ninth centuries that were not preserved in the *Huajian ji*. But in this small body of 363 Tang literati lyrics, we have further imbalances. Only four poets—Bai Juyi, Liu Yuxi, Xue Neng, and Sikong Tu—have more than a dozen lyrics extant; the 130 lyrics of these four, however, constitute over a third of the entire body of extant literati lyrics. From the opposite perspective, the great majority (84) of the 109 poets represented in the Tang literati lyrics have only a few lyrics extant. In sum, the evidence from the 441 total Tang literati song lyrics that we isolated from the *Quan Tang Wudai ci* is highly skewed: it represents largely ninth-century practice, it is scattered

---

80. For the most recent and thorough challenge to this attribution, see Bryant, "On the Authenticity of the *Tz'u* Attributed to Li Po."

81. There are ten lyrics by Huangfu Song and four lyrics by Wen Tingyun that were not collected in the *Huajian ji* but were preserved elsewhere. The *Quan Tang Wudai ci* editors treat Wei Zhuang as a Five Dynasties poet, as will I.

unevenly across a disparate group of poets, and a sizeable chunk of the evidence is the body of lyrics preserved in the *Huajian ji*.[82]

Interestingly, the Dunhuang lyrics reveal similar kinds of distributional imbalances. Ren Bantang has argued that, of the 545 Dunhuang lyrics, only 248 can be dated, either from internal references (which can identify the date of composition) or external indications such as taboo words (which can only be used to approximate the date of transcription). However, of these 248 datable lyrics, only a few dozen can be dated to the Tang at all; the remaining datable lyrics can be placed in the tenth or eleventh centuries.[83] Most scholars simply assume that the remaining few hundred undatable lyrics include Tang lyrics—indeed, most scholarly discussions of Tang song lyrics include undatable Dunhuang lyrics—and yet these assumptions are not substantiated in the texts themselves. It seems far more likely that the composition dates of the undatable Dunhuang lyrics follow a pattern similar to that of the datable lyrics, which is the same pattern described by the literati lyrics: a few lyrics from the High Tang, perhaps a few dozen from the mid- and late Tang, and then the rest from the Five Dynasties and early Northern Song. Despite our knowledge that popular musicians were writing song lyrics in the eighth century, a conservative interpretation of the textual evidence from both literati and popular lyrics suggests that poets at all levels of Tang society may have been slow to preserve their songs *as song lyrics*—which is to say, as words written to a fixed tune whose tune title would have been attached to the poetic text. In other words, what we see in the extant evidence for Tang *quzi ci* may not be composition or prevalence at all, but rather a question of preservation practices.

---

82. In contesting some of the inclusions in the *Quan Tang Wudai ci* and assessing numbers of lyrics, I am following the example of Murakami Tetsumi, who argued some of the same points I make here regarding the lateness of the song lyric as a genre. Since his work was published in 1976, however, he did not have Zhang's more comprehensive 1986 work and was instead using the smaller 1936 *Tang Wudai ci* of Lin Dachun as his base text. Murakami, *Sō shi kenkyū*, 99–103.

83. The dating of the lyrics appears in Ren, *Dunhuang qu jiaolu*, 220–65, and throughout the commentary for individual lyrics in his *Dunhuang geci zongbian*; also discussed in Liu, *Tang Wudai ci de wenhua guanzhao*, 75.

The increase in song lyrics in the ninth century has a complex relationship to the use of heterometric verse in song lyrics, one of the critical formal features that came to define the genre of *ci*. In this discussion, I have placed the issue of verse form outside the consideration of whether or not a text can be labeled a *quzi ci* because of the problems in the evidence for the development of heterometric verse in the Tang. The use of heterometric verse in *quzi ci* is meaningful, but not as a way of dating the "rise of song lyrics" in the Tang. The prefaces to lyrics by Bai Juyi and Liu Yuxi and other accounts of mid-Tang song tell us that some mid-Tang poets changed their composition practice from setting poems to tunes to composing new words for popular tunes, a practice sometimes labeled *yisheng tianci* 倚聲填詞 (following the music to fill in words).[84] The belief that the compositional practice of song lyrics shifted in the mid-Tang was widely held by Song dynasty poets.[85] From the many discussions of music and performance in poems and other texts by mid-Tang writers, we know that Bai, Liu, and their contemporary Yuan Zhen were interested in and apparently proficient at musical composition and performance; so their desire to have their lyrics fit closely to the tunes they performed seems reasonable. And yet, in the works of the four poets with more than a dozen lyrics who are not included in the *Huajian ji*—Bai Juyi, Liu Yuxi, Xue Neng, and Sikong Tu—the majority of their extant lyrics appear as isometric quatrains composed to "Yangliu zhi." If this important change in compositional practice occurred in the mid-Tang, then why are the majority of extant Tang literati lyrics—including those of the ninth century—found in isometric verse?[86]

---

84. The clearest statement of this shift appears in the mid-Tang poet Yuan Zhen's account of contemporary song practices, in his "Preface to Music Bureau Poetry on Old Topics" 樂府古題序. Yang, ed., *Yuan Zhen ji biannian jianzhu*, 266–93.

85. Shi Yidui summarizes the three stages of musical development for song lyrics as: selecting music to accompany poems, selecting poems to go to music, and "filling in lyrics according to tune." Shi, *Ci yu yinyue guanxi*, 5.

86. Ren, *Tang shengshi*, 371–74, argues that poets who were more musically proficient might have used heterometric verse to match the rhythms of tunes more closely, which may account for the changing forms of song-texts. Picken argues

Ren Bantang's efforts to establish the subgenre of *shengshi* demonstrated that the literati use of heterometric verse for song was a late ninth-century development. We can confirm his conclusions simply by examining the group of Tang literati lyrics we isolated above, the group of 441 lyrics that excludes works attributed to Lü Yan, Yi Jing, and Li Bai. In this set of lyrics, 177—or 40 percent—are in heterometric verse. However, if we exclude from this set of 441 Tang lyrics the 78 lyrics from the Tang poets Wen Tingyun and Huangfu Song collected in the *Huajian ji*, we discover that only 57 lyrics—or a mere 15 percent of the 363 Tang lyrics preserved outside the *Huajian ji*—are in heterometric verse.[87]

By disaggregating the lyrics of the *Huajian ji* poets from the Tang data, we get a very different picture of the formal development of *quzi ci*: in this smaller group of 363 Tang literati lyrics, we see *no significant increase* in the use of heterometric verse in literati lyrics over the course of the ninth century. Instead, we find heterometric verse concentrated in a few tunes, such as "Yi qi ling," or "Yi Jiangnan." But by far the most common tune titles in the lyrics of Tang poets are those, like "Yangliu zhi" and "Zhu zhi" 竹枝 (The bamboo

---

from a different angle that it was the new Central Asian music that forced the change from isometric to heterometric verse. Chinese song tended to be syllabic, one syllable sung to one note; Central Asian music was heterorhythmic ("composed of notes of two or more different durations arranged in different patterns in different musical lines"). If Chinese song were still to remain syllabic, Picken argues, then lyricists had to develop heterometric verse to match the music. Picken's conclusion complements Ren's argument: we know that Bai and Liu Yuxi were competent musicians, and thus they might have been interested in writing lyrics that more closely matched the tunes. The fact remains, however, that the majority of these poets' lyrics are in isometric verse. Picken, "The Musical Implications of Chinese Song-Texts with Unequal Lines."

87. Here I am construing isometric verse as loosely as possible to include, for example, heptametric quatrains that have only one line with an extra character. Such lines should strictly be considered violations of isometric patterns rather than different heterometric patterns, but even using this broader definition, we see that isometric verse was the standard, and heterometric verse still occurs in only a few tune titles such as "Yi qi ling" and "Yi Chang'an." If we use tune titles rather than lyrics for comparison, of the 68 tune titles used by Tang poets (excluding those used only by Li Bai, Lü Yan, Yi Jing, Wen Tingyun, and Huangfu Song), 29 tune titles have lyrics in heterometric verse, or 38 percent.

branch), whose four-line, heptametric, single-stanza lyrics were formally indistinguishable from isometric quatrains. If we focus on the Tang lyrics in the *Huajian ji*, the implications of this reassessment stand out even more clearly: of the 78 lyrics by Wen and Huangfu collected in the *Huajian ji*, 63 of those lyrics—or 81 percent—are in heterometric verse. The same proportions appear if we examine tune titles instead of lyrics: of the 22 tune titles used by these two poets in the *Huajian ji*, 18 tunes—or 82 percent—use only heterometric verse. Therefore, in contrast to the rest of Tang literati lyrics, the *Huajian ji* lyrics present heterometric verse as the norm, not the exception, for *quzi ci*. The differences between the extant Tang literati lyrics preserved outside the *Huajian ji* and those collected in the *Huajian ji* make it clear that the two sets of lyrics do not provide the same kinds of evidence for the development of the song lyric as a genre. Whether the differences were due to changes in composition, transcription, or preservation, the two sets of lyrics give us remarkably different pictures of Tang *quzi ci*.[88]

What then can we conclude from the distribution of literati lyrics and the use of heterometric verse in literati lyrics across the Tang? The evidence of the distribution of lyrics over the Tang at first seems to suggest a late rise in popularity of lyrics composed to tune titles—that despite the presence of *quzi* in popular entertainment,

---

88. I have excluded the consideration of stanzas from this formal analysis partly for simplicity but also because the practice of composing "sung to match," *changhe* 唱和, poems or *lianju* 聯句, linked-couplet sets, which could be sung or chanted and were popular among ninth-century poets, could create a stanzaic song. Although the bibliographic sources from the Tang and Song contain dozens of titles to *changhe* collections, the collections themselves have not survived, and we assume that most of these verses have been handed down in individual poets' collections, *bieji*. Prefaces and anecdotes tell us about linked verse practices and assign poems to specific poets (see also the *Wenyuan yinghua*), but this information is not usually reflected in the *bieji* themselves. This practice of preserving linked verse "unlinked," as it were, suppresses the original stanzaic structure of such compositions from our textual record and hides potentially useful evidence for the use of stanzas in Tang song. If we compare the *Huajian ji* lyrics, 90 percent of which are in two-stanza form, to the Dunhuang *zaqu*, we find that most Dunhuang lyrics are also in two-stanza form—but, as noted before, most of the Dunhuang lyrics are undatable, and the majority of the datable lyrics are not of Tang origin.

literati were slow to become interested in composing lyrics for these tunes. We could also consider other explanations. The most probable explanations for the rise in extant literati song lyrics between the ninth and tenth centuries are changes in composing songs, transcribing song-texts, and preserving those texts for circulation. We saw above that the argument for a change in compositional practice is supported by descriptions of "filling in words according to music" from mid-Tang poets such as Bai Juyi, and yet the extant lyrics do not substantiate this argument. This may raise the issue of transcription practice. Given the associations of popular song with frivolous entertainment, poets may have preserved their songs as other kinds of poetic texts in order to mask their origin as song. Thus, a text that began as a *quzi ci* (whether isometric or heterometric) might have been preserved under another title (not the tune title to which it had been composed) so that a poet could protect his poem from the taint of performed song. If the lyric were composed or even later transcribed in isometric verse, it would be indistinguishable from other isometric poems in a poet's collected works. The content of these literati verses was certainly conventional enough to allow such texts to be preserved under common or unspecific titles.

Finally, we may also be facing a failure of song-texts to be handed down from the Tang, either through historical chance or due to the reputation of the practice. One example of such a text that did not survive the Song is the *Hanlin geci* 翰林歌詞, attributed to the mid-Tang literatus Wang Ya 王涯 (ca. 765–835), and also discussed by the Song scholar Shen Gua 沈括 (1031–95). According to Shen, this lost text collected lyrics in heterometric verse, which Shen concluded were composed by fitting words to tunes.[89] What we may be seeing, therefore, in the "rise of song lyrics" attributed to the ninth century is the coincidence of two developments: an increase in the practice of fitting words to tunes (which encouraged the use of heterometric verse) and a decrease in the stigma attached to preserving one's songs *as songs*, which would appear in one's collected works as lyrics, attached to a tune title. One last, largely unconsid-

---

89. Cited and discussed in Wu, *Tang Song ci tonglun*, 27–28.

ered, possibility remains: that the heterometric lyrics of the late Tang and Five Dynasties period, even those to tune titles found in Tang texts from both the eighth and ninth centuries, may have been composed to new melodies that were attached to old titles. If this last possibility were true, it would make the entire argument about the rise of heterometric verse irrelevant, since we would simply be faced with a ninth-century musical practice that is not adequately documented in the historical texts.

Without the discovery of a new trove of song lyric texts or Tang music manuals, the answers to the questions of why and how heterometric verse became the preferred form for song lyrics from the ninth to the tenth centuries will remain elusive. But with respect to the interest in *quzi ci* of any form by Tang poets, the numbers of song lyrics from poets whose work was not collected in the *Huajian ji* still do not support the argument for a gradual rise in popularity of the composition of *quzi ci* over the course of the ninth century. What we have instead are lyrics scattered over poets of mostly the ninth century and a small group of poets who either preserved their lyrics themselves, like Bai Juyi and Liu Yuxi, or whose lyrics were preserved by others. Furthermore, we find neither topical nor formal coherence within the body of extant Tang literati *quzi ci*. The available evidence shows that the significant rise in numbers of extant song lyrics occurs in the tenth century, in the realms of the Five Dynasties and Ten Kingdoms, and not in the Tang. At the same time, in the lyrics of the poets and works of the tenth century, we discover a clear narrowing of topical interests and formal possibilities, whether we look to Shu or to the Southern Tang. The tenth-century states were the sites of the birth of *quzi ci* as a literati genre. More specifically, the *Huajian ji* stands as the first extant—and likely the first—collection to regularize *quzi ci* with respect to both content and form. As we will see in the next two chapters, the compilers of the *Huajian ji* defined *quzi ci* as a genre for the purposes of their specific historical moment, but the *Huajian ji* model continued to influence and stimulate the poets of the Song.

To conclude, I would return to the issue of the status of song lyrics in Tang culture, because it is there that the two problems of the content of *quzi ci* and the reputation of poets who wrote them appear intertwined. The *Jiu Tang shu* description of the most influential Tang literati composer of *quzi ci*, Wen Tingyun, gives us a sense of how song lyrics might have endangered one's reputation in the Tang.

> Wen Tingyun was from Taiyuan, and his honorific was Feiqing 飛卿. At the beginning of the Dazhong era 大中 [847–60], he should have passed the *jinshi* examination. He labored over his studies and was particularly good at poetry and rhapsodies. When he first came to the capital, many literati praised him greatly. But then he began to move in miscellaneous, seedy circles, and did not attend to his attire; he was skilled at following the sounds of strings and flutes to make lascivious and erotic lyrics (測艷 之詞). . . . Pei Cheng accompanied him in drinking, and they spent their days in a drunken stupor. Because of this, the years went by without his ever passing an examination.[90]

Here, song lyrics are not depicted as the cause of Wen Tingyun's dissipation, but they are a revealing sign of how far he had fallen from his early promise, and their eroticism is a measure of his corruption. Drunkenness and licentiousness are inextricably linked in this portrait of the dissolute playboy. Later texts go beyond this brief portrait to record anecdotes of specific instances of Wen Tingyun's bad behavior that were sometimes connected to his song lyrics; these later stories may have some truth in them, but they may also be circularly derived from the erotic content of Wen Tingyun's lyrics and poems.[91] Although we have no biography for him, Huangfu Song, the other late Tang poet whose work is collected in the *Huajian ji*, was known as the author of a text now extant only in fragments, the *Zuixiang riyue* 醉鄉日月 (Days and months in the land of drunkenness).[92] Since we know very little of Huangfu Song's life, we cannot judge the effect of these texts on his career in the short or long term, though there is no record of his passing an exam or serving in an office.[93] But the connection between his romantic

---

90. *JTS* 190.5078–79. His friend Pei Cheng also has five lyrics extant, collected in *QTWDCSZ*, 222–25.

91. See, for example, the stories collected in *Tang shi jishi jiaojian*, 54.1474–78.

92. *Shuofu* 58.24a–28a.

93. For a summary of the evidence for Huangfu Song's life, see Chen Shangjun, "*Huajian* ciren shi ji," in *Tangdai wenxue congkao*, 370–73.

song lyrics and his text on the realm of drunkenness seems apparent: both kinds of texts would be appropriate for a literatus who frequented the entertainment quarters.

Even for poets like Bai Juyi and Liu Yuxi, for whom we have dozens of lyrics, we find no approving comments on those pieces in their official biographies, and more commonly find no comment at all on the matter.[94] From the viewpoint of official historians, the practice of songwriting seems to have been either unimportant or a source of embarrassment for Tang literati, given its association with popular entertainment culture and singing girls. However, the same stigma did not necessarily obtain in literati social life. In stories and poems of the ninth century, the rakish playboy attitude and behavior known as *fengliu* 風流, adopted by certain elite men in their youth, appears to have been one way to attract both male and female attention in a competitive social environment. This behavior could be abandoned, of course, once a young man attained a good post or perhaps achieved a socially advantageous marriage, and the literary artifacts of earlier days, such as licentious poems or songs, would be left out of collections compiled for political advancement. These cultural forces surely affected the preservation of literati song lyrics in the Tang: just as many disincentives dissuaded elite men from composing such lyrics, there was little further incentive to preserve them in collections or to otherwise encourage their circulation.

My emphasis on the cultural contexts for *quzi ci* in the Tang is intended to draw attention to the status of song lyrics vis-à-vis other literary forms, and to highlight discrepancies in the evidence we have for song lyrics from the ninth and tenth centuries—both the song lyrics collected in the *Huajian ji* and those transmitted otherwise. Without an understanding of the range of Tang song lyrics, we cannot appreciate the continuities and innovations of the *quzi ci*

---

94. One exception would be the mention of Liu Yuxi's "Zhuzhi ci," in his *JTS* and *XTS* biographies. However, they are simply mentioned as his works and not presented as a demonstration of musical ability or interest. For a discussion of the place of Liu's *quzi ci* in his biography, see Qu, ed., *Liu Yuxi ji jianzheng*, 1575–76. Neither Bai Juyi's lyrics nor his interest in music are mentioned in his official biographies, despite the importance of music as a topic in many of his works.

found in the *Huajian ji*, whether those are from the ninth or tenth centuries. In the *Huajian ji*, Wen Tingyun's "lascivious and erotic lyrics" establish the topic and the mood for much of the Shu collection, and the forms that Wen used appear as the standards for other *Huajian ji* lyrics. If the new interest in romantic song indeed represents a change in cultural tastes from the ninth to the tenth century, from Tang to Shu, we must next explore what prompted it.

TWO

Poets in Their Place

Court and Culture in Tenth-Century Shu

In the summer of 940, Ouyang Jiong, a drafter (*sheren* 舍人) in the service of the ruler of Shu, described the creation of the *Huajian ji* in his preface to the collection:

Now the Vice Minister for the Court of the Imperial Regalia, cognomen Hongji 弘基 [Zhao Chongzuo 趙崇祚],[1] by picking up kingfisher feathers from the banks, has found the finest quills, and from the woven floss of the springs' depths has singled out [the dragon-weavers'] best work.[2] He has

---

1. Zhao Chongzuo's family name is not given in the preface, but his identity can be confirmed through two sources: *Jiuguo zhi* 7.5a, and *SGCQ* 51.757–8. Translations of offices and titles come from Hucker, *A Dictionary of Official Titles in Imperial China*, unless otherwise noted.

2. The "woven floss" of the dragon-weavers refers to a marvelous fabric woven by southern water-dragons (a kind of *jiaolong* 蛟龍) that dwelt in deep pools and

gathered often with many guests who have proffered excellent arguments and has thus collected 500 lyrics to tunes (*quzi ci*) of recent poets and has divided them into ten chapters.³

By noting the cognomen and the official title of the *Huajian ji* compiler and by showing the collection to be the product of ongoing social events, Ouyang Jiong suggested that this collection of *quzi ci* represented the tastes of Shu elites. But who were these elites, and why were they discussing song lyrics, rather than poetry (*shi*) or rhapsodies (*fu* 賦), two of the orthodox genres of elite literature? More importantly, why would this imperial official, Zhao Chongzuo, think a compilation of 500 song lyrics in ten *juan* worth making?

Although Ouyang's description seems to ignore the censure that Tang officials might have suffered performing or discussing song lyrics, such censure was directed toward Ouyang Jiong himself only decades later, after the fall of Shu to the Song. Under the Latter Shu regime, Ouyang Jiong rose to be a grand councilor (*pingzhang shi*), one of the highest-ranked officials in the Shu government. After he was captured by the Song in 965, Ouyang was summoned once by the first Song emperor to perform a few songs. On hearing about the incident, the Director of the Censorate Liu Wensou remonstrated heatedly, arguing that this was inappropriate behavior for the emperor. Song Taizu replied:

> I have heard that Meng Chang and his ministers indulged themselves in music and song. Ouyang Jiong rose to be a high minister while still practicing this skill, and thus he was captured by us. I summoned him because I wanted to see if what had been said [about Meng's court] was a false accusation.

Liu Wensou then acknowledged his mistake in remonstrating too hastily, not having recognized the emperor's superior understanding—and Ouyang was never summoned again.⁴ In the eyes of Song

---

coastal waters. See Schafer, *The Vermilion Bird: T'ang Images of the South*, 217–21; *The Divine Woman*, 26–27.

3. *HJJZS*, 1.
4. *Song shi* 479.13,894.

historians, Ouyang embodied all that was corrupt about the kingdom of Shu: not only did he gain position through his entertainment skills, but he then rose to high office while continuing his music-making. The distance between Ouyang's description of Shu elites discussing and collecting *quzi ci* and the later criticism of Shu officials points to the heterodox nature—Song historians would say decadence—of Shu political and cultural life.[5] In this chapter, I explore the intimate nature of Shu court culture, in which rulers and courtiers together "indulged in music and song." It was in this fluid, pleasure-oriented world that literati poets found writing, singing, and compiling song lyrics to be an appropriate and worthwhile pursuit.[6]

It is important to keep in mind the questionable status of *quzi ci* in the Tang precisely because Ouyang Jiong and the other compilers of the *Huajian ji* strove to efface the entertainment practices that song lyrics represented: learning and performing light popular music, associating with singing girls, and having casual romantic encounters with them and other kinds of courtesans. Investigating the cultural contexts of Shu allows us to see the environment in which such a collection might even have been framed as an orthodox literary effort. If the *Huajian ji* not only worked to establish song lyrics as an elite literary practice but also served as a kind of cultural capital—a claim to the status of *shi*, or literati—then we must look more closely at the conditions in which such a claim was made possible. As we saw in the previous chapter, even if composing and performing song lyrics was a popular activity for elite men in certain entertainment contexts, Tang poets associated with romantic song lyrics were sometimes criticized for their frivolity. In contrast, in both the Former and Latter Shu periods, we find song lyrics

---

5. A similar story about Li Yu, second ruler of the Southern Tang, appears in *Song shi* 478.13,862.

6. The title of this chapter, "Poets in Their Place," is an adaptation: it was used by Pauline Yu, in her article on anthologies and the Chinese canon, "Poems in Their Place," a title she borrowed from Fraistat, *Poems in Their Place: The Intertextuality and Order of Poetic Collections*. Although I consider the ordering and selection of the *Huajian ji* in Chapter 3, here I focus on the historical contexts for the collection.

being composed at the Shu courts, by some of the highest officials in the regimes. Clearly, there must have been some changes that made this challenge to literary orthodoxy possible between the late ninth century and the mid-tenth century. Here, I hope to lay out a few of the germane social and political developments in tenth-century Shu.

Although it is now generally acknowledged that the Tang-Song transition brought about sweeping social, political, and cultural changes in China, those changes are difficult to trace in tenth-century documents, in part because of the fragmentary and partial nature of historical records from the period. Another difficulty in tracing the developments in the southern kingdoms stems from the claims made by the southern rulers: each independent ruler lay claim not only to the Mandate of Heaven held by the Tang but also to the Tang cultural heritage. Claims for regional distinctiveness thus had to be balanced with perhaps the more pressing political need to claim continuity with the Tang. As a consequence, extant records from the southern kingdoms tend not to emphasize their particular innovations, but rather highlight the presence of Tang elite descendants, Tang political offices, and Tang literary practices. The Sichuan region is unique among the Chinese provinces in that its relative geographical isolation, along with periods of political independence, has heightened its cultural distinctiveness over the course of Chinese history. In the tenth century, for the first time since the Cheng Han state of Shu (302–47), a succession of men were able to take advantage of Sichuan's isolation and the power struggles in the Central Plain to create an independent kingdom. Two successive regimes, separated by an "interregnum" when Sichuan was under the control of the Latter Tang (925–34), claimed the kingdom of Shu: the Former Shu regime (907–25), founded by Wang Jian 王建 (r. 907–19), who was succeeded by his son Wang Yan 王衍 (r. 919–25), and the Latter Shu regime (934–65), founded by Meng Zhixiang 孟知祥 (r. 934), who was succeeded by his son, Meng Chang 孟昶 (r. 934–65). The regime changes were of course important to the political history of Shu, but, as I explain below, many important social and political figures continued to exercise influence through both Former and Latter Shu regimes. We should rightly understand the years from 907 to 965 as a culturally coherent era, one that could even be extended back into the late ninth century, from the time of Wang Jian's rise to power in the region.

In the following sketch of tenth-century Shu culture, recent scholarship on the social and political changes of the Tang-Song transition has been especially useful for tracing the potential connections among social status, political office, and literary skill in the fragmentary historical documents of the tenth-century kingdoms. A wide range of literary talent was required of ninth-century officials, and the scarcity of positions with respect to the available pool intensified the literary competition of the period. During the eighth and early ninth centuries, the center of this competition was certainly the capital, Chang'an, where the examinations were held and the most prestigious posts were to be found. However, over the course of the second half of the ninth century—a time of growing political corruption at the center, a series of rebellions in various parts of the country, and increasing influence and independence of provincial capitals—we can discern a cultural decentralization that affected literary activity as well. The "courts" of provincial military governors (*jiedushi* 節度使) offered employment and a cultural niche to elite men who could not find a spot in the stream of imperial positions in Chang'an. The cultural environments of the regional centers were not in competition with the capital, but instead flourished simultaneously, and likely fostered different regional tastes. As the preceding discussion of the entertainment districts of late Tang China demonstrated, poets' interest in song lyrics was not simply a literary phenomenon, but rather grew from political disincentives (the potential liability of being associated with the entertainment quarters) and social incentives (songs as a part of literati social intercourse and competition). Tenth-century poets' interest in song lyrics was also influenced by the dramatically altered political and social contexts for literature. Throughout the new "centers" in the old periphery of Tang China, we find flourishing local elite cultures, most of which had developed considerably in the latter half of the Tang. Although Song and later historians deprecated the governments of the "usurping" states, the independence of the kingdoms of the tenth century was critical to many subsequent developments in Song society and culture and should be studied with an eye to their positive contributions.[7]

The most important of the new independent cultural centers in the tenth century were Chengdu, long the provincial capital and later the capital of both the Former Shu (907–25) and Latter Shu (934–65) kingdoms, and Jiangling, the capital of the Southern Tang (937–75). In the ruling courts of Shu and the Southern Tang, we find poets of varying social and political backgrounds writing and circulating song lyrics much more publicly than Tang poets ever did. In this chapter, I draw connections among the worlds of politics, society, and literary culture in Shu in order to reveal the poets of the *Huajian ji* as active participants in an unusual political environment, one in which talent, rather than birth or examination success, was enough to win office and rewards, and in which the definition of "talent" itself was rather broad, and came to include literary, artistic, and even musical skills. The local and independent court culture that fostered the lyrics of the Shu *Huajian ji* poets did not survive the Song conquest of Sichuan, but its influence would still be felt in the Northern Song, in the reception of the *Huajian ji* and other artifacts of Shu court life. An exploration of the cultural contexts for the Shu composition and collection of song lyrics cannot fully explain the popularity of song lyrics among Shu elites. However, a closer examination of the Shu courts and courtiers can help us understand how high-ranking officials of Shu might also have been well known as composers of song lyrics, a phenomenon that we do not find even in the last decades of the Tang.

Problems of Historiography

Before sketching the cultural history of tenth-century Shu, I must first note the limitations of the extant historical sources for the period. Given the Shu regimes' independence, the history of Shu as told by succeeding generations of Confucian historians was bound

---

7. This point is made explicitly by Franciscus Verellen in his study of the use of Daoism to legitimize the Wang rule of the Former Shu kingdom. Verellen, "Liturgy and Sovereignty," 59.

to be biased. However, the historiographical picture of tenth-century Shu is something more than mere Confucian polemic. In Chinese historiography, victorious successor states compile the *zhengshi* 正史, orthodox histories, for the preceding regimes; for periods of division, which were considered to be undesirable if not by definition morally corrupt, the historiography is generally more complicated and difficult to analyze. In the case of the Five Dynasties and Ten Kingdoms era, the historiography is further confused by the fact that only the "Five Dynasties" of the north Central Plain (Liang, Latter Tang, Jin, Han, and Zhou) were considered to be the legitimate successors to the Tang throne. The "Ten Kingdoms" of the south were all considered by historians of the Song to be separatist—and thus completely illegitimate—regimes.[8] Fortunately, some histories of the southern kingdoms written as unofficial accounts have survived to balance the generally censorious tone of Song accounts. Among extant historical sources for the Ten Kingdoms, the sources for the Southern Tang are by far the most numerous and complete.[9]

Histories of the southern kingdoms seem to have been written in two waves, the first coming at the end of the tenth century, just after Song reunification, and the second over the course of the eleventh century. Although we do have Song bibliographical records of histories written in the southern states with the sanction of the local regimes, almost all of those have been lost. Among the extant texts, the first wave of accounts was composed by private scholars, who were often more interested in recording events that fascinated them than in laying out moral lessons. The second wave of histories came from Song officials, who were necessarily committed to constructing a pro-Song reunification narrative in which separatist impulses

---

8. The "Ten Kingdoms" are usually identified as the Former and Latter Shu, Min, Wu-Yue, Southern Tang, Jingnan, Southern Han, Ping, Chu, and Wu.

9. For an excellent introduction to the historiography of the tenth century, see Kurz, "A Survey of the Historical Sources for the Five Dynasties and Ten States in Song Times." See also Kurz's earlier study of the Southern Tang texts, "Sources for the History of the Southern Tang (937–975)." For a study of the culture of another southern kingdom, see Schafer, *The Empire of Min*.

were harshly condemned. As time passed, the critical tone grew more severe.

In the kingdom of Shu itself, history-writing seems to have coincided with the periods after the fall of the Former and Latter regimes. Although the first ruler of independent Shu, Wang Jian, did not order a *Tang shi* 唐史 (Tang history) written, Meng Chang ordered the writing of a *Qian Shu shi* 前蜀史 (Former Shu history) and also commissioned Veritable Records (*shilu* 實錄) to be made for his own reign, some of which remained extant into the Yuan dynasty. According to Song bibliographies, there existed as many *juan* of historical records from Shu as there did for some of the Five Dynasties.[10] Still extant in fragments are two contemporary anecdotal accounts. The first, the *Jianjie lu* 鑒誡錄 (Record of examined warnings), was written by He Guangyuan (fl. 950), an official at Meng Chang's court. The other, a private account called the *Jinli qijiu zhuan* 錦里耆舊傳 (Accounts of the elders of the Brocade City), was written by Gou Yanqing, a magistrate of Jianrong district in the capital prefecture, shortly after the fall of the Latter Shu. Both accounts are quite miscellaneous, combining stories of supernatural happenings with accounts of battles and political events featuring important figures at court, and neither is favorable to the Former Shu regime. Two other, somewhat less useful, sources for Shu history are the *Shu Taowu* 蜀檮杌, from the mid-eleventh century, and the *Shu jian* 蜀鑒 (Mirror of Shu), from the mid-thirteenth century.[11] These anecdotal works shed light on the foibles of individu-

---

10. See the bibliography chapter of *Song shi* 203.5090, which records Li Hao, author of the *Hou Shu Gaozu shilu* (Veritable records of the Grand Progenitor of the Former Shu) in 30 *juan*, and *Hou Shu zhu shilu* (Veritable records of the Ruler of the Latter Shu) also in 30 *juan*. This number of Veritable Records for 31 years of rule surpasses the figure for the Liang Veritable Records, recorded to have existed in 34 *juan* for 16 years of rule. Wang Gungwu, in "The *Chiu Wu-tai shih* and History-Writing During the Five Dynasties," 17, demonstrates that the number of *juan* of Veritable Records correlates closely to the coverage of Five Dynasties in the *Jiu Wudai shi*. We can only conclude that the relative lack of specific detail on Shu results from Song historians' desire to ignore the regimes, not from lack of data.

11. The *Shu Taowu*, named after the annals of Chu cited in the *Zuo zhuan* (where "*taowu*" means "inhuman monster"), was written by Zhang Tangying, a Song official from Sichuan, and prefaced in 1071. The book's title reveals its agenda: to

als in Shu and the interests of their authors, but are generally less useful for understanding the larger history of tenth-century Shu.

In the early Northern Song, other private historians penned general accounts such as the *Jiuguo zhi* 九國志 (Account of the Nine Kingdoms) and the *Wuguo gushi* 五國故事 (Anecdotes from the Five Kingdoms), both of which are extant in fragments today.[12] Other works, such as the *Bei Meng suoyan* 北夢鎖眼 (Gossip from North Meng) by Sun Guangxian, one of the *Huajian ji* poets, focus exclusively on humorous or striking stories of famous people from the Tang through the Five Dynasties and Ten Kingdoms period. This private history-writing activity seems to have fallen off quickly after Song reunification and to all but cease by the Southern Song.[13] A comparison of the bibliographical essays of the *Song shi* and the *Yuan shi* (compiled in the Ming) reveals that histories of the southern kingdoms and historical records from Shu that existed during the Song disappeared from imperial archives, at least, over the succeeding centuries.

The gradual shift in Song official historians' attitudes toward the southern regimes can be seen most clearly in the two "Five Dynasties" (*Wudai* 五代) histories: the *Jiu Wudai shi* 舊五代史 (Old History of the Five Dynasties), completed in 974, relegates the southern states variously to the "hereditary houses" *shijia* 世家 and to the

---

demonstrate the monstrosities of the two Shu regimes for posterity. Zhang acknowledges having read and owned the *Jianjie lu*, the *Jinli qijiu zhuan*, and even some of the Veritable Records of the Latter Shu (which he wanted to burn but couldn't bring himself to do). His account, however, is aimed at presenting only the "fundamentals" of the Shu rulers' mistakes. (See Zhang Tangying, preface to *Shu Taowu* 1.1a–2b.) The *Shu jian*, written sometime in the mid-thirteenth century, after the retreat of the Northern Song to south of the Yangzi, is instead concerned with the military history of the Sichuan region, as a guide for immediate future use. For a list of the sources of these texts, see Kurz, "Survey of the Historical Sources for the Five Dynasties and Ten States," 205.

12. Kurz, "Survey," 192–93.

13. Xu Minxia et al., preface to *SGCQ*, 1–2. Kurz ("Survey," 197) suggests that the appeal of oral, eyewitness accounts of tenth-century events was great in the early part of the Northern Song and stemmed from contemporary interest in that history. This perhaps accounts for the survival rate of some of the smaller and more miscellaneous texts in comparison to the many *juan* of individual state histories that were lost.

"usurpers" *jianwei* 僭偽 sections.¹⁴ One hundred years later, the "Ten Kingdoms" were expanded and placed at the end of Ouyang Xiu's *Wudai shi ji* 五代史記 (later known as the *Xin Wudai shi* 新五代史, New history of the Five Dynasties), again arranged by "hereditary houses." The information on the southern kingdoms in these chapters is confined to thin basic annals (*benji* 本紀) for each ruler of each kingdom; however, the pieces of information Ouyang chooses to include seem carefully selected to demonstrate the fundamental corruption at the heart of each illegitimate regime.¹⁵ In the other major Song historical work that covers the tenth century, Sima Guang's late eleventh-century compilation *Zizhi tongjian* 資治通鑒 (Comprehensive mirror for aid in government), references to events in the southern kingdoms are found scattered among the events of the northern regimes, as suits the format of the text.¹⁶ However, as in the *Xin Wudai shi*, the events that are selected for this history—things such as inauspicious portents, court intrigues, and rulers' excesses—appear to be part of a larger moral lesson on the evils of separatism and power grabs.

The early Qing scholar Wu Renchen attempted to bring together the fragmentary history of the southern kingdoms in his work *Shiguo chunqiu* 十國春秋 (The springs and autumns of the Ten Kingdoms), in which he employed the composite history format of basic annals and biographies for each of the ten southern kingdoms. Although Wu's account includes sources of all sorts, he did not document the sources for his entries unless there were conflicting accounts, and some of his biographical entries have since been

---

14. Kurz, "Survey," 189.

15. Ouyang privately compiled this history under the title *Wudai shiji* between 1036 and 1053; it was not officially published until after his death. See the introduction to Richard Davis's translation of the work for an analysis of Ouyang Xiu's approach to the historiography of the era. Ouyang was especially interested in legitimation theory and found many examples of illegitimate rule in the Five Dynasties through which to explore the problem of moral leadership in an era of political chaos. Ouyang, *Historical Records of the Five Dynasties*, translated and with an introduction by Davis, xlv–lv.

16. The two early Song anthologies of anecdotal and geographical material, the *Taiping guangji* and the *Taiping yulan*, contain information on Shu, but they are less helpful in reconstructing political history.

shown to contain some unreliable information. Wu Renchen was not a historian by training, although he was a scholar of many different kinds of texts; so his work is perhaps less critical of sources than it might have been and must be used with caution. Nonetheless, his biographies provide the greatest single collection of data on men who made up the ranks (ranging from military officers and high ministers down to court painters) at the two Shu courts. For the Former Shu, which lasted 18 years, Wu collected biographical notes on 89 men (this number excludes the Wang clan, consorts, and the dozens of men whom Wang adopted as sons); for the Latter Shu, which lasted 31 years, he found material on 86 men. Even though the Latter Shu endured almost twice as long as the Former Shu, the *Shiguo chunqiu* basic annals for the two regimes are roughly the same length.[17]

Wu's proportionally larger amount of material for the Former Shu reflects the lesser coverage of the Latter Shu regime in all extant sources on tenth-century Shu. This disparity in coverage between the Former and Latter regimes would appear to have two causes. First, officials of the Latter Shu—many of whom were holdovers from the Former Shu court—took it upon themselves to record the failures of the previous regime as lessons for Meng Chang. But after Song reunification, few officials wanted to write about the events of an obviously illegitimate Latter Shu regime outside the broader context of "secessionist southern kingdoms." Second, the extant sources all tend to agree that the Latter Shu regime was both peaceful and prosperous. It therefore seems likely that the available information on the Latter Shu, particularly if it recorded Shu's stability and prosperity, could not support an argument for the moral illegitimacy of separatist regimes. Therefore, Song historians might well have chosen to simply ignore this era of Shu history.

---

17. Taken together, the materials for the Former Shu and Latter Shu amount to less than what Wu Renchen collected for the individual regimes of the Wu-Yue (907–78), Wu (902–37), or Southern Tang (937–75), kingdoms that covered approximately the same geographical region. However, the Shu materials constitute the third largest group of data among the Ten Kingdoms of the *Shiguo chunqiu*.

The discrepancy in the amount of material dedicated to the two regimes must be considered when reconstructing the cultural history of Shu and the biographies of the poets of the 940 *Huajian ji*. We have a better picture of the Former Shu court, but information on the Latter Shu is both sparse and inconsistent. Of the eighteen poets in the *Huajian ji*, fourteen were officials in either one or both Shu courts, and at least five, and perhaps eight, poets were alive in Shu in 940, in the early years of the Latter Shu.[18] The success or failure of the *Huajian ji* in court circles would very likely have affected the political careers of the poets and patrons involved, yet due to the relative scarcity of information on the second regime, it is almost impossible to document the reception of the anthology and its subsequent effects on the poets' careers (with the sole exception of Ouyang Jiong, who prefaced and contributed to the collection). The anthologists' literary and political agenda can be discerned without additional historical data; the achievement or frustration of their anticipated results unfortunately cannot. Therefore, due to the limitations of the extant source material, the description of the Shu courts that follows is necessarily partial.

Beyond the textual problems outlined above, there remains one important but elusive problem in the historical sources on the Former and Latter Shu: the degree to which historians wanted to portray the Shu regimes as recreating the politically corrupt and morally decadent Southern Dynasties (Eastern Jin–Chen, 317–589). The resonances of the Southern Dynasties' historical model can be perceived in almost every text, whether or not historians mention it explicitly. The sense that Shu was recreating the "southern" court life was felt even by Shu contemporaries: Ouyang Jiong openly evokes the aristocratic splendor of the Southern Dynasties when he describes the elegance of the Shu court in the preface to the *Huajian ji*. But historians showed more interest in the archetype of the

---

18. Sun Guangxian (d. after 968) and He Ning (898–955), two poets in the collection who did not live in Shu (although Sun was born and spent his youth in Shu), were alive in 940; their careers, however, were tied to the rulers of other regimes, Sun to Gao Jichang, the ruler of Jingnan, He to the successive northern dynasties of Liang, Latter Tang, Jin, Han, and Zhou.

profligate southern ruler—such as the last ruler of the Chen, or the infamous Emperor Yang of the Sui—who ignored his political responsibilities to pursue his pleasures, thereby destroying himself and his kingdom. It is impossible to ignore the echoes of the Southern Dynasties in the historical accounts of Shu, but this does not mean that we must discard all Shu history as a retelling of the "southern" mythology. Instead, it is best to compare different accounts of events, considering their authors' political allegiances, to reveal this bias when it seems present. As a rule, I assume that anecdotes about the rulers' excesses are likely to be less reliable (if still useful) than records concerning matters such as building projects, titles of works, or biographical information on men other than Shu rulers, for which we have more than one source. In what follows, I take the potential influence of the decadent "southern" model into account where appropriate.

Creating the Shu Courts: Social and Political Contexts for Shu Culture

The Shu regimes that flourished between the founding of the Former Shu in 907 and the fall of the Latter Shu to the Song in 965 patterned themselves in many ways on the Tang, which they believed they were replacing as inheritors of the Mandate of Heaven. We find evidence that the rulers of both the Former and Latter Shu deliberately evoked the Tang by replicating to some extent the organization of the Tang bureaucracy, by naming buildings and offices with Tang titles, and by interpreting omens as signs of the transfer of power to Shu from Tang.[19] But what these rulers created in

---

19. A story in the *Xin Wudai shi* provides a clear example of signs revealing the transfer of power: in 912, the Tang seal of imperial succession was discovered at the residence of the late Tang eunuch official Tian Lingzi, who stole it during Emperor Xizong's flight to Chengdu. The seal was accepted by Wang Jian as a sign of his legitimate succession. *XWDS* 63.788. For a discussion of this and other events that were interpreted as omens of beneficent rule in the early years of Wang Jian's reign, see Verellen, *Du Guangting (850–933)*, 157–61. Verellen's study of Du Guangting also includes the broader cultural history of the Former Shu kingdom, in particular, the ways in which Du's service as a "court Daoist" helped legitimate the Wang clan rule.

Chengdu was in no way an exact replica of the Tang model; in terms of Shu politics, society, and culture—which were inextricably intertwined—the rulers and courtiers of Shu were making a new world. Even with the incomplete biographical data on Former and Latter Shu officials and famous men, it is clear that Shu rulers and officials were a miscellaneous group: in these biographies, we find refugees from the Central Plain, peasant-class military men, local elites, Daoist and Buddhist court priests and monks, actors, painters, and others seeking a way up in the world. The culture that grew out of these miscellaneous and self-fashioned Shu courts seems to have been similarly multifarious.

The history of tenth-century Shu falls into three parts: the Former Shu regime of Wang Jian and his son Wang Yan (907–25); the brief period between the fall of the Former Shu to the Latter Tang and the declaration of a new independent regime by Meng Zhixiang, which I call the Interregnum (925–33); and the Latter Shu regime of Meng Zhixiang, who died less than a year into his tenure as "emperor," and his son Meng Chang, who ruled until conquered by the Song (934–65). Despite the changes in regime, we discover a great deal of political, social, and cultural continuity from the late ninth century down through the tenth century, as many men from one regime survived to serve the next. Although the formal independence of Shu lasted less than a century, the decades of isolation from the political control and culture of the Central Plain alone guaranteed a sense of cultural independence, which had been growing throughout the ninth century. The record of the successive reigns showed that, along with the homage paid to Tang models, the rulers and their courtiers were happy to follow their own tastes in creating and sponsoring literature, art, and music. It would be easy to simply summarize the verdict of Song historians who dismissed Shu culture as decadent and corrupt—the anecdotes I cite below express this view clearly—but the historical record suggests something more complex and interesting. The literary, religious, artistic, and musical artifacts of Shu certainly reveal the hedonistic tastes of the era; at the same time, they point to a cultural vitality, and a level of engagement in cultural pursuits, that was seen in only one other tenth-century kingdom, the Southern Tang. Thus, the fact that the *Hua-*

jian ji was put together by a group of officials at the court of the Latter Shu seems strange only in comparison to the Tang exclusion of song lyrics from official records. When contextualized amidst other literary and musical court entertainments from Shu, it seems merely another example of contemporary local taste.

To answer a question provoked by Ouyang Jiong's preface to the *Huajian ji*—who were the men who created Shu culture?—we must rely on the fragmentary biographies of men found in the sources outlined above, and then offer tentative conclusions. However, the biographical evidence strongly suggests conclusions largely compatible with those proposed by other scholars: that the political, social, and cultural elites in Shu were overlapping and extremely mixed; that in kingdoms founded by ambitious and resourceful men, any talented person willing to work for a regime was readily employed; and that success (which, in many of the southern kingdoms, was measured by affluence and rank, rather than birth or family reputation) was easily achieved by those who mastered the skills to serve their self-made sovereigns.

Wang Gungwu, a historian of the Five Dynasties regimes of northern China, examined the changing political and military structures of the north and concluded that the Five Dynasties governments awarded great civil and military responsibilities to men who had been previously outside of the bureaucratic world—men with peasant backgrounds, non-Chinese, and men of purely military experience.[20] Wang did not assess the cultural impact of these new political actors; however, Peter Bol has offered some strong general arguments on the social and cultural trends in the tenth century. Drawing on scholarship by Japanese and Chinese social historians, Bol argues that the literati, whom he refers to as the *shi* 士, underwent a serious transformation in this period. Bol notes that "there seem to have been families, distinct from military families, at the court and prefectural levels with traditions of holding scholarly and administrative positions that required education and literary abil-

---

20. Wang, *The Structure of Power in North China During the Five Dynasties*.

ity."²¹ Such men, he suggests, emerged to fill the ranks of the newly formed bureaucracies scattered across China. Their claim to *shi* status was no longer based on birth or even degree status, but on their claim to a shared Chinese culture. As a new "cultural elite," the members of this transformed *shi* class gained access to political position through culture and education and, as such, were useful to "men with power who lacked their literary talents, knowledge of history, and repertoire of classical forms."²² In other words, the transformation of the *shi* class depended as much on the abilities of the independent rulers—their ability to identify and use men of talent—as it did on the skill of the *shi* in adapting to changing times.

The first independent Shu state was founded in 907 by such a ruler, Wang Jian, who distinguished himself throughout his extraordinary life by his ability to transform himself and to use others. Born of a family of cake-sellers, Wang Jian is said to have spent his youth as a black-marketeer and local bandit in Wuyang, Xu prefecture, Henan circuit.²³ He joined the troops enlisted by the Tang to fight the rebel forces of Wang Xianzhi from 874 to 877. His success in that and subsequent campaigns speeded his rise to the top of the Tang military structure and gained him the patronage of the powerful eunuch Tian Lingci, the military governor of Jiannan circuit (Sichuan). After the Tang emperor Xizong returned to Chang'an (following his 880 retreat to Sichuan during Huang Chao's attack on the capital region), Wang Jian rose to the position of commander of one of the five Palace (*Shence* 神策) Armies. In 886, he was made the prefect of Li prefecture, in western Sichuan.²⁴ Over the course of twenty years, through a combination of careful alliances, troop-building, strategic strikes, and clever manipulation of his enemies, Wang Jian was able to destroy and supplant the Tang military governors of both the Jiannan East and the Jiannan West circuits. By 905, he controlled the entire region from the capital,

---

21. Bol, *'This Culture of Ours': Intellectual Transitions in T'ang and Sung China*, 50, and n64.
22. Ibid., 52. Bol points to the example of the Southern Tang in this discussion.
23. *SGCQ* 35.481.
24. *SGCQ* 35.482.

Chengdu. After the execution of the Tang puppet ruler by Zhu Wen in 907 and the subsequent founding of Zhu's Liang dynasty, Wang Jian, in the ninth month of that year, on the *yihai* day (3 November), declared himself emperor (*di* 帝) of the kingdom of Shu.[25] Charles Hucker's summary of the leadership patterns that emerged throughout China in the tenth century, though focused on northern China, also applies to Wang Jian's rule of Shu:

> ... the creation of reasonably effective central governments was facilitated by the fact that the founder of each new state or dynasty after Tang was a warlord who had developed his own personal staff of relatives or dependents; they were hungry for prestige and power and had some measure of practical experience.[26]

Success or failure in this kind of political structure depended heavily on the capabilities and longevity of the ruler and on the abilities of those closest to him.

Although little detailed research has been done on the composition of Wang Jian's government and his use of power, scholars generally agree that his success in establishing a separate kingdom in Shu was based on three strengths: his military experience and troop-building skills; his bonds of personal loyalty forged with a close circle of compatriots; and his intelligent use of émigré literati in his government.[27] It is in this final area—the use of *wen*, or civil, officials—that Wang Jian seems unusual among tenth-century rulers. In the wake of Zhu Wen's usurpation of the Tang throne, many elite families fled the Tang capitals and the Central Plain entirely, seeking better prospects in the provincial capitals. This emigration, which continued sporadically throughout the tenth century, reshaped societies across the Chinese mainland. Certainly, former Tang officials sought places where their talents and training would be of use, and many were welcomed by men like Wang Jian. Ouyang Xiu, in the *Xin Wudai shi*, described the situation in this manner:

---

25. *ZZTJ* 266.8685.
26. Hucker, *Dictionary*, 38.
27. Yang, *Qian Shu Hou Shu shi*, 55–63. See also Zeng, "Bashi niandai yilai Wudai Shiguo shi yanjiu xuyi," 19.

Shu had the advantage of its inaccessible position and so grew wealthy. During the decline of the Tang, many of the literati wanted to ally themselves to Jian in fleeing the upheavals. Although Jian came up from banditry, he was a very intelligent and crafty person, and he was very good at retaining literati. Thus, in his usurpation of the imperial throne, in all cases he used descendants of famous Tang ministers.[28]

The *Zizhi tongjian* assesses the Shu founding somewhat differently:

At this time [the founding of the Shu kingdom], the clans of many Tang capped-and-gowned officials fled the upheavals and came to Shu. The emperor [Wang Jian] revered and employed them there, and he had them manage the affairs of his government. Thus, the civil elements [of government], such as the institutions and documents [of Shu], retained an air of the Tang.[29]

Sima Guang points to the great influence on the Shu government of Tang institutions and practices, as transmitted by émigré literati. However, one account from Shu reveals that Wang Jian did not limit his search to "descendants of Tang ministers" or even to émigrés from the Central Plain: in the early days of his reign, Wang Jian openly advertised for any men with talents in government, remonstration, education, and disputation to come out from wherever they lived in the kingdom to serve in his government.[30] Wang Jian also made skillful use of religious means to legitimate his place as ruler of Shu; as Franciscus Verellen has demonstrated, the important Daoist figure Du Guangting, who rose to prominence under the Tang, served the Wang regime in Shu by providing rituals of investiture and oracular proof of the Wang claim to the throne.[31] Wang Jian's awareness of his need to establish legitimacy in many ways, and his quest for men who had both experience and education to help him do so, surely contributed to the early stability of his regime.

Tang literati certainly found places in Shu government: the biographical information on the men in the *Shiguo chunqiu* shows that

---

28. *XWDS* 63.787.
29. *ZZTJ* 266.8685; also cited in *SGCQ* 35.501.
30. *Jinli qijiu zhuan* 5.8b–9b.
31. See Verellen, "Liturgy and Sovereignty," and *Du Guangting (850–933)*.

some civil officials of Wang Jian's government came from Tang families with ancestors in official service. However, the biographical evidence does not support the argument that Chengdu was merely a shadow version of Chang'an: among the 89 civil and military officials who have a biography in the *Shiguo chunqiu*, only 17 of those officials claimed forebears who had held office under the Tang, and of those 17, only 9 can be identified as members of the "great clans" of medieval China.[32] Some of these 9 great-clan members, such as *Huajian ji* poet Wei Zhuang, held very high positions in the Shu court; others, such as a certain Du He, of the Duling Du clan, simply presumed upon their family background to gain a low position and, lacking other skills, remained there.[33]

The pattern of Tang official families having some, but not exclusive, influence on the shape of the government seems to have been more common in the southern kingdoms than in the regimes of the northern "Five Dynasties." In tracing the tenth-century fate of one great clan, David Johnson has argued that strong anti-aristocratic feeling among the Northern Dynasties usurpers led to the deliberate destruction, in the Central Plain, of many officials of aristocratic background.[34] Such persecution did not occur in the

---

32. The term comes from Johnson, *The Medieval Chinese Oligarchy*, 33. My identification of great-clan officials is made on the basis of choronyms, that is, clan regional affiliation. I exclude the imperial sons and adopted sons of Wang Jian and 5 eunuchs from my count of 89. Out of 89 men, 13 are not given regional provenance. Aside from the problem of the loss of documents, the absence of regional affiliation in biographies is also probably due to inadequate record-keeping in the tenth century, a time when many people from different regions and with little or no documentation were entering Wang Jian's government (which itself must have taken some time to organize). However, given Wang Jian's desire to use men with ancestors in the Tang officiate or with aristocratic backgrounds, and the wish of those with such clan affiliations to have that known, it seems unlikely that many of the men of *unknown* regional provenance had such backgrounds.

33. Du He resented his low position and was said to have complained about the new socio-political order in Shu: "In years past, when entering service, one served under the virtuous ancestors of the flowering tree of Wei [Zhuang]. Now, when submitting one's dossier, one is ranked beneath the petty descendants of Feng [Rui] from Xinjin [a Shu prefecture]." *SGCQ* 42.625.

34. Johnson, "The Last Years of a Great Clan: The Li Family of Chao-chün in Late Tang and Early Sung," 67–68.

Former Shu, but neither do we see in the extant records of the Former Shu a strong preference for Tang elites. In fact, among the 89 biographies, the largest group of men of the same regional provenance—23 men—comes from Shu.[35] A few of the biographies of men from Shu include ancestors who had served in Shu prefectural or district offices under the Tang, but the majority have no such claims. It is true that the officials of Shu provenance did not occupy the topmost positions in the political hierarchy; rather, they were clustered in lower-rank (but sometimes higher-prestige) positions that required literary skills, such as secretary or administrative assistant in the Chancellery, Secretariat, or Imperial Library. Some of them had concomitant appointments in the Hanlin Academy (a mark of demonstrated literary talent).[36] Although we cannot track the social backgrounds of the Shu officiate over time without specific dates of service (most biographies simply report "served the Former Shu ruler Wang Jian" or "served the Former Shu"), if we compare the biographies of officials in the Former Shu to those of the Latter Shu, we find in the second group fewer men who claim Tang great-clan status or claim forebears who were Tang officials. This suggests that the Shu government and court society were becoming more heterogeneous in terms of social class, and perhaps also more local, with successive rulers and waves of emigration to Shu.[37]

---

35. Of the 89 men in the biographies, 49 come from some region other than Shu or Xu prefecture, Wang Jian's home.

36. Yang Weili, a contemporary historian, has analyzed Wang Jian's use of literati (*shiren* 士人). He identifies 49 of the officials with biographies in *SGCQ* as such. Of his 49 *shiren*, 14 come from Shu, making them 28 percent of his total literati count, a figure close to my count of 23 officials from Shu out of 89—or 26 percent. In Yang's analysis of literati, Shu is the best-represented region. However, Yang does not identify his criteria for *shiren*, and he excludes some lower-level office-holders (such as the *HJJ* poet Yin E) without explanation; so I have presented my conclusions in the larger context of the 89 total officials for whom we have biographies. Yang, *Qian Shu Hou Shu shi*, 59–62.

37. The question of successive waves of emigration to Shu only complicates understanding the composition of the Shu officiate. Meng Zhixiang himself was originally from Taiyuan, as were some of the men who accompanied him to Shu (according to their biographies in the Latter Shu records), but he and many in his

The implications of this social heterogeneity for Shu culture are significant and appear clearly when we look at the career paths of various Former Shu and Latter Shu officials. First, in the absence of Tang aristocratic hegemony and in light of the failure of the Former Shu to reinstitute the examination system, the primary path to high rank was that of demonstrated personal service to the rulers—not birth or degree status.[38] Furthermore, once an official had gained rank for himself, he often was able to place his sons and nephews in good positions as well. Next, the definition of "service" became quite broad, comprising military skill, intelligent debate, composition, and remonstration.[39] Finally, many officials of both Shu kingdoms attained positions via their literary ability, which included the composition and performance of songs. Of course, none of this was

---

entourage had spent much of their lives in the central capital region. Thus, if in fact Johnson's argument that the rulers of the northern regimes actively extirpated former Tang official families is true, the influence of the Tang aristocracy—or even of men with ancestors in the Tang officiate—would have only been further diluted by the time of the Latter Shu, meaning that the members of the Latter Shu officiate would likely have been even more heterogeneous. The influence of "local" talent—meaning men of literati skills who had lived in Shu from early in the tenth century—would also likely have risen, as the Latter Shu government drew upon such men to staff its offices.

38. There is strong evidence that Meng Chang reinstituted the examination system, awarding at least the *jinshi* degree, during the Latter Shu, although there are no detailed descriptions of the frequency or extent of its use. There are four Shu literati whose *SGCQ* biographies indicate attainment of the *jinshi* during the Latter Shu (*SGCQ* 53.785–86, 814). Further evidence is provided in the record of a Shu text by Yang Jiuling, the *Shu guitang bianshi* (The compiled affairs of the Cassia Halls of Shu), a collection of examination compositions and biographical notes on candidates, noted in Chao Gongwu's *Junzhai dushuzhi*, 2B.2a and in the *Song shi* bibliographic essay, 203.5116. Yang's collection is described in *SGCQ* 56.817.

39. Two examples of this kind of promotion are found in the biographies of Wang Xiancheng and Pu Youqing. Wang, of Xinjin district in Shu, gave up his studies to become a soldier. During Wang Jian's campaign to take Shu, Wang Xiancheng offered unsolicited strategic advice that helped Wang Jian's campaign, and he was later awarded a prefect position for his service. *SGCQ* 42.618. Pu Youqing was a commoner who "liked direct speaking" and was not afraid to criticize Wang Jian. Despite opposition from powerful officials at the Shu court, Wang Jian awarded Pu the post of right rectifier of omissions (in the Tang, a remonstrance post at court, attached to the Chancellery). *SGCQ* 43.632.

unknown in the Tang; rewards for personal service—both military and literary—were often given in the Tang, and the institution of the *yin* privilege, which allowed the sons of officials of rank five and above to enter the "stream" of service without taking an examination, ensured nepotism as well. The other perennial threat to Tang stability, nefarious eunuch and consort cliques, was also a problem in Shu. However, unlike the Tang central government, the Former Shu government, at least, seems to have functioned entirely on the basis of imperial favor.

At its best, this system created an environment in which ambitious and capable men without birth or wealth to recommend them could make a name at the Shu court with their particular skills; at its worst, imperial favoritism meant that the Shu court was governed by whim. Thus, under Wang Jian's rule, the talented and experienced Wei Zhuang served as high minister, shaping Former Shu policies and the composition of the officiate. Wei Zhuang only passed the *jinshi* in 894, when he was perhaps past sixty; in 901, he was appointed chief secretary to Wang Jian, who was then the Commissioner of West Sichuan.[40] Wang Jian appreciated Wei Zhuang's work so much that he petitioned to keep him in Sichuan when Wei was summoned to the capital.[41] After the establishment of the Shu kingdom in 907, Wei quickly acquired high offices and responsibilities, finishing his years as the vice-director of the chancellery and the joint manager of affairs with the secretariat-chancellery, and as the vice-director of the ministry of personnel, which effectively made him Wang Jian's top civil official. The *Shu Taowu* states that Wei held the enormous responsibility of establishing "the regulations and rules, the commands and orders, the

---

40. There is no biography of Wei Zhuang in any of the standard histories of the Tang or Five Dynasties. Robin Yates suggests that the loss of documents in the Huang Chao rebellion and its aftermath, as well as historians' prejudice against Shu, lay behind this omission. Yates, *Washing Silk: The Life and Selected Poetry of Wei Zhuang (834?–910)*, 11. The information on Wei Zhuang's examination dates and official posts comes from Xia, "Wei Duanji nianpu," in *Tang Song ciren nianpu*, 58ff.

41. Noted by Wei Zhuang's brother, Wei Ai, in the preface to a collection of Wei Zhuang's own work, *Huanhua ji*; *QTW* 889.5b. See also *Tang shi jishi jiaojian*, 68.1020.

punishments and rites and music for the government."⁴² Such talented and literary-minded men could indeed blow the "air of the Tang" through the Shu court. In his years at Wang Jian's court, Wei Zhuang was an active poet as well as high-ranking official, presiding over literary discussions and extending his literary influence even to locating and restoring the poet Du Fu's fabled "thatched hall," located on the banks of Flower-Washing Stream outside Chengdu. Wei Zhuang was known for his generous attitude toward men of talent who had either come from low class backgrounds or had suffered misfortunes in their careers, and he surely extended this to his patronage of officials, with Wang Jian's approval.⁴³ It is impossible to calculate the influence that Wei Zhuang must have had on the cultural tone of Wang Jian's court, but it was surely considerable.⁴⁴ Robin Yates offers a useful counterargument to the view of other scholars that Wei Zhuang's sorrowful lyrics expressed feelings of sadness at being in Sichuan: Yates argues that Wei instead "felt he was fulfilling his life's ambition to be at the center of the political stage and to participate in what he hoped would be an imperial restoration."⁴⁵ Given the kinds of men represented in Wang Jian's court, I suggest that this feeling of fulfillment and realized political ambition was shared by others in the Shu officiate, whether they were émigrés or Shu natives.

---

42. *Shu Taowu* 1.5; translation from Yates, *Washing Silk*, 35. Wei Zhuang died in the eighth month of 910, according to *Shu Taowu* 1.4–5 and *SGCQ* 40.593.

43. In 900, a year before Wei Zhuang was first sent to Shu to serve as chief secretary to then-regional governor Wang Jian, Wei composed a memorial requesting that fourteen talented poets be posthumously awarded the *jinshi* degree and an official title, and that Luo Yin (who was still alive) be given emoluments as well. The earliest source of the story surrounding the memorial is Wang Dingbao (870–940), *Tang zhiyan*, 116–19, but the *Tang zhiyan* gives Wen Tingyun's brother, Wen Tinghao, instead of Tingyun as one of the possible honorees. The *QTW* 889.3b–4a version gives Wen Tingyun, as do all later citations of the memorial. For a discussion of the text, see Yates, *Washing Silk*, 14, 31, and n132; Yates concludes that the *Tang zhi yan* is in error. See also Xia, *Tang Song ciren nianpu*, 21–22.

44. For a brief discussion of his influence on the selection of the Shu officiate, see He and Zhong, "Wei Zhuang yu Qian Shu zhengquan," 34–35.

45. Yates, *Washing Silk*, 39.

Wang Jian left his kingdom in the hands of Wang Yan, the son of a consort from a Shu lineage, who had not in fact been Wang Jian's first choice as heir. In the hands of lesser administrators, the political model of imperial license meant that a weak ruler like Wang Yan could spend his reign in the pursuit of pleasure, to the point where—according to both Shu and Song historians—the culture of the court became one long musical party with imperial favorites and concubines.[46] It is in the reign of the second Shu ruler, Wang Yan, that we discover the strongest evidence of the popularity of song lyrics and other kinds of musical entertainment at court.

"Indulging in Music and Song" in Shu

Under Wang Yan, Shu became famous—or infamous—for music and song. This reputation, which the Latter Shu ruler Meng Chang upheld, is well-documented by Song historians. One story from the *Zizhi tongjian* captures the historians' unanimous condemnation of Wang Yan's tastes and his poor skills as a ruler:

[After the fall of Shu to the Latter Tang] the Prince of Wei [Li Jiji] sent Li Ting'an to have an audience with the emperor [Zhuangzong, Li Zunxu] to present the [captured] musicians of Shu, over 200 people. Among them was one Yan Xu, whom Wang Yan had made the prefect of Peng prefecture. The emperor asked him, "How did you get to be a prefect?" He replied, "By singing." The emperor made him sing, and enjoyed it, and he permitted Yan Xu to take up his former duties.[47]

The resemblance between this anecdote and the one about Ouyang Jiong and the Song emperor is likely not coincidental: both stories

---

46. Two of Wang Yan's most successful companions were Han Zhao and Pan Zaiying, whose biographies are given in *SGCQ* 46.660–61. Han became the governor of Chengdu city and the chief minister of the Ministry of Rites; Pan became the capital security commissioner, apparently the head of a "secret service" agency for the court. Both men, in short, held highly lucrative and prominent posts based at court.

47. *ZZTJ* 274.8955. Sima Guang here takes the chance to make two points with one story: one about the corruption of the Shu government, and another about the weakness of the Latter Tang emperor, who failed to see the error of Wang Yan's appointment.

make the same point, which is that the Shu rulers inappropriately appointed musicians of little or no administrative skill to high office (the office of prefect being the highest regional rank, outside the central bureaucracy, in the Shu kingdom). In almost every account of the decadence or bad governance of the Former and Latter Shu we find music or singing, but in many cases the historians' emphasis on music more likely stems from the demands of historiography rather than from reality. The closest historical model for Wang Yan's reign was that of the profligate final reign of a corrupt Southern dynasty, in which a pleasure-loving emperor "indulged in music and song" to the great expense of the kingdom. (The oldest model for this was, of course, the songs of Zheng and Wei from the *Classic of Odes*, but historians writing about Shu relied more heavily on the Southern Dynasties version.) In order to read past this model, or at least to balance it, we should flesh out these musical-political anecdotes with other kinds of evidence for the popularity of singing at the Shu court, such as that provided by records of pleasure palaces and musical performers, or by the song lyrics of the poets of the *Huajian ji* and their official titles.

The evidence of building projects from the very first years of Wang Jian's reign suggests that the Wang rulers' taste for musical entertainment predated the reign of the weaker son, though Wang Yan was apparently the most licentious of musical devotees. Upon founding the Shu kingdom in 907, Wang Jian constructed new buildings and renamed an array of palaces, bridges, and other buildings in Chengdu. One change he made was to refashion the "music garrison," *yueying* 樂營—the title given to the musical quarter of a provincial capital or military governor's office—into the "Instruction Quarter," *jiaofang* 教坊—the name given to the imperial music quarters of Chang'an.[48] Scattered references to musicians from the Former Shu suggest that the quarter must have housed performers similar to those in the Tang imperial *jiaofang*, such as singers, actors, and instrumental musicians. Another piece of evi-

---

48. *SGCQ* 35.501–2. *Yueying* was the title given to the organization of musicians attached to the offices of a *jiedushi*, military governor, in the Tang. The change in title is thus Wang's self-conscious "promotion" of the institution to imperial status.

dence illustrating Wang Jian's fondness for musical entertainment comes from his own tomb, the Yongling 永陵 (Mausoleum for eternity), which was excavated in 1941: the walls of the tomb were decorated to a degree uncommon for the period, featuring 24 sculpted panels of female musicians and dancers, and effectively creating a musical motif for the entire tomb.[49] But it is in records of Wang Yan's reign that stories of music and singing at the Shu court appear most often. Tangible evidence of Wang Yan's tastes can be found in his expansion of the imperial gardens in order to construct Xuanhua Park. Built between 919 and 921, this pleasure park housed elaborate and expensive palaces, compounds, and pavilions.[50] Later, he built a special canal running through the park to the imperial quarters, to facilitate floating parties staffed by musicians and performers of both sexes.[51]

In stories about Wang Yan's parties at Xuanhua Park and at sites around the Shu kingdom, songs and song lyrics—words sung to a tune that is denoted by a fixed tune title—figure prominently, and these stories show Wang Yan to be a composer as well as an appreciative listener.

The ruler of Shu took the Grand Scholar of the Wensi Basilica, Han Zhao, the Capital Security Commissioner, Pan Zaiying, and the Commissioner for the Militant and Brave Army, Gu Zaixun, as his intimate companions; they accompanied him on his roaming and parties, sitting all mixed together with the palace women. Sometimes they would make licentious songs [*yan'ge* 艷歌] and match them [that is, create new lyrics to the same tune]; sometimes they would mock and ridicule one another. In their mean vulgarity and indecent laziness, there was nothing they might not do. The ruler of Shu delighted in this.[52]

---

49. Feng, "The Tomb of Wang Jian," 15. For a general study of the tomb, see also Qin, *Wang Jian mu zhi mi*.

50. *Shu Taowu* 1.14a.

51. *Jinli qijiu zhuan* 6.7a. Yang Weili, in *Qian Shu Hou Shu shi*, discusses the layout and history of Xuanhua Park, whose remains are still yielding artifacts (86–88).

52. *ZZTJ* 272.8892. As the grand scholar of the Wensi Basilica, Han Zhao replaced *Huajian ji* poet Mao Wenxi, who had originally been appointed to the post

In this story, Wang Yan is guilty of a host of sins: he is excessively fond of parties; he takes unworthy men as his "intimate companions" and allows them access to his palace women; and finally, he and his friends stoop to making licentious songs and mocking one another. In this inappropriate mixing of inner and outer worlds, it seems, "there was nothing they might not do."

The traveling parties of Wang Yan often included his mother, his aunt, and their cronies, who were also seen as a source of the corruption at court. Bibliographies, extant poems, and historical texts reveal that Wang Yan, his mother, and his aunt were all poets of one sort or another. In fact, one of the charges leveled against Wang Yan by historians was that he allowed women to participate so publicly in court literary activity, a charge that was later made against the Latter Shu ruler Meng Chang, whose consort Lady Huarui 花蕊夫人 became known as a poet for her 100 "palace lyrics," *gongci* 宮詞.[53]

In the eighth month of the second year [of the Qiande 乾德 reign period, 920], Wang Yan toured northward. . . . The empress [Wang's mother] feasted at Ascending Transcendents Bridge and, with twenty of the palace women, followed him. When they arrived at Han prefecture, they stopped at West Lake and with the palace women they boated on the lake, playing music, drinking, and feasting all day long. In the ninth month, they journeyed to Junxi county; from there they returned to Yichang [prefecture], where they all boated down to Langzhong. The boatmen were all attired in damask and embroidery. Wang Yan himself made [*zhi* 制] "River Tune of the Silver Han" lyrics and commanded his musicians to sing them.[54]

---

by Wang Jian. Mao was dismissed when he held a betrothal party in imperial palaces without permission from Wang.

53. He Guangyan, in *Jianjie lu*, places some of the blame for the fall of the Former Shu at the feet of Wang Yan's mother and aunt, the Xu sisters. In his discussion of this same "Northern Tour," a voyage that included visits to important Daoist sites in Sichuan, and for which the two women composed memorial poems, He proclaims that "righteous people understand that the ability of writing is not an affair for wives or girls." *Jianjie lu* 5.1a–b.

54. *Shu Taowu* 1.13b–14a.

A later passage in the same text describes a different musical event at court, during which Wang Yan "ordered his palace woman Li Yuxiao [the sister of *Huajian ji* poet Li Xun] to sing the 'palace songs' [*gongci* 宮詞] that Yan had collected."[55] According to some sources, Wang Yan was not only a connoisseur of song and poetry but a poet himself as well. A Song bibliography, Chen Zhensun's 陳振孫 *Zhizhai shulu jieti* 值齋書錄解題 (An explanation of book titles recorded in the Upright Studio), records a collection of Wang Yan's verse, titled *Yanhua ji* 煙花集 (Collection of mist and flowers), that was said to have 200 pieces in five *juan*. The *Shiguo chunqiu* states that Wang Yan's poems were so popular, "all he composed was transmitted and recited by the people of Shu."[56] Only two of his song lyrics are extant today; no others seem to have survived the fall of the Song.[57]

The *Zizhi tongjian* and *Shu Taowu* anecdotes present singing as only one feature of Former Shu corruption; other stories show singing to be the most serious symptom of the disease. He Guangyan, an official at the court of the Latter Shu, provides a detailed account of Wang Yan's debauchery in a short piece entitled "Tones of the Fallen Kingdoms," *wang guo yin* 亡國音. There, he makes explicit reference to the Southern Dynasties model of the debauched final ruler.[58]

[Wang Yan's] inner minister Yan Ningyue and others competed to sing "Flowers in the Rear Courtyard" and "Longing for the Woman from Yue," and they sought out seductive and beautiful quatrains of nobles to secretly make into "Willow Branch" lyrics. Lord and ministers sitting together all would remove their court raiment; from day into night, strings and pipes and throats and tongues resounded with one another. When the company

---

55. Ibid., 1.14a.
56. *SGCQ* 37.531.
57. The crudeness of the first extant song lyric attributed to Wang Yan, "Zui zhuang ci" 醉妝詞 ("Lyric on the drunken makeup," referring to a style of cosmetics that made women seem flushed and drunk) seems almost too exaggerated to be credible. See the comments on it included in Shi, *Tang Wudai ci jishi huiping*, 765–67.
58. In the opening to this story, He Guangyan goes so far as to state that Wang Yan was a kind of shape-shifter, or a werewolf. *Jianjie lu* 7.2b.

was flushed with wine, then the concubines were allowed to take the goblets, and the consorts filled in words (*tianci* 填詞). Hands beckoned, drunken eyes met—it would come to the point where shoes were lying about, and cups and bowls were tumbled in disarray.

At this time, the wind of debauchery blew strong in Shu and thus toppled the kingdom. "Flowers in the Courtyard" is the tune of the fall of the Chen [dynasty]. . . . "Longing for the Woman from Yue" is the tune of the fall of the Wu [kingdom]. . . . "Willow Branch" is the tune of the fall of the Sui [dynasty].[59]

In this account of Wang Yan's parties, we again find both ruler and highly placed officials drunk and disorderly with the forbidden imperial palace women. The inappropriate mixing of inner and outer, men and women, continues unabated.[60] To strengthen his critique of the Former Shu court's political corruption, He Guangyan lists the songs that were sung— "Flowers in the Rear Courtyard," "Longing for the Woman of Yue," and "Willow Branch"—all three of which were indeed associated with the downfall of kingdoms.[61] Furthermore, all three kingdoms were believed to have

---

59. Ibid., 7.2b–3b.
60. This inappropriate mixing seems to have been another of Wang Yan's serious flaws, or at least one of the historians' greatest concerns; a similar story is repeated in the brief biographical notice of another Shu courtier, Li Guizhen, who reprimanded Wang Yan and warned of the inevitable invasion of Shu if Wang continued his licentious and unheeding ways. *SGCQ* 43.638.
61. "Flowers in the Rear Courtyard" ("Houting hua" 後庭花) was associated with the final emperor of the Chen, and He Guangyan goes on to cite the late Tang poet Du Mu's poem "Lodging on the Qinhuai Canal," which uses a reference to the same song to point to the weakening of the Tang. "Longing for the Woman of Yue" ("Si Yueren" 思越人) refers to the story of the famous beauty Xi Shi, who was blamed for the downfall of Wu. The "Willow Branch" tune, according to He Guangyan's version of its origin, dates from the Sui and was written about the willow dike planted by the last, extravagant emperor of the Sui. This explanation was one popular story about the tune, though contemporary scholars have differing opinions as to its actual origins. Four lyrics to "Longing for the Woman of Yue" are found in the *HJJ*; the *HJJ* also contains thirteen lyrics to the tune "Yangliu zhi," all of which are heptametric quatrains, and another nine lyrics to the tune "Liu zhi" (the "Willow Branch" of the story), all but one of which are heptametric quatrains. During the Tang and Five Dynasties / Ten Kingdoms period, "Liu zhi" was probably a common abbreviation for the "Yangliu zhi" tune.

been lost because of their rulers' depraved behavior or excessive desire for a woman.⁶² He Guangyan can thus attack the practice of songwriting and the licentious behavior that surrounded it by noting the historical parallels.

From a literary standpoint, however, we should note that these stories depict at least four, if not five, different methods of composing songs: in the *Zizhi tongjian* passage, the men are "making licentious songs," *wei yan'ge* 爲艷歌, and "matching [them] back and forth," *xiang changhe* 相唱和; in the *Shu Taowu*, we find Wang Yan "making," or "creating," *zhi*, lyrics to the preexisting "River Tune of the Silver Han"; in the *Jianjie lu* story, the ruler and his courtiers are singing established tunes, perhaps with fixed lyrics, and also taking "seductive and beautiful quatrains (*yanli jueju* 艷麗絶句) of nobles and secretly making them into 'Willow Branch' lyrics" (*yinwei Liu zhi ci* 隱爲柳枝詞; "secretly" in this context meaning "without attribution"), but then the concubines themselves "fill in words," *tianci* 填詞, to tunes. "Making licentious songs" could have meant composing original tunes and words together or may have simply been a way of saying "writing new licentious words to preexisting tunes." The practice of "matching," *changhe*, when used for songs, however, indicates that the composer would use the same tune and create new words. In the *Shu Taowu*, the use of *zhi* ("to construct or create") for lyrics confirms original composition on Wang Yan's part.⁶³ In the *Jianjie lu* story—which we should recall was written in

---

62. Zhang Tangying, in *Shu Taowu*, increases He Guangyan's count by adding the song "Rainbow-Feathered Cloak," known as the favorite of Tang Xuanzong during his association with Precious Consort Yang, who was famous for performing it. Zhang's addition of this song to the list is an excellent example of a case in which a historian was more likely responding to the moral imperatives of Confucian historiography than working from facts. *Shu Taowu* 1.16a. The need for careful scrutiny of these anecdotal sources can be seen in Rao Zongyi's use of this *Shu Taowu* passage to date the tune "Si yueren" to before 923, the date given in *Shu Taowu* for this story. Rao, *Airs de Touen-houang*, 234. He Guangyun, who was alive in Shu in 923, does not date his story in *Jianjie lu* so precisely, though the event, if true at all, had to have occurred between 919 and 925, during Wang Yan's reign.

63. For parallel uses of this verb for composing song lyrics and tunes, see *XTS* 22.476 and 22.478, in a story about Tang Xuanzong 宣宗 and his courtiers.

the Latter Shu, probably within a decade of the appearance of the *Huajian ji*—we see men singing (potentially) new lyrics to preexisting tunes and stealing others' quatrains to put to the four-line, heptametric "Willow Branch" tune, with concubines "filling in" their own words (which also suggests original composition) to the tunes that had just been sung. The variety of song composition practices in the *Jianjie lu* reflects what we know about late Tang practices, though we do not have a similarly useful story from the Tang showing these different methods all being used at the same time.[64] At the very least, this range of composition practice suggests a great enthusiasm for song on the part of ruler and courtiers and a high degree of musical ability at the Shu court.

As any good Confucian reader would expect, the climax to the story of Wang Yan's debauchery was the fall of the Former Shu kingdom. In the 920s, the Latter Tang regime of the Central Plain sent spies to Shu to assess the chances of a successful invasion. In the fourth month of 924, the Latter Tang emissary Li Yan visited Chengdu for this purpose.

Wang Yan received Li Yan at his court in Upper Clarity Palace. Nobles and commoners of the Shu capital, in their curtained carriages decorated with kingfisher feathers and pearls, crowded the roads without a break. Li Yan saw that the people and things of Shu were rich and splendid and that Wang Yan was arrogant and depraved. He returned [to the Latter Tang emperor] and presented a strategy for invading Shu.[65]

The Latter Tang conquest of Shu took only two months. Wang Yan, his relatives, consorts, and highest officials were taken captive and sent to Luoyang. The imperial family was executed outside of Chang'an in the fourth month of 926, and the ministers handed over their offices in the sixth month.[66] Niu Xiji, one of the *Huajian ji* poets, was among the officials captured and taken to Luoyang, and

---

64. It may, however, be the case that He Guangyan conflated these practices in his story simply to tar them all with the same brush.

65. *XWDS* 67.792–93. A slightly different version of the story is found in *ZZTJ* 273.8921.

66. *ZZTJ* 274.8956ff; *SGCQ* 37.555–56.

his poem about that defeat became widely known in the Central Plain (he went on to serve the Latter Tang regime):[67]

The city was filled with officials wishing to pay court,	滿城文物欲朝天
yet none perceived the smoke of neighboring armies crossing the borders.	不覺鄰師犯塞煙
Once the Tang ruler had unfurled a new sun and moon,	唐王再懸新日月
the Shu king then renounced his former mountains and streams.	蜀王還卻舊山川
It had nothing to do with the inept support of generals and ministers;	非干將相扶持拙
it was a matter of course that our lord counted out his final years.	自是吾君數盡年
From ancient times till now, it's always been like this:	古往今來亦如此
as many once made merry, just as many now shed tears.[68]	幾曾歡笑幾潸然

Another poet from the Former Shu, the Buddhist monk Yuan Gong, expressed similar sentiments in his poem, "Grieving over the Fall of the Kingdom": "When the music was at its height, grief came upon us endlessly; / the sounds of singing had barely ceased, when cries of sorrow arose...."[69] The "sounds of singing" is not just a familiar metaphor: the *Zizhi tongjian* records that no fewer than 200 musicians were also sent to the Latter Tang emperor from Shu.[70] To

---

67. Along with his more well-known lyrics, Niu left behind seventeen prose texts, collected in *QTW*. They concern historical events and contemporary politics and stand in contrast to the lightness of his lyrics. See Liu, "Yu 'Huajian' xiangfeng zhongxing 'jiaohua zhi dao.'"

68. This translation is based on the text of the poem given in *Jianjie lu* 7.4b. Two other versions are found in *QTS* 760.8631 and *Quan Wudai shi*, 847. The *QTS* version is identical to the *Jianjie lu* text except for the second character of the last line, which *QTS* has as *hui* 會 instead of *ceng* 曾.

69. *Jianjie lu* 5.4b.

70. *ZZTJ* 274.8955. A rough comparison of the numbers of musicians in the mid-ninth century *jiaofang* and those sent to the Latter Tang suggests that the Shu *jiaofang* was small compared to the great Tang imperial musical instruction quarters, which employed thousands of musicians. However, when compared with

the sorrow of these men, and perhaps to the relief of others, the Wang lineage of the Former Shu ended ignominiously and completely.

The "sounds of singing" from the Shu court were indeed silenced by the Latter Tang conquest, though only for a short while. In the Interregnum that followed (925–34), the Latter Tang official Meng Zhixiang quickly consolidated his control over the region. In early 926, the Latter Tang emperor Zhuangzong enticed Meng, a man of high rank and considerable military experience, and a former Taiyuan native, to oversee Shu as the military governor of Western Sichuan.[71] Unfortunately for the Latter Tang, Meng Zhixiang was impressed by the wealth of Chengdu and the surrounding region and, over the eight years of his representing the Latter Tang government in Sichuan, grew less and less willing to share that wealth. As Meng accrued more powers and titles from the Latter Tang and enjoyed the splendors of the largely undespoiled imperial palaces, he apparently began to plot his secession with his close advisors.[72]

In 934, immediately following the death of the Latter Tang emperor Mingzong, Meng Zhixiang declared himself emperor of Shu.[73] He filled many of the highest offices of the new Shu government (which was likely an extension of the military governorship bureaucracy) with the men who had accompanied him to Shu, some of them compatriots from Taiyuan or other officials from the Central Plain.[74] But like Wang Jian, Meng Zhixiang also employed literati from Shu in many official posts, particularly those requiring literary skills. Some of them were even holdovers from the Former Shu re-

---

musicians captured from other southern kingdoms during the Song conquest, a group of 200 musicians from Shu was sizable (and probably did not include all the musicians of the *jiaofang*).

71. *SGCQ* 48.680.

72. *XWDS* 64.798. After the conquest of Shu, huge indemnities in both cash and textiles were sent to Chang'an, but there is no record of burning or looting of the imperial palaces. After he assumed command in Chengdu, Meng Zhixiang in fact opposed beggaring the country for indemnities above what had already been sent. *SGCQ* 48.682, 48.699.

73. *ZZTJ* 278.9102.

74. For accounts of some of these men, see *SGCQ* 51.757–63.

gime. At the time of the conquest in 925, the Latter Tang emperor Zhuangzong had extended amnesty to many Former Shu officials in an edict:

> The emperor declared that those who had held office in Shu at rank four and above must surrender their duties; those who had been at rank five and below, if they had not [unlawfully] taken land or goods, were free to return to their fields and villages. Those who had surrendered earlier [before the final capture of Chengdu] and had demonstrated other merit were to submit themselves to the discretion of Guo Chongtao [the commanding general] to receive their rewards or positions.[75]

Outside the few hundred imperial relatives and high ministers who were executed or held captive in the Central Plain, then, the great majority of the Former Shu officiate not only survived the conquest but also may have applied to Meng Zhixiang's military governor offices, and then to his Latter Shu regime, for posts.[76] Between the staff he brought with him to Chengdu and the local men willing to serve a conquering military governor, Meng was well supplied with

---

75. *ZZTJ* 274.8951. See also *Wudai huiyao* 17.281–82 for a longer version of the edict, which the *Zizhi tongjian* seems to paraphrase. The *Wudai huiyao* version suggests the Latter Tang need for skilled officials, since it reserves punishment only for the most highly ranked civil and military officials; those with no talent on record were merely dismissed.

76. One prominent example of a literatus who served throughout the Former Shu, the Interregnum, and the Latter Shu is Li Hao, who was a director of the Secretariat and a Hanlin academician in the Former Shu (and a member of a Tang great clan). He accompanied Wang Yan to the surrender in Luoyang, and there was awarded a position in Chengdu serving the Latter Tang. Upon his return, he worked for the Meng regime, where he seems to have wielded great advisory power. Under the Latter Shu, Li rose quickly to the top of the official hierarchy, eventually becoming a chief minister. *SGCQ* 52.775–76. David Johnson has examined his case in "The Last Years of a Great Clan," 70–72. Another example is that of Ouyang Bin (who may have been related to Ouyang Jiong—sources differ), who was "skilled at songs and rhapsodies" and was made a Hanlin academician during the Former Shu on the basis of one of his rhapsodies. After the fall of the Former Shu, he served under Meng Zhixiang; then, during the Latter Shu, he rose to be left assistant director of the Department of State Affairs. *SGCQ* 53.779–80. It seems probable that skilled and experienced literati were too valuable not to be used, even if they had served different masters.

experienced and ambitious men.⁷⁷ But Meng Zhixiang had little time to enjoy his throne in Shu: he fell ill and died within months of founding his kingdom, leaving a son, Meng Chang, aged only fourteen *sui*, to take his place.⁷⁸

Despite his youth, Meng Chang was fortunate in his coterie of advisors and, after spending the early years of his reign edging out the more corrupt officials, slowly came to control his court.⁷⁹ Unlike Wang Yan, he had no ambitious maternal relatives (at least none with local connections or influence), and, more importantly, he seems to have been well educated and prepared for a career of official service. This preparation perhaps made him more eager and able to shape the culture of his court. Even though the historical records for the Latter Shu are sparse and uneven, a variety of historical and bibliographical sources show Meng Chang's regime to be full of literary, artistic, and musical activity. In one anecdote from 941 (the year after the preface to the *Huajian ji*), we find him swearing to two officials, "Wang Yan was frivolous and flighty, and he loved light and licentious songs. I will not be this way."⁸⁰ Although the evidence from various Latter Shu and Song dynasty texts suggests that as Meng Chang grew, he too enjoyed singing, there is no evidence of the kind of debauchery that historians accuse Wang Yan of pursuing.

---

77. Meng Zhixiang began his post in Shu without his own troops, but after Zhuangzong's death, the men who served under Meng transferred their allegiance to him. For a study of Meng Zhixiang's career and his followers, see Amthor, *Meng Chih-hsiang (874–935), der Erste Kaiser von Hou-Shu*.

78. *ZZTJ* 279.9123. The *Shu Taowu*, which so harshly condemns the Former Shu regime, admits that Meng Zhixiang's tenure in Shu was a good one: "The emperor [Meng Zhixiang] comforted the people with humanity and benevolence, led his soldiers with compassion and strength, and treated the literati and officials with [appropriate] ritual. On the day he died, the people of Shu greatly mourned him." *Shu Taowu* 2.3b.

79. The *Xin Wudai shi* suggests that it was not until 948, upon the death of one powerful minister, Zhang Ye, that Meng Chang truly began to rule Shu himself with the aid of his own appointed and trusted ministers (Meng Chang would have been in his late twenties at the time). *XWDS* 64.804.

80. *Shu Taowu* 2.6a. Wu Renchen cites this passage verbatim, adding, in a note, that Meng Chang went back on his word, pointing out Meng's authorship of one lyric to "Xiang jian huan" (an attribution which is debated). *SGCQ* 49.712.

Instead, the record of Meng Chang's 31-year rule of the Latter Shu suggests that he was successful in reestablishing something that more resembled Tang elite culture in Chengdu. The books dating to his reign that are found scattered throughout Song biographies reveal him and his advisors to have been interested in preserving and fostering the study of the orthodox literary tradition. According to records of official titles and Shu books whose titles indicated that they collected examination compositions, Meng Chang reinstituted an examination system.[81] He also appointed a historian, the powerful Li Hao, to keep "Veritable Records" of his reign. A wealthy official at Meng Chang's court, the Hanlin Academician Wu Zhaoyi supplied personal funds for the engraving of the Nine Classics and the printing of the *Wen xuan*, the Tang encyclopedia *Chu xue ji* 初學記 (Record for early learning), and the Tang poet Bai Juyi's *Baishi liutie* 白氏六帖 (The six papers of Mr. Bai).[82] The engraving and printing of such texts points to the need for standard texts in a reconstituted examination system. Meng Chang was also said to have commanded the compilation of a rhyme dictionary, the *Gujin yunhui* 古今韻會 (Compilation of ancient and recent rhymes), in 500 *juan*.[83] Meng Chang's own consort, Lady Huarui, became

---

81. Working largely from titles of officials found in his source texts, Wu Renchen reconstructed bureaucratic charts for the Ten Kingdoms of his history. Among the Shu literati offices for which he found evidence, Wu notes the Hanlin Academy (which housed literati and painters and is attested to in many sources), a Hongwen Bureau, and also a Chongwen Bureau (given that these were both bureaus that traditionally housed literary men, it is unlikely that a Hongwen Bureau existed contemporaneously with a Chongwen Bureau; this likely indicates a name change or a scribal error; see *Wudai huiyao* 18.305 for a similar name change in the Latter Tang period). For imperial instruction, he notes the presence of a College for the Sons of the State (Guozi jian), for which there were at least four classical scholars. He also notes the existence of an imperial library. *SGCQ* 114.1655.

82. *SGCQ* 52.768. See Li, *Lidai keshu kaoshu*, 35–40, for a discussion of this and other printed texts in tenth-century Shu. Li particularly emphasizes the importance of the cultural and economic environment to the development of printing in Shu, noting that the Latter Shu regime provided unparalleled support to such projects. See also Twitchett, *Printing and Publishing in Medieval China*, 30–31.

83. *SGCQ* 49.712. Given the diverse regional backgrounds and, presumably, accents or dialects of the Shu officiate (the Meng family was from Taiyuan), a rhyme dictionary might have met a need for new standards. The tenth century was

known as a poet who presided over an inner court of talented women. This interest in a wide range of literary compositions is indicated not only by titles in Song bibliographies but also through the scattered pieces of prose and poetry by Latter Shu officials found in the *Quan Tang wen* and the *Quan Wudai shi*. Throughout the Northern Song, Shu was a source of editions of Tang literature, demonstrating that not only were many works preserved by individuals in Shu (perhaps by refugee literati) but interest in collecting and preserving Tang works must have remained strong throughout the period.[84]

The aesthetic interests of the Latter Shu court extended in all directions, to classical literary studies, to musical performance, and even to painting. One important early Northern Song text on painters and painting in the tenth and eleventh centuries, Guo Ruoxu's *Tuhua jianwen zhi* 圖畫見聞志 (Record of experiences in painting), gives brief biographies of important painters from the Five Dynasties and Ten Kingdoms era. Of the 59 painters with known provenance documented by Guo, 31 are from Shu, and many of those held the position of "Hanlin painter-in-attendance," an indication of activity at the Shu court.[85] The most famous of these painters, Huang Quan 黃筌 (ca. 903–65), served the Latter Shu and was an influential figure in the development of Song court painting; his sons also served Meng Chang and the Song emperors.[86] The notes on a father-and-son pair of painters show the kind of service such men gave:

---

a period of great linguistic change throughout the Chinese mainland due in part to widespread emigration. For further discussion of the tenth-century linguistic developments and interest in rhymes, see Nakata, "Tō Godai shiin kō," and Bryant, "The Rhyming Categories of Tenth-Century Chinese Poetry."

84. For a Song perspective on early Northern collection practices, see Kurz, "The Politics of Collecting Knowledge: Song Taizong's Compilations Project." Kurz discusses the transfer of the Shu library holdings to Kaifeng: approximately 13,000 *juan* of texts ("books, charts, seals, and scriptures") were transported to Kaifeng from Chengdu, in comparison to the roughly 20,000 *juan* produced from the libraries of the Southern Tang (295–97).

85. Guo, *Tuhua jianwen zhi*, trans. Soper, *Experiences in Painting*.

86. *SGCQ* 56.818–20.

Yuan Zhihui: Native of Shu prefecture. Skilled at painting the children of princely households, and also excellent at portraiture. He served the Wang regime in Shu as Hanlin painter-in-attendance and did a portrait of the first Wang ruler which was truly outstanding. . . .

Yuan Weide, son of Zhihui, who continued and refined his father's work. He served the Meng regime as Hanlin painter-in-attendance. Very good at catching the look of palace apartments, the forbidden park, imperial consorts and relatives, and wealthy and great personages in general.[87]

The imperial palaces and favored temples were thus gorgeously decorated, and then carefully documented, by the hands of a bureau of imperial painters in Shu. At the same time, brief descriptions in the biographies of Shu painters suggest that the connoisseurship of the visual arts was integrated with other kinds of aesthetic appreciation. In the *Shiguo chunqiu* biography of Huang Quan, for example, we find Meng Chang commanding Ouyang Jiong to compose a text to describe the effects of one of Huang Quan's bird paintings.[88] Ouyang Jiong was also known for having composed an *ekphrasis*, a long poem on painting, on the subject of the Buddhist monk Guan Xiu's paintings of arhats.[89] Another anecdote in the Latter Shu painters' biographies notes that the Hanlin scholar Xu Guangfu composed a set of songs to praise a series of paintings of autumn mountains painted by Huang Quan and his sons.[90] The titles of paintings done by Latter Shu painters-in-attendance evoke the same world we see described in other sources: "Appreciating Spring in the Palace" 宮中賞春, "A Princely Evening Banquet" 公子夜燕, "The Drunken Guests of Changmen [Palace]" 長門醉客, and "Performing Music" 按樂.[91] Thus, we see in the Shu sponsorship of

---

87. Ibid., 33-34. *SGCQ* includes biographies of six painters in the Former Shu and sixteen from the Latter Shu, some of whom served both regimes. The son, Yuan Weide, does not appear in *SGCQ*; the father's biography appears in *SGCQ* 56.820.

88. Ibid.

89. Ouyang Jiong has two long poems on paintings extant, in *Quan Wudai shi*, 1169-70. His poem on Guan Xiu's paintings of arhats (*luohan* 羅漢), Buddhist saints, exemplifies the blending of arts common at the Shu court.

90. *SGCQ* 56.820.

91. Ibid.

painting a desire on the part of Meng Chang and his courtiers to use every artistic endeavor to adorn their courtly life.⁹²

The records from the Latter Shu also reveal the "frivolous and flighty" side of Meng Chang's reign, citing stories of court musicales, extravagant building projects, and patronage of the *jiaofang*.⁹³ Meng Chang's support of the *jiaofang* is borne out by the *Song shi* music monograph, where historians note that no fewer than 139 musicians were captured from the Latter Shu *jiaofang*, compared to the 32 and 26 taken, respectively, from the kingdoms of Jingnan and the Southern Tang when they were conquered by Song forces.⁹⁴ The pictures of the Shu court painted with words in the "palace lyrics" of Lady Huarui confirm the image of the Shu court as one replete with literary and musical talent sponsored by the ruler and his intimates. Her *gongci* give us glimpses of imperial palace life that often involved musical entertainment, as in the following two lyrics:

"Palace Lyric" 宮詞 (11th of 157)
Lady Huarui

No sooner is the imperially commanded, newly arranged song done,	御製新翻曲子成
than the "six palaces" ladies sing it without knowing its title.⁹⁵	六宮纔唱未知名
They finish copying it in tablature for the *bili* horns,⁹⁶	盡將觱栗來抄譜

---

92. Records of similar painting subjects from the Southern Tang and copies of such paintings, most famously the "Night Entertainment of Han Xizai," provide a useful comparison to the accounts of music and painting from Shu. See the discussion of the textual record of the "Night Entertainment" in Wu, *The Double Screen: Medium and Representation in Chinese Painting*, 29–71. Whether later commentators understood the painting to be evidence of Han Xizai's decadence or Li Yu's bad governance, they frequently condemned the "indulgence" in wine, women, and song that the painting represents, in terms identical to those used by critics of Shu culture.
93. *SGCQ* 49.718–20.
94. *Song shi* 142.3347–48.
95. The "six palaces" was an ancient reference to the palaces of imperial consorts.
96. The *bili* 觱栗 was a bamboo-necked, gourd-headed instrument of Central Asian origin; it first became popular in imperial circles during the reign of the Tang empress Wu. It was known for its melancholy tone and was particularly associated

after following the ruler's playing it first upon his flute.[97]	先按君王玉笛聲

(55th of 100)

The lead dancers all wear colorful gauzy clothes,	舞頭皆著畫羅衣
as they sing a newly arranged, imperially commanded song lyric.	唱得新翻御製詞
Every day in the inner courts, one hears the troupes of performers—	每日內庭聞教隊
the sounds of music fly up and over to the dragon steps.[98]	樂聲飛上到龍墀

In these lyrics, we see the hand of the Shu ruler in the musical life of his court, through his "commanding," *yuzhi* 御製, the arrangement of music and the composition of melodies, *quzi*, and song lyrics, *ci* 詞, and through his own performance on the flute. Although there is only one lyric extant that is attributed to Meng Chang, the reputation of the Latter Shu court was apparently widely known.[99] What is less frequently acknowledged either by Song sources or even modern historians is the breadth of Shu literary and cultural

---

with songs of parting. Duan Anjie, in *Yuefu zalu*, tells of its popularity in the Tang and gives names of some of the most famous players in the mid-Tang (*Yuefu zalu*, 34–35). By the Song, it had become the lead instrument in the wind section of musical ensembles.

97. *QTS* 798.8972. The dating and lineage of Lady Huarui have been debated in modern times; see Pu, "Huarui furen gongci kaozheng." I accept the traditional identification of her as Meng's consort, but I would also point out that the palace life she describes seems to have existed throughout the tenth century in Shu.

98. *QTS* 798.8977.

99. For this lyric of Meng Chang, see *QTWDCSZ*, 1132. The story of the lyric, "Mulan hua" (for which the attribution, original title, and original words are all debated), has received a great deal of attention due to Su Shi's account, given in his preface to "Dong xian ge," of having heard the opening lines from an old nun in Chengdu when he was a child. As one Su Shi scholar has argued, it seems more likely that a later poet reworked Su's lyric and placed it in Meng's collection. Wang, *Su Shi xuanji*, 287–91. For the relevant sources and versions of this story, see *Quan Tang Wudai ci jishi huiping*, 923–26. For a translation of Su's lyric and a discussion of its relation to its "source," see Egan, *Word, Image, and Deed in the Life of Su Shi*, 345, and n78.

activities. Latter Shu culture appears to have continued some of the trends from the Former Shu, such as the popularity of singing and other kinds of musical performance, and yet it seems to have gone substantially beyond the Former Shu in sponsoring the literary, as the emperor and other literati sponsored a return to canonical texts and studies. The first Song emperor himself tells us that "Meng Chang and his ministers indulged themselves in music and song," and the *Huajian ji*, among other texts, records the evidence of Shu courtiers doing precisely that. With the context provided by this partial but suggestive picture of Shu culture, we can now turn to the *Huajian ji*, which dates from the early years of the Latter Shu, and see more clearly the social and political implications of this courtly collection of song lyrics.

"Among the Flowers" of Shu: The Huajian ji *in Context*

In the summer of 940—the season and year of Ouyang Jiong's boastful preface to the *Huajian ji*—Meng Chang was only twenty *sui* and likely was still forming his own literary and musical tastes, just as he was learning his role as "emperor" of Shu. It is in this context that some features of the *Huajian ji*, puzzling to commentators over the centuries, take on meaning. In light of the competitive and heterogeneous court environment of the Latter Shu, outlined in this chapter, a collection of works by Tang and Shu officials should be read not only as a literary text but also as a political and social document. Along with Ouyang Jiong, who was a secretary in the service of the Latter Shu, perhaps as many as ten of the *Huajian ji* poets were alive in Shu in 940, though we cannot determine if anyone other than Ouyang played a part in the discussion or selection of lyrics for the anthology. Even if Ouyang Jiong had not taken such pains in his preface to call attention to the elite company that produced the anthology, his inclusion of men who had been quite famous in Shu would itself have drawn notice to the work. Some of the poets—men such as Wei Zhuang, Mao Wenxi, Niu Qiao, and his nephew Niu Xiji—had made names for themselves during the Former Shu, which had fallen fifteen years before. Ouyang Jiong was himself an ambitious junior official in 940; the men later considered part of the "Five Devils" coterie were also active at this time, including Ouyang and the three *Huajian ji* poets Yin E, Yan Xuan, and Lu Qianyi (see Table 1).

It seems probable that Wang Jian's minister, Wei Zhuang, 48 of whose song lyrics are collected in the *Huajian ji*, was instrumental in promoting music at the Former Shu court before his death in 910. Along with Wei Zhuang, we know that at least ten *Huajian ji* poets had some post in the Former Shu government (one other, Zhang Bi, may have served the Tang but not the Former Shu, and two others, Yan Xuan and Li Xun, lived during the Former Shu but may not have held office). The ten *Huajian ji* poets who served the Former Shu are: Wei Zhuang, titled "minister" in the *Huajian ji*; Mao Wenxi, titled "minister of education";[100] Niu Qiao, titled "Supervising Secretary Niu," whose *jinshi* date of 878 suggests he did not live to serve the Latter Shu;[101] Gu Xiong, titled "defender-in-chief," who may have served the Latter Shu;[102] Wei Chengban, also titled

---

100. According to *SGCQ*, Mao Wenxi was a descendent of one Mao Guifan, chamberlain of the Imperial Stud (rank 3b) in the Tang. He had the reputation of precociousness, passing the *jinshi* at age 14, and might have served the Tang before serving Shu. He was made a Hanlin scholar upon the founding of Shu, and then rose to the positions of minister of rites and supervisor of the Bureau of Military Affairs. In 914, he was appointed grand scholar of Wang Jian's newly built hall of literature, the Wensi Basilica. However, in 916, he was demoted by Wang Jian for throwing a betrothal party for his daughter in an imperial palace. According to the monk Guan Xiu, who was a long-term visitor in Shu, Mao was talented at the *qin*, and was known for his poetry. Chen, 383-88.

101. Niu Qiao was a grandson of the famous Tang minister Niu Sengru and thus a member of the Anding Niu clan. He passed the *jinshi* in 878, the only secure date we have for his biography. Niu served as an administrative assistant to Wang Jian before 907 and then, after the establishment of Shu, rose to the post of supervising secretary, the title given here. In the *Jianjie lu*, he is identified as the director of the Palace Library, which position he may have held concurrently. According to the Song bibliography *Junzhai dushu zhi*, he left 30 *juan* of collected works. Chen, 376-80.

102. Of Gu Xiong we know very little other than this title; he served as a prefect and as a military official in the Former Shu, and he avoided execution at the fall of the regime, which means he may have been alive in 940. The title of "defender-in-chief" may also be a posthumous honorary title. Chen, 400-402.

Table 1
Huajian ji Poets from the Former or Latter Shu

Name	Dates or period of service	Official title given in *HJJ*	*HJJ* lyrics
Wei Zhuang 韋莊	834?–910; Tang, Former Shu	Minister (*xiang* 相)	48
Niu Qiao 牛嶠	*jinshi* of 878; Former Shu	Supervising secretary (*jishi* 給事)	32
Zhang Bi 張泌	Tang, Former Shu(?)	Secretary (*sheren* 舍人)	27
Mao Wenxi 毛文錫	d. after 934; Former Shu	Minister of education (*situ* 司徒)	31
Niu Xiji 牛希濟	Former Shu, Latter Tang	Scholar (*xueshi* 學士)	11
Ouyang Jiong 歐陽炯	896–971; Former Shu, Latter Shu	Secretary	17
Gu Xiong 顧敻	Former Shu, Latter Shu(?)	Defender-in-chief (*taiwei* 太衛)	55
Wei Chengban 魏承班	d. 925; Former Shu	Defender-in-chief	15
Lu Qianyi 鹿虔扆	Former Shu, Latter Shu(?)	Grand guardian (*taibao* 太保)	6
Yan Xuan 閻選	Former Shu, Latter Shu(?)	Retired gentleman (*chushi* 處士)	8
Yin E 尹鶚	Former Shu, Latter Shu(?)	Associate minister (*canqing* 參卿)[1]	6
Mao Xizhen 毛熙震	Former Shu, Latter Shu(?)	Librarian (*bishu* 秘書)[2]	29
Li Xun 李珣	Former Shu, Latter Shu(?)	Licentiate (*xiucai* 秀才)[3]	37

NOTES: Where available, dates of birth, death, or *jinshi* examination are given. Most of these men have scant biographical data available. Chen Shangjun has exhaustively examined the extant material for each of these poets in his article "*Huajian* shiren shiji," in *Tangdai wenxue congkao*, 368–420. Given the thoroughness of Chen's work, I will not provide complete biographies for each poet, but include only the information most relevant to my discussion. In the table, the poets are listed in the order in which they appear in the collection; I discuss this order and its implications in Chapter 3.

1. This translation is tentative, since there is no Tang or Song equivalent for the title. It is possibly an abbreviation or an honorific title. Chen, 413.

Notes to Table 1, cont.

2. Chen (414) suggests that *bishu* is an abbreviation not for *bishu jian*, Director of the Imperial Palace Library, rank 3b, as the *Quan Tang shi* editors have it, but *bishu lang*, Assistant Librarian, rank 6a.

3. The title "Licentiate" suggests that Li Xun passed the *jinshi* examination, but Chen (415) suggests that this was an honorary awarding of the degree, similar to the practice in the late Tang. It is less likely that he served the Latter Shu, but he may have lived into the Latter Shu period.

"defender-in-chief," a son of one of Wang Jian's adopted sons, killed in 925;[103] Mao Xizhen, titled "librarian," who was likely a relation of Mao Wenxi;[104] Ouyang Jiong; Niu Xiji, titled "scholar," who served the Former Shu and composed a poem at the fall of the kingdom to the Latter Tang;[105] Yin E, titled "associate minister(?)"; and Lu Qianyi. The *Huajian ji* poets Yan Xuan (titled "retired gentleman," which was likely an honorary title for someone who had not held office) and Li Xun (a man of Persian ancestry who is given the

---

103. Wei Chengban was the son of one of Wang Jian's adopted sons, Wang Zongbi, who was executed at the fall of the Former Shu, along with Wei and the rest of his family. In 918, Wei held the title of commander-escort, a position in the imperial bodyguard. The title "defender-in-chief" may reflect a later post or it may also be a posthumous honorary title. Chen, 410–11.

104. Chen speculates that Mao Xizhen was alive in the Latter Shu, perhaps even as late as the fall of Shu to the Song in 965. Given the nepotistic appointment practices of both regimes, it seems likely that Mao Xizhen was a descendant of Mao Wenxi, although there is no evidence of that relationship.

105. Niu Xiji was the nephew of Niu Qiao, and was thus of the same great-clan status, but it is not clear when he arrived in Shu. He was born sometime around 872; at the fall of the Tang, he fled to Shu and served the Former Shu regime as a Hanlin scholar, then later as the vice-censor-in-chief (rank 4a), according to the *Beimeng suoyan* and the *Jianjie lu*. He went with the Wang imperial family to Luoyang at the fall of Shu in 927 and was then reemployed by the Latter Tang emperor Mingzong. The emperor was apparently impressed with Niu's poem on the fall of Shu, which, unlike other poems composed by former Shu officials to Mingzong's command, did not slander the Wang regime. Mingzong appointed him assistant military governor for Yongzhou. Chen speculates that Niu died not long after the surrender, since there is no further information about him from records of the Latter Tang. Chen, 388–90.

perhaps honorary title of "licentiate")[106] lived in the Former Shu and may have also survived into the Latter Shu.

Adding these latter two poets to the ten men who were known officials in Shu, we have twelve poets associated with the Former Shu who were responsible for 295 of the 500 lyrics in the *Huajian ji*. These twelve men were also the attributed authors of 75 more lyrics in the anonymous, later collection patterned after the *Huajian ji*, the *Zunqian ji* 尊前集 (Collection from before the wine-cups). Although Wei Zhuang's lyrics, and perhaps the lyrics of some of the older poets such as Niu Qiao and Mao Wenxi, may have been written before the fall of the Tang, the remaining *Huajian ji* lyrics were likely composed between 907 and 940, the year of the *Huajian ji* preface.[107] To draw a relevant comparison: the body of 360 extant lyrics of these twelve poets associated with Shu—most of which were likely composed over the first three decades of the tenth century—almost equals the 363 extant Tang literati lyrics that exclude the Tang *Huajian ji* lyrics, or the extant literati lyrics for the entire three centuries of the Tang. Clearly there were significant incentives—whether political, social, or cultural—to compose and preserve song lyrics in tenth-century Shu.

Here, however, I must note that despite the presence of anecdotes about song lyrics, nowhere in the extant tenth-century records do we find notice of the *Huajian ji* itself. From the perspective of tenth-century historiography, this is not surprising, given the patchy coverage of the Latter Shu regime in all extant historical works on the southern kingdoms. However, from the perspective of the claims and rhetorical intensity of Ouyang Jiong's preface, one might expect the collection to have made a bigger splash in the rec-

---

106. Li Xun's sister, Li Xunxian, was a consort to Wang Yan and was also herself a poet. Li Xun had one collection of his own song lyrics, entitled *Qiongyao ji* (Collection of rosegem and turquoise), that circulated at least in Shu and was discussed by Wang Zhuo, the Chengdu-based Northern Song author of an important early *cihua*, *Biji manzhi*. Chen, 415–16. Li Xun also has another eighteen lyrics that are collected in *Zunqian ji*.

107. For a discussion of the dating and contents of the *Zunqian ji*, see Bryant, "Messages of Uncertain Origin: The Textual Tradition of the *Nan-T'ang erh-chu tz'u*," in Yu, ed., *Voices*, 299–307.

ords passed down to the Song historians. From the numerous editions of the *Huajian ji* produced in the Northern and Southern Song, as well as from its consistent appearance in Song bibliographies, we know that the collection became very popular.[108] And references to *Huajian ji* lyrics found in Song *cihua* (comments on lyrics) confirm that the anthology was widely read after the fall of Shu, whereas many other Shu texts for which we have bibliographical notations have long since vanished. The silence of the historical record regarding the Latter Shu regime is illustrated in the uneven account provided by the *Shiguo chunqiu*, the most comprehensive text to cover the period. Of the very few stories about Meng Chang's reign in the basic annals of the *Shiguo chunqiu*, the majority date from after 948, and most of those focus on events immediately preceding the Song invasion.[109] It is possible that the appearance of the *Huajian ji*, coming in 940 or thereabouts, was simply lost along with the other events of the first decade of Meng Chang's rule. It is also possible that this kind of literary collection would not have been mentioned in the generally political sources that were transmitted after the Song conquest, but might have been noted in more literary or informal sources that did not survive. From the perspective of historians, whether official or amateur, the *Huajian ji* might have appeared a minor and frivolous court production of little note, but the anthology's popularity at the Shu court, and then later among Song readers, would not have been affected by this oversight.

---

108. The colophon to one of the oldest known editions, from 1148, states that there were many other editions of the text at the time. Zhao Qianzhi, the author of the colophon, who apparently oversaw the 1148 edition, calls the lyrics of the collection "all long-and-short-lines of talents from the end of the Tang" (*Tang mo caishi* 唐末才士), preferring to ignore the Shu provenance of the text. *Tang Song ciji xuba huibian*, 339. In contrast, the Southern Song poet Lu You took pains in his colophons to link the collection to the decadence of the "Five Dynasties" era. The appearance of the *Zunqian ji* also testifies to the circulation and popularity of the *HJJ* in the Northern Song.

109. As a rough measure, of the 38 pages of basic annals for Meng Chang's reign compiled by Wu Renchen, only 5 pages concern events from 934 to 940.

Even if the historical record shows no sign that the *Huajian ji* helped the careers of poets it included (other than perhaps Ouyang Jiong), the preface and ordering of the *Huajian ji* clearly reveal the text's social ambitions and political ties to Shu government. In the passage from the preface that opened this chapter, Ouyang Jiong vaunts the company that discussed the *quzi ci* (lyrics to little tunes), and the official, Zhao Chongzuo, who collected them. The rank of Zhao Chongzuo, "vice minister for the Court of the Imperial Regalia," was a Tang rank that, by the Song, had dwindled to a sinecure.[110] We cannot determine what the rank might have meant in Shu, but the history of the office and the title both suggest intimacy with the imperial quarters, if not with the emperor himself. More importantly, from the *Jiuguo zhi* we learn that Zhao Chongzuo was the younger son of Zhao Tingyin, an official who had accompanied Meng Zhixiang to Shu, continued to be very important to Meng Chang, and was known for his lavish parties and literary gatherings.[111] The air of elegance and nobility that Ouyang Jiong wished to impress upon readers thus came from a real coterie environment closely associated with the Latter Shu court.

Ouyang Jiong's concern for official rank extends throughout the *Huajian ji*, and constitutes one of the features of the anthology that later readers found disingenuous, if not downright deceptive: without noting which poet served under which regime (the Tang, Former Shu, Latter Shu, Liang, and Latter Tang regimes—at least—are represented by the eighteen poets), he arranges the lyrics chronologically by poet and gives each poet a title, either his official rank or an honorary title (see Table 2).

The anthology begins with the late Tang poet Wen Tingyun, titled "Instructor Wen," a position that he may not have ever held.[112]

---

110. Hucker, *Dictionary*, 565.

111. *Jiuguo zhi* 7.5a. In 948, Zhao was ennobled by Meng as "Prince of Song"; it was said that whenever Meng Chang had an important affair of state, he went to Zhao's mansion to consult with him.

112. Xia Chengtao presents the evidence (which he accepts as credible) for Wen's having held this position in *Tang Song shiren nianpu*, 411–13.

Table 2
Titles Given to All 18 Poets in the *Huajian ji*
and Their Tang Ranks, If Known

Poet (*HJJ* order)	Official title	Dates or period of service
Wen Tingyun 溫庭筠	Instructor (*zhujiao* 助教), rank 7b-8b	ca. 812–ca. 866
Huangfu Song 皇甫松	Elder (*xianbei* 先輩, a title given to *jinshi* degree holders), no rank	Tang
Wei Zhuang	Minister, rank 1a	834?–910 Tang, Former Shu
Xue Zhaoyun[1] 薛昭蘊	Vice director (*shilang* 侍郎), rank 3a	d. ca. 906 Tang
Niu Qiao	Supervising secretary, rank 5a1	878 *jinshi* Former Shu
Zhang Bi	Secretary, no rank	Tang, Former Shu?[2]
Mao Wenxi	Minister of education, rank 1a	d. after 934 Former Shu
Niu Xiji	Scholar, no rank; often held concomitantly with other ranked position	Former Shu, Latter Tang
Ouyang Jiong	Secretary	896–971 Former Shu, Latter Shu
He Ning 和凝	Scholar[3]	898–955 Liang, Latter Tang, Jin, Han, Zhou
Gu Xiong	Defender-in-chief, rank 1a	Former Shu, Latter Shu(?)
Sun Guangxian 孫光憲	Assistant librarian (*shaojian* 少監), rank unknown[4]	ca. 894–d. after 968 Former Shu, Jingnan
Wei Chengban	Defender-in-chief, rank 1a	d. 925 Former Shu
Lu Qianyi	Grand Guardian, rank 1a	Former Shu, Latter Shu(?)[5]
Yan Xuan	Retired gentleman, no rank	Former Shu, Latter Shu(?)
Yin E	Associate minister(?), rank unknown	Former Shu, Latter Shu(?)
Mao Xizhen	Librarian, rank 6b1 or 9a1	Former Shu, Latter Shu
Li Xun	Licentiate, no rank	Former Shu, Latter Shu(?)

Notes to Table 2

1. This man's name was most likely Xue Zhaowei 薛昭緯, not Zhaoyun 昭蘊, an identification first substantiated by Wang Guowei in his *Renjian cihua*. See Chen, 373–74, for additional evidence that the poet's name was in fact Zhaowei.

2. This poet may have served the Former Shu, but he may also have served other southern regimes. Chen, 381–82. His presence in both the *Huajian ji* and the *Caidiao ji* suggests that he was in Shu for some time after the fall of the Tang.

3. He Ning was made a Hanlin scholar in 935, in the reign of the last Latter Tang emperor, and held other posts concurrently. In 939, he was made the director of the Jin Hanlin Academy. Chen, 396–97.

4. Sun Guangxian was a Shu native and had held a prefect position (rank 3b–4a) in the Former Shu; after 937, he went to Jingnan, where he had a long, successful literary and political career. He persuaded the ruler of Jingnan to submit to the Song and was rewarded with a post after the surrender. Although he held the position of acting director of the Palace Library (*jianjiao bishu jian*, rank 3b) in Jingnan, that post likely came after 940. This *HJJ* title may thus reflect a lower position Sun held in Jingnan for which we have no other record. Chen, 404–6.

5. There are conflicting records as to whether or not Lu Qianyi served the Latter Shu regime. Chen, 412, summarizes these accounts.

The poets then flow without comment from one dynasty to the next, though the order is perhaps not precisely chronological, since the lowest-ranked poets fall at the end of the collection. The impression that Ouyang creates with this ordering is that of a coherent body of "poets" (*shike* 詩客), as he calls the literati of the anthology, all of whom composed lyrics in similarly elegant settings. However, the earliest of the poets in the collection, Wen Tingyun, was born around 812, more than a century before the *Huajian ji* itself came into existence; some of the poets may never have had an official position at all. Although the editors of the *Siku quanshu zongmu tiyao* note that this somewhat resembles the practice of the Liang anthology *Wen xuan*, which gives poets' honorific titles before their personal names, there are no precedents in any extant medieval anthology for Ouyang's innovation.[113]

---

113. The 1148 edition of the *Huajian ji* and the 1188 source edition for the *Siku quanshu* catalogue both preserve this curious and thus probably original feature of the collection. Modern editions generally retain the titles. The *Siku quanshu zongmu tiyao* editors state, "As for the authors, the captions give not their personal names but their offices, somewhat after the precedent of the *Wen xuan*, which gives the honorific titles." Cited in *HJJZS*, 403. However, there may have been Tang precedents for this also; see the discussion of the collection of poetry compiled under Empress Wu, the *Zhuying xueshi ji*, in Wu, "'Tang ren xuan Tang shi'

Ouyang's titling of poets by rank is more ingenious than its simple meddling with chronology might suggest. His ordering and titling also mask another feature of the anthology that would reveal its tenth-century origins: the heterogeneous social backgrounds of its poets. Although he implicitly claims for all of them the status of *shi*, one could argue that he stretches the definition of the word past its Tang boundaries. On one end of the social spectrum, there are two Tang great clans represented in the anthology by the poets Wei Zhuang, Niu Qiao, and his nephew Niu Xiji; the Tang poet Huangfu Song came from a respected Tang official family, and Mao Wenxi also came from a family that had served in the Tang. At the other end of the spectrum, we find Li Xun, a poet from a Persian family that had moved to Sichuan before the fall of the Tang, Yan Xuan, a poet who was a commoner, and—perhaps the strangest inclusion of all—Wei Chengban, the son of one of Wang Jian's adopted sons, who was massacred with the rest of his family in 925, at the fall of the Former Shu, for his father's greed and cruelty.[114] The regional backgrounds of the poets are equally miscellaneous, but they also follow patterns noted before: although some men lived only in the Tang or were émigrés to Shu, as many as eight of the eighteen poets may have been Shu natives. Only Ouyang Jiong is identified as such by more than one source, but other poets who are noted as being Shu natives in at least one source include Gu Xiong, Lu Qianyi, Yan Xuan, Yin E, and Li Xun. Zhang Bi may have been a Shu native or may have been an émigré literatus; Sun Guangxian was originally from Shu and served the Former Shu government as a prefect, though he was no longer in Shu in 940. Thus, to a degree that many scholars have not acknowledged, the *Huajian ji* was fundamentally a local production, involving men who had lived and had been well known in Chengdu in the early decades of the tenth century.

Beyond Ouyang's political connections and his social climbing, the *Huajian ji* also reveals its regional coloration in the praise of its

---

chuanliu, sanshi kao,'" 131–32. The Yuan scholar Ma Duanlin noted that Cui Rong, the compiler, ordered his anthology according to the rank of the poets, and included details of their offices and titles in the collection.

114. *ZZTJ* 274.8945.

preface. In the closing lines of Ouyang Jiong's preface, he explains the title and purpose of the anthology, revisiting an earlier allusion to the story of the Warring States courtier Song Yu and the reputed singers of Ying, the capital of the southern state of Chu.

Long ago, among the people of Ying, there were those who could sing "Yang Spring" who were called the greatest singers.[115] Thus I have declared this [collection] to be *The Collection from Among the Flowers*. I hope that it will make the talented and wise of the Western Gardens use it to increase their pleasure on outings in their feathered-awning carriages, and [I hope that it will make] the charmers of the southlands cease singing the lays of the lotus boat. Prefaced in the third year of the Guangzheng 廣政 era of the Great Shu, summer, fourth month, by Ouyang Jiong.[116]

The point of the allusion to Chu is clear: the poets of Shu, like those few talented singers from Chu who could sing "Yang Spring," represent their generation's best composers and performers. Furthermore, Ouyang suggests that the songs of the *Huajian ji* should be considered the best songs in the country. A historical parallel also seems implicit here: Ying, the capital of the southern state of Chu, was renowned for its musicians and artists, as Ouyang suggests Chengdu is or soon will be. Ouyang extends these comparisons with the title he chooses for the anthology, *Huajian ji* (The collection from among the flowers). We can understand this as both "Songs Collected While Sitting Amid the Flowers" and "Songs Collected from Among the Flowers," where the "flowers" themselves have multiple referents. The flowers may suggest the literati, the "flowery talents," *xiucai* 秀才, of the Shu court, but they certainly refer to the beautiful women of the court by whom and among whom such songs would be performed. The flowers could even represent the songs themselves, the best that were culled from a

---

115. In the *Wen xuan* (45.981) we find the text "Song Yu Responds to the King of Chu," in which Song Yu tells the king that there are few singers who could "match" (*he* 和) the songs "Yang Spring" and "White Snow."

116. Ying was the capital of the Warring States southern state of Chu, and Ouyang implies a comparison between Ying and Chengdu. The "Western Gardens" refer to the imperial gardens of the capital of the Wei and Western Jin, where rulers and their courtiers entertained themselves.

"garden" of song—recalling the notion, from earlier in the preface, of Zhao Chongzuo's selecting from among the "finest quills." My sense is that Ouyang intended all these readings of the title.

Ouyang Jiong concludes by likening the young Meng Chang and his courtiers to Cao Pi and his entourage, the renowned literati of the Jian'an era, and he offers the collection up to "increase the pleasure" of the ruler and his courtiers and to serve as a substitute for the common "lays of the lotus boat" sung by southern women. In the next chapter, I investigate the literary claims Ouyang makes in these lines, but here let me note his social and political claims. Not only does he suggest that the collection of song lyrics is worthy of the emperor (a claim no Tang poet had ever made about song lyrics), but, by comparing Meng Chang to Cao Pi, he also implicitly figures himself (since he is a contributor) and his peers as the talented Wei poets consorting with courtiers in the Western Gardens. As I noted above, we have no record of a *Huajian ji* presentation to Meng Chang, but that does not preclude the possibility that the anthology was offered to him, as the preface seems to suggest. Meng Chang himself is noticeably absent from the collection, which may simply mean that in 940, at age twenty, he had not yet composed many song lyrics (he was known for doing so later in his reign); also missing is Wang Yan, who was much more famous for having composed song lyrics, but whose inclusion would surely have been an affront to Meng Chang. However, several features of the anthology—the title, the preface, the ordering and titling of poets—seem intended to flatter the poets included in the collection, the society they represent, and the ruler who presides over their court. The problem of the *contents* of the anthology—the morally suspect nature of its romantic topics and erotic scenes—I examine in subsequent chapters.

Over the course of six decades, successive rulers of Shu created a culture devoted to artistic pleasures, from the construction of parks to literary competitions in the imperial gardens. Music and singing formed one strand of the fabric of Shu court life, but, as the evidence from different sources has shown, they made up an especially brilliant piece of the culture of the "Brocade City," as Chengdu had long been called. The evidence from a variety of sources also shows that Shu officials of all stripes were involved in the cultural life of its court. From one perspective, the society in which Shu culture developed was a new one, made up of men from diverse social classes and regional backgrounds, and the unusual careers of many Shu officials testify to the new rules under which that society operated. And yet Shu was only one kingdom of many in which similar kinds of social and political relationships were being forged, with similarly diverse consequences for local cultures. If prospective officials of the southern kingdoms could draw on a range of cultural skills—including poetry and music—to win attention and office, as we see in the Shu regimes, then we should not be surprised to find frivolous compositions among the more serious political texts from the period.

The culture of Shu was not unique among the independent kingdoms in the decades after the fall of the Tang, but it was perhaps unusual with respect to its rulers' great fondness for light musical entertainment. The Southern Tang provides ample evidence of other rulers' tastes in music and singing, and scattered evidence of song lyrics can be found in almost every northern and southern regime of the tenth century. Unlike any other collection from the tenth century, however, the *Huajian ji* provides a tantalizing glimpse of Shu poets in their social and political places, allowing us to see how one group of men might have exploited their literary talents in a time of cultural transition. The fact that these poets chose song lyrics as their favorite form reflects the musical culture of Shu and also suggests how far and how publicly Shu literati were prepared to stray from their Tang literary antecedents, even while acknowledging them as models.

THREE

Gathering the "Flowers" of Poetry and Song

Anthologies in Tang and Shu

Just as the lyrics of the *Huajian ji* have most often been read as early texts in the history of *ci*, so too has the anthology as a whole most often been examined by scholars as the first in a line of *ci* anthologies. Since the *ci* genre was, as Pauline Yu has argued, one "whose own status within the tradition was ineluctably compromised by the questionable nature of its origins," the history of *ci* anthologies reveals a persistent concern with establishing legitimacy for the genre.[1] The claims made by Ouyang Jiong in the preface to the *Huajian ji* offer one set of strategies for dealing with the problem of *quzi ci*'s origins in the Tang entertainment world, and as Tang and Five Dynasties *quzi ci* became Song *ci*, literati poets and collectors developed still more. However, the Shu court compilers of the *Huajian ji* probably did not see themselves as innovators for collecting *quzi ci* texts. Instead, they more likely saw themselves as engaging in

---

1. Yu, "Song Lyrics and the Canon," 71.

a commonplace activity of Chinese literati culture—creating a volume of their own and other poets' literary work as proof of their talent. In this chapter, I examine the *Huajian ji* from that perspective: as a collection of poetic texts that can be filiated to a range of earlier collections and collecting practices of the medieval period.[2] In particular, I compare the *Huajian ji* preface to the prefaces of two important anthologies of Tang poetry with Shu connections, Wei Zhuang's *You xuan ji* 又玄集 and the Shu official Wei Hu's 韋縠 *Cai diao ji* 才調集, in order to demonstrate the continuities and influences among these three collections. Although the scarcity of extant anthologies and prefaces from the Tang makes it difficult to do more than sketch the collecting practices of three centuries, the available evidence suggests a growing diversity in kinds of collecting over the course of the dynasty, particularly through the ninth century. When we view the tenth-century *Huajian ji* in the context of earlier anthologies and against the *You xuan ji* and *Cai diao ji*, both the *Huajian ji*'s links to earlier modes of literary collecting and its truly innovative features become much clearer. With respect to earlier collections of poetry, the *Huajian ji* compilers made some unusual choices, but those choices tell us less about the emerging genre of *quzi ci* than they do about the literary tastes of tenth-century Shu.

The prefaces to the *Youxuan ji*, the *Caidiao ji*, and the *Huajian ji* examined in this chapter demonstrate similar approaches to collecting—most importantly, they share a concern for selecting only "the best" for their collections (a concern often voiced in anthology prefaces), and they rely on individual taste or on the taste of a small group, rather than literary or moral precedent, as their guide. The praise of connoisseurship that we find in all three prefaces is consistent with the cultural environment of Shu surveyed in Chapter 2, a culture of court entertainment and coterie taste. But each writer

---

2. I use "anthology" and "collection" interchangeably here. Although the *Wen xuan* is indeed a *xuan*, "selection," the term *ji*, "collection," was used throughout the Tang for both the compilation of all extant works of an individual writer and for collections of works by different writers (commonly referred to as *zongji* 總集). If a collection of Tang poetry uses a term other than *ji*, such as the late Tang collection *Tang shi lei xuan*, discussed below, I note it. It may be that the *Wen xuan*'s canonical status made Tang collectors reluctant to imitate its title.

defines his motives and the purpose of his anthology slightly differently: Wei Zhuang sees himself as the necessary polisher and sifter of the heap of Tang poetry for the edification of future readers; Wei Hu presents his work as the product of his individual pleasure, meant to pleasure others; and Ouyang Jiong, writing a preface at another's request, not only defends the song lyrics of the anthology but, more importantly, defends the social practice of court-centered songwriting as the hallmark of an elegant literary society. Each of these writers expresses confidence in his own or his coterie's ability to determine "the best" of poetry and song from careful reading and discussion. The two Shu authors, Wei Hu and Ouyang Jiong, present the texts of their collections as potential sources of pleasure to a certain kind of person in a certain kind of place, a defense that can be traced back to the Liang collection *Yutai xinyong*. Later critics condemned the tenth-century views as frivolous at best and immoral at worst. But just as the new society of the Shu court manifested the substantial social changes of the Five Dynasties and Ten Kingdoms, even as its courtiers claimed to be heirs of the Tang, the literary choices of these tenth-century anthologists reveal their full awareness of the literary tradition they had inherited—and a willingness to ignore elements of the tradition as they saw fit.

Anthologies in the Tang

In Tang documents before 900, we find two kinds of evidence about poetry anthologies, or collections of poetry that include works by more than one poet. One kind of evidence—the most powerful but also the least common—is poetry anthologies and their prefaces.[3]

---

3. Among the useful studies of collections in the past decades, I have found the following especially helpful: Knechtges, ed. and trans., *Wen xuan, or Selections of Refined Literature*, 1–70; and Knechtges, "Culling the Weeds and Selecting Prime Blossoms," 200–241; Yu, "Poems in Their Place: Collections and Canons in Early Chinese Literature," 163–96, and "Song Lyrics and the Canon: A Look at Anthologies of *Tz'u*," in Yu, ed., *Voices*, 70–103. For Tang anthologies, see Wu Qiming, " 'Tang ren xuan Tang shi' chuanliu, sanshi kao" and "Tangdai shixuan xue luelun," in *Tang yin zhiyi lu*, 127–83; and also Chen Shangjun, "Tangren bian xuan

Only eight Tang anthologies are extant from the 300 years of the dynasty, and only six of these have prefaces. The periodization of these anthologies also poses a problem: of the eight extant anthologies, five come from the latter half of the eighth century, two from the first decades of the ninth century, and the last—Wei Zhuang's *You xuan ji*—from 900, at the very end of the Tang. In other words, one stretch of the dynasty—the several decades between the end of the High Tang and the early ninth century—is well represented, but collections from other periods that might help to create a history of poetry collections in the Tang are lost. The other kind of evidence is what we might call "trace" evidence, and it ranges in precision from bibliographic entries of titled works to extant prefaces without anthologies to references in texts to anthologies no longer extant. From the ninth century, the period most relevant for the three later collections, we have only one anthology preface extant without its collection, and bibliographic notices of collections whose contents and principles are unknown to us. Given that the evidence for literary anthologies is both scarce and unevenly distributed across the dynasty, we can only survey the models of Tang literary collecting represented in the extant texts and prefaces and offer some speculation on ninth-century developments.[4] We can also consider other kinds of literary collecting—such as the compilation of individual collections in the ninth century—that may have played a role in the diversification of literary taste.[5]

---

shige zongji shulu," in *Tangdai wenxue luncong*, 184–222. David McMullen's survey of Tang literary developments, in *State and Scholars in T'ang China*, includes some discussion of anthologies. For a broader survey of the relationship between collecting and literary trends, see Wang Yao, "Zhongguo wenxue piping yu zongji."

4. Fu Xuancong's own prefaces to each of the Tang collections in his edition of *Tang ren xuan Tang shi* are important sources of bibliographical information for each collection, and they also include some discussion of the literary value of individual collections. See Fu, ed., *Tang ren xuan Tang shi xin bian*.

5. Chen, in "Tang ren bian xuan shige zongji shulu," distinguishes Tang anthologies into seven types: poetry anthologies spanning an entire era (通代詩選), period anthologies, anthologies that collected both poetry and prose, anthologies of couplets, *changhe* (poems composed to match) collections, collections of parting poems, and collections composed by members of the same family. His categoriza-

Tang literati inherited two influential but very different anthology models from the Southern Dynasties: the *Wen xuan* 文選 (Selections of refined literature) and the *Yutai xinyong* 玉臺新詠 (New songs from the Jade Terrace). These two works are quite different in nature and scope. Of the two, the much broader *Wen xuan*, which collected texts from an intentionally wide range of genres, influenced literati throughout the Tang, both as material for study and as a model of collecting. Early Tang scholars supplemented the *Wen xuan* with other comprehensive compilations, such as the 1,200-scroll anthology *Wensi boyao* 文思博要 (The wide-ranging and the essential in literary thought), but the *Wen xuan* held pride of place among its successors both for its royal compiler and for its contents.[6] The imperial and literati interest in anthologies, despite the paucity of extant examples, is well documented in historical records of the decades before the An Lushan rebellion, when literary anthologies generally received much imperial attention and sponsorship—particularly under Empress Wu and Emperor Xuanzong, whose courts were filled with literary talents.[7] In bibliographies from the Song, we find reference to thousands of *juan* of collections made at imperial command before the rebellion, such as the 1,300-*juan* collection compiled under Empress Wu, *Sanjiao zhuying* 三教珠英 (Pearls and blossoms of the three teachings), from which was compiled a five-*juan* collection of poetry, the *Zhuying xueshi ji* 珠英學士集 (Collection of the pearls and blossoms of the scholars).[8]

---

tion is useful for understanding unique features of different kinds of collection—for example, that *changhe* collections tended to have no more than three poets represented—and the periods in which certain kinds of collections appear to have been more numerous, which I comment on below. My discussion here is meant to introduce some broad issues at stake in the act of compiling a collection of literary works that included other writers during the Tang, and therefore I point to examples from different kinds of works.

6. McMullen, *State and Scholars*, 212. See Chen, "Tang ren bian xuan," 199–201, for notes on the bibliographic records of three Tang anthologies titled as continuations or imitations of the *Wen xuan*, and several others clearly modeled after it. The Tang compilations of poetry and prose tended to be large—most of the titles Chen discusses are twenty *juan* or more.

7. McMullen, *State and Scholars*, 218–20.

8. Ibid. See also Wu, "'Tang ren xuan Tang shi' chuanliu, sanshi kao," 131–32.

From the reign of Taizong through that of Xuanzong, rulers of the seventh and eighth centuries studied and promoted the *Wen xuan*. Their lead was followed by court literati, who submitted numerous commentaries to the anthology and also supplemented its works with collections of their own.[9] However, we find little evidence of similarly broad, court-centered compilations after the An Lushan rebellion; instead, we find records of smaller collections of poetry that focused on shorter periods, specific regions, certain poetic styles, and select groups of poets.

Tang readers and collectors found a very different model in the *Yutai xinyong*, the specialized collection of medieval romantic *yuefu* and Liang court "palace-style" poetry. Where the *Wen xuan* was meant to be comprehensive, the *Yutai xinyong*, according to its own preface, had a more modest aim—to provide pleasurable diversions for palace ladies.[10] Where the *Wen xuan* intended to conserve the great works of the tradition, the *Yutai xinyong* explicitly promoted its commitment to contemporary taste, from the "new" of its title to the actual newness of its contents.[11] The *Yutai xinyong* gives us a specialized example of literary collecting—it is a collection of court poetry from a narrow time span, created by a courtier-poet himself. Its focus on beautiful women and romance, along with its Liang court taste for the ornate "palace style," were despised as decadent, southern verse by the northern scholars at Tang Taizong's court, yet the collection was admired by Tang Taizong himself, who composed in the "palace style."[12] In the early decades of the Tang, Southern Dynasties verse came under attack, and the *Yutai xinyong* was implicated in this criticism; though poets certainly continued to read and imitate its works, Xu Ling's collection did not again enjoy the imperial attention it received under Tang Taizong or the court popularity of the *Wen xuan*.[13] However, the perennial criticism that the *Yutai xinyong* received in the Tang suggests that the work re-

---

9. Ibid., 223–24.
10. Knechtges, "Culling the Weeds and Selecting Prime Blossoms," 233–34.
11. Ibid., 236.
12. McMullen, *State and Scholars*, 214.
13. Knechtges, "Culling the Weeds," 239, and n161.

mained popular, or at least quite visible, throughout the dynasty.¹⁴ In the mid- to late eighth century, a literatus of whom we know little, one Li Kangcheng 李康成, compiled a remarkably large "continuation" of the *Yutai xinyong*, entitled the *Yutai houji* 玉臺後集 (Later collection for the Jade Terrace), which was said to have contained 670 poems from 209 poets.¹⁵ This evidence for a late eighth-century collection of romantic verse, itself presented as a continuation of the much older anthology, suggests that the *Yutai xinyong* poetic taste remained appealing to Tang poets, in spite of criticism voiced from some quarters. Furthermore, the creation of a mid-Tang *houji* to the Liang anthology also indicates that the *Yutai xinyong* was still perceived as a model of a certain kind of literary collection, one worth following in a later age.

The crisis and aftermath of the An Lushan rebellion provoked a strong conservative reaction among certain literati in the late eighth century, a reaction whose influence can also be seen in a few extant poetry collections.¹⁶ In her article on medieval anthologies, "Poems in Their Place: Collections and Canons in Early Chinese Literature," Pauline Yu examines three anthologies from just before and after the rebellion: Yin Fan's 殷璠 *He yue yingling ji* 河嶽英靈集 (Collection of the eminences of our rivers and peaks; 753), Rui Tingzhang's 芮挺章 *Guo xiu ji* 國秀集 (Collection of the floriate [talents] of the state; late 750s–60s), and Yuan Jie's 元結 *Qiezhong ji* 篋中集 (Portfolio collection; preface dated 760).¹⁷ Yu's discussion of the Tang anthologies focuses on an emergent "oppositional nature" that characterizes the poetics of collectors, by which she means opposition, grounded in Confucian arguments, to the perceived

---

14. For example, in the preface to the Tang collection *Zhongxing jianqi ji*, the prefacer alludes to the "[poems of] the *Jade Terrace* that fell into lascivious excess," and attacks other anthologies in the same vein. Fu, *Tang ren xuan Tang shi xinbian*, 456.

15. Fu, 316. Fu collects 79 complete poems and 10 fragments that were attributed to this collection in *shihua* and other sources. The text was apparently lost in the Ming.

16. On the conservative reaction, see McMullen, *State and Scholars*, 243–48.

17. Yu, "Poems in their Place," 163–96.

decadence of contemporary taste.[18] Beginning with Yin Fan's influential work, Yu traces the development of a defense of poetry that supersedes current trends and finds its roots in "a moral and political stance associated with earlier poetry."[19] Of the three anthologies, the one compiled soon after the outbreak of the rebellion, Yuan Jie's *Qiezhong ji*, has the most strident preface. Yuan Jie invokes the values of the *Odes* in defense of his selections, but he also turns on his contemporaries fiercely.

Writers of recent ages increasingly copy one another. . . . Indeed, they . . . describe in song the phenomena of the seasons and set them to the music of strings and pipes. For singing boys and dancing girls who produce lewd and bewitching sounds in private rooms this may be permissible. But as for the upright scholar of today—a gentleman of the Great Elegances [of the *Odes*]—I have never found it permissible for him to listen or to chant them himself.[20]

Yuan Jie's vehemence is perhaps more comprehensible in light of the moment of his writing, only five years after the outbreak of the rebellion that devastated the brilliant, and to Yuan's mind decadent, literary culture of the Kaiyuan and Tianbao periods. But even as these compilers lamented the ill winds of the age, they simultaneously called attention to the many other kinds of poetry that the literati wrote, read, and collected. Furthermore, their vociferous criticism documents the popularity of other kinds of anthologies, such as those which catered to the abhorred contemporary taste. Although there are only a few of these other anthologies extant, in them we find an approach to collecting that is neither oppositional nor polemic.

Three extant anthologies from the late eighth and early ninth centuries, the *Zhongxing jian qi ji* 中興間氣集 (The collection of the spirit of the restoration; late 780s), the *Yulan shi* 御覽詩 (Poems for imperial perusal; Yuanhe reign period, 806–20), and the *Jixuan ji* 極玄集 (The collection of the ultimately mysterious; early ninth

---

18. Ibid., 195–96.
19. Ibid., 189.
20. Ibid., 193.

century), give us a range of approaches to collecting Tang poetry. These works are relatively modest—the *Zhongxing jianqi ji* has 142 poems by 26 poets, the *Yulan shi*, 286 poems by 30 poets, and the *Jixuan ji*, 98 poems by 21 poets—and the poetic subjects and styles they collect is notably limited.²¹ Although the preface of the *Zhongxing jianqi ji* seems to echo Yuan Jie's preface to the *Qiezhong ji*, the contents of the anthology, rather than imitating the "old style," unornamented verse of the earlier work, belie the collector's preference for current poetic taste.²² Stephen Owen, in his analysis of the poets of the later eighth century represented in these anthologies, argues that the era's poetry was marked by a stylistic conservatism in contrast to the innovation of Kaiyuan and Tianbao poets. Of the poets collected in the anthologies, Owen remarks that "they did not see themselves as the preservers of an invariable standard of excellence, but as the inheritors of the mainstream of the poetic art."²³ The poetry in these anthologies is characterized by smoothness and competence in the regulated verse form, particularly in couplet craft.

Rather than being comprehensive in terms of period or style, these three anthologies provide us with narrow slices of poetic taste from the late eighth and early ninth centuries. For example, the *Yulan shi*, which can be dated to between 814 and 817 and was compiled by the drafter and Hanlin scholar Linghu Chu 令狐楚 (766–837) at the command of Tang Xianzong 憲宗 (r. 806–20), collects only regulated verse in pentametric and heptametric forms. Its poems are divided equally between quatrains and eight-line verses,

---

21. I give here the number of poems and poets in the editions compiled by Fu Xuancong. The *Zhongxing jianqi ji* originally was said to contain 140 poems, the *Yulan shi* 310 poems by 30 poets, and the *Jixuan ji* 100 poems. For discussions of the various editions of these collections, see Fu, *Tang ren xuan Tang shi*, 363–67, 451–55, 527–31.

22. The preface to the *Zhongxing jianqi ji* is vehement in its avowal of allegiance to the standards of the "Airs and Elegances" and in its criticism of other collections, which makes the contrast between its rhetoric and the collection's contents even more remarkable. One might wonder if the author of the preface was imitating Yuan Jie's Confucian tone, which was lauded at the time, simply to advertise the *Zhongxing jianqi ji* itself.

23. Owen, *Great Age*, 253–54.

and it largely collects the works of poets no longer on the Yuanhe-period literary scene.[24] From the perspective of the Tang periodization developed by Song and later readers, the *Yulan shi* seems especially unusual because even though it was compiled during the Yuanhe period, it contains none of the poets that later became associated with the era—such as Bai Juyi, Yuan Zhen, or Han Yu 韓愈 (768–824)—and instead compiles poems on light topics composed by well-known craftsmen of earlier decades.[25] Parting, boudoir laments, and seasonal reflections are the most common topics of the *Yulan shi*; none of its poems challenge the conventional range of these topics. The *Jixuan ji* attempts a slightly broader range: Yao He 姚合 (781–ca. 859), the compiler of the collection, begins with poems by the High Tang poet Wang Wei 王維 (699–761), but most of his selections come from the works of well-known Dali 大曆 reign period (766–80) poets, such as Li Duan 李端 (738?–86) and Qian Qi 錢起 (722?–85). He also includes poems from monks of the late eighth century known for their talent in poetry, such as Jiaoran 皎然 (720–805?). Although the *Jixuan ji* contains no boudoir verses, the collection's poems are largely regulated verses on common topics—partings, banquets, and poems presented to companions. In short, these two early ninth-century collections give us glimpses of particular compilers' tastes in the poetry of a few decades; they also provide a useful balance to more polemical collections such as the *Qie zhong ji*.

After the group of extant anthologies from the late eighth and early ninth centuries, we have few texts with which we might assess changes in poetry collecting in the last decades of the Tang. The functions of anthologies in the early and High Tang are attested by the variety of anthologies extant or described in Tang documents, from the imperially commissioned bouquet of court poems on a specific event, to the comprehensive, education-oriented tomes that sought to preserve and circulate works perceived as critical to the

---

24. For a study of some of the distinctive features of the *Yulan shi*, see Pauline Yu, "Poems for the Emperor: Imperial Tastes in the Early Ninth Century." See also Fu, *Tang ren xuan Tang shi*, 363–67.

25. Yu, "Poems for the Emperor."

tradition, to the small collection of a poetry circle. In the first half of the dynasty, court-centered collections dominated the scene, whether large-scale projects like the *Wensi boyao* or the coterie collections of Empress Wu. Judging from references in Song bibliographies and Tang historical texts, imperially commissioned and court-presented anthologies declined in number in the ninth century. However, in the bibliographic chapter of the *Xin Tang shu* and bibliographic records of the Song dynasty, we find records of dozens of titles of smaller poetry collections (five *juan* or fewer) from the ninth century, most of which appear to be compiled by individuals or small groups of poets.[26] We know from their titles and sometimes from brief notices in other sources that these collections include linked-verse compilations as well as *changhe* 唱和 collections, volumes of poems that were composed responsively by two or more poets.[27] From brief notes in literati biographies, we can speculate as to the contents or compilers of some of these collections;[28] few appear to be wide-ranging or comprehensive in nature.[29]

---

26. From the two bibliographical chapters of the *Jiu Tang shu* and *Xin Tang shu*, Wu Qiming compiles more than 60 titles of poetry collections that are no longer extant, and he adds several other titles found in various Song texts. Wu, "Tangdai shixuan xue luelun," 162–64.

27. The bibliographic essay of the *Xin Tang shu* contains fourteen collections that are identified in their titles as containing *changhe* verse, most by ninth-century poets. *XTS* 60.1623–24.

28. For example, see the *San sheren ji* 三舍人集 (Collection of the three [secretariat] drafters), a collection of pentametric and heptametric quatrains by Linghu Chu and two other officials of the Yuanhe era, Wang Ya and Zhang Zhongsu 張中素. These collections compiled by a small group of friends or colleagues were often meant as self-advertisement. See Jiang, "Linghu Chu zuopin chuanliu ji sanshi kaoshu," 60. Noted also by Wu, "Tang ren xuan Tang shi," 151. See *Tangshi jishi*, 42.1152, for a record of this collection.

29. One remarkable exception to these smaller collections can be found in a mid-ninth-century preface to a lost anthology that was explicitly Confucian in nature. The lost work was titled *Tang shi leixuan* 唐詩類選 (Selections of Tang poetry by categories) and was compiled by the literatus Gu Tao 顧陶, with a preface dated 856 (*QTW* 765.21b–23a). In his preface, we hear echoes of Yin Fan and Yuan Jie (both of whose works Gu praises), as well as harsh criticism of "shallow, specious, popular seductive language" and "the songs of Zheng and Wei" seen by Gu as common in his era. He acknowledges his debt to the *Odes* explicitly in his preface and his title, which refers to "categories of stimulus," *xinglei* 興類, a crite-

These smaller collections of compiled exchange poetry are distinctive in scope, even alongside brief anthologies such as the *Jixuan ji* and the *Yulan shi*. Where a work such as the *Jixuan ji* aimed to present a view of the poetic "best" of a short period, a poet who compiled a collection of his own work in conjunction with other poets advertised the literary talents and social ties enjoyed by himself and his companions.[30] In these smaller ninth-century collections of verse composed by a few poets, we see the new importance of contemporary literary fame in Tang culture, and the utility of literary collections as means of circulating one's name and of associating oneself with other, perhaps more influential, literati.

The nature of the evidence for Tang collections of poetry—few extant works, and sketchy bibliographical records for dozens of others—precludes a more precise portrait of Tang literary collecting. However, we can discern a few trends from our understanding of other ninth-century cultural developments and by recalling the possible audiences for which collections were designed. As I noted in Chapter 1, the ninth century saw more poets writing in provincial centers outside the capital, whether as a consequence of exile, provincial employment, rebellions, or the desire to steer clear of the increasingly dangerous politics of the imperial court. One result of these new contexts for literary composition was a sharp growth in private literature. In the absence of a literary center or a strong consensus on literary values, poets would have felt free to rely upon their own tastes and ambitions in compiling poetry collections, without reference to capital trends, the sanction of literary tradition, or even current taste, if they so chose. Titles tell us little about the contents of works; without prefaces, moreover, we are unable to reconstruct the principles that might have governed the compilation of any given work. The increasing privatization of literature

---

rion of selection and arrangement that points to the first of the Six Principles (*liu yi* 六義) of the *Odes*. Gu uses the word "selection," *xuan*, over the more common "collection," *ji*, to emphasize his stringent standards of compilation. But he also aimed to be comprehensive: the work contained twenty *juan* and no fewer than 1,232 poems.

30. For a close analysis of the composition and the compilers of such collections, see Jia, *Tangdai jihui zongji yu shiren qun yanjiu*.

likely had an unforeseen textual consequence: unlike the court-commissioned anthologies of literature of the seventh and eighth centuries, which often earned a mention in a variety of historical records even if they did not survive the Tang, many such private collections were surely lost in the upheavals at the end of the dynasty and did not survive even to be listed in Song bibliographies.[31] After the *Yulan shi* and the *Jixuan ji*, the collections of the early ninth century, we do not have another extant poetry anthology until the year 900, the date of Wei Zhuang's *Youxuan ji*.[32] But this work, unlike its ninth-century predecessors, is extant in a version that appears close to the original;[33] more importantly, the collection opens with a preface in which Wei Zhuang describes in detail the process of compilation. With a historical perspective unique among Tang collections, Wei Zhuang's work reveals his interest in preserving the best of Tang poetry for the benefit of future readers.

Collecting Tang Poetry for Posterity: The Youxuan ji

When seen in the late Tang context, the claims and selections of Wei Zhuang's *Youxuan ji* take on greater meaning. Wei Zhuang's anthology differs in key ways from the late eighth- and early ninth-century collections discussed above: first, in the preface to the anthology Wei Zhuang eloquently defends his own qualifications as a compiler, persuading the reader of his own refinement and the quality of his collection; second, the collection contains works from

---

31. Chen, "Tang ren bian xuan," 184, points out that the extant Tang anthologies represent only 10 percent of those mentioned in historical records and bibliographies.

32. The discovery of a collection of song lyrics, the *Yunyao ji*, at Dunhuang provides evidence of nonliterati anthologies, but this collection cannot be dated more precisely than before 922. For the dating of this anthology, see Ren Erbei, *Dunhuang qu chutan*, 204. I follow Murakami, *Sōshi kenkyū: Tō Godai Hoku Sō hen*, 162–68, for the attribution of these lyrics to nonliterati composers.

33. The transmission of Wei Zhuang's *Youxuan ji* in China after the Tang can be traced in other texts through the Yuan, but it disappeared after that time, only resurfacing in the 1950s in a Japanese library, missing apparently only one poem from its original 300. Modern editions are based on this text. Fu, ed., *Tang ren xuan Tang shi*, 574–75.

almost two centuries of Tang poetry rather than from Wei's recent past; third, it includes poems from a wider range of people, including more monks and women poets, than any known Tang collection. Wei Zhuang openly links his work to Yao He's *Jixuan ji* in the preface to his *Youxuan ji*: "Some time ago, Yao He compiled the *Collection of the Ultimately Mysterious* in one *juan*, which circulated in his era and was entirely refined and subtle. Now I again compile the 'mysterious' (*xuanzhe* 玄者) to complete this *Collection of the Ever-More Mysterious* in three *juan*."[34] Wei Zhuang's collection is intended not only to continue Yao He's work but also to expand it in terms of both scope and number of poems. Wei Zhuang collects 300 poems in comparison to Yao's 100, and 150 poets to Yao's 21;[35] Wei's collection includes Du Fu 杜甫 (712–70) and Li Bai, among other High Tang poets excluded by Yao, and extends forward in time to include many late Tang poets. Although it clearly pays homage to Yao He's work, the title also alludes to lines from the opening passage of the received *Laozi*, "Mystery upon mystery, the gate of many wonders" 玄之又玄, 眾妙之門.[36] In the center of the preface, Wei Zhuang directly explains his title by praising the power of poetry to inspire extraordinary responses in readers and in the natural world, a quality that was both mysterious and ineffable.

In compiling this anthology, Wei Zhuang seems to have been seeking to create a collection that would represent the work of the greatest Tang poets, demonstrating an unprecedented concern with preserving the "best" of the dynasty.[37] All anthologists were convinced of their own good judgment, whether that judgment reflected or opposed current tastes in poetry. They would not have collected otherwise. In some of the eighth-century anthologies

---

34. For this preface, I rely upon the notes of Gao, *Tang Song wen ju yao*, 1582–85, and also Li, ed., *Wei Zhuang ji jiaozhu*, 559–75.

35. The extant collection today contains 299 poems by 146 poets. Fu discusses this discrepancy and other differences between the preface, table of contents, and the actual numbers of poems and poets in the collection, noting the cases in which poems are not correctly divided or misattributed. *Tang ren xuan Tang shi*, 576–78. Wei Zhuang's poems include twelve poems also selected by Yao for the *Jixuan ji*.

36. Lou, *Laozi Zhouyi Wang Bi jiaoshi*, 1.

37. Fu, *Tang ren xuan Tang shi*, 573.

examined by Pauline Yu, Confucian precedent guided the collectors and protected them from being deluded by mere fashion in poetry. In the case of anthologies that capture a specific period or style, such as the *Yulan shi* or the *Jixuan ji*, it may be that little defense was needed: they merely present what are generally acknowledged as the finest works of their age. In the case of the *Youxuan ji*, however, Wei Zhuang defends not only his own favorites among Tang poems but also his right to choose favorites on the grounds of personal taste rather than precedent. We hear Wei Zhuang's claims echoed a few decades later, in Wei Hu's preface to his *Caidiao ji*. Many of the favorites chosen by the two were in fact poems whose Tang popularity is well documented in other texts, but there are also idiosyncratic choices in both works that beg some justification. We can consider below whether the rationales offered by the two men are convincing or not. First, the preface to Wei Zhuang's *Youxuan ji*:

Xie Xuanhui's 謝玄暉 [Tiao 眺] collected writings fill scrolls, but people recite only the "Limpid River" line; Cao Zijian's 曹子建 [Zhi 植] reputation as poetic master surpasses all others of antiquity, yet people only chant his "Clear Night" piece.[38] From this, one can understand that among the excellent grain stored in a thousand boxes, double-awned grain is rare; amid the nine changes of the strummed strings, songs like "Great Aid" are scarce.[39] When I enter the flowery forest [of literature], I find that pearly trees are very few. I have surveyed the many pipes, but there was only one purple panpipe.[40]

---

38. Wei Zhuang is referring to Xie Tiao's "Climbing Third Mountain Late and Turning to Gaze at the Capital" and Cao Zhi's "The Duke's Banquet," both of which were collected in the *Wen xuan* and were very well known. *WX* 27.589–90 and 20.423.

39. The "double-awned grain" was auspicious grain presented to the throne, mentioned in *Hou Han shu*, 31.1100; the "nine changes" refer to the sequencing of musical pieces in *Zhou li* 22.71. The song *Da hu* 大護 is noted in the *Lüshi chunqiu* and the *Zhou li* as a folk piece sung by Yi Yin at the court of Tang. Chen, ed., *Lüshi chunqiu jiaoshi*, 5.5/286. Here it signifies a musical piece of outstanding excellence.

40. The "many pipes" and "purple panpipes" may echo the *Zhuangzi*'s comparison (2/3–8) of the "pipes of earth," "pipes of men," and "pipes of Heaven." All references to *Zhuangzi* are to chapter and line number in the Harvard-Yenching index, *A Concordance to Chuang Tzu*. "Purple panpipes" appear in three ninth-

Thus have I plucked flowers in the forest and gathered kingfisher feathers by rocky crags. Only after sifting through the sand and stones did I begin to recognize the jewel that drives away cold, and only after I recorded what was carved and chiseled into shape did I finally complete [a work as] precious as a ritual vessel.[41] Thus we know that in plucking the pearl under the jaws [of the black dragon], one can't go after ten bushels of them.[42] Or it's like looking at a leopard through a pipe—one can only see one spot.

From our imperial court's [the Tang's earliest] skilled and famous [writers] down to today's authors, out of some who have one hundred works, I occasionally noted down one piece; from some collected works, I only solicited several poems. But in collecting their fresh words and beautiful lines and recording them in my Western Studio, I could not exhaust their great floods and had to let most of them return to the Eastern Sea. When I united what I had noted down, I had 150 Talents; of the pieces I had recited, I had 300 famous poems. . . .

My only concern is that I have eaten the horse's liver—and moreover, I might be said to have "dyed my finger" in it.[43] How could I not worry that, in getting rid of the *yi* bone when boiling the fish, I might have ruined its scales?[44] I'm ashamed that my "mole's belly" of a mind is so easily filled; it's

---

century poems and not before, suggesting that Wei's use of the term as a figure of excellence is contemporary.

41. The "jewel that drives away the cold" (*bihan* 避寒) appears in the ninth-century anecdote collection, *Youyang zazu*, in a story from the Wei. The state of Kunming presented a magic bird that spit out bits of gold, which the palace ladies then made into hairpins, saying they were made of "gold that drives away the cold," since the bird did not fear cold. See Duan Chengshi, *Youyang zazu* 16.8a/b. Wei's use of the term suggests a rare and priceless jewel (or other decorative object). The "ritual vessel," *hulian* 瑚璉 appears in *Lun yu* 5.4.

42. The pearl under the mouth of the black dragon comes from *Zhuangzi* (32/44) in a passage describing the unattainability of precious things—pearls worth a thousand in gold are only found in the deepest depths, or under the jaws of black dragons.

43. The horse's liver was said to be poisonous; see *Shi ji* 26.1390. "Dyeing the finger" refers to a story in *Zuo zhuan*, in which someone dipped his finger in a delicacy not meant for him; see Yang, ed., *Chunqiu Zuozhuan zhu*, 677–78.

44. This line may contain allusions to two fish stories. The first, "getting rid of the *yi* 乙 bone," refers to the practice, noted in the *Liji*, of removing a small bone that was dangerous if eaten; see *Li ji zhengyi* 8.21a. The second, "ruining its scales," may refer to the Heshang gong commentary to *Laozi* 60, which begins: "Ruling a big kingdom is like cooking a small fish." The commentary elaborates: "In cooking

not that I relish only the singular excellence of bears' paws. In this way, I have selected from among the regulated and discarded the excessive.[45]

[One might ask:] How could I tell the black goose from the white by taste?[46] I force myself to try and distinguish the taste of the waters of the Zi River from the Min River.[47] Zuo Taizhong 左太沖 [Si 思] over ten years [produced] a tripartite rhapsody on the capitals; yet it could not be without flaws.[48] Liu Muzhi 劉穆之 produced a hundred volumes a day—how could they have been entirely beautiful?[49] From this, we know that Ban [Gu] 班固, Zhang [Heng] 張衡, Qu [Yuan] 屈原, and Song [Yu] 宋玉 also had weedlike verbiage; Shen [Yue] 沈約, Xie [Lingyun] 謝靈運, Ying [Yang] 應瑒, and Liu [Zhen] 劉貞 moreover had many tedious lines. Although we may regret the excluded lovely [pieces], a comprehensive collection would have been difficult. It is like taking an axe and clearing a mountain just to get one fine tree, or taking a cup to the ocean only to draw what one could have from a sweet spring. It's the same with the wind, the moon, the mist, the flowers—or quinces, pears, tangerines, and pomelos.[50]

Some time ago, Yao He compiled the *Collection of the Ultimately Mysterious* in one *juan*, which circulated in his era and was entirely refined and subtle. Now I again compile the 'mysterious,' to complete this *Collection of the Ever-More Mysterious* in three *juan*. Noting where the currents flow at

---

a small fish, you do not remove the guts, and the scales are not taken off. You dare not scratch it, for fear it might fall apart." Zheng, ed., *Laozi Heshang gong zhushu zheng*, 407.

45. Although the bulk of the poems in Wei Zhuang's anthology are regulated, "the regulated" here does not refer to metrics but stands in contrast to the "excessive" or "lush" that was pruned away.

46. The *Taiping yulan* 919.3a cites a lost text, the *Qin ji*, that tells the story of one Fu Yin 符殷, who could tell whether a goose had been black or white feathered by taste.

47. The *Lüshi chunqiu* cites Confucius as saying that one Yiya 易牙 was able to tell the two rivers apart by taste. The commentary notes that Yiya was a minister "who understood tastes." *Lüshi chunqiu jiaoshi*, 18.3/1168.

48. The reference is to Zuo Si's "Rhapsody on the Three Capitals," collected in the *Wen xuan*.

49. Liu Muzhi was a literatus of the Southern Dynasties' Song period, noted for his writing a hundred letters a day as secretary to the emperor. *Song shu* 42.1305.

50. Wei alludes to a passage from the *Zhuangzi* (14/40) in which Zhuangzi says that the mores and laws of the rulers of antiquity were distinct and not comparable, like quinces, pears, tangerines, and pomelos—although each had a different flavor, they were all good.

right angles, my eyes are dazzled;[51] I have surveyed the beauteous waters until now my spirit is weary.[52] Since the fish and the hare are hard enough to keep, I have abandoned the fishtrap and snare.[53] Thus, when using golden dishes to drink dew, one gathers only the essence of the mists and fogs.[54] When one sups on treasures in the "flower world," one relishes only the taste of ghee.[55] Therefore, making this collection is not just for the benefit of my own perusal; it is also to be handed down to posterity. As for gathering the substance and eliminating the excesses [of other poets in other eras?], that must await those to come. [Written in] the third year of the [Tang] Guanghua 光化 reign period [900 C.E.], seventh month.

There are a number of remarkable elements to this preface, but the most striking is the prominence of the anthologizer himself, Wei Zhuang. Rather than praising the kind of poetry that he has chosen for his collection, or tracing back the history of poetry collection to the *Odes*, Wei Zhuang has chosen instead to explain not only the importance but indeed the necessity of his role as discriminating connoisseur and collector. Wei begins the defense of his collection with the observation that people generally acknowledge the existence of a "best" in poetry and nature—the constant citing of only one of Xie Tiao's and of Cao Zhi's poems is proof—and that the task of selecting the best is therefore not impossible, if challenging. In a cascade of metaphors, Wei tells us how he "reviewed," "plucked," "gathered," and finally "recorded" the precious treasures of Tang poetry. His series of allusions reinforces two ideas: first, the task of "sifting through the sand and stones," *shatai* 沙汰, is one that

---

51. According to Li Shan's 李善 commentary to a poem by Yan Yannian 嚴延年 in the *Wen xuan*, water flowing at right angles (*fang liu* 方流) marks the location of jade.

52. "Beauteous waters" (*li shui* 麗水) contain gold, according to the *Han Feizi*.

53. The "fishtrap" and "snare" refer to the *Zhuangzi* (26/48) discussion of useful means—once the fishtrap and snare are used to catch their prey, they can be discarded.

54. The "golden dishes" refer to the bronze statues of transcendents of the Han, which held up golden bowls to collect dew (drunk by the emperor for immortality).

55. Wei refers to the "treasures" consumed in the "flower world" of Buddhist temples on the path to enlightenment. Ghee, refined butter, is a symbol of the highest stage on this path.

takes great labor and skill. The product of all that labor (i.e., his collection) is priceless and marvelous, as the references to the "jewel that drives away cold" and the "ritual vessel" suggest. Furthermore, he argues that such a work of sifting could *only* produce a small, refined collection—this is the point of the analogies of plucking a pearl from beneath the jaws of a dragon and of looking at a leopard through a pipe. Although Wei laments the difficulty of sorting through the "great floods" of works, his final tally is hardly arbitrary: he claims his collection contains 300 "famous poems," a number that echoes the 300 poems of the *Odes* and hints at Tang canon-making on Wei's part.

Wei's use of metaphors of flavor and taste in itself is not unusual in the context of defending selections, but his heaping of example upon example does seem oddly excessive. Rather than locating his principles in sanctioned precedent, he argues that his own "taste" (literally) can be his guide in the quest for a purified, "regulated" sample of Tang poetry. He begins, however, by using metaphors of taste to modestly deprecate his own skills: he fears that he may have "eaten the [horse's] liver" by not knowing what to consume or discard or that he has ruined the "fish" of poetry through his effort to clean and sort it. But—as in the opening section, where he turned a potential difficulty (the great volume of poetry to be sorted through) into an argument supporting his work (a necessary task if we wish to discover the best poetry)—he tells us that he does not only value the "singular excellence of bears' paws," and that he has, in fact, "discarded the excessive," or used his discrimination to select appropriate poems. The next two "taste" allusions set up a key transition between one line of argument and another. Wei refers to the story of a man who could tell whether a goose had white or black feathers when tasting it, and to that of someone who could tell apart the waters of two rivers by taste. He questions his own ability to do such a thing, saying he "forced himself" to accomplish it. And in the lines that follow, he cleverly shifts the ground from his own qualifications (to which he will return) to the work of the poets from which one can select.

Wei Zhuang anticipates those who might question his qualifications as a purifier of poetry with an implicit comparison of his anthology to the work of Xiao Tong in the *Wen xuan*, a comparison in which Xiao Tong comes off the worse. He points to renowned poets of the Warring States, the Han, and the period of division, all of whom are found in the *Wen xuan*, stating that even the great ones had their "weedlike verbiage" and "tedious lines." His anthology, however, since it aims to present only "the best," must exclude anything slightly flawed. Wei Zhuang's implication here is that the *Wen xuan*, in its breadth, was too inclusive and insufficiently discriminating. In his statement, "a comprehensive collection would have been difficult," "difficult" certainly can be read as "undesirable." One must match one's efforts to one's goals, Wei argues—why hack down a mountain for one tree? If one is aiming for perfection, why waste time on the excessive? Although he ends the passage with a metaphor that evokes equality among fellow collectors—like different fruits, each has its own "flavor"—his own stronger claim to excellence has already been made.

Wei Zhuang acknowledges the mid-Tang collector Yao He, compiler of the *Jixuan ji*, as the source of his title and the inspiration for his collection. Wei takes up the subject of his own efforts again in the closing lines, this time describing his collection as a labor of keen visual perception—akin to sensing the presence of jade or gold by the flow of the current or the appearance of water. He returns to metaphors of taste and consumption to defend the "refinement" of his collection: like the dew collected in the golden pans of the bronze transcendents of the Han, or the ghee consumed by Buddhists in the "flower world," his collection preserves the essence of poetry. The analogies can be extended beyond Wei's efforts as collector, to the reader's benefits in "consuming" the anthology: just as would-be transcendents sup on auroras and dew, and would-be Bodhisattvas consume ghee, so the poetry connoisseur can approach Wei's anthology assured that he will find only the best poetry. Wei Zhuang closes by disclaiming any selfish motive in making the collection—"it is also to be handed down to posterity"—and invites future readers to do likewise.

Although Wei refers to the work of other collectors in passing, he makes no reference to the Great Collector, Confucius, and his tradition; he spends almost no time describing the actual poetry he

Gathering the "Flowers" of Poetry and Song 139

has collected and what it represents; and he makes no reference to poetic standards outside of those he has conceived within himself. His qualifications for the task seem to be hard work and an understanding of refinement. And yet he seems supremely confident in having accomplished his self-prescribed task of "gathering the substance and eliminating the excesses." This emphasis on the amount of "excess" in poetry is unusual, and it appears throughout the preface, from the opening invocation of the "flowery forest" and "many pipes" to the historical examples of excess found in even the best poets from before the Tang. Ultimately it serves to reinforce Wei's argument for the importance of his role as discriminating connoisseur. It is difficult to find precedents for this assumption of independent aesthetic judgment in extant Tang anthology prefaces; however, we might filiate Wei's position to similar statements made by ninth-century compilers of smaller collections of their own or others' verse, which were often created while an author was still living and circulated before the late or posthumous compilation of complete works. In prefaces to these smaller collections of works by a single writer, poets could defend their selections simply on the basis of taste or pleasure.[56] Wei Zhuang certainly intended his work to be representative, and yet he was clearly convinced of his own ability to refine the essence of Tang poetry by himself.

In the year 900, before the fall of the Tang, there was as yet no Tang canon—it would be the task of Song poets and literati to create one by ranking and selecting among the "floods" of Tang poems handed down in manuscripts. Certainly some poems were collected in more than one work—which suggests that they were consistently appreciated by readers over the course of the dynasty and had a better chance at survival—but it is impossible to determine the relative fame of individual poems in the late ninth century. As a

---

56. Two contemporaneous examples of prefaces to small collections in which this position is articulated are Sikong Tu's 司空圖 preface to the collection *Zhuoying ji* 擢英集 (Collection of plucked blossoms) and Han Wo's 韓偓 preface (attributed) to the *Xianglian ji* 香奩集 (The fragrant satchel collection). For Han Wo's preface, see Gao, 1578–81.

collection of Tang poetry made by an individual, we must assume that the *Youxuan ji* documents Wei Zhuang's personal tastes. First, Wei prefers regulated, occasional verse over "old-style" verse, *yuefu*, or other song forms. His few selections of *yuefu* are poems that had been collected in other works, suggesting that they were relatively famous. The High Tang is well represented (Du Fu, Li Bai, and Wang Wei 王維 open the collection), but poets from the late eighth century, such as those so prominent in the *Jixuan ji*, are also quite numerous. It seems as though Wei Zhuang wished to preserve those texts that best recalled the image or reputation of a given poet. For example, Du Fu is represented by, among other works, five- and seven-character regulated verse, including the rebellion poem "Gazing at Spring" 春望, Li Bai by his "Road to Shu Is Hard" 蜀道難, Wang Wei by regulated verses, including "Observing the Hunt" 觀獵 (also found in the *Jixuan ji*), Gao Shi 高適 (716–65) by his "Song of Yan" 燕歌行, Du Mu 杜牧 (803–52) by his "Qin Huai" 秦淮, and Yuan Zhen by his "Lianchang Palace Lyric" 連昌宮詞. Some of the late eighth-century capital poets, such as Lu Lun and Qian Qi, are represented by the same poems found in Yao He's *Jixuan ji*. And poems dedicated to or composed about other poets are common, such as Jia Dao's 賈島 (779–843) "Weeping for Meng Jiao" 哭孟郊, and Bai Juyi's and Liu Yuxi's exchange poems. When viewed through our eyes—looking backward over the millennium of collecting and ranking of Tang poetry that began in the Song—it is a broad but unsurprising collection of "greatest hits." Although Wei Zhuang includes monks' and women's poetry, his selections are again almost all previously collected works by famous monks and women, such as the Buddhist monks Qingjiang 清江 and Jiaoran 皎然, and the women poets Xue Tao 薛陶 (768–ca. 832) and Yu Xuanji 魚玄機 (844–68). In the end, Wei's selections, which he so strenuously defends as the work of the connoisseur, seem to have been mediated by decades, if not centuries, of other readers' approval.

Over the course of his lifetime, Wei Zhuang took other steps on behalf of poets he considered worthy of defense or promotion, from writing a memorial advocating poets whose work and persons he believed had been unfairly slighted to rebuilding and preserving Du

Fu's "thatched hut" in Sichuan.⁵⁷ On the one hand, these are all gestures in tune with the "air," *feng* 風, of Wei's chaotic time, an early articulation of the need to preserve the Tang's glory for posterity; on the other, they can be seen as an intervention in an era of divergent and weakened literary standards, when a definition of "the best" of the age gone by is more elegiac than controversial. There are hints of canon-making in Wei's preface, but his efforts are chiefly aimed toward his own pleasure and the pleasurable edification of other reader-connoisseurs, present and future. His anthology might have been lost along with many others after the fall of the Tang but for one critical career move: his 901 posting to Shu as a secretary in the military governor's offices of Wang Jian. As demonstrated in Chapter 2, many sources suggest that Wei Zhuang strongly influenced Shu culture in its early years as an independent kingdom. Certainly his literary works, including the *Youxuan ji*, escaped the fate of other texts in the Tang capitals and survived due to his presence in Shu. But the mid-tenth century Shu anthology *Caidiao ji* shows that Wei Zhuang's anthology was also a model for Shu literary collecting.⁵⁸

"Taking Delight in What One Loves": The Caidiao ji

The fall of the Tang by no means marked an end to the collecting of poetry; if anything, the records of tenth-century literary activity suggest that the practice continued to flourish and diversify. The Southern Tang has perhaps the best bibliographical documentation of any of the "southern" regimes, though this documentation too is quite partial; it gives evidence that the kingdom produced many kinds of collections—from small compilations of individual poets' works to coterie collections made at court to more comprehensive

---

57. For a discussion of these achievements, see Yates, *Washing Silk*, 31, and n132.

58. Wei Zhuang's anthology was also a model for literary collecting in the Southern Tang, as evidenced by the bibliographical record of a *Jiangnan xu Youxuan ji* 江南續又玄集 in ten *juan*, compiled by one Liu Ji 劉吉. Noted in Tang, "Nan Tang yiwen zhi," 349; also discussed by Chen, "Tang ren bianxuan shige zongji shulu," 197.

and even retrospective anthologies.⁵⁹ Since they are much less complete than those for the Southern Tang, the historical records from the Former and Latter Shu give us only a glimpse of the range of literary, musical, and artistic activity at the Chengdu court; scattered references from Wu Renchen's *Shiguo chunqiu* suggest that Shu literati pursued similar kinds of literary collecting. From the Former Shu, we have records of texts such as an eight-*juan* collection entitled *Shuguo wenying* 蜀國文英 (The literary blossoms of the state of Shu), compiled by one Liu Zan 劉贊;⁶⁰ Wang Yan's own two hundred–*juan* collection *Yan hua ji*; and various collections of the works of individual writers, such as the *Huajian ji* poet Li Xun's *Qiong yao ji* 瓊瑤集 (Collection of rosegem and turquoise). In the Latter Shu, although there are records of dozens of texts, we have only the *Caidiao ji* and the *Huajian ji* as extant examples of collections of verse that included more than one poet's work. Both of these anthologies proved significant in literary history, though in quite different ways.

Unlike Wei Zhuang's anthology, which may not have been widely read after the fall of Shu, the Latter Shu official Wei Hu's *Caidiao ji*, a collection of 1,000 poems by 178 poets, has been an important—and in some cases exclusive—source for the work of many late Tang poets. It seems to have enjoyed uninterrupted transmission from the tenth century to today. Although its particular vision of the Tang may not have influenced the tastes of Song readers, the *Caidiao ji* came under scrutiny in the seventeenth century for what some perceived as misguided judgments and a shallow understanding of what late imperial readers considered to be the best of Tang poetry.⁶¹ The *Shiguo chunqiu* states that Wei Hu was an official in the Latter Shu regime and that he served both Meng Zhixiang and his son Meng Chang, reaching the rank of Censor and then perhaps

---

59. See Tang, "Nan Tang yiwen zhi," 349–56, for titles of anthologies (*zongji*) and individual writers' collections (*bieji*) attributed to Southern Tang literati.

60. *SGCQ* 43.637.

61. Fu notes this critical scrutiny in his prefatory remarks to the anthology (*Tang ren xuan Tang shi*, 687–88). However, he also cites an eighteenth-century commentator's praise of Wei Hu's taste.

head of a ministry; no further biographical information is available.⁶² If Wei Hu did indeed serve in such high positions in the Latter Shu regime, he likely would not have known Wei Zhuang (who died in 910), but he would surely have known Ouyang Jiong—who rose to the highest ranks of the Latter Shu government—as well as the courtiers whose discussions of *quzi ci* are described in the *Huajian ji* preface. The Shu culture of music and other artistic pleasures sketched in Chapter 2 should be understood as the backdrop for Wei Hu's collection.

In his preface to the *Caidiao ji*, Wei Hu imitates Wei Zhuang's air of connoisseurship and moderates it with gentle self-deprecation. Wei Hu is perhaps less certain of his qualifications for the task of compiling an anthology of Tang poetry, but he is no less convinced of the excellence of his selections. In addition, despite his slightly defensive tone, Wei Hu's collection is more than three times larger than his predecessor's work, and so achieves a comprehensiveness of its own, though from the perspective of late imperial or even modern tastes in Tang poetry it could in no way be called representative. Here is his preface in full:

From a young age I have widely surveyed the masses of words, finding always my aspirations achieved therein.⁶³ Although the autumn firefly's glow did not go far, even the perception of insect-carving was excellent on its own.⁶⁴ An ancient once said, "Returning [to oneself] and listening is called 'acuity'; contemplating things internally is called 'enlightenment.'"⁶⁵ Then why should I take blame from the stupid and crude or be ridiculed by mere book-hoarders?⁶⁶ Thus in my leisure days I reviewed the collections

---

62. *SGCQ* 56.811.

63. Reading *suo* 所 as *qu* 取, according to the *SKQS* and *QTW* emendation.

64. The "firefly's glow" may refer to student reading by firefly light; the "insect-carving" here means good writing. "Insect-carving" can be both a positive or (more often) a negative reference to literature. Wei Hu's use is clearly positive.

65. The citation comes from the biography of Shang Yang in *Shi ji* 63.2233; the words are spoken by Shang Yang's advisor, Zhao Liang, who is counseling Shang Yang on the means of controlling Qin. His emphasis, as the lines indicate, is on self-reliance and self-control.

66. "Book-hoarders" (*shu chu* 書廚) comes from the *Nan Qi shu* as a label for a scholar who studies diligently but makes no progress; see *Nan Qi shu* 39.685–86.

of Li [Bai] and Du [Fu] and the poems of Yuan [Zhen] and Bai [Juyi]. In them, there are the vastness of the heavens and seas and an *esprit* that was absolutely unprecedented.

Then I selected the secretly wondrous among them, together with the many worthies' perfect stanzas and lines.[67] I could not record them all, but each one has its order and rank. Some are for unscrolling while sitting idly by the window, others for chanting while strolling by a moonlit gazebo. Their consonance is lofty, vying with the cassia spirit [the moon] in brilliance; their words are lovely, contending with spring's beauty in fairness.

But although I value taking delight in what one loves [*zi le suo hao* 自樂所好], how dare I pass anything down to posterity? I have here gathered various persons' songs and poems, 1,000 pieces altogether. Each 100 works makes up a chapter, dividing the collection into ten sections. I call it *The Collection of the Tunes of the Talents*. I hope those to come will not call me long-winded and that in future ages there will be those who will not deride my insights.[68]

Wei Hu's preface falls neatly into three parts: the first section addresses Wei's fitness for the work of anthologizing; the second explains the nature and quality of the collected verse and outlines the function of the collection itself; the last section addresses future readers. In the opening line, Wei asserts his experience with and love of literature. His anxiety about his qualifications can be seen in his use of the two insect metaphors, describing his study, by "firefly light," of the "insect-carving" of the fine writing he preferred. The metaphor of "insect-carving" is a well-established figure for "precious and useless literary activity," dating back to Yang Xiong's 揚雄 attack on the Han rhapsody and later to the Qi scholar Pei Ziye's 裴子野 critique of his era's excessively ornate style ("Essay on Carving Insects" 雕蟲論). However, Wei Hu defends his enjoyment of "insect-carving" by saying that it was "excellent on its own," or "in itself," *zi jia* 自佳. This phrase not only contrasts with the image

---

67. The rhyming binome "ʔaw-mjiaw" 奧妙 (using Pulleyblank's LMC reconstruction) combines the meaning of "secret, deep" with "excellent, wonderful." Wei Hu certainly echoes Wei Zhuang's "mysterious" here, and his allusion to the *zhong ao*, "many wonders," of the *Laozi* passage.

68. My text for the preface is taken from *Tang ren xuan Tang shi*, 691.

of the "borrowed" light of fireflies by which he studied as a youth but also implies that his own pleasure in reading was sufficient to justify his selections. Wei Hu develops this line of argument further with a citation from the *Shi ji* biography of Shang Yang that advocates turning to one's own senses for understanding. Whereas Wei Zhuang catalogued his hard work of collecting and purifying, Wei Hu defends the importance of self-reliance in forming judgments. This argument, though it had a few precursors in the literary tradition, runs counter to the more conservative approaches to collecting in the Tang, which draw either on literary precedent or on the necessity of defending the "true way of poetry" against vulgar popular taste (both arguments usually led back to Confucius and the *Odes*). Wei Zhuang claims the right to compile by virtue of his hard work and understanding of true "refinement." Wei Hu, in contrast, makes light of his own talents and yet argues for the right of the well-read individual to make his own distinctions. The defensive tone of his remark, "Then why should I take blame from the stupid and crude or get ridiculed by mere bookhoarders?" hints at some anxiety on his part, but he has made his anthology nonetheless.

And what kind of poetry does he find worthy of his collection? Wei Hu calls it "secretly marvelous," a phrase that comes from a family of esoteric terms for excellence in poetry that developed in ninth-century critical writing, and alludes also to the "mysterious" of Wei Zhuang's *Youxuan ji*. More revealing is Wei Hu's description of the *uses* of the "poems and songs": "some [are for] unscrolling while sitting idly by the window; others for chanting while strolling by a moonlit gazebo." Pleasure is certainly the point of these poems. If this collection were the only work of poetry extant from after 850, its one-note (or perhaps one-chord) version of Tang poetic subjects would radically alter our picture of Tang poetry. The selection of poets is decidedly lopsided: late Tang poets dominate the anthology. Half of the collection is dedicated to the work of only 20 poets (12 percent of the collection's total of 178). Wei Hu's high estimation of ninth-century poets is obvious from the list of poets for whom he collects the greatest number of poems: Wei Zhuang (63 poems), Wen Tingyun (61), Yuan Zhen (57), Li Shangyin (40), and Du Mu

(28).⁶⁹ Wei Hu was also fond of poets with Daoist tendencies, men such as Cao Tang 曹唐 (ca. 797–ca. 876), Xu Hun 許渾 (ca. 788?–ca. 854?), Luo Yin 羅隱 (833–910), and Gu Kuang 顧況 (ca. 727?–820). As we find confirmed in the *Huajian ji* song lyrics, Wei Hu's decided preference for the work of Wei Zhuang and Wen Tingyun seems to have been a Shu taste, although we cannot prove which collection first advocated the work of the two Tang poets.

What is most remarkable about the collection as a whole is the sameness it creates out of the work of extremely different poets. From the "great floods" of Tang poetry, Wei Hu has almost exclusively chosen poetry on romantic topics, many of them either *yongwu* 詠物 pieces on women, seasons, or flowers, or light occasional pieces on parting or separation, with a sprinkling of *huaigu* 懷古 (meditations on the past) throughout. Despite his token acknowledgment of the "Li-Du" pairing in his preface, Wei Hu in fact compiled a collection of a thousand Tang poems with no Du Fu poems in it.⁷⁰ There are also only two poems each by High Tang poets Wang Wei, Meng Haoran 孟浩然 (689–740), and Gao Shi, but there are 50 poems by one "anonymous" poet—supposed by some to be Wei Hu himself.⁷¹ For some poets, Wei Hu preserves poetry others did not, the most important example being that of Yuan Zhen, whose "sensuously beautiful poems" (*yanshi* 艷詩) are today

---

69. Among the remaining fifteen poets of Wei Hu's "top twenty," only Li Bai, Wang Jian, and Gu Kuang were active primarily in the eighth century.

70. This and other niggling inconsistencies seem to have annoyed the editors of the *Siku quanshu*, who point out several misattributions, line differences, and title discrepancies in the *zongmu tiyao* entry on the collection. However, they do note the presence of poems extant only in Wei Hu's collection, and they state that the work is therefore worth consulting for reference. As for the character of the work, they conclude that "Wei was born at the moment of literature's exhaustion in the Five Dynasties. Therefore, in his selection criteria, he took the late Tang lush and beautiful style and the expansive, insubstantial style as preeminent, and he preserved the practices of the vulgar and shallow." The passage is included in *HJJZS*, 403–4.

71. Li Tiaoyuan 李調元, the Qing compiler of the *Quan Wudai shi*, went so far as to include many of the anonymous pieces under Wei Hu's name in the Shu section of his compilation. *Quan Wudai shi*, 1190–98.

extant only in this collection.[72] For other poets, such as the prolific Du Mu and Bai Juyi, Wei's selections create a narrow image of the poets' actual literary interests and abilities. Like Wei Zhuang, Wei Hu also gives us two *juan* of poems (81 total poems) by monks and women; but Wei Hu simply takes 31 of Wei Zhuang's selections and adds 50 more poems to them.[73] More importantly, Wei Hu's anthology also contains many pieces that are now the only extant works for a number of late Tang poets—men of whom we know nothing else. Some of these men, such as Zhang Bin 張蠙 and the song lyric poet Zhang Bi (whose song lyrics are in the *Huajian ji*) can be traced to Shu, but for most of the poets represented by one or two pieces we have no clues to era or region.

Another remarkable characteristic of Wei Hu's anthology is the prominence of song-forms but the concomitant exclusion of *quzi ci* from the collection. This formal feature of the *Caidiao ji* strongly suggests that by the mid-tenth century in Shu, *quzi ci* were regarded as a verse form distinct from the various forms of *shi*. Wei Hu signals his interest in song forms in his title—*Collection of the Tunes (diao* 調*) of the Talents*—and this interest is substantiated in the anthology itself. We find many poems to *yuefu* titles, as well as dozens of poems with song words in their titles, such as *ge* 歌 (songs), *geci* 歌詞 (words for singing), *qu* 曲 (tunes), *yao* 謠 (ditty), and even *ci* 詞 (lyrics). For example, out of 63 poems of Wen Tingyun collected by Wei Hu, 34 contain one such song word in their titles. Many other poems concern singing or singing girls, and literally hundreds of poems describe scenes of musical entertainment. However, with the exception of some "Willow Branch" songs—the "Liu zhi" and "Yangliu zhi" seven-character, isometric quatrain form that, as

---

72. See Hanabusa and Maegawa, *Gen Shin kenkyū*, 194–202, for a discussion of the reasons behind the partition of Yuan's poetry and the meaning of *yanshi*, and Shields, "Defining Experience," for a discussion of the place of these poems in Yuan Zhen's larger corpus.

73. The overlap is perhaps more striking when seen the other way: of the 43 poems by monks and women collected by Wei Zhuang, 31 were incorporated into Wei Hu's work. Fu discusses this overlap and suggests that Wei Hu was simply copying Wei Zhuang's selections (*Tang ren xuan Tang shi*, 688–89).

noted in Chapter 1, are metrically identical to regulated quatrains—Wei Hu does not collect any work written to the tune titles found in the *Huajian ji*, nor does he include any poems in heterometric verse. We cannot know how many of the poems with titles indicating singing were actually sung, nor can we rule out the possibility that some of the poems without such titles were sung, particularly the regulated quatrains. However, Wei Hu's exclusion of lyrics written to tunes—other than the two that used the seven-character regulated quatrain form—as well as the absence of any heterometric verse in the collection, demonstrates that he is making a distinction between *quzi ci* and other kinds of sung poetry.

The influence of the *Youxuan ji* as an anthology on the *Caidiao ji* selections can be seen in Wei Hu's inclusion of many *Youxuan ji* poems; Wei Zhuang's personal influence is obvious from the fact that he has the greatest number of poems of any poet in the anthology. Despite the formal difference between the *Caidiao ji* pieces and those of the *Huajian ji*, the similarities between the language of the prefaces to the two Shu anthologies are striking, particularly their shared conception of the function of verse and song. Wei Hu claims that his selections are suitable for "unscrolling while sitting by a window" and "chanting while strolling by a moonlit gazebo"; Ouyang Jiong offers his song lyrics as pleasure for courtiers who wander in the gardens in feathered carriages and to singing girls in their lotus boats. The thematic overlap of the two is also considerable: both anthologies collect primarily romantic verse. From the perspective of period and regional taste, Wei Hu's collection of Tang poetry and the *Huajian ji* represent two sides of the same literary coin. However, Ouyang Jiong, in his preface to the *Huajian ji*, remakes Wei Hu's defense of personal taste into the defense of an elite collective taste, the literary and social praxis of an elite group of connoisseurs. In its defense of "the best of the age," the *Huajian ji* recalls similar Tang anthologies, but the grounds on which Ouyang defends "the best" are unlike any from the Tang anthologies we have today.

The Defense of Shu Court Taste: The Huajian ji

In Chapter 2, I traced the poets and makers of the *Huajian ji* to their social and political contexts, arguing that the collection reveals its strong regional interests in the preface and in the ordering and titling of its poets. But these local allegiances are somewhat overshadowed by Ouyang Jiong's strenuous efforts to link the anthology to the Tang and, more importantly, to the Southern Dynasties. Scholars who have studied the preface suggest that Ouyang's attempts to filiate the collection to the poetic tradition were part of his legitimizing efforts for *quzi ci* as a new literary genre. Although I agree that the *Huajian ji* preface became an important defense of *ci* in the history of the genre, I would argue that Ouyang Jiong was less concerned about advocating *quzi ci* as a literary form and much more interested in portraying his court as a refined literary arena and in defending the lyrics themselves as evidence of Shu aesthetic refinement.

In its form and its depiction of the anthology contents, the *Huajian ji* preface assembles a distinctive set of literary interests. First, the form of the preface is parallel prose, which, though unusual in comparison with the extant prefaces of the eighth century, was the preferred form for a number of late ninth- and early tenth-century prefaces. By writing in parallel prose, Ouyang Jiong clearly aligned himself with the element of the high literary tradition that found the allusive difficulty of parallel prose to be a strength, not a weakness, of elite writing. Although some mid-Tang writers had rejected *pianwen* for plainer prose forms, it was a taste that enjoyed late Tang popularity in the hands of writers such as Wen Tingyun, famous for his *pianwen*, and others.[74] Second, Ouyang Jiong the prefacer was not the compiler—though he probably helped to select

---

74. Wei Zhuang's preface, for example, is made up of many parallel prose passages. Other examples of ninth-century parallel prose prefaces include Sikong Tu's preface to the collection *Zhuoying ji* and Han Wo's preface to his *Xianglian ji*. The use of parallel prose is important, not as an element of prefaces to literary collections, but rather as one way of expressing a set of aesthetic values that included elegant, allusive language.

lyrics, as we discover when he explains the compilation process—and his own song lyrics are included in the collection. Aside from the references to the Southern Dynasties that Ouyang makes in the preface, the inclusion of the prefacer's own song lyrics points to the model of Xu Ling's *Yutai xinyong*; echoes of the Southern Dynasties' anthology resonate throughout the piece (which may also link the *Huajian ji* to the Tang "continuation" of the *Yutai xinyong*, the *Yutai houji*). In commenting on a collection in which his own work was included, Ouyang could not be excessive or direct in his praise of the Shu song lyrics themselves. Instead, as we see below, he promotes the collection as a whole by tracing the lineage of song lyrics, identifying the kinds of people who wrote the works, and offering the collection as pleasurable entertainment for his fellow courtiers and his ruler. His arguments follow the outlines of earlier poetry anthology prefaces, but his substance is quite different.[75]

In engraving jade and carving rosegem, one imitates the transforming craft [of nature] and exceeds it in artifice; in clipping flowers and cutting leaves [from paper], one seizes the allure of spring in order to contend with it in freshness. Thus, when singing the "[White] Cloud Ballad," the Spirit-Mother's lyrics were fresh; when she poured out the roseate liquor, King Mu's heart was intoxicated.[76] He whose name was known for singing "White Snow" note upon note naturally blended with the song of the simurgh;[77] those whose voices' echoes stilled the passing clouds, word after

---

75. Interesting formal and argumentative parallels to the *Huajian ji* preface can be seen in the preface and postface for a brief Southern Tang anthology that is no longer extant, the *Yu zhi chunxue shiji* 御製春雪詩集 (Collection of "spring snow" poetry made on imperial command). Xu Xuan 徐鉉 (916–92), an important tenth-century writer, composed both documents for presentation to the Southern Tang emperor and, according to his own preface, has works included in the 21-poem collection. The poets of the collection were officials of the Southern Tang court, and their titles are given in the preface. Xu Xuan's language is just as florid as Ouyang's, though his collection is much smaller. *QTW* 881.11a–14a.

76. The Spirit-Mother is Xiwang mu 西王母, who sang the "White Cloud Song" to King Mu of Zhou 周穆王 during his legendary trip to the queen's kingdom, as recorded in the *Mu tianzi zhuan*, an anonymous text recovered in the third century, traditionally believed to date from the fourth century B.C.E.

77. In the text "Song Yu Responds to the King of Chu," collected in the *Wen xuan*, the courtier Song Yu tells the king that there were few singers who could

word harmonized with the pitches of the phoenix.[78] Lines to "The Willow" and "The Great Dike" were passed down by the Music Bureau;[79] verses to "Lotuses" and "The Winding Sandbar" were crafted by grandees themselves.[80] There were none who did not vie in the great courts with their "three thousand tortoise-shell hairpins";[81] they competed in wealth before the wine jars, with their "dozens of coral trees."[82]

And so there were lords of the gorgeous feasts, fair ladies behind embroidered silk screens, exchanging leaf after leaf of flowered paper, drawing out works from beautiful brocade sleeves. When the ladies lifted their lissome fingers of jade and kept time with fragrant sandalwood [clappers], there was no lack of fresh and wondrous words to enhance the charming

---

"blend with" or "match" (*he* 和) the song "Yang Spring and White Snow" 陽春白雪. A famous Tang anecdote about the poets Gao Shi, Wang Changling, and Wang Zhihuan alludes to these two songs as examples of elite songs that commoners, particularly common singing girls, would not know. See Wagner, *Lotus Boat*, 106–7, for a discussion of this story.

78. The *Liezi* tells the story of the musician Qin Qing, who was able to "still the passing clouds" with the power of his music. The "pitches of the phoenix" refer to the pitches ascertained by the musician Ling Lun, who was said to have lived during the time of the Yellow Emperor.

79. "The Willow" 楊柳 and "The Great Dike" 大堤 are two tune titles from the Southern Dynasties recorded in Guo Maoqian's *Yuefu shiji*. According to Guo, both tunes emerged in the late Southern Dynasties period, long past the end of the historical Han Music Bureau. *Yuefu shiji* 48.705.

80. There is no agreement among commentators as to the referents for these two songs; neither is found in the *Yuefu shiji*, and modern commentators strain to find lines in various poems that may have given Ouyang the titles. Fusek, *Among the Flowers*, 34, n10, suggests that general topics rather than tune titles are meant here. However, the strong parallelism of this line and the one preceding inclines me to believe that Ouyang is referring to actual tune titles that were known to him but lost to us.

81. The hairpins come from the *Shi ji* (78.2395) story of Lord Pingyuan of Zhao (third century B.C.E.), who sent his envoy to Lord Chunshen of Chu. The envoy wished to display his elegance and so wore pins made of tortoiseshell and a decorated sword. However, when he arrived in Chu, he was embarrassed to find that the courtiers all wore shoes of pearls and tortoiseshell hairpins.

82. The trees come from a story in the *Jin shu* (33.1007) and the *Shishuo xinyu* (30.8) about rivalry in ostentatious display. Emperor Wu of the Jin and his uncle, Wang Kai, vied for extravagance with Shi Chong. The emperor presented Wang Kai with a coral tree; upon seeing it, Shi Chong shattered it and then ordered his retainers to bring out all of his own coral trees, all of which surpassed Wang Kai's shattered tree in size and beauty.

grace of their demeanors. But the "palace style" of the Southern Dynasties was fanned by the style of the songstresses of the northern quarter.[83] How could this have been merely a case of words without elegance [not going far]? [It was also] what is called "blossoming without bearing fruit."[84]

Since the Tang began, in all the land, on the fragrant paths in the spring wind of every house, one could find a "Beauty of Yue," and every red tower beneath the moon held a "Chang E."[85] In the era of the Brilliant Emperor, there was Li Taibai's "Qingping Tune Composed to Imperial Order" in four pieces;[86] in the recent age, Wen Feiqing [Tingyun] moreover has his *Gilded Gauze Collection*.[87] Our composers since then are not shamed by their predecessors.

Now the Vice Minister for the Court of the Imperial Regalia, of the cognomen Hongji [Zhao Chongzuo], by picking up kingfisher feathers from the banks, has found the finest quills and, from the woven floss of the springs' depths, has singled out the [dragon-weavers'] best work. He has gathered often with many guests who have proffered excellent arguments and has thus collected the lyrics [*quzi ci*] of recent poets, 500 works, and has divided them into ten chapters. Since I, Jiong, am roughly conversant with the "knowledge of the tone," he requested me to declare a title and further to provide a preface.[88]

Long ago, among the people of Ying, there were those who could sing "Yang Spring" who were called the greatest singers. Thus I have declared this [collection] to be *Huajian ji*. I hope that it will make the talented and wise of the Western Gardens use it to increase their pleasure on outings in their feathered-awnings carriages, and [I hope that it will make] the

---

83. A reference to the *Beili zhi*; see Rotours, *Courtisanes chinoises*.
84. Both "words without elegance" (*Zuo zhuan*, 1106) and "blossoming without bearing fruit" (*Lun yu* 9.22) are attributed to Confucius.
85. The "Beauty of Yue" is Xi Shi 西施. Chang E 嫦娥 is the mythical woman who stole the elixir of immortality from her husband and fled to the moon.
86. QTS 164.1703. See Bryant, "On the Authenticity of the *Tz'u* Attributed to Li Po," 105–36.
87. The *Gilded Gauze Collection* (*Jinquan ji*) was first cited as a collection of Wen Tingyun's poetry in this preface. It is also found in XTS 60.1607. Since the collection is no longer extant, it is not clear whether it contained both song lyrics and poems or song lyrics alone. For discussions of the evidence, see Rouzer, *Writing Another's Dream*, 60–61; and Wu, *Tang Song ci tonglun*, 178.
88. In this line, the phrase *zhiyin* 知音 (knowledge of the tone) means an understanding of music.

charmers of the southlands cease singing the lays of the lotus boat.[89] Prefaced in the third year of the Guangzheng era of Great Shu, summer, fourth month, by Ouyang Jiong.[90]

Before I comment on Ouyang's text, I would like to summarize the central points made by other scholars about the preface. Three elements of the preface have attracted the most critical attention: Ouyang's evocation of the elegant courts of the Southern Dynasties, his echoing of Xu Ling's claim that the point of the collection is to give pleasure, and the singling out of Wen Tingyun as the immediate Tang forerunner to the works of the Shu poets.[91] I follow these arguments, but I think that Ouyang Jiong's social and political claims are as important—to him, at least—as his literary arguments.

Rather than defending a literary genre, Ouyang Jiong's preface defends the *social practice* of writing songs at court, characterizing it as an activity that epitomizes an elegant, artistic, and refined society. In defending song-writing as an elite skill, Ouyang Jiong chooses to create a history of the genre and its practitioners. But if we look closely at the examples he uses to build his argument, we find that he is less concerned with the formal boundaries of the song lyric genre (the concern of most contemporary scholars) and much more intent on presenting the song lyric as the expression of a certain kind of person in a certain place. Furthermore, if we compare the arguments Ouyang uses with the prefaces of earlier Tang antholo-

---

89. The scene of these two lines references the "Western Garden" of the Western Jin and thus alludes to courtiers and poets such as Cao Pi 曹丕 and Wang Can 王粲.
90. *HJJZS*, 1.
91. A number of scholars have examined this preface closely and have offered many useful conclusions about its claims. Wu Xionghe is most interested in Ouyang's evocation of the Qi-Liang "palace style" as model for the song lyric, and he argues that the ultimate purpose of the collection is to be a songbook. Wu, *Tang Song ci tonglun*, 283. Yang Haiming, whose approach focuses on the cultural and economic implications of the collection, considers Ouyang's evocation of the aristocratic nature of the Southern Dynasties' court to be the real goal. I follow Yang in arguing that the social status of the Southern poets is important to Ouyang, though my grounds for doing so are somewhat different. Yang, *Tang Wudai ci shi*, 102. And Pauline Yu has pointed out the numerous strategies Ouyang adopts in his defense of the song lyric as a literati genre. Yu, "Song Lyrics and the Canon," 73–75.

gies, it becomes even more apparent that Ouyang esteems the context of the song lyrics' composition and the uses of song more than the quality or nature of individual songs. Given the dubious moral status of the lyrics, Ouyang assiduously avoids the model, important to other anthologists, of Confucius and the *Odes*. Where some anthologists would argue that the poetry they collected revealed the moral character of poet and state, Ouyang Jiong attempts to locate value in the poets themselves—their sophistication and talent, manifested in their work, he suggests, mirrors their cultured society.

In the opening statements of the preface, we find a surprising claim: Ouyang Jiong states that artifice is superior to nature. The two metaphors of craft he uses, carving gems and clipping flowers, are carefully chosen to show the ways in which artists take raw materials and shape them into things of beauty. When practiced by masters, this "transforming craft" enables artists to "contend (*zheng* 爭) with spring." Ouyang's defense of artifice over nature had relatively few precedents in the Chinese literary tradition. Even in the preface to the *Yutai xinyong*, Xu Ling takes pains to distinguish his collection as a separate stream, like the waters of the Jing and Wei rivers—not to put his palace poems forward as competition to other kinds of literature.[92] And yet we saw in the preface to the *Caidiao ji* that Wei Hu made a similar claim about the poems he collected: "Their rhymes are great, contending (*zheng* 爭) with the cassia spirit in brilliance; their words are lovely, vying (*dou* 鬥) with spring's beauty in fairness." In both prefaces, the authors assert the power of literature to compete with and even exceed the beauty of the natural world. But, as we see below, this is only Ouyang's first move in his bold creation of a "history" for his art. Singing, in Ouyang's definition, is one manifestation of the practice of artifice; as the examples of Xiwang mu and King Mu, Song Yu, and Qin Qing demonstrate, it is also one of the most ancient. These examples of performances before rulers seem deliberately chosen to please a desired audience of the *Huajian ji* songs—the Shu sovereign. In his summary of the evolution of song lyrics, Ouyang focuses on its

---

92. Mu, ed., *Yutai xinyong jianzhu*, 12. See also Knechtges, "Culling the Weeds," 233–34.

practitioners, men from "the best families." Here, Ouyang launches his effort to valorize song (specifically, romantic song) as social praxis. In the southern setting, the power of song was domesticated: songs make up one part of the elegant scene, an essential element of the interplay between court literati and court ladies. However, over the course of the era, as Ouyang declares, domestication became vulgarization, and "the 'palace style' of the Southern Dynasties fanned the style of the songstresses of the northern ward." In this line, Ouyang reveals his elitist allegiances: the quality of the song lyrics is degraded by the lower social status and sex of the writers. But even as he denigrates the lesser practitioners of song, he establishes a clear line of development that begins with the aristocrats of the Southern Dynasties, goes through the "songstresses" of Chang-an, and continues (it is implied) with its original elite flavor refreshed in Shu.

The closing lines of this discussion reveal another, even bolder step in Ouyang's defense of artifice. Ouyang uses Confucian terms to underline the contrast between the elegant songs of male court poets and the ditties of paid songstresses: "this was not just 'words without elegance' [not going far], [but it was also] what is called 'blossoming without bearing fruit.'" Ouyang's borrowing of Confucius's words from the *Zuo zhuan* is clever and deceptive. In context, Confucius was discussing the importance of communicating one's "intent," or "aim," *zhi* 志, and the need for *wen* 文, "patterning," or what I have translated here as "elegance," in such communication. Without some *wen*, Confucius says, one's words "do not go far," or are ineffective. Ouyang's use of the second phrase, "blossoming without bearing fruit," subtly alters its meaning. In a Confucian context, the phrase means that *wen*, patterning or ornamentation, for its own sake, is pointless and wrong. However, just as he argued that artifice could surpass nature in beauty, Ouyang seems to subversively claim the virtue of ornamentation—beauty for its own sake—for the practice of songwriting.

For Ouyang, the Tang represents a recovery from the vulgarity of the late Southern Dynasties, because it possessed abundant wealth and beauty (necessary ingredients for song composition) as well as talented court poets. He points to two Tang examples to support his case: the High Tang poet Li Bai, ornament of Tang Xuanzong's luxurious court entertainments, and the late Tang playboy-literatus Wen Tingyun. But after noting these important Tang predecessors, Ouyang brings the history of song lyrics up to date with the rather immodest statement (given that his lyrics are also included in the anthology), "Our more recent composers are not shamed by their predecessors." Having suggested that the Shu poets engaged in the aristocratic pastimes of the Tang and southern courts, Ouyang goes on to support that by describing the making of the anthology, discussed in Chapter 2, as a collaborative effort of Shu elites. He closes by explaining the anthology's title and purpose, comparing the talented composers of song lyrics to the singers of ancient Chu, and offering up the collection to those who wander in the Western Gardens, an allusion that recasts the Shu court as the Jian'an entourage of talents. Ouyang then ends with what seems like a casual line, "and the lovely ones of the southern countries can stop singing the refrains of the lotus boat," but he is in fact echoing the words of Xu Ling, in the preface to the *Yutai xingyong*. In his preface, Xu Ling praises the palace women who populate his collection's "palace-style" poems as women of learning, and proposes that the anthology could be enjoyed by them: "[The palace lady] having nothing else to cheer her spirits during idle moments, / Solely devotes her mind to new verse, which can / Serve as a substitute for the day lily and the herb of oblivion [used as anodynes], / And relieve somewhat the malady of melancholy."[93] Ouyang Jiong aims higher than Xu Ling: he seeks to circulate his songs among the courtiers of Shu. However, by offering the elegant *Huajian ji* songs to the lotus-picking women as a substitute for the presumably vulgar "songs of the southland," he both alludes to the *Yutai xinyong* and, once again, promotes the anthology's song lyrics as elite literature. The apparently modest closure to the preface is the finishing touch to a well-constructed, ambitious argument for the social standing and literary talent of the Shu court poets.

Ouyang Jiong's skillful and elaborate defense conceals the degree to which the song lyrics of the *Huajian ji* exceeded even the *Yutai*

---

93. Translation from Knechtges, "Culling the Weeds," 233.

xinyong in "allure," *yan*, a term that in both anthologies points to the romantic, sometimes erotic, content of its works. This allure was the collection's flaw. Ouyang Jiong attempted to seize the high ground in his preface, ignoring the problem of moral value in his praise of beauty, but he opened himself up to an inevitable twofold critique. For some readers, the elegance of the *Huajian ji* song lyrics was nothing but artifice, *qiao*, without depth of feeling; for other readers, the lyrics' very content was offensive. Once the insular, hedonistic world of the Shu court disappeared, the argument that Ouyang had developed so assiduously—the argument for composing, discussing, and collecting *quzi ci* as a social activity fit for literati poets—became pointless at best. Although the place of song lyrics in literati culture was no less problematic in the Northern Song, after the *Huajian ji*, the defense of what came to be called *ci* took very different paths, just as *ci* branched into different styles.[94] Instead of describing lyrics as an activity pursued by a certain person in a certain place, poets like Li Qingzhao defended *ci* as the literary vehicle for particular kinds of feeling, giving lyrics a "separate sphere" of literary expression. In the Northern Song we see the maturation of the genre of *ci* in the emergence of both descriptive and prescriptive discourses on song lyrics. Ouyang Jiong's discussion of the *quzi ci* of Tang and Shu is certainly one of the earliest descriptive discourses on song lyrics, but the practice he describes changed greatly in the Song.

Ouyang Jiong's preface stands as the first attempt to establish a place for the literati *practice* of composing song lyrics. What we discover when we read the contents of the anthology is that the Shu poets, following their chosen Tang predecessors, also articulated a coherent vision of *quzi ci* as a formal entity—lyrics written to songs, primarily but not exclusively composed in heterometric verse— with clear topical boundaries and conventions. This coherent presentation of song lyrics is why the *Huajian ji* has long been considered a critical collection for the genre of *ci* as it was practiced by literati poets—a watershed moment. What I hope I have dem-

---

94. For a study of the status of *ci* in a later period, see Egan, "The Problem of the Repute of *Tz'u* during the Northern Sung."

onstrated in these three chapters is how the poets of Shu came to compose song lyrics and why they might have wanted to participate in this novel kind of literary collection. The Shu poets of the *Huajian ji* had a complex relationship with the Tang literary tradition that had preceded them; in the composition, preface, and song lyrics of the *Huajian ji*, we see these tenth-century poets both filiating themselves to and distancing themselves from elements of that tradition as they saw fit. In some sense, all poets after the Tang had to negotiate their places in an increasingly crowded and burdensome tradition; but in the case of Shu, the poets of *quzi ci* claimed a cultural independence and a literary freedom that allowed them to craft song lyrics to their own tastes. In the chapters that follow, we will see what they made of the practice they inherited from the Tang.

PART II

Poetic Practice

FOUR

From Imitation to Innovation

The Poetic Craft of the *Huajian ji*

Ouyang Jiong reveals his aesthetic priorities in the opening lines of his preface to the *Huajian ji*:

> In engraving jade and carving rosegem, one imitates the transforming craft [of nature] and exceeds it in artifice; in clipping flowers and cutting leaves [from paper], one seizes the allure of spring in order to contend with it in freshness.[1]

In these lines, Ouyang confesses his belief in the primacy of artifice, *qiao* 巧, and craft, *gong* 工, in artistic endeavor. Like others in the literary tradition before him, Ouyang grounds art in the imitation of nature, and yet he goes further to suggest that the works of men, through skillful imitation, could "contend" with the rarity and freshness of the natural. As we saw in Chapter 3, Ouyang significantly appropriates a Confucian defense of *wen*, "patterning," in his

---

1. *HJJZS*, 1.

arguments for the *Huajian ji*'s romantic song lyrics, but most of his energy is spent relocating the grounds of the argument from aesthetics to social praxis. In his vision of elite literary pursuits, artifice is the hallmark of writing by talented courtiers. These opening lines tell us that craft, particularly the skill of "imitation," *ni* 擬, is essential for successful artifice; if one is to contend with the beauty of nature, one must possess the skills of observation to study and reproduce it. This activity is not simply making axe handles with an axe; rather, the result should be a better, more beautiful version of "the allure of spring" itself.² Ouyang Jiong goes on to give us examples of famous artists of myth who excelled at their skills, but he does not return to the question of how an artist perfects this imitative craft. Instead, the imitative poetics of the *Huajian ji* song lyrics substantiate his argument. What we find in the lyrics of the *Huajian ji* is not a concern for adequate mimesis, but a narrow and shared range of literary techniques designed to create convincing portraits of romantic melancholy.

The poets of the *Huajian ji* imitate styles and borrow language from one another in lyric after lyric of the anthology. Although the most important stylistic model for imitation in the collection is its earliest poet, Wen Tingyun, the later poets do not confine themselves to his corpus alone. On the contrary, they raid the riches of medieval romantic poetry, both folk and elite strains, for their compositions. In a twist on the traditional claim of "transmitting but not creating," Ouyang openly admits his lack of interest in originality, and the song lyrics support him. The lyrics of the *Huajian ji* are built on creaky conventions, decorated with the imitation of masters, and enlivened with the vivid language of popular song. The resulting style is homogeneous but it is also, perhaps unexpectedly, unique. The poets of the anthology reveal themselves to be skilled craftsmen, not only in their ability to imitate and play with one another's lines but also in their conceptualization of the song lyric as a literary form. As we saw in Chapter 1, with the exception

---

2. "Axe handles" refers to a line of *Odes* 158, "In making an axe, in making an axe, / the model is not far away." Ouyang's defense of the "transforming craft," however, suggests that the thing made can exceed its model.

of the lyrics of Wen Tingyun, the extant song lyrics of Tang poets are brief and generally unremarkable as poems. The impression one gets from reading the *quzi ci* of Tang poets outside the *Huajian ji* is that this was indeed a casual and inconsequential practice, suitable for light topics and witty language and not the focus of serious poetic effort. The song lyrics of the *Huajian ji*, although often as light in tone, reveal a concern for detailed images, coherent mood, innovative rhetorical structures, the interplay of poetic and vernacular language, and even rhyme and tonal balancing that was new to *quzi ci*. As we will see, an essential element of the *Huajian ji* poets' presentation of song lyrics as an elite practice was their ability to appropriate techniques from the *shi* tradition for their song lyrics. Ouyang Jiong advertised himself and his fellow *quzi ci* writers as "poets" (*shike* 詩客), and the lyrics reveal the truth of his claim.

Our view of the *Huajian ji* song lyrics should not merely assume the vantage point of their Song successors but should also frame them against the backdrop of the Tang songs and poems that preceded them—in that light, the *Huajian ji* regains its "freshness" and originality. Apparently speaking on behalf of the Shu elites who compiled the anthology, Ouyang Jiong presented its *quzi ci* as a literati practice with a respectable history, which was simply not true. The attempt to disguise the newness of the *Huajian ji* was part of the larger claim to literati status for the poets themselves and for the composition of *quzi ci* as a social practice. In this and the following chapters, I will challenge Ouyang Jiong's claim of continuity in order to explore the many poetic accomplishments of the *Huajian ji* song lyrics. I do not suggest that the poets selected for inclusion in the *Huajian ji* were the only ninth- or tenth-century literati poets composing song lyrics in this fashion, despite the lack of evidence of other late Tang poets' song lyrics. But the effort made by Shu poets to compose in the manner of select Tang models and then to create an anthology of those song lyrics shows that they had a particular stake in defining the genre. For them, the collection captured the particular talents and refined tastes of the Shu court.

As I demonstrated in Chapter 1, the *Huajian ji* song lyrics are different from extant Tang lyrics in some significant ways. In the *quzi ci* of the *Huajian ji*, we can perceive a coherent set of formal and topical preferences, and we can begin to discuss the poetics of *quzi ci* as a genre. In what follows, I examine sets of lyrics to different tune titles in order to delineate the most prominent achievements of the anthology. Two assumptions guide my analyses throughout: first, the formal features of *quzi ci* gave rise to some subtle but critical shifts in the representation of "romance" in the Chinese literary tradition. In particular, the use of heterometric verse and the prevalence of two-stanza songforms changed the way poets created romantic vignettes. For example, the heterometric lines of *quzi ci* gave rise to more fragmented ways of creating a visual or modal scene; stanza shifts allowed poets to move about in time or space or even to change speakers from one stanza to the next. Although the use of a dense, highly paratactic style can already be seen in the *shi* poetry of certain late Tang poets, such as Li Shangyin and Wen Tingyun (the latter of course being the most important poet of the *Huajian ji*), as we will see, the varied lengths of *quzi ci* lines encouraged this stylistic preference across the form itself, not merely in the works of specific poets. The second assumption that guides my reading is that these *quzi ci* were intended to be sung as well as read. The formal changes from *shi* to *quzi ci* are quite visible in the texts themselves, but the implications of performing particular lyrics must sometimes be explored. When we do so, however, specific tendencies of the emergent genre—such as the use of anonymous subjects or the interest in "speaking" or "telling out" one's feelings—take on greater meaning. As I hope to demonstrate, the literary rewards of exploring the performance of the *Huajian ji* lyrics are considerable: by reimagining the interplay of form and theme as it might have been voiced by a singer and heard by an audience, we can better understand the appeal of this new genre to Chinese poets, and the influence of the *Huajian ji* on the later *ci* genre.

Formal and Stylistic Innovation in the Huajian ji

Although the content of the song lyrics of the *Huajian ji* owes much to the Tang culture of romance, the anthology must be credited with important formal and stylistic innovations in the history of Chinese poetry. The *Huajian ji* lyrics use heterometric verse as the preferred metrical form for song lyrics and use two-stanza forms more often than single-stanza forms. Whether we look at numbers of lyrics in heterometric verse or tune titles that use heterometric verse, the *Huajian ji* preference is clear: 392 of the 500 lyrics (78 percent) in the collection are in heterometric verse, and 66 of the 77 tune titles (88 percent) have only heterometric lyrics.[3] This preference for heterometric verse appears remarkable when we recall the number of heterometric lyrics composed by Tang literati that were not collected in the *Huajian ji*: only 57 lyrics contain lines of uneven length. As I noted in Chapter 1, most scholars agree that this shift from isometric to heterometric verse represents, at the very least, a change in literati composition practice and musical ability, as poets became more skilled and more fond of composing lyrics that closely matched the rhythmic structures of the tunes. I also suggested that the shift may represent a change in transcription practice or perhaps simply a new interest in recording song lyrics in their original forms, which may have been more commonly heterometric than the textual record would indicate.

The *Huajian ji* preference for two-stanza short songforms known as *xiaoling*, some of which are undocumented until the *Huajian ji*, was also new among literati song lyrics.[4] The evidence for this innovation is even stronger: among tune titles used by Tang literati poets outside those titles found in the *Huajian ji*, only 8 of the 68 tune titles (11 percent) have two-stanza lyrics, accounting for a mere 11 lyrics out of 363 total (3 percent).[5] But in the *Huajian ji*, 52 of the 77 tune titles (68 percent) have *only* two-stanza forms, and another 7 tune titles have both one- and two-stanza forms. The impression of the *Huajian ji* preference for two-stanza songs only

---

3. Three of the 77 tune titles have both heterometric and isometric forms in the anthology.

4. Twenty-four tune titles occur first in the *Huajian ji*, and are not found in the *Jiaofang ji*, the Dunhuang corpus, or in extant lyrics by Tang literati poets. Of the 24, 21 occur in the two-stanza form in the *Huajian ji*.

5. The eight tune titles for which we have two-stanza songs outside the *HJJ* are: "Zhexian yuan," "Yi Qin e," "Chang xiang si," "Ba liu zi," "Pusa man," "Jiu quanzi," "Wushan yiduan xia," and "Huanxi sha." This number excludes the tune titles of lyrics attributed to Li Bai, Lü Yan, and Yi Jing (unless, as in the case of "Pusa man," there are other extant Tang lyrics to the tune title).

increases if we look at numbers of lyrics: there, the count is 373 of 500 lyrics (75 percent) in the two-stanza form. The *Huajian ji* preference for two-stanza songs is echoed by the same preference among the popular songs discovered at Dunhuang. Among the Dunhuang songs, both those of the *Yunyao ji* and the other miscellaneous short songs, 34 of 53 tune titles (65 percent) are preserved as two-stanza forms.[6] The similar proportions of two-stanza forms in the *Huajian ji* and the Dunhuang corpus cannot be explained solely by the overlap in tune titles, since only 16 of the *Huajian ji*'s 77 tune titles are also found in the Dunhuang songs. The preservation of two-stanza forms in the *Huajian ji* is thus a genuinely new feature of the anthology, though it probably also represents the widespread popularity of two-stanza forms in the tenth century.[7] During the Song, the two-stanza form became the dominant form for both short (*xiaoling* 小令) and long (*manci* 慢詞) songs.

As I noted in Chapter 1, the preservation of literati songs as individual poetic texts disguises the well-known performance practice of singing consecutive lyrics to a single tune, a practice that would have generated a multi-stanza performed song. There is unfortu-

---

6. Zhang (following Ren, *Dunhuang geci zongbian*), *QTWDC*, 856–955. I am excluding the Dunhuang songs for which tune titles have been lost, fragments of songs, and suites of songs written to a single tune title, the "Guiqulai" and the "Wugeng zhuan" series. However, I am not certain that the distinction between one- and two-stanza forms is particularly useful in analyzing the song practices inscribed in the Dunhuang texts. A change in lyrics to the same tune (*quzi*) in the Dunhuang manuscripts is marked by spaces between iterations of a song (sometimes preceded by *you* 又, "again," indicating a musical repeat, or *tong qian* 同前, "to the same [tune] as before," or, *you tong qian*) but stanza divisions are often not marked in two-stanza songs, nor does the rhyme always change between "repeats." See Rao, *Airs de Touen-houang*, esp. Pelliot 2838, P3836, P3333, P3821. Relying on one- versus two-stanza forms to date a tune title also seems risky, given the likely differences in transcription and preservation of songs in the popular and elite traditions. See, for example, the discussion of "Yu meiren," *QTWDC*, 856.

7. The popularity of two-stanza forms in the tenth century is also supported by texts from the Southern Tang. In Feng Yansi's *Yangchun ji* and the two Li rulers' *Nan Tang erzhu ci*, both of which postdate the *Huajian ji*. Of the 34 tune titles found in the two collections, 25 (74 percent) are given as two-stanza forms. Only 18 of these 34 titles are found in the *Huajian ji*.

nately no documentation, either at the elite or popular level, of the reasons for the shift from single-stanza to two-stanza forms among elite poets, a change that the *Huajian ji* clearly reveals. As in the case of the move toward heterometric verse, however, I would speculate that the poets' increased interest and skill in composing to music prompted the change. The two-stanza forms found in the *Huajian ji* are generally not doubled metrical units (*shuangdie* 雙疊)—that is, the second stanza does not repeat the first stanza's metrical form—which suggests that the structure of the music, itself in two different parts, was shaping the metrical structure of the lyrics.[8] It may have been the case that the more popular songs among these literati were composed of two segments of differing rhythmic and melodic structures, to which the poets were composing lyrics that would match closely.

In the history of the song lyric as a Chinese literary genre, the importance of these two formal innovations—the preference for heterometric verse and two-stanza metrical forms—can hardly be overstated. These formal changes engendered new rhetorical approaches to the romantic scenes of the *Huajian ji* lyrics and affected poets' construction of such scenes from the largest unit, the lyric as a whole, down to the smallest, the line. Although there are plenty of five- and seven-character lines among the heterometric verse patterns of the *Huajian ji* song lyrics, heterometric verse required poets to master the use of other lines and to deploy them sometimes in parallel, sometimes singly, sometimes in linked sets. The repeated, balanced line and predictable caesurae of pentametric and heptametric *shi* were interrupted by lines of two, three, and four characters. These shorter lines had, of course, survived into the Tang from ancient verse and medieval *yuefu* and had long been the syntactic components of five- and seven-character lines (which divide two/three and four/three, respectively, at the caesura), but in the

---

8. However, without musical notation for *shuangdie* lyrics, we cannot rule out the possibility that the two stanzas were not sung to the same melody—in other words, the metrical structures of lyrics, given the potential gaps between performance and transcription, are not sufficient evidence on which to base conclusions about musical settings.

heterometric lines of song lyrics, they were detached from preceding or succeeding syntactic units in new ways.[9]

Scholars have long studied the link between heterometric verse patterns and the syntactic fragmentation of song lyrics, and the resulting fragmentation of emotional expression and visual imagery, but these developments have generally been seen as Song innovations.[10] However, the move toward this kind of discursive fragmentation, or the practice of collage, which can be seen already in Tang *shi* poetry by the likes of Li He, Li Shangyin, and Wen Tingyun, appears fully developed in the song lyrics of the *Huajian ji*. In song lyrics with the greatest metrical variation and length, the Song *manci*, the discursive continuity of *shi* forms is replaced by discontinuities of narrative, scene, time, and voice. We find some of this kind of experimentation in the smaller framework of *xiaoling* in the *Huajian ji*. In the *xiaoling* form, continuity tends to be descriptive and modal: the imagery of the shorter and varying syntactic units coheres to create a single mood for the lyric. In the anthology as a whole, these coherent modal elements, in combination with the simple and unvarying romantic story that underlies the collection, provide intelligibility. At the same time, we should always keep in mind the importance that music must have played in holding together what seem to be fragmented images and emotions. Before one word was sung, instruments would have established a tempo and a mode in which the vignette would unfold and would likely have evoked a mood as well, one that could carry the audience through unexpected shifts in the lyrics.

---

9. Irregular verse forms can be found throughout Tang poetry, but they are overshadowed by the dominance of five- and seven-character isometric verse. Poets who were particularly skilled in music, such as Li Bai, are also known for their experiments with irregular forms. The Tang poetic subgenres in which we find more heterometric verse were particularly those marked as "old" or "folk," such as *yuefu* and other songforms.

10. One discussion of this substantive generic difference between *shi* and *ci taxis*, the arrangement of words and periods, is found in Owen, "Meaning the Words: The Genuine as a Value in the Tradition of the Song Lyric," in Yu, ed., *Voices*, 58–62.

The two-stanza form of *xiaoling* allowed the *Huajian ji* poets to exploit the *huantou*, the change from one stanza to the next.[11] Dramatic shifts within a single poetic form were not unknown in the *shi* tradition, of course. The shifts of point of view or subject prompted by stanzas were also an important part of the early medieval tradition of *yuefu*, particularly *yuefu* from the anonymous popular tradition or those written by literati poets in imitation of the popular tradition. Long *shi* forms of the Tang allowed poets to change voices or moods and to move across long stretches of space or time, often through rhyme changes. Tang linked verses (composed by two or more poets) and quatrain series (composed by a single poet) also exploited changes in scene or voice, particularly those quatrain series that foregrounded poets' wit and competition. In the short song lyric forms of the *Huajian ji*, however, shifts of scene and voice were compressed, sometimes even suppressed, and the stanza break became the critical space of transition. As we will see, the *Huajian ji* poets experimented with shifts in time, place, and voice across the stanza break to varying degrees in different tune titles. No single practice emerges as dominant among the lyrics; instead, poets chose from a range of options, according to the demands of the style in which they were composing.

These formal changes are matched by the *Huajian ji*'s stylistic innovations in the realm of romantic poetry.[12] The romantic lyrics of the *Huajian ji* have long roots in the medieval tradition of romantic poetry, reaching back to folk and literati *yuefu* of the period of division; as I argued in Chapter 1, however, the direct antecedents of the Shu song lyrics are ninth-century romantic poems and the culture that fostered them. In these ninth-century texts, we find poets imagining and documenting romantic experiences in many different ways. In the interactions between literati and women of

---

11. Strictly speaking, *huantou* refers to the stanza break between stanzas of different metrical structures, but not all scholars observe this distinction. See Shi, *Ci yu yinyue guanxi*, 193.

12. For a recent and useful introduction to the style of the collection, including some of the key terms used by traditional and modern readers in discussions of the collection, see the preface to Gu and Zhong, *Huajian pai ci zhuan*, 1–32.

the entertainment quarters, romantic poems were a form of currency: they were written by male literati to be given to particular courtesans and also performed in front of an audience of both men and women. The poems were shared and imitated, and their "stories" were often integrated into a poet's biography, whether or not they originated there. Much of the poems' value lay in their perceived individuality and particularity: they were read as communications between two (or more) real people involved in the elaborate game of romance. Titles of these poems often revealed the names, or sobriquets, of the female addressees, and many poets were more than willing to have their romantic poems widely circulated with their own names attached. A certain degree of notoriety, or *fengliu* reputation, was acceptable in the intense competition for patronage. In contrast, the "boudoir laments" and quatrains on beauties that litter the collections of many ninth-century poets rarely venture beyond the well-worn tropes of those topical categories, although they, too, played a part in the exchanges of the entertainment quarters. The material of such poems was thus highly conventional, and the poems themselves manifested a narrow set of acceptable emotions and actions.

Rather than representing an entirely new trend in literary culture, the content of the *Huajian ji* song lyrics can be traced to the literary tastes of the mid- and late Tang. But the song lyric, as the *Huajian* poets conceived it, was not simply a musicalized version of romantic poetry. In terms of their topical boundaries, the song lyrics of the late Tang and Shu resemble the more conventional Tang romantic poems on the topics of "boudoir laments" and "parting" in that they remain completely within the world of generic lovers and anonymous participants. In the *Huajian ji*, the historical romantic game of some ninth-century poems is replaced by the game of performing song lyrics *about* romance. The pleasure of eavesdropping on the trials of love is itself staged, and song lyric poets and their audiences play all the roles—participant, narrator, and spectator. The exploration of sentiment in song lyrics, which in romantic *shi* forms is usually restricted to one lover's view, could be expanded to include both lovers; the description of meetings and separations could embrace past and present and could occur in a constantly shifting array of settings. Coded references to the participants of Tang romantic poetry, intended both to mask identity and to reveal a poet's skills, are replaced in the *Huajian ji* song lyrics by an anonymous female figure, represented to suggest a courtesan or other sexually available woman, and an anonymous male, who, when speaking, represents the generic playboy-lover and is either lamenting his lost love or actively pursuing her. As we will see in Chapter 5, the voices of song lyrics offer us a poetic subjectivity that is generic rather than particular; they are coded male or female, but, even if delivered in the first person, they are not presented as a specific author's experiences. This anonymity surely grew out of the performance of song lyrics: unfettered by historical specificity or circumstance in the lyrics, any singer could inhabit the voice of the observing narrator or the complaining lover and make the song his or her own.

The conventional and anonymous nature of the *Huajian ji* romantic vignettes is in part a result of the language of the collection. Ninth-century poets often experimented with syntax and word choice, striving for arresting images and memorable couplets. However, with the important exception of Wen Tingyun, who was not particularly influential in this regard, the *Huajian ji* poets tended to avoid the semantically dense language of some ninth-century verse in preference for a hypotactic, or syntactically loose, style. Although they still cherished the power of a well-crafted and carefully placed "poetic" couplet, they also developed a fondness for vernacular phrases and comments, which were often presented as direct speech. Hypotaxis is marked by the use of "empty," *xu* 虛, words and logical connectors, particularly those indicating time; as we will see, with such devices, poets could move between styles from lyric to lyric or even within a single stanza. The clever interplay of poetic density and spoken casualness, "high" and "low," itself became part of the song lyric genre. Finally, although the dominant tone of the *Huajian ji* song lyrics is melancholic, there is a surprising amount of wit and humor, often couched in colloquial phrases, throughout the anthology. What scholars have not sufficiently studied, however, is the degree to which this language use and the styles of the *Huajian ji* song lyrics more broadly considered are creations of the Shu poets' imitation and borrowing practices.

Imitation and influence in poetry are notoriously difficult to gauge. The copying of descriptive technique or word choice is the easiest type of imitation to identify, but in a genre such as the romantic song lyric, it is sometimes difficult to distinguish stylistic imitation from sheer lexical repetitiveness, particularly when both are common.[13] Influence is subtler and more elusive in a poetic form still in its early development. The inherently conventional nature of romantic poetry and the remarkable consistency of its tropes over the course of centuries might sometimes lead us to misperceive thematic convention as influence. Edward Schafer, in his discussion of the conventions of the *Huajian ji* lyrics to "Nü guanzi" (which he translated as "The Capeline Cantos," and I translate as "The Daoist Nun"), set aside the problem of influence by arguing that such conventions were best understood as shared tools:

> Perhaps it is best not to think of these phrases as "clichés" or "stereotypes" at all, but as the constituents of a technical vocabulary which the writer is required to use. They challenge his craft; they test his skill; they try his fancy. It was incumbent on him to make the most of his talent in shaping excellent verses under the restrictions imposed by lexical conventions and concomitant limitations of tone and atmosphere.[14]

Given that the *Huajian ji* poets were working within the limitations imposed by convention and vocabulary, there were certain to be lyrics in which images and phrases recur almost repetitively. Identifying influence and imitation in the *Huajian ji* is not a hopeless task, but it does require careful consideration of individual cases.

---

13. In a generally excellent article, one scholar seems occasionally to conflate these two phenomena. Sawazaki Hisayoshi, in his study of imitation in the *HJJ*, points to the repetition of two-character phrases such as "faded red" (or "bits of petals," depending on specific context), *canhong* 殘紅, "melancholy," *chouchang* 惆悵, or "dawn orioles," *xiaoying* 曉鶯, in different lyrics as imitation (he uses the traditional term, *yanxi* 沿襲). However, some of these are fixed binomes that often appear in romantic verse, and others are phrases that appear so frequently in the *HJJ*'s limited lexicon that, due to their constant use and inconsistent location within a line or stanza, their appearance should not be considered imitation. Sawazaki, "*Huajian ji* de yanxi," 90–120.

14. Schafer, "The Capeline Cantos: Verses on the Divine Loves of Taoist Priestesses," 20.

My approach to these obstacles is to address the problem in sets of lyrics to a single tune and to read a number of lyrics in a set against one another. There are three important reasons to analyze the *Huajian ji* song lyrics in this way. First, and most importantly, although the compilers of the anthology collected each individual poet's lyrics separately, singers, as we saw in the stories discussed in Chapter 2, would have performed several iterations of a tune, using their own lyrics or someone else's as they chose. Reading tune title sets thus allows us to recreate tenth-century performance practice.[15] Second, as a close examination of the lyrics reveals, the Shu poets tended to borrow lines and images from other poets *within* tune title sets (although there are also examples of phrase-borrowing across tunes). This stems in part from metrical demands: it seems to have been easier for a poet to borrow another poet's three- or four-character phrase from a lyric to the same tune (hence, metrical structure)—"plugging it into" his own line, often in the same position—than to plunder lyrics of different metrical structures. At the same time, the borrowed phrase might also be a better fit in terms of rhyme and tonal pattern. It seems probable that music was another consideration—that there were rhythmic, melodic, or even vocal reasons for borrowing within tunes as well. Finally, by comparing lyrics that follow the same metrical structure, we can isolate stylistic imitation more precisely, on the levels of rhetorical structure, syntax, and word choice. Different metrical structures demanded different rhetorical approaches. By reading lyrics within a tune title set, we exclude the problem of formal variation, and we can more easily perceive imitation in the ways poets structured their lyrics. The Shu poets skillfully imitated their Tang masters, but went beyond them to create a coherent style of their own. Reading their

---

15. This was not a practice limited to Shu, nor was it a tenth-century invention, as the lyrics by Bai Juyi and Liu Yuxi demonstrate. Evidence of the practice can also be found in the lyrics composed by the northern poet He Ning included in the *HJJ*. For example, He Ning's two lyrics to the tune "He manzi" contain the same introductory phrases for the final two lines. The two lyrics appear to be describing the same woman, with the second giving us a new variation.

lyrics against one another allows us to identify specific poetic choices and to distinguish innovation from imitation.

Reading tune title sets thus brings us closer to the poets' composition and performance demands on a number of levels. At the same time, it provides another unexpected benefit: it reveals the central themes of the collection as they play out within sets and across the anthology as a whole. In my discussion of the stylistic range of the anthology, I focus on features that recur frequently. In terms of form, I examine the rhetorical structure of lyrics within sets and the connections between stanzas created by the stanza break. I also focus on the relationship of lines within stanzas and the syntax of individual lines. Although I will discuss rhyming practices in specific lyrics, I do not address the subject of rhyme for the collection overall, nor do I discuss tonal patterns except in a few cases. As other scholars have argued, there are interesting uses of rhyme and tonal euphony in the *Huajian ji*, but the evidence from this collection—created *before* the establishment of "regulations" for song lyrics—cannot be fairly assessed by the standards that emerged in the Song. Scholars such as Nakata Yūjiro, in 1936, and, more recently, Daniel Bryant and Aoyama Hiroshi have examined tenth-century *shi* and *quzi ci* rhyming either in analyses of rhyme and tonal patterning in the period or in studies of individual poets or collections.[16] These studies have tended to confirm the kinds of phonological changes that have been hypothesized as occurring between the Tang and the Song and have even suggested the possible influence of regional dialects on rhyme practice. However, without a greater body of datable evidence of ninth- and tenth-century literati *quzi ci* against which to compare the *Huajian ji*, I am hesitant to

---

16. Aoyama Hiroshi examines both rhyme and tonal patterns in the *Huajian ji*. He notes the originality and diversity of rhyme tonality in the collection in comparison to Tang literati song lyrics, which underlines the uniqueness of the anthology against its Tang background. Aoyama, *Tō Sō shi kenkyū*, 227–67. For the suggestive phonological features of the *Huajian ji* rhymes, see Bryant, "The Rhyming Categories of Tenth Century Chinese Poetry"; and Nakata, "Tō Godai shi'in kō," 551–88. Tonal patterns of the *Huajian ji* generally appear as part of broader examinations of early tonal patterns in song lyrics, as in Shi, *Ci yu yinyue guanxi*, 208–16, and the many works on *ci* prosody since the Song.

make broad conclusions about rhyme and tonal patterns in the anthology and will only comment on specific usages—such as a poet's straying significantly from a pattern that others follow—where appropriate.

Although the core content of the *Huajian ji* lyrics was not itself new, close readings of the lyrics reveal that certain elements of the romantic story came to dominate the collection to a degree unprecedented in the medieval poetic tradition. In this chapter and the two chapters that follow, I examine the elements that I find central to the *Huajian ji* as a literary work, and I draw connections between the formal and stylistic innovations of the collection and the new importance of these thematic elements. In the lyrics to "Pusa man" discussed in this chapter, the poets' voyeuristic approach to the scene of the abandoned woman foregrounds the spatial and temporal liminality of the boudoir. Liminality—the period or space of transition between one state and another—is both an underlying assumption of the "abandoned woman" narrative and constantly evoked in the lyrics through the use of seasonal imagery and temporal cues. Among the many liminal states and moments depicted in the lyrics, dreams are the most common and most important in the collection. The isolated, otherworldly space of the abandoned woman also allows poets to add erotic touches to their lyrics. In Chapter 5, I examine the use of voice and gender in lyrics to "Jiu quanzi" and "Huanxi sha." In lyrics to these tune titles, poets seem to experiment more often with changes of voice between iterations of lyrics and to use male voices as well as female voices. As a result, the lyrics reveal the poets' interest in gendered perspectives on the romance, and show them revising, in part, the traditional subjectivities they had inherited. Finally, in Chapter 6 I explore lyrics to tunes with Daoist overtones, an important subset of the song lyrics of the *Huajian ji*, to demonstrate the range of uses of supernatural or religious narratives, images, and objects in the anthology. Although similar uses of Daoism can be found throughout the medieval literary tradition, the *Huajian ji* poets were the first—and perhaps really the last—poets to import this material into romantic song lyrics in such a thoroughgoing fashion. These lyrics not only incorporate the themes and problems raised in other tune title sets but also disturb the anthology-wide depiction of romance. By invoking the altered power relationship between goddess and mortal man, a few poets of the "Daoist" lyrics offer a different view of those who suffer in romantic love. Thus, although the *Huajian ji* offers us a narrow range of topics, reading tune title sets gives us access to the sometimes subtle differences in style, technique, and theme within a single tune, allowing us to make connections and distinctions across the collection as a whole.

Models for the Huajian ti *(Among the flowers style):* Wen Tingyun and Wei Zhuang

The question of the style of the *Huajian ji* has been a problem for readers of song lyrics from as early as the Northern Song. For Song literati familiar with the history of Shu, the style of the collection was filiated to its "decadent" era and kingdom. Late imperial readers and writers of song lyrics attempted to trace the development of the anthology's style more precisely. From Qing-era *cihua* (comments on song lyrics) through the most recent scholarship on the *Huajian ji*, most readers have argued that the song lyric style of the collection, sometimes called the *"Huajian ti"* 花間體 (style of the *Huajian [ji]*), was a creation of the late Tang poet Wen Tingyun that was then slavishly followed by the Shu poets.[17] The style of Wei Zhuang's song lyrics, quite different from that of Wen Tingyun, is generally read as a secondary and less interesting influence. As the preface revealed, Ouyang Jiong and the Shu anthology collaborators acknowledged Wen as one forefather of the song lyric—along with Li Bai, Wen Tingyun is specifically praised as an early composer of *quzi ci*. The ordering and selections of the text further testify to the Shu poets' regard for both Wen Tingyun and Wei Zhuang: in the body of the *Huajian ji*, Wen is placed first in the collection, with 66 lyrics, and Wei is third, with 48. Wei Zhuang's prominence

---

17. Wen Tingyun's importance as a stylistic model for the *Huajian* poets has been discussed by *ci* poets and commentators since the Qing. For a view of the evolution of Wen's reputation, see the comments on Wen collected in *Tang Wudai ci jishi huiping*, 230–36.

in the collection likely stems from his high position in Wang Jian's Former Shu government and his general influence on Shu culture. I consider Wen Tingyun's importance below. I should also note two other factors that likely influenced the style and shape of the *Huajian ji*, factors for which we have no external textual evidence. The first is the influence of popular song on the Shu poets, which can be perceived in their use of vernacular phrases throughout their lyrics. The second is the influence that salon discussions of song lyrics must have had on the *Huajian ji* compilers' choices for the anthology. It may be that the process of selecting song lyrics for the anthology produced a more homogeneous body of lyrics—and one that clearly manifested the influence of Wen and Wei—than might otherwise have been preserved. We do, however, have lyrics from some of the *Huajian ji* poets in the anonymously compiled *quzi ci* anthology *Zunqian ji*, which was itself modeled upon the *Huajian ji* and includes many of the same poets. There are 120 lyrics from *Huajian ji* poets in the *Zunqian ji*, placed in the same order as they are found in the Shu anthology. Although I agree with the scholarly consensus that sees Wen and Wei as the two stylistic poles of the anthology, I suggest that the styles of the other *Huajian ji* poets are more syncretic than either extreme. Space does not allow a comparative analysis of the styles of the *Huajian ji* and the *Zunqian ji* lyrics, but, as other scholars have noted, the styles of individual poets collected in both anthologies seem quite consistent between the two.[18]

Let me juxtapose two lyrics by Wen Tingyun and Wei Zhuang to show the two poets' styles at their most disparate. The tune title set "Pusa man" contains examples of each poet at his most extreme, whether that extreme is characterized by rich description or a hearty casualness.

---

18. See, for example, Jiang, "Zunqian ji he zaoqi wenren ci," 39–41.

"Pusa man" 菩薩蠻 (1st of 14)
Wen Tingyun

Hills in many layers, golden glow flickering,[19]	小山重疊金明滅
Clouds of hair poised to fall across the snow of her fragrant cheeks.[20]	鬢雲欲度香腮雪
Languidly rising to paint her moth-brows,[21]	懶起畫蛾眉
to her makeup and toilette she finally stirs.	弄妝梳洗遲
Reflected flowers in mirrors front and back;	照花前後鏡
flowery faces shine upon each other.[22]	花面交相映
Newly stitched on her embroidered gauze gown:	新帖繡羅襦
pair on pair of golden partridges.[23]	雙雙金鷓鴣

For generations of critics, Wen's "Pusa man" lyrics have exemplified his style, and this lyric in particular is most commonly discussed.[24] The layering of closely observed images lacking narrative context, the voyeuristic focus on the figure of the woman, and the avoidance of direct emotional statements found in this lyric are seen as Wen Tingyun's trademarks. The relations between the objects Wen describes are often obscure: where exactly are the "hills in many layers"—in the woman's hair, outside the woman's window, or on a bedroom screen? The "reflected flowers in mirrors front and back"

---

19. The debate over this line is irresolvable. Li Yi provides the two most popular readings of this line in a note: one reading states that the "hills" represent the woman's hair, done into a layered chignon; another argues that they are hills painted on a screen in her bedroom. *HJJZS*, 4, n2. Zhang Yiren discusses the origins of these readings in his analysis of all of Wen's "Pusa man" lyrics in "Wen Feiqing jiushuo shangque," collected in his *Huajian ci lunji*, 2–3.

20. Both hair as clouds and cheeks like snow are common in poems describing women. See Ye's detailed discussion of the images of this opening couplet in *Tang Song ci shiqi jiang*, 24–29.

21. The "moth-brows," another common figure in poetry describing women, refer to eyebrows painted or shaped to be long and curved, like moth antennae.

22. Li Yi reads this line as describing a woman, flowers pinned in her hair, who is reflected in mirrors both in front and behind her. Another possibility is that there are flowers not only in the woman's hair but also carved or painted on the back of the mirror itself. In the next line, however, the woman's face is certainly one of the "flowery faces" that is shining.

23. *HJJZS*, 4.

24. For the generations of commentary on this lyric and the series, see *Tang Wudai ci jishi huiping*, 253–70.

pose a similar interpretative problem: is this simply the woman's face reflected in two mirrors, or are there flowers in her hair, or perhaps on a dressing table? There are a number of plausible readings of both lines, but none of those alters the nonlinear, elliptical style of the lyric as a whole. The lack of strong verbs in the opening couplet of the first stanza and the opening line of the second stanza enhances the static quality of the lyric. Readers of this lyric conclude that Wen Tingyun excels in rich description but is less interested in narrating action, or even in evoking the emotions of his female subjects.

Wei Zhuang, in contrast, eschews Wen Tingyun's obscurity in favor of a more direct style, as we see in his fifth of five to the same tune:

"Pusa man" (5th of 5)
Wei Zhuang

In Luoyang City, spring scenes are fine;	洛陽城里春光好
but the Luoyang talent in other lands grows old.[25]	洛陽才子他鄉老
Willows darken by the Wei King's dike,[26]	柳暗魏王堤
at this moment, one's heart is beguiled.	此時心轉迷
Peach blossoms by spring waters' green—	桃花春水綠
on the water, ducks and drakes preen.	水上鴛鴦浴
Fixed in regret, I face the fading glow,	凝恨對殘暉
I remember you, but you do not know![27]	憶君君不知

In contrast to Wen Tingyun's dazzling array of images, Wei Zhuang's lyric gives us a simple, almost folk-song rendition of "the beauty of Luoyang." The opening couplet of the first stanza, with its refrain-like "Luoyang city . . . / the Luoyang talent . . ." immediately

---

25. The "Luoyang Talent" was originally the Han literatus Jia Yi 賈誼. Here, Wei Zhuang uses the phrase to refer to himself.

26. The "Wei King's dike" was built in Luoyang during the Tang; it was lined with willows and became a popular spot for Tang literati in Luoyang. Willows were, of course, also linked to lovers' parting because of the homophony of "willow," liu 柳, and "to detain," liu 留. They became associated with romantic trysts and entertainment and were found in other provincial cities. During his reign, Wang Yan had a willow dike constructed in his new Xuanhua Park. *Jinli qijiu zhuan* 6.7a.

27. *HJJZS*, 77.

clarifies the topic (beauty of Luoyang) and theme (Luoyang is a place for youthful love) of the lyric, and the second couplet completes the description. The second stanza gives us a closer look at the "fine" Luoyang spring scene and the typical Luoyang beauty abandoned by the "talent" who is growing old elsewhere.[28] Where Wen Tingyun creates a striking portrait by focusing on the intimate details of the anonymous woman's appearance, Wei constructs his lyric around the contrast of Luoyang (where the speaker is not) and the spring scene—the memory and the present moment. Wei's lyric also offers us a number of possibilities of voice: although the final couplet strongly suggests a first-person speaker (the use and placement of the verbs "face," *dui* 對, and "remember," *yi* 憶, indicate direct speech, and the use of the second-person pronoun "you," *jun* 君, confirms it), the gender of the speaker is ambiguous. Is it the woman who has been abandoned by the "Luoyang talent" or the "Luoyang talent" himself who is recalling the lost love? The conventions of romantic verse favor the speaker's being a woman—men were not usually the ones who were "fixed in regret" over a lost love, since their mobility was part of their gendered, generic identity—but there are no other gender markers in the second stanza to settle the question definitively. In a song that could be performed by a man or a woman, Wei's lyric does not require us to make a choice between male or female speaker. As I explore more fully in Chapter 6, this ambiguity of gender was one feature of Wei Zhuang's style that some *Huajian ji* poets exploited.

Many twentieth-century scholars of the song lyric have contrasted the styles of these two poets, to the point where the two men have become opposite ends on the spectrum of the *Huajian ji* style.[29] To some extent, I support this view of Wen and Wei as stylistic op-

---

28. Owen suggests that Wei Zhuang's "Pusa man" lyrics make up a series on "the Southland" (the Jiangnan region) and the pleasures of Luoyang, as in this lyric. Owen, *An Anthology of Chinese Literature*, 566–67. Ye Jiaying also notes that the "Jiangnan" of these lyrics is a place of memory and imagination, not the place where the lyrics were composed. Ye, *Wen Tingyun, Wei Zhuang, Feng Yansi, Li Yu*, 74–75.

29. The Qing commentator Zhou Ji, in *Jiecun zhai lunci zazhuo*, discusses them as two complementary but different talents. Cited in *Tang Wudai ci jishi huiping*, 231.

posites, and I have made much use of recent scholarship on their styles in this and subsequent chapters. Let me summarize the central arguments about Wen and Wei made by scholars in the past few decades. Adapting terminology from Wang Guowei's influential *Renjian cihua* in her many works on song lyrics, Ye Jiaying has labeled Wen Tingyun's style "objective" and Wei Zhuang's style "subjective." She argues that Wen's close observation of women and their appearances gives an impersonal and "objective" quality to his description. In contrast, Wei's uses of male and female first-person voices make his lyrics "subjective," since they tell the romantic story from the point of view of the subject who experienced it. Borrowing the language of traditional criticism, Ye also labels Wen's style "richly beautiful" and Wei's style "light and thin," terms that suggest each poet's use of descriptive imagery.[30] In *The Evolution of Chinese Tz'u Poetry*, Kang-i Sun Chang's analysis follows similar lines, but Chang instead locates the stylistic difference in the poets' syntax. Chang argues that Wen Tingyun's style is paratactic, or syntactically dense and lacking connective devices, and Wei Zhuang's style is hypotactic, or syntactically open and full of phrases that indicate logical progression and connection. In Wen Tingyun's lyrics, the lack of speakers, the disconnection between two stanzas of a single lyric, and the emphasis on description over emotional content leads to intriguing ambiguity. Chang labels Wen's practice the "rhetoric of implicit meaning," in which the significance of a scene must be carefully assembled from the bits and pieces of image and scene the poet provides. On the other hand, Wei Zhuang's use of speakers and logical connectors to create a narrative flow from line to line creates what she calls the "rhetoric of explicit meaning."[31]

In his *Sōshi kenkyū: Tō Godai Hoku Sō hen*, Murakami Tetsumi traced Wen Tingyun's poetic style to his biography and the culture

---

30. Ye, *Wen Tingyun, Wei Zhuang, Feng Yansi, Li Yu*, 16–17, 60–62, and see also her *Jialing lun ci conggao*, 18–20. Ye's language echoes the terms used by Long Yusheng, *Tang Song mingjia cixuan*, in which he describes Wen's language as "beautifully dense," *limi*, and Wei's language as "lightly diffuse," *qingshu*. Cited in *Tang Wudai ci jishi huiping*, 233.

31. Chang, *Evolution of Chinese Tz'u Poetry*, 33–62.

of the late Tang. He also saw Wen as the dominant influence on the collection, though he points to Wei Zhuang as a "counter-style." Murakami also made an important connection between Wen Tingyun's influence on the Shu poets of the *Huajian ji* and the influence of the late Tang poet Li Shangyin on the early Northern Song poetic group known as the "Xikun" group, after the *Xikun chouchang ji* 西崑酬唱集, an anthology that collected their poetry. Both Wen and Li, Murakami suggested, made stylistic innovations that proved enormously influential, but only long after their deaths, through later poets' reading and imitation.[32] Paul Rouzer, in his study of the poetry of Wen Tingyun, has followed Murakami's lead in emphasizing the importance of later poets' appropriation of Wen Tingyun, suggesting further that Wen Tingyun's style has been summarized too simply. Rouzer argues that Wen's song lyric style is not as different from his poetry style as critics have claimed and that both Wen's poetry and song lyric styles are in fact quite heterogeneous. Rouzer demonstrates that many of Wen's song lyrics have "syntactically 'open' phrases, are less imagistically dense, and make explicit reference to the emotions of their subjects."[33] Rouzer notes that the critics' identification of Wen's style as "richly beautiful" is based on their repeated reading of the same small set of lyrics, particularly the "Pusa man" lyrics, when in fact other, less often examined, lyrics by Wen contradict this judgment.[34] Acknowledging that Wen's "richly beautiful" hypotactic style greatly influenced the Shu poets, Rouzer suggests that it was through their imitation that the Shu poets were

---

32. Murakami, *So shi kenkyū*, 134–43.
33. Rouzer, *Writing Another's Dream*, 62.
34. Aoyama Hiroshi provides further evidence for the similarity between Wen and Wei in his analysis of certain lexical items such as "dream" (*meng*) and the use of specific times (night) and seasons (spring) in the two poets' *HJJ* lyrics, and concludes that the similar frequency of these features in the two poets' works links rather than distinguishes them (*Tō Sō shi kenkyū*, 65–70). Although I agree on the significance of the shared lexicon (a feature that runs throughout the collection, as Aoyama demonstrates in further analyses of lyrics by the poets Li Xun and Gu Xiong, 117–227), I would argue that the overall stylistic difference between Wen and Wei is still quite apparent.

able to create a new *genre* style—a development that occurred within a reading tradition long after Wen's death.³⁵

Wen Tingyun's influence over the *Huajian ji* poets makes him curiously prominent in the history of song lyrics, and that prominence is, as Rouzer points out, probably exaggerated precisely because of the *Huajian ji*.³⁶ The scholar Liu Zunming also emphasizes Wen's influence, noting that without Wen Tingyun's lyrics, the body of Tang song lyrics—and, consequently, our understanding of the early genre—would be completely altered.³⁷ In different ways, these scholars both highlight Wen Tingyun's uniqueness by contrasting his style and formal proficiency with the works of other late Tang poets, none of whom had his diverse talents. The distinctiveness of Wen Tingyun in comparison with other late Tang poets should certainly raise the question of why Wen Tingyun was so important for the *Huajian ji* poets. Was his particular song lyric style more popular in the Tang than either the historical records or extant poetry would suggest? Within his varied corpus, Wen Tingyun does not make clear stylistic distinctions *among* genres in the way that the imitative practice of the Shu poets might suggest. Instead, as Rouzer demonstrates, Wen created a "personal style through the use of dense imagery and diction, 'objectivity,' and the reinvention of the erotic tradition."³⁸ Was Wen Tingyun then particularly well known in the late Tang for a song lyric volume? We have no evidence from the Tang to support such a hypothesis. The lapse of time and the historical disruptions between Wen Tingyun's death (ca. 866) and the compilation of the *Huajian ji* in 940 argue against the likelihood that his song lyrics survived only in the oral, performed tradition, pointing instead to the existence and circulation of a text that contained his song lyrics—perhaps the *Jinquan ji* 金筌集, mentioned in the preface to the *Huajian ji*, or another col-

---

35. Rouzer, *Writing Another's Dream*, 68.
36. Ibid., 61.
37. Liu, *Tang Wudai ci di wenhua guanzhao*, 135–39; Rouzer, *Writing Another's Dream*, 15–16, and throughout.
38. Rouzer, *Writing Another's Dream*, 68.

lection, the *Wolan ji* 握蘭集.³⁹ Yet Rouzer, following Ye Jiaying, cautions us against concluding that Wen Tingyun had prepared his own collections of song lyrics or that the *Jinquan ji* was composed exclusively of song lyrics.⁴⁰ His song lyrics were more likely preserved as texts along with other texts in one of these named collections. Wen Tingyun's reputation as a song lyric poet is supported by the existence of his song lyrics in the *Huajian ji* and by his brief biographies in the two Tang histories, both of which mention his "licentious lyrics."⁴¹ However, there are no late Tang documents that celebrate or censure Wen Tingyun specifically on the basis of his song lyrics.

Why then did the Shu poets, almost a century after Wen Tingyun's death, come to take this distinctive poet as a stylistic model for their own song lyrics? In the absence of evidence from the late Tang, I can only speculate on the means by which Wen Tingyun's lyrics might have been transmitted to and circulated within Shu. Wen Tingyun's son, Wen Xian 溫憲, was apparently a low-ranking subofficial in the Shannan circuit (Sichuan) in 886 or 887; his son Wen Yi 溫顗, Tingyun's grandson, served in the Former Shu government under Wang Jian, a fact that suggests the family had settled

---

39. For an analysis of the possible contents of the collections attributed to Wen, see Stephen Owen's discussion in *The Late Tang: Chinese Poetry of the Mid-Ninth Century (827–860)*, 530–33.

40. Rouzer, *Writing Another's Dream*, 61, and n36. He also suggests that certain of Wen's poems "were kept out of his official *shi* collection because they dealt with 'improper' (i.e., erotic) subject matter" (n37), which might mean that the *Jinquan ji* to which Ouyang Jiong refers and the *Wolan ji* were collections of erotic poetry and may have included song lyrics.

41. *JTS* 190.5078–79 and *XTS* 91.3787–88. Another early mention of Wen as a song lyric composer comes in the anonymous work *Yu quanzi*, dated to the Tang (cited in *Tang Wudai ci jishi huiping*, 229). Perhaps the most famous story about Wen as a song lyric composer—in which the minister Linghu Tao steals one of Wen's "Pusa man" lyrics to pass off as his own to Emperor Xuanzong—appears first in *Bei Meng suoyan* 4.29 (again later in *Tang shi jishi*), over a century after his death. Xia Chengtao includes the story in his *Tang Song ciren nianpu*, 406. Rouzer discusses the difficulty of reconstructing a biographical account based on the sparse, inconsistent, and contradictory evidence, in *Writing Another's Dream*, 11–15.

in Sichuan permanently by the fall of the Tang.⁴² The grandson, Wen Yi, was perhaps the source of a copy of Wen Tingyun's *Jinquan ji*, which may have contained some of Wen Tingyun's song lyrics. Ouyang Jiong's reference to Wen's text by name in his preface suggests that it was available in Shu. Moreover, Wei Zhuang was known to have defended Wen Tingyun as an overlooked talent, and if he had known of a collection of Wen Tingyun's work that included song lyrics (since Wei Zhuang was himself fond of composing them), he would likely have obtained and circulated them at the Former Shu court.⁴³ Or Wei Zhuang may himself have possessed a text that contained Wen Tingyun's lyrics. The prominence of Wen Tingyun in the *Caidiao ji*, which collects 61 of Wen Tingyun's poems (none of which are duplicated in the *Huajian ji*), also points to a textual source for Wen Tingyun's work in Shu that might not have been available in other regions.⁴⁴ Without other textual evidence, it is impossible to determine the transmission of Wen's lyrics from his death to 940, the year of the *Huajian ji*. What is quite clear from the *Huajian ji* and the *Caidiao ji* is that Wen Tingyun's poetry and song lyrics were known and admired by Shu poets.

---

42. *SGCQ* 42.625 identifies Wen Xian as a *congshi*, a "retainer," perhaps an abbreviated title or simply a low-ranking, probably secretarial post. Xia, *Tang Song ciren nianpu*, 396–97, discusses the stories about Wen Xian in various sources.

43. *QTW* 889.3b–4a for one version of Wei Zhuang's memorial, also noted in Chapter 2. See Yates' discussion, *Washing Silk*, 30–31, and the extensive n132.

44. *Caidiao ji* in Fu, *Tang ren xuan Tang shi*, 730–46. The Shu taste for Wen's poetry was also tilted toward his musical pieces: 28 of the 61 pieces collected in the *Caidiao ji* have titles indicating musicality, such as *yao*, *qu*, *xing*, and *ci*. These pieces do not fall within the boundaries of *quzi ci*, since they are not written to fixed tunes whose titles are recorded elsewhere; instead, they are part of Wen Tingyun's distinctive work in the *yuefu* tradition (other pieces of the 61 could also be considered *yuefu*, but they do not have titles that link them to music). The existence of separate textual sources for different kinds of poetic texts by Wen in the tenth century is also supported by the fact that none of Wen's *yuefu* appear in the *Wenyuan yinghua*, suggesting that the *Wenyuan yinghua* compilers did not have access to a text that was available in Shu. This point is made by Owen, *The Late Tang*.

Imitating Wen Tingyun: Lyrics to the Tune "Pusa man"

Wen Tingyun's "richly beautiful" style is particularly associated with the fourteen lyrics to "Pusa man" (Bodhisattva barbarian). Although this tune is recorded in the High Tang document of the court music quarters, the *Jiaofang ji*, outside of the lyrics by Wen and Wei, only five literati lyrics to the tune are extant from the Tang, and the authorship of three of those is contested.[45] After Wen's 14 lyrics, however, we find 27 others in the *Huajian ji*, by the poets Wei Zhuang, Niu Qiao, He Ning, Sun Guangxian, Wei Chengban, Yin E, Mao Xizhen, and Li Xun (see Table 3).

Table 3 demonstrates the Shu editors' great admiration for Wen Tingyun's "Pusa man" lyrics: they included 14 of them (the largest number of lyrics in the anthology by an author to a single tune title), and they placed them first among Wen's lyrics, which are themselves placed first in the anthology. Furthermore, the inclusion of 27 "Pusa man" lyrics by other poets makes a total of 41 "Pusa man" lyrics, the second-largest number of lyrics to a single tune title (after "Huanxi sha," with 57 lyrics). The "Pusa man" lyric has two stanzas; the first stanza contains two lines of seven characters

---

45. Li Bai is credited with three "Pusa man" lyrics in the *Zunqian ji*. Daniel Bryant has convincingly demonstrated the many problems with this attribution in his article, "On the Authenticity of the Tz'u Attributed to Li Po," see n85. However, Zhang Zhang includes them without reference to the debate over attribution in *QTWDC*. The ill-fated last Tang ruler, Li Ye, is also credited in the *Zunqian ji* with two "Pusa man" lyrics. As is true for many Tang lyrics, the origins of "Pusa man" are obscure, but they were almost certainly foreign. One anecdote that connects the title with a beautiful foreign woman's hairstyle seems to originate in the mid-ninth century, despite the *Jiaofang ji* record of the tune's High Tang existence. The association of the tune with the appearance of a beautiful woman may indeed have been a late Tang invention and may explain the focus, in the lyrics of Wen and his successors, on the face and figure of the woman. See the reconstruction of some features of the "Pusa" tunes and dances in Picken, ed., *Music from the Tang Court*, vol. 4, 59–70. Ren summarizes four theories of origin for this tune title in *Jiaofang ji jianding*, 89–90. There are thirteen lyrics to "Pusa man" in the Dunhuang corpus, though the lyric is not found in the *Yunyao ji*.

Table 3
Huajian ji Poets with Lyrics to "Pusa man"
(in order of appearance)

Poet	Number of lyrics	Poet	Number of lyrics
Wen Tingyun	14	Wei Chengban	2
Wei Zhuang	5	Yin E	1
Niu Qiao	7	Mao Xizhen	3
He Ning	1	Li Xun	3
Sun Guangxian	5		

followed by two lines of five characters, and the second stanza contains four lines of five characters each. Since the five- and seven-character line were the standard lines for regulated verse, most *Huajian ji* poets follow the usual caesurae for those lines (after the second and fourth characters, respectively) and end-stop their lines. The four-line stanzas tend to fall into couplets, which often show some parallelism. The rhyme scheme of the two stanzas, however, runs counter to the rhymes of *shi* forms, since the rhymes fall at the end of each line, rather than alternating lines, thus occurring in couplets, and they change after each couplet: the first stanza rhymes AA (a *ze* rhyme) BB (a *ping* rhyme), and the second stanza rhymes CC (a new *ze* rhyme) and DD (a new *ping* rhyme). The use of five- and seven-character lines arranged in quatrains, in conjunction with the stability of the rhyme and tonal patterns in the *Huajian ji* "Pusa man" lyrics, suggests an early date of origin.[46] However early the form of "Pusa man" may have been, the lyrics to the tune by Wen Tingyun are the earliest extant from the Tang. And, when we examine the *Huajian ji* set of "Pusa man" lyrics as a whole, it quickly becomes clear that Wen Tingyun's set influenced the compositions of other poets in the anthology.

---

46. In *Tō Sō shi kenkyū*, 258–63, Aoyama Hiroshi examines the rhyme and tonal patterns of all the "Pusa man" lyrics in the *HJJ* and contrasts their stability with the many metrical and rhyme variants for tunes such as "He zhuan" and "Jiu quanzi" in the anthology.

The content of Wen Tingyun's fourteen "Pusa man" lyrics is consistent and includes three basic elements: a description of the setting, whether the natural world or the enclosed chamber; a description of the woman, focusing on her clothes and face; and sometimes a brief expression of feeling from the woman, perhaps accompanied by a narrative detail. Aoyama Hiroshi has analyzed the contents of all of Wen's "Pusa man" lyrics, and he notes that the season is usually spring, the time is the evening, and the setting is the woman's decorated chambers. He also notes that the subject of most of Wen's lyrics is female, whether the lyric appears to be in the first person, which is less common, or is "about" the woman, with some suggestion of her emotions.[47] The woman's emotion is sometimes articulated in the form of a question (such as "Where is the wandering man?"), but is just as often stated less directly. One could certainly argue that these three are the basic components of all medieval verse, but more specifically, the interplay between emotions and scene (*qing* 情 and *jing* 景) became a central part of *ci* poetics in the Song and afterward. In the hands of Wen Tingyun and his followers, each of the three elements is used to strengthen the impact of the other two. The natural world is used to stage the characters' emotions; the interior setting is alluringly mysterious and concealing; and the emotions are communicated through scenic detail and overheard plaints from the hidden or only partially seen female subjects.

In his reading of Wen's erotic *yuefu*, Rouzer points out that the highly descriptive style derived in part from the romantic tradition, which valued decorative presentation. Wen Tingyun's poems and lyrics in the late Southern Dynasties style were both a response to the tradition and a transformation of it. Where the description of the Southern Dynasties *yuefu* tended to be formulaic and repetitive, Wen reworked the descriptive technique by withholding certain details and offering only partial glimpses of the private scene. His technique resulted in more suggestive and ambiguous romantic vignettes than had yet been seen in romantic poetry.[48] Wen's ap-

---

47. Aoyama, *Tō Sō shi kenkyū*, 14–16.
48. Rouzer, *Writing Another's Dream*, 79–94.

proach to the romantic vignette also exploited fully the longstanding thematic conventions of concealment and the passage of time. Of these conventions, however, Wen explored a few thematic elements more frequently than others, and his selections greatly influenced the lyrics of other poets in the anthology. One prominent element we find throughout Wen Tingyun's lyrics is liminality, the period of transition or suspension between one state and another; the single most common representation of this state is the dream, *meng* 夢. The notion of liminality derives from anthropological studies of ritual, and most importantly from Arnold van Gennep's early studies, which were developed in the work done on performance and "social drama" by Victor Turner.[49] In their use of the term, liminality describes the bounded time and (sometimes) space of transition between one state and another, found in rituals such as rites of passage or collective seasonal rites. Van Gennep's influential tripartite division of ritual into separation, transition (liminal phase), and reincorporation offers a way of understanding the transformations that human rituals enact and signify for their participants. In anthropological descriptions of liminality, people who enter such periods are often physically separated from others and exist in a realm in which the normal rules of social life seem to have been suspended.[50] In the logic of ritual, this period of freedom within boundedness destabilizes the participants, unmooring them from their previous states and allowing them to be transformed.

In the lyrics of Wen Tingyun and many other *Huajian ji* poets, liminality appears as both the conventional depiction of the lover's state and a theme articulated across a range of images. The romance, as depicted in medieval Chinese poetry through the Tang, emphasizes the separation phase—the period after the original romantic encounter or relationship but before a final resolution or termination. The tension of the medieval romantic vignette, such as it is,

---

49. Van Gennep, *The Rites of Passage*; Turner, *From Ritual to Theatre: The Human Seriousness of Play*, and *The Anthropology of Performance*.

50. See Turner's expansion of van Gennep's definition in *From Ritual to Theatre*, 26–27.

stems from the fact of the subject's waiting to hear or know of the beloved. In keeping with the conventional imagery of romantic poetry, as we saw in the Tang quatrains of Chapter 1, the mood is often questioning and uncertain, whether the question is spoken directly by a subject or simply posed by the ambiguity of the scene, and details of the unspecific but evocative setting are used sparingly. In poems that depict abandoned women, the women are usually secluded in a bounded space; at the same time, they seem suspended outside the social worlds in which medieval women would normally have moved.

When we look at the *Huajian ji* vignettes, we find that liminal spaces, moments, and seasons are so common as to appear standard to these lyrics. Women are not only trapped within boudoirs but are framed behind windows, poised at the edge of railings, and half-illuminated in lamplight. The scenes of melancholy often occur at dawn or in the early evening, at dusk; the seasonal moment, when it is announced, is frequently transitional—most often the end of spring. With respect to the women's physical liminality, they often hover on the threshold of two spaces—on the verge of being seen by a suppressed observer, but not fully disclosed. Boundedness is thematized by the poets' emphasis on the doors, gates, and walls that enclose the women and cut them off from others and by their use of elements that penetrate and thereby draw attention to those boundaries, such as wandering dream-souls, birds in flight, scents, and sounds that enter the bedchamber. This physical liminality is mirrored throughout the "Pusa man" lyrics—and indeed throughout the collection—by the poets' concern for other kinds of in-between states: between waking and dreaming, between drunkenness and sobriety, and, in emotional terms, between the loss of hope for the lover's return and its perpetual rebirth. As in the liminal phase of ritual, the liminality of the boudoir and its latent eroticism allow a certain kind of transforming freedom. Within the seclusion and anonymity that the poets create for their female subjects, the women take actions that might in other circumstances be excessive, such as drinking too much wine or sleeping the days away, and voice complaints or wishes that might not be spoken outside the chamber. As I demonstrate in the lyrics that follow, the

Huajian ji poets' exploration of liminality on many levels is a potent poetic technique that helps to define the romance of the collection.

Wen Tingyun's response to the conventions of the romantic poetry tradition was to break them down into discrete elements, discard the most obvious among them, and reassemble the most decorative and evocative pieces as collage. The reader of these lyrics must use his or her knowledge of the tradition's conventions to create some kind of narrative for the scene—but Wen Tingyun's static scenes generally resist narrative coherence.

"Pusa man" (3rd of 14)
Wen Tingyun

Stamen yellow powder all over the peak of her forehead—[51]	蕊黃無限當山額
last night's makeup and hidden smiles blocked by the window screen.	宿妝隱笑紗窗隔
When they saw each other in peony season,[52]	相見牡丹時
he came but for a moment, then had to depart.	暫來還別離
Kingfisher hairpins with gilded stems—	翠釵金作股
on the hairpins, pairs of butterflies dance.[53]	釵上蝶雙舞
Who knows the affairs of her heart?	心事竟誰知
The moon is bright: flowers fill the branches.[54]	月明花滿枝

---

51. Zhang Yiren discusses the four most common readings of this line, *Huajian ji ci lun*, 22. I follow that proposed by Li Yi and others, that "stamen-yellow powder" refers to a face powder used by Tang women.

52. "Peony season" occurs at the end of spring, which is also the end of the traditional time for lovers' meetings. Apparently not domestically cultivated before the Tang, they enjoyed a tremendous vogue in the eighth and ninth centuries. Peonies, particularly the most popular red peony, became a common metaphor for alluring women. See Schafer, "Passionate Peonies."

53. The hairpins had stems, or "thighs," *gu*, of gold or gilded metal, and kingfisher feathers were inlaid on the pins. The butterflies, often also made from gilded metal, were attached to the top of the pins, often by long, thin pieces of metal so that they would wobble, or "dance," when the wearer moved.

54. *HJJZS*, 6–7.

(6th of 14)

In the jade tower, under bright moonlight, always remembering him.	玉樓明月長相憶
Willow silk swirls about, listless in spring.	柳絲裊娜春無力
Beyond the gates, grasses are thick and rich.	門外草萋萋
While seeing you off, I hear the horse neigh.	送君聞馬嘶
On the painted gauze, gilt kingfishers;[55]	畫羅金翡翠
perfumed candles melt, turning to tears.[56]	香燭銷成淚
Flowers fall, the cuckoo calls—[57]	花落子規啼
at the green window, lost in a fading dream.[58]	綠窗殘夢迷

The setting and subject for both lyrics are the same: the boudoir of an abandoned woman, described in close detail. In Wen Tingyun's third "Pusa man" lyric, we find weak parallelism on the level of couplet lines, but a stronger parallel structure between the two stanzas: both stanzas contain an opening couplet that describes the woman's appearance followed by a couplet that tells us about the romantic situation. This parallel stanza structure helps us to integrate the two sudden sharp images of the woman into the whole scene. The opening line focuses on the woman's "stamen yellow" powdered forehead; the following line goes on to tell us that it was "last night's makeup," but after the caesura we seem to pull away from the woman's face—we are seeing her from behind the "window screen." Then we are given a bit of story—a late spring meeting and a quick parting—that helps us understand the source of the

---

55. The gilt kingfishers are sewn on the "painted gauze" of the woman's robes, just as the "golden partridges" were stitched on the gown of the woman in Wen's first "Pusa man."

56. In the Tang, candles were scented with perfumes whose aroma would be intensified when the candle was burned.

57. The cuckoo has many associations and names. In romantic poems, the reference is often to the belief that the cuckoo was a transformed betrayed lover (a king of Shu), who wept tears of blood. Its cry was associated with lovers' grievances. This reference to the cuckoo uses the term *zigui* 子規, which puns on the phrase "your return," *zi gui* 子歸. Other puns are found in the stanza: willow silk, *si* 絲, which puns on "longing," *si* 思, for the beloved; the grasses' thickness and richness, *qiqi* 萋萋, pointing to the *qi* 妻 of "wife."

58. *HJJZS*, 9.

woman's slept-in makeup. When the second stanza opens again with an even tighter close-up of the woman's hair ornaments, we can add that to our picture of this adorned demimondaine. And when, in the couplet that follows, she (or the poet) wonders, "Who knows the affairs of her heart?" we can integrate that line with our knowledge of her emotional state, intimated in the first stanza. The last line of the lyric turns outward to the natural scene: bright moonlight shines, illuminating the flowers that fill the branches. The artfulness of the image is difficult to miss: the flowers, long a clichéd figure for women, are illumined—like the woman in the moonlight—for our gaze, and the woman's heart—like the branch—is "filled" with emotion. The final line is not an answer to the question, but an indirect response that reveals Wen's mastery of the quatrain craft, in which the closing line often deflected the reader's attention to a resonant image.

The content of Wen's third "Pusa man" is very simple: a beautiful woman sits alone in her boudoir after a lover's meeting. The lyric challenges on the level of descriptive technique, as the "quick cuts" that Wen makes—from the woman's face, to the course of the romantic affair, back to the woman's hairpins, to her thoughts, and then to a scene outside her chamber—are difficult to put into a logical sequence. The chronology of the story is unsettled by the rapid shifts: "last night's makeup" seems to refer to the night before her lover left, but the second stanza seems to occur in a different moment, after her lover has been gone some time. The close description of the woman's face and elegant butterfly-ornamented hairpins tells us that it is probably spring and that she is well-off enough to afford expensive baubles, but it reveals nothing of her feelings. This lyric shows us Wen's expert use of the gaze. Above, I noted Ye Jiaying's use of the term "objective" to characterize Wen's description of the female figure. Paul Rouzer addresses Ye's use of this term and offers a different explanation of "objectivity": the removal of the poet's explicit presence from the scene he describes.[59] This technique is voyeuristic: it takes the reader inside a private, prohibited space—the woman's bedchamber—without suggesting

---

59. Rouzer, *Writing Another's Dream*, 21.

the presence of a male participant, or narrator. The technique creates the basic erotic appeal of Wen's poems on women in their boudoirs. The penultimate line of this lyric—"Who knows the affairs of her heart?"—is ironic, in that we understand her distress only partially. We, the listeners or readers, may guess at her feelings, and yet the beautiful surfaces themselves reveal little emotion. Wen and other *Huajian ji* poets were particularly sensitive to the ironies in this poetry that portrayed private experiences.

Wen Tingyun's sixth "Pusa man" lyric could be describing the same woman in the same condition as the third lyric, but it offers two possible points of view. In song lyrics, the common lack of pronouns in Chinese verse often combines with the use of voices in romantic poetry to produce a provocative ambiguity: many of the romantic lyrics in the *Huajian ji* can be read coherently in both first and third person. As we saw in Wei Zhuang's fifth "Pusa man" lyric, first-person voices are often signaled by the presence of transitive verbs without stated subjects, particularly those of emotion; but as in Wen's lyric, the point of view could shift from stanza to stanza without warning. The opening line of Wen's sixth "Pusa man" lyric is most plausibly read in third-person voice: "always remembering *him*," *chang xiang yi* 長相憶, or even "always remembering one another." The two observations on the natural world that follow—the listless willow silk that mirrors her tangled feelings, the lush spring grasses that flourish in contrast to her idle sorrow—could be read either as her perceptions or as the omniscient poet's description.[60] The last line of the first stanza, however, suggests a first-person voice in its use of the pronoun *jun*, "you": "While seeing you off, [I] hear the horse neigh" (*song jun wen ma si* 送君聞馬嘶). The use of the verb *wen*, "hear," further marks the line as a first-person statement of a sensory perception—only the speaker could experience the "hearing" described in the line. In this first stanza, Wen reveals a looser, more narrative approach to the scene of abandonment than we have seen, but he shifts again with the stanza break.

---

60. See Zhang's discussion of a range of readings of this line, *Huajian ci lunji*, 37–38.

The opening couplet of the next stanza returns to the "objective" observer's voice, as it describes the woman and her chamber. We find in this stanza a deliberate layering of stock images: the candle weeping tears (of sadness), the flowers falling (signifying the end of spring and betrayal of the woman), a cuckoo crying (signaling separated lovers). Wen makes no attempt to integrate the images, but instead piles them atop one another. The final line shows that the woman's only means of contact with her lover—traveling in dreams, through her *hun*-soul—has failed. She is "lost in a fading dream." The verb *mi* 迷 tells us not only that her dreaming soul has gone astray from its destination, but also that she is distracted by her dreams, allured, and even bewitched.[61] The modifier of "dream" that I have here translated "fading," *can* 殘, also suggests "fragments, remnants" of something that was once whole. These remnants of the dream of happiness have been prefigured in the stanza by the dripping candles and falling flowers, images of the evanescence of all things, and markers of the romance that has just ended. The juxtaposition of the dream in the last line and the constant remembering of the first line disorients the scene—the two moments seem to occur simultaneously, in the same space. After the woman's lover has left, her private space is regulated not by normal time and causality but by the time-distorting forces of memory (*yi*) and dream (*meng*) that frame the lyric in the opening and closing lines.

Wen Tingyun's layering of images that are themselves poignantly articulate seems to preclude the direct expression of emotion by his generally silent female subjects. Other *Huajian ji* poets, though they copied Wen's skilled imagery, seem to have been more interested in the mood of the poetic subject (whether observed or speaking), and in this respect, they resemble the other strong voice in their collection, Wei Zhuang. The emotions Wei expresses in his lyrics are not very complex, but they are plainly and directly stated:

---

61. For similar uses of the verb *mi* in connection with the dream-soul, see Wen's own second "He chuan," Xue Zhaoyun's sixth "Huanxi sha," and "Libie nan." See also Wei Zhuang's line from his fifth "Pusa man," translated above: "At this moment, one's heart is beguiled" 此時心轉迷.

"Pusa man" (3rd of 5)
Wei Zhuang

Today I yet recall the delights of Jiangnan—[62]	如今卻憶江南樂
back then I was a young man, in spring clothes so light.	當時年少春衫薄
Riding my horse, I'd lean from the bridge to see	騎馬倚斜橋
towers filled with red sleeves beckoning.[63]	滿樓紅袖招
The gilded kingfisher screen around me,	翠屏金屈曲
drunk, I'd enter the "flowery groves" to sleep.[64]	醉入花叢宿
Now when I see the flowering branches,	此度見花枝
this white-headed old man vows he'll never go home![65]	白頭誓不歸

Wei Zhuang's casual recitation of melancholy mixed with pleasurable remembrance is distinctive and a sharp contrast to Wen Tingyun's highly staged erotic scenes. The bluff, masculine voice that tells of romantic encounters in many of Wei Zhuang's lyrics has led critics to read them as autobiographical.[66] Whether or not they are confessions by the elderly Wei of his youthful adventures, the hearty style of the lyrics appealed to some *Huajian ji* poets, as did Wei's longing for bygone happiness. Although his influence is felt most strongly in the lyrics to "Huanxi sha" (as we will see in the next chapter), even in the Shu poets' "Pusa man" lyrics we find evidence of Wei Zhuang's strong male voice and *carpe diem* gaiety. His fondness for colloquial language is also a minor, but perceptible, influence in the Shu "Pusa man" lyrics, especially his hypotactic syntax filled with deictic particles and expressions not commonly

---

62. Here, Wei Zhuang refers to Jiangnan partly as a trope for "the south," a place of warm weather and an abundance of wine, women, and song. But Wei Zhuang also spent many years in the actual "south of the river" capital, and he often refers to his carefree days there.

63. The towers of red sleeves are multi-leveled buildings that held wineshops and songstresses. The women are waving for his business.

64. Wei Zhuang is recalling a visit to a singing-girl's chambers, which are decorated with ornate screens. The "flowery grove" is her inner room.

65. *HJJZS*, 74.

66. Ye, *Jialing lunci conggao*, 53–56, and Xia, *Tang Song ciren nianpu*, 30, are examples of scholars who take this view. Robin Yates counters it in *Washing Silk*, 45–47.

found in regulated verse. For example, the opening phrase of Wei's lyric, "Today I yet recall . . ." *ru jin que yi* 如今卻憶, is made noticeably wordy by the compound phrase *ru jin* and his use of *que*, an adverbial particle that emphasizes the contrariness of his "recalling" youthful experience. His use of other compound temporal markers such as "at that time," *dang shi* 當時, and "this time," *ci du* 此度 (translated in the lyric as "back then," and "now," respectively), also reveals Wei Zhuang's deep interest in the passage of time and the contrast between past and present.

Most of the Shu poets were, above all, skilled imitators and craftsmen, able to select elements from the broader tradition of romantic poetry, as well as from their "mentors" Wen and Wei, and to combine those elements coherently and evocatively. Two "Pusa man" lyrics by the poet Niu Qiao show Niu's mastery of both Wen Tingyun's descriptive style and Wei Zhuang's direct voices:[67]

"Pusa man" (1st of 7)
Niu Qiao

Her dancing skirt's fragrance warms the gilt-glittered phoenixes;[68]	舞裙香暖金泥鳳
swallows' chatter in the painted beams startles her from a fading dream.[69]	畫梁語燕驚殘夢
Beyond the gates, willow flowers fly—	門外柳花飛
the jade gallant still has not returned.[70]	玉郎猶未歸

---

67. Throughout this discussion, I will refer to Niu Qiao as a Shu poet, despite the fact that he attained the *jinshi* in the late Tang. Niu Qiao lived well into the Former Shu and held high office under Wang Jian, and I believe that his prominence at the Shu court would have been directly responsible for the circulation and preservation of his lyrics in Shu. Conversely, although the poets Zhang Bi and Xue Zhaoyun may have lived in Shu and held office in the Former Shu—speculations for which there is little evidence other than their inclusion in the *Huajian ji*—they do not seem to have been known as Shu courtiers. Therefore, I will refer to them as late Tang poets.

68. Like Wen Tingyun's expensively garbed women, this woman's "gilt-glittered phoenixes" are stitched on her skirt, which is being warmed by her exertion.

69. Swallows are common in romantic poetry, since they return in their spring migration, while lovers generally do not.

70. The "jade gallant" (*yulang*) refers to the aristocratic, anonymous lover.

Two sorrowful lines of red-powdered tears—	愁勻紅粉淚
eyebrows cut into spring mountains' bright green.	眉剪春山翠
Where is this place "Liaoyang"?	何處是遼陽
Behind brocade screens, the spring day stretches on.[71]	錦屏春晝長

Niu Qiao's first lyric is such a consummate imitation of Wen's style that it might easily be taken for Wen's own work.[72] The lyric opens with a couplet describing the woman, much like Wen Tingyun's third "Pusa man": the first line focuses tightly on the woman's clothing, erotically warmed and scented, and the second line backs away to see the chatter of swallows "startling" her from her "fading dream," *can meng* 殘夢 (the same phrase that Wen uses in his sixth "Pusa man"). The next line contrasts the fixed sadness of the interior with the green, dynamic lushness of the external world, via a view of the willow flowers flying from "beyond the gates," *men wai* 門外柳花飛 (the same line from Wen's sixth lyric: *"Beyond the gates, the grasses are thick and green"* 門外草萋萋). The last line of Niu's first stanza tells us the situation: the lover has not returned (the same line from Wen's third lyric: "he came for a moment, but then had to depart"). Structurally and lexically, Niu Qiao's first stanza is an exercise in copying Wen Tingyun's "Pusa man" style.

Niu's second stanza strongly resembles the second stanza of Wen's third "Pusa man" lyric: the opening couplet describes small details of the woman's appearance, the third line is a question spoken by (or for) the woman, and the closing line gives us a final, silent image. The parallels are clear if we juxtapose the two stanzas:

Niu Qiao's 2nd stanza "Pusa man" #1	Wen Tingyun's 2nd stanza "Pusa man" #3
Two sorrowful lines of red-powdered tears—	Kingfisher hairpins, with gilded stems—
eyebrows cut into spring mountains' bright green.	On the hairpins, pairs of butterflies dance.
Where is this place "Liaoyang"?	Who knows the affairs of her heart?

---

71. *HJJZS*, 141.

72. The Qing commentator Chen Tingzhuo, commenting on this lyric in his *Ci ze*, calls Niu an inferior version of Wen Tingyun (noted in *Tang Wudai ci jishi huiping*, 786).

| Behind brocade screens, the spring day stretches on | The moon is bright: flowers fill the branches. |

愁匀紅粉淚　　　翠釵金作股
眉剪春山翠　　　釵上蝶雙舞
何處是遼陽　　　心事竟誰知
錦屏春畫長　　　月明花滿枝

Niu even echoes Wen's fondness for symmetry, pairs, and doubled objects (we recall Wen's "pairs of butterflies" dancing) in his couplet on the woman's painted face: the woman's tears course down her powdered face in "two sorrowful lines," and her two eyebrows are arched, like mountains. The influence of Tang quatrain *taxis* is apparent in these two second stanzas: in each, the opening couplet (which avoids parallelism) serves to establish the scene and subject of the stanza; the rhetorical question serves as the "twist" or pivot of the stanza; the final line, with its single image, adds a delicate emotional overtone. (Either stanza, in fact, could stand alone as a quatrain, with a title along the lines of "Boudoir Lament.") In his closing lines, Wen Tingyun emphasizes the woman's isolation: "Who knows the affairs of her heart? / The moon is bright: flowers fill the branches." The woman's heart full of untold feeling is mirrored by the fullness of the flowered branches. In Niu Qiao's lyric, the closing line mirrors the woman's emotions in the same manner. Niu's woman asks the question, "Where is this place 'Liaoyang'?" which only seems to underline the spatial dislocation of the woman herself. Moreover, the reference to Liaoyang by a tenth-century poet is a deliberate anachronism, a reference to a world that no longer existed. It implies that the lover is on campaign in the far northeast—where Tang men traveled but Shu literati would not. Niu's use of "Liaoyang" in the line is thus a clear tribute to his Tang predecessors and perhaps even suggests the boundedness of Tang boudoir poetry, in which Niu participates but does not challenge. The final line, "Behind brocade screens, the spring day stretches on," adds a temporal dimension to the isolation of the boudoir. Where Wen's flowering branches revealed the woman's full heart, Niu's screens illustrate the lovers' separation, and his use of the verb *chang* 長, "stretches on," to describe the passage of the spring day, emphasizes not only the woman's boredom and sense of dragging time but also the distance that separates the two lovers.

In Niu Qiao's first lyric, we see that his imitation of Wen Tingyun is not limited to imitating the rhetorical structure of his stanzas but extends even to imitating couplet and line structure and includes outright borrowing of phrases. In Niu Qiao's second lyric to "Pusa man," however, he reveals his ability to imitate more than one master—in this case, Wei Zhuang.

"Pusa man" (2nd of 7)
Niu Qiao

When willow flowers have flown away, orioles' calls quicken;	柳花飛處鶯聲急
on a bright street amid spring hues, a fragrant carriage stands.	晴街春色香車立
The golden phoenix curtain opens—	金鳳小簾開
anger and regret appear in her gaze.	臉波和恨來
Tonight I try to envision her in a dream—	今宵求夢想
so hard to make it to the blue tower!	難到青樓上
I only get a sceneful of sorrow.	贏得一場愁
Under the duck-and-drake quilt, whose head lies next to hers?[73]	鴛衾誰並頭

This lyric implies a male observer in the fashion of Wei Zhuang by the second line: "on a bright street amid spring hues, a fragrant carriage stands." Women of the demimonde were commonly the inhabitants of such "perfumed carriages," and the people likely to be on the street watching them were young men. When, in the next two lines, we see the "golden phoenix curtain" part and reproaching glances emerge, we know that the observer is the rejecting or faithless male lover. The syntax of the second stanza is straightforward (with a time phrase to locate the action in contrast to the preceding stanza, and full verbs followed by direct objects), and the logic of the lines follows quite clearly: "Tonight I try to envision her in a dream—/ so hard to make it to the blue tower [where she is]." And in the following lines, we hear a voice echoing Wei's casualness

---

73. *HJJZS*, 142.

quite clearly: "I only get a sceneful of sorrow. / Under the duck-and-drake quilt, whose head lies next to hers?" The verb phrase "I only get," *yingde* 贏得, is a strong first-person construction and noticeably colloquial, as is the "sceneful," *yi chang* 一場, of sorrow that follows.[74] The colloquial tone continues in the closing line, which I have probably translated far too decorously—its tone is much closer to a wry "who's she sleeping with tonight?"

The talkative manner of Niu's second "Pusa man" lyric contrasts sharply with the delicate, melancholy air of the first, and the contrast can only have been deliberate on Niu's part, or perhaps on the part of the anthology's editors. In these two lyrics, it appears that Niu has adopted Wen's style for one view of romance—that from the woman's hermetic chamber—and taken Wei's style for another—that of the man on the outside, envisioning the woman from whom he is separated. Moreover, the arrangement of the two lyrics—they are the first and second of Niu's lyrics to "Pusa man" and presented consecutively in the text—offers the possibility of reading them as a sequence. The first lyric's description—"beyond the gates, willow flowers fly"—is extended in the second lyric, which opens with the phrase, "where the willow flowers fly." The "gilt-glittered phoenixes" of the woman's skirts in the first lyric are further echoed in the "golden phoenix" curtains of the carriage in the second. The reward of reading the lyrics in sequence, whether or not that was intended, is found in the satisfaction of hearing two

---

74. The careful use of colloquial constructions and so-called leading words, *lingzi* 令字, quickly became part of the *ci* poet's art: too much, and one's lyric would sound vulgar; too little, and one was merely writing a regulated verse to a song lyric pattern. The use of colloquialism and strongly marked first-person phrases also became part of the vexed issue of "authenticity" in the song lyric. Kang-i Sun Chang's chapter on the Northern Song poet Liu Yung discusses the development of *lingzi* (*Evolution of Chinese Tz'u Poetry*, 123–33), and Stephen Owen comments on the implications for the genre in his essay "Meaning the Words." With respect to Chang's discussion of Liu Yung's use of *lingzi*, in particular his use of "verbs of thought" (130) in the first position of a line, I would note that we will see the same usage in the lyrics of this and the following chapters. In other words, the feature of *lingzi*, considered critical to the *manci* form of the Northern Song, may have been important to the genre even in tenth-century *xiaoling*.

sides of a story usually told from a single point of view, a pleasure that other poets exploited even more fully.

Wen Tingyun's use of discrete lines of close and discontinuous description is perhaps the most obvious stylistic element in his lyrics and in the Shu lyrics that imitate him. But among the thematic elements of Wen Tingyun's style that appealed to other *Huajian ji* poets, we should note the poets' repeated use of liminal psychological states, especially those of dream and drunkenness. As I argued above, the stock romantic situation—the abandoned woman separated from her lover—is itself a liminal state between loving and complete rejection. Such a state is rife with anxieties and fears and always threatened by the loss of memory and the unreliability of dreams: if she cannot summon memories or travel in dream, then nothing remains of the romance. Dream-states, moreover, are themselves liminal phases between waking consciousness and complete unawareness, whether in sleep or death; as such, they echo the transitional state the lover is experiencing in separation. As we saw in Wen Tingyun's sixth "Pusa man" lyric, the dream is one device the *Huajian ji* poets used to portray the confusion of the real and unreal in the romantic realm.[75] Images of concealment and seclusion create a sense of the otherworldliness of the woman's chamber, they suggest that her dwelling exists outside of normal time or space. Mythical (or quasi-historical) and religious allusions do occur in song lyrics—in Chapter 6, I examine an entire subset of these—but they tend to be well within the range of an educated reader's basic knowledge. The lack of allusions to classical texts or historical events enhances the "otherworldliness" of the song lyric setting, but this practice also requires poets to find emotional resonances for their romantic scenes outside the rhetorical conventions of regulated verse. Exploiting the potential of the in-between states of dream, dusk, and separation is one method poets used; experi-

---

75. My argument that "dream" is a critical thematic element of the *Huajian ji* can be quantitatively substantiated through Aoyama Hiroshi's index to the *Huajian ji*, *Kakanshū sakuin*. The lexical item *meng* 夢 appears no fewer than 112 times in the *Huajian ji*, in 110 separate lyrics. Thus almost a quarter of the song lyrics in the anthology refer to a dream-journey or dream-state.

menting with changes of voice is another; yet another involves constructing elaborate parallels and echoes between the emotions of the poetic subject and the scene in which s/he was placed. Later in the song lyric tradition, an entire discourse on the use of the latter method in song lyrics emerged, revolving around the terms "feeling," *qing*, and "scene," *jing*. Since the *Huajian ji* poets stand at the beginning of the genre's history, it is unwise to use criteria laid down much later to assess their work. However, we should try to identify their contributions to this practice in the genre, particularly in the exploration of liminality and the construction of the settings of the romance.

Just as he uses small details of the boudoir or natural world to establish a mood, Wen Tingyun uses similar details to enhance the liminality of his lyrics.

"Pusa man" (8th of 14)
Wen Tingyun

Peony blossoms bid farewell, sounds of orioles cease;	牡丹花謝鶯聲歇
green willows fill the garden, moonlight in the courtyard.	綠楊滿院中庭月
Recalling him, her dreams are hard to form—[76]	相憶夢難成

---

76. This line—"Recalling him, her dreams are hard to form," *xiang yi meng nan cheng* 相憶夢難成—is an excellent test case for the question of whether or not poets were deliberately citing Wen Tingyun, intending a reference to Wen's lyric, or merely borrowing a phrase. There are four other instances of the three-character phrase "*meng nan cheng*" in the *Huajian ji*. In order of their appearance, they are: Xue Zhaoyun, "Sorrow at its height—dreams are hard to form" ("Xiao chongshan," *HJJZS*, 119); Mao Wenxi, "Dreams are hard to form" (a discrete line of "Yu meiren," 174); and two uses by Wei Chengban, "In sorrow and resentment, dreams are hard to form" ("Sheng chazi," 331), and "In longing and imagining, dreams are hard to form" ("Su zhongqing," 329). Among these, only the lines from Wei suggest a deliberate imitation of Wen Tingyun's line, since Wei contrasts first feeling and then longing to the dreams' being hard to realize, just as Wen Tingyun suggests that the act of remembering is what makes the dreams hard to realize. The three-character phrase is a useful one to "plug into" the last three places of a five- or seven-character line, due to its tonal structure (仄平平) and the level tone and easy rhyme category of its final word, *cheng*.

behind the window, the lamp
    gutters.[77]   背窗燈半明
Kingfisher filigreed "dimples" on her face—[78]   翠鈿金靨臉
lonely and still, the fragrant chambers are closed off.   寂寞香閨掩
For the one far away, tears crisscross her face—[79]   人遠淚闌杆
the swallows fly, as spring wanes again.[80]   燕飛春又殘

    The lyric is a study of liminal states: as the "farewell" of the peony blossoms, the green poplars, and the waning spring tell us, the season is poised between spring and summer. The orioles' falling silent suggests that they have left for the season, but it also suggests the arrival of evening or twilight. The woman is even denied the dream-journey of memory, since her dreams are "hard to form," *nan cheng* 難成; she is caught between her desire to recall him and her difficulty in doing so. Even her figure is half-lost in shadow, as the lamp shines only dimly. In both stanzas, her figure is poised between states, either between darkness and illumination or understanding (*ming* 明), or between the outside and inside worlds, at the balustrade. The conventional "spring comes again but he does not return" theme, signaled so strongly in the last line, is made more effective by Wen's choice of the moment of spring's departure, rather than its arrival, for his setting. The contrast between the passage of time in the outside world and the unchanging stillness of the boudoir enhances the sense of isolation and otherworldliness in the lyric.

    One Latter Shu poet, Mao Xizhen, imitates Wen Tingyun's close description without his abrupt shifts in focus and copies Wen's use of the natural world and its sights and sounds as means to evoke the plight of his female subject. With these borrowed descriptive techniques, Mao Xizhen also explores the theme of liminality in Wen's

---

    77. See Zhang, *Huajian ci lunji*, 47–48, for a discussion of the meaning of *bei* in this line.
    78. The gilt "dimples" were small ornaments pasted on the face to draw attention to certain features (such as one's snowy cheeks) or to cover up others.
    79. Li Yi notes the phrase *lei langan* also occurs in Bai Juyi's famous "Song of Eternal Regret," in a description of Yang Guifei's face when she appears to Tang Xuanzong's envoy in the other world. The image of a barred balustrade suggests tears running across the woman's face. *HJJZS*, 11.
    80. Ibid.

own manner.⁸¹ Two of Mao's three lyrics to "Pusa man" show him at his most deft:

"Pusa man" (1st of 3)
Mao Xizhen

Pear blossoms fill the courtyard, floating fragrant snow;	梨花滿院飄香雪
in the evening stillness of the high tower, wind chimes clatter.	高樓夜靜風箏咽
Waning moonlight shines on shades and curtains—	斜月照廉帷
though I recall you, I'm rarely with you in dreams.	憶君和夢稀
By the little window, the lamp's flicker put out,	小窗燈影背
swallows' chatter startles her sorrowful demeanor.	燕語驚愁態
Enclosed by screens, cut off from the flight of fragrance—	屏掩斷香飛
the traveling clouds have gone beyond the mountains.⁸²	行雲山外歸

Like most of the Shu poets, Mao Xizhen constructs a temporally and emotionally coherent scene: both stanzas are set in late spring, on a moonlit night, when the woman is up in her "high tower." None of the images Mao uses are new, but he selects them carefully, so that each image strengthens the preceding ones, and the whole creates a single mood. The sight of the white pear blossom "snow" that blows about the courtyard, signaling the waning of spring, is paralleled synesthetically by the sound of the wind chimes calling through the "evening stillness." The moonlight shining on the shades and curtains of the woman's chamber picks up the "whiteness" of the first line and suggests the image of a heavily curtained, perhaps darkened room. In this poorly lit chamber, we find that, despite the speaker's turn to memory, her dreams are infrequent. In the final line of the stanza, Mao brings together the passage of time and the wearing down of spring, memory, and dream.

---

81. Chen Tingzhuo remarked of this lyric that "in its implicit allure (*youyan* 幽艷), it achieves Wen Feiqing [Tingyun]'s intent." Cited in *Tang Wudai ci jishi huiping*, 889.

82. *HJJZS*, 369.

At the stanza break, Mao begins an interesting reversal of a common strategy in boudoir poetry: instead of penetrating the woman's chamber, he uses each line of the second stanza to move away from the woman whose voice we heard in the final line of the first stanza. In contrast to the external world filled with the whiteness of moonlight and the sounds of wind chimes, the woman inside the tower now is perceived only dimly, like the woman in Wen Tingyun's eighth "Pusa man" lyric, who sat in guttering lamplight. As in Niu Qiao's lyric, she is "startled" from her sadness by the chatter of swallows. (Niu, first "Pusa man," l. 2: "Swallows' chatter in the painted beams startles her from a fading dream.") The bright sounds of the swallows awaken the woman to her own loneliness; the third line shows the screens that cut her off from the "flight of fragrance," the flying pear blossoms described in the first stanza. The sense of isolation is doubled in this line: the woman is separated from her lover and sorrowful, and she is further concealed from sight (or seeing) by screens. The final line pulls back one more step: the "passing clouds," a trope for sexual intercourse or, in this case, the lover, "have gone beyond the mountains." This line alludes to the "passing clouds and rain," signifying dalliance with transcendents, and reinforces the image with the use of the phrase "beyond the mountains," suggesting inaccessibility and distance. The clouds go off, or "return," *gui* 歸, while the lover does not. Taken individually, these images are stock elements of romantic poetry; Mao's accomplishment lies in his linking each image to another and binding the whole around the contrast of the open, active external scene and the dark, static scene of the woman's chamber. This contrast of the activity of the natural world and the stasis of the interior realm is one that the *Huajian ji* poets explored frequently. Implicit in the dynamic/static opposition is the sense that although the seasons are passing in their normal course outside, time has stopped in the boudoir. The woman is fixed between the two worlds, able to perceive the liveliness outside and yet unable to engage it.

In his third "Pusa man" lyric, Mao uses the same juxtaposition of exterior and interior worlds to depict the woman's liminal state.

"Pusa man" (3rd of 3)
Mao Xizhen

Heaven-held fragments of blue fuse into spring colors;	天含殘碧融春色
of the faithless nobleman, there's no news.	五陵薄幸無消息
Passing the days hidden behind red doors—	盡日掩朱門
separation's sorrow secretly breaks her spirit.	離愁暗斷魂
Orioles call from the warmth of blossoming trees;	鶯啼芳樹暖
swallows skim the winding pond's brimming waters.	燕拂回塘滿
Still and silent, she faces the screen mountains,	寂寞對屏山
longing for him in a drunken dream.[83]	相思醉夢間

Mao's opening couplet gives us a provocative contrast between the first, highly controlled line, "Heaven-held fragments of blue fuse into spring colors," and his looser, almost matter-of-fact second line, "of the faithless nobleman, there's no news." With this couplet, Mao establishes the tension between exterior and interior that governs this lyric and others. The exterior is the warm, active, and colorful spring scene, representing vitality; the interior holds the still, quiet, and sorrowful woman. The beauty of the natural scene outside is countered by the line that introduces the interior, where the woman is "passing the days hidden behind red doors." Not only is she "hidden," *yan* 掩, but her spirit is broken, *duan* 斷. "Severing the soul," *duan hun* 斷魂, refers to the belief that the *hun*-soul was able to travel in dreams to visit loved ones; this line suggests that even the avenue of contact offered by the dream is cut off. The phrase *duanchang* 斷腸, which is often translated "heartbreak" or "heartache" (given the awkwardness of "guts" or "bowels" in English), is more common in the *Huajian ji*, but the use of *duan hun* (and *hun duan*) seems to be preferred by some poets because of the association of dream-travel.[84]

---

83. Ibid., 370.

84. There are 25 uses of *duan chang* and its variations, such as *chang duan*, in the collection. There are 5 uses of *duan hun*, another 11 instances of *hun duan* or *meng hun duan*, and many more of dreams, *meng*, alone being cut off, which implies the dream-travel of the soul. The clearest example of this among the five uses of *duan*

The second stanza structures the contrasts of the first stanza differently: the opening parallel couplet returns to the natural world, and the closing couplet focuses again on the abandoned woman. Like the opening line of the first stanza, the natural images of the second stanza suggest burgeoning life: orioles calling from the warmth of trees in full blossom, the winding pond full with spring rains. To close, Mao returns to the hidden woman, who is now facing the barrier of the screens, whose mountains, like the real mountains separating her from her lover, enclose her. The last line returns to the hazy, threshold state between dream and consciousness seen in other lyrics, but this time, the woman uses wine as a means to escape into a reverie of "longing for him." Since Mao has earlier suggested that she is unable to send her *hun*-soul to meet him, he seems to say here that wine-induced dreams are all she has left. The woman Mao Xizhen describes, like the woman of Wen Tingyun's eighth "Pusa man" lyric—whose dreams were "hard to realize"—is desperate to remember the fading romance. Wine offers an avenue of fantasy that is otherwise cut off.

Wen Tingyun's lyrics dwell on what seem to be the rich interiors associated with courtesans; his women's chambers are filled with elegant fabrics, jewelry, scented candles, incense, and other baubles. Although the Shu poets depict the same kinds of objects, their gaze is turned as much outward as inward. For Wen Tingyun, the details of a woman's dress are mute: they are striking and memorable images, but they reveal little of the woman's emotional state unless they are "tearstained" or otherwise marked. Later *Huajian ji* poets emulate Wen's attention to feminine finery, particularly when it can be used to erotic effect, but when they turn to the natural world—which they do more often than does Wen—they have a clear preference for telling detail. We saw in Mao Xizhen's lyrics his attention to the repetition of related natural images, such as the whiteness of the pear blossoms and moonlight, or the chatter and movement of birds as a contrast to interior stillness. At its weakest, this technique is mere pathetic fallacy: rain "weeps" and branches

---

hun in the *Huajian ji* is in Sun Guangxian's "He manzi": "With my soul cut off [from you], where shall we find one another?" 斷魂何處相尋. *HJJZS*, 310.

are "severed" or "broken off," like lovers' ties. At its most subtle, however, the technique creates a mood synesthetically, before any word of emotion—or, indeed, any human figure—is introduced. In most cases, the poets' goal was to overdetermine the mood of a lyric, but the line between labored, obvious overdetermination and subtle, integrated overdetermination could be very fine.

An example of the subtler form can be found in the first stanza of the Shu poet Li Xun's first "Pusa man" lyric:

"Pusa man" (1st of 3)
Li Xun

A breeze rises on the winding pond, ripples grow fine;	回塘風起波紋細
amid thorny paulownia blossoms, the gates slant shut.	刺桐花裏門斜閉
Fading sunlight shines on leveled rushes—	殘日照平蕪
pair on pair of flying partridges.	雙雙飛鷓鴣
Where goes that traveler beneath the departing sail?	征帆何處客
They saw one another, and then separated.	相見還相隔
Not speaking, about to melt in sorrow—	不語欲魂銷
in her gaze, misty waters recede into the distance.[85]	望中煙水遙

The "winding pool" of Li Xun's opening line is the same as the one on which the swallows played in Mao Xizhen's lyric; its name, *huitang* 回塘, introduces the idea of returning into the opening line of this lyric about parting. In this line, Li Xun seems to be echoing the second line of Wen Tingyun's fourth "Pusa man" lyric. Li Xun writes: "Wind rises on the catchpool, ripples growing fine" 回塘風起波紋細; compare Wen: "Ripples on the water rise lightly on the azure of the spring pond" 水紋細起春池碧. But in Wen Tingyun's lyric, it is unclear whether the line refers to a real pond or to a scene embroidered—like the water birds he describes in the lyric's opening line—on the woman's clothes. As subsequent lines reveal, Li Xun's scene is part of the natural world, not a painted or stitched panorama. The "thorny paulownia" trees are often found in parting

---

85. Ibid., 388.

poems, since they are equipped with sharp thorns, and they bloom in autumn, the season most associated with partings. Amid these trees that warn us of an imminent separation, we see the gates "slant shut"; the "fading sunlight" of the following line suggests that they are closing for the evening, but perhaps they also are closing behind a departing traveler. The wind rises, the gates shut, the sun sets, and in the last line of the first stanza, we see "pair on pair of flying partridges" (雙雙飛鷓鴣). The pairs, of course, remind the reader of the human "pair" that is about to be separated. But this line is also perhaps Li Xun's most clever imitation of Wen Tingyun. In Wen Tingyun's first "Pusa man" lyric, the final line gave us "pair on pair of *golden* partridges" (雙雙金鷓鴣) stitched on the woman's gown. In his lyric, Li Xun has picked up Wen's artificial object, itself taken from nature, and turned it back into a natural object. Considered alone, Li Xun's line is not necessarily more effective than Wen's, but his clever adaptation of Wen's line must have impressed his fellow poets and the *Huajian ji* compilers.

In the second stanza, Li Xun uses the natural scene to mirror the woman's desires: just as she is about to "melt in sorrow," *hun xiao* 魂銷 (a phrase used often in the *Huajian ji* to describe a moment of emotional crisis, such as ultimate melancholy or, occasionally, ultimate happiness in memory), the "misty waters" she is gazing into seem to dissipate, as they recede into the distance. In these lines, Li Xun is playing with the potential of the verb *xiao* to describe the melting or dissipation of ephemeral substances (fragrance, *xiang* 香, can also evaporate, *xiao* 銷) as well as an intense emotional state. The motions of departure, signaled by the elements of the first stanza, are carried out in the second: the sail departs, and her gaze follows it out until it can no longer be seen. The liminal features of the lyric are different than those of the boudoir lyrics seen above: here, the woman stands poised, at sunset, on the edge of a river or bank instead of at her bedroom window. The emphasis in the second stanza is different also: instead of gazing at the woman, we see (or hear) what *she* is seeing: "Where goes that traveler beneath the departing sail? / They see one another, yet still are separated." The lyric ends as her gaze fails her: "In her gaze, misty waters recede into the distance."

Kinds of Qing: Eroticism and Carpe Diem Sentiments in "Pusa man"

As we see in the lyrics of Wen and his imitators, liminality is one of the most important themes of the anthology as a whole, and in the subset of the "Pusa man" lyrics more specifically; it underlies the romantic story of the lyrics and is also articulated in spatial and temporal images throughout the collection. From one perspective, the liminal space of the boudoir confines and isolates the abandoned woman; but from another perspective, this bounded, private space also seems to allow some emotional and sexual license. The poets of the collection exploit this license in different ways. One kind of license is a voyeuristic and sometimes quite explicit eroticism, very present in certain "Pusa man" lyrics, particularly those by Wen Tingyun; another is an obsession with comparing the past and present moments, a favorite topic of Wei Zhuang, which appears even more frequently in the "Huanxi sha" lyrics examined in the next chapter. The eroticism of the *Huajian ji* might be compared to the visible spectrum, where violet would be the "coolest," or least salacious, representation of a woman's sensual appeal, and red the "hottest," most explicit representation of a sexual encounter. Most of the *Huajian ji* lyrics fall in the yellow-green part of the spectrum—showing us only glimpses of skin or hinting at well-spent nights—but a few Shu poets seem to have specialized in the red-hot version of romantic lyrics. Wen Tingyun, despite his obsession with minute, erotic details of a woman's dress and appearance (an obsession that certainly influenced later *Huajian ji* poets), did not portray sexual encounters in his lyrics. As we have seen, Wen Tingyun's eroticism is static and descriptive—it is the voyeur's pleasure in the unexpected, brief exposure of flushed skin or tumbled hair. Such as it is, the "action" that occurs in his lyrics is usually as slight as a woman stepping onto a balcony to gaze outward.

On the whole, the Shu poets depicted events that involved considerably more than merely leaning from a window. The handful of poets who portrayed sexual encounters used this more narrative approach quite skillfully, as these two lyrics by the Former Shu poet Wei Chengban demonstrate:

"Pusa man" (1st of 2)
Wei Chengban

Her gauzy lapels are thin and fine, "autumn waves" her eyes;	羅裾薄薄秋波染
on her brow are painted two dots of mountain.	眉間畫得山兩點[86]
Seeing one another on the banquet mats,	相見綺筵時
they secretly know their share deep passion.	深情暗共知
Kingfisher feathers shake in her clouds of hair;	翠翹雲鬢動
demurely, she strums the "Golden Phoenix."[87]	斂態彈金鳳
After the party, they enter the orchid chamber—	宴罷入蘭房
she invites him to unclasp her girdle-pendants.[88]	邀人解佩璫

(2nd of 2)

On her gauzy robes, gilt glitters dimly—	羅衣隱約金泥畫
one song on the tortoiseshell mats suits the autumn night.	玳筵一曲當秋夜
Her voice quavers as he looks her over—	聲顫覷人嬌
her clouds of hair entwined with kingfisher feathers.	雲鬟裊翠翹
When the wine has gone to her head, her flushed jade-face softens;	酒醺紅玉軟
in the darkness of her brows, "autumn mountains" seem distant.	眉翠秋山遠
Behind embroidered hangings, musky smoke thickens—	繡幌麝煙沉
who can know these two hearts?[89]	誰人知兩心

In both lyrics, Wei Chengban uses close description to give us the same kind of detail that interests Wen Tingyun—the look and feel of the woman's robes ("gauzy" robes revealing both the figure and possibly the skin of the woman), the makeup on her face, and the

---

86. Li Yi notes that *de* 得 is a variant character in this line, but he gives *shi* 時 in his text. I take *de* to be correct, given that *shi* is used again in the next line. Ibid., 321.

87. The "Golden Phoenix" refers to a stringed instrument such as the *pipa*, commonly played by women entertainers.

88. As I explain below, the line is unclear as to whether she invites him, or he invites her, to "loosen girdle-pendants." I have chosen the female lover as the "inviter," since it is her actions and appearance that we have observed up to this point. *HJJZS*, 321.

89. Ibid., 322.

color of her skin. These details are as erotic in Wei's lyrics as they are in Wen's. But Wei Chengban goes beyond Wen in portraying the progress of the romantic game: Wei gives us not only the first glimpse and the flirtation but also the subsequent encounter. Using the same contrasts of openness and concealment that other poets use in portraying the abandoned woman, he heightens his audience's sense of having entered a truly private scene. Instead of contrasting the external, natural world and the interior, artificial world of the boudoir, however, he juxtaposes the public meeting and the private rendezvous in the two stanzas of both lyrics. We—Wei Chengban's audience, whether listeners or readers—are made party to the exchange of desire and drawn into the action.

In the first stanza of the first lyric, the woman is displayed for other men and for us. Wei Chengban contrasts the openness of the woman's performance with the secret knowledge the man and the woman have of each other's desire (but we, of course, are in on the secret). The second stanza gives us another look at the woman performing for the secretly chosen partner, and then takes us into the "orchid chamber" of the encounter. Most poets would turn away at this point, but Wei Chengban adds a final titillating detail of someone "inviting" someone else to "loosen girdle-pendants," or get undressed. No matter which person is doing the inviting (the wording seems deliberately ambiguous: *yao ren* 邀人), the explicitness of the gesture is startling when read against other poets' avoidance of the sexual encounter. The second lyric seems to be a replay of the same scene from another angle. In this lyric, the display of the woman's beauty and talent are made even more obvious, as her potential partner looks her over while she is singing, making her voice quaver in nervousness or anticipation. But by the second stanza, we see that the wine she has drunk at the party has relaxed her, flushing her face and smudging her brows, making them seem "distant." Wei then veils the scene in the smoke of musk incense, as if to give the lovers their privacy. But the closing couplet cleverly relocates the lyric in the context of our enjoyment of the couple's "performance" and seems to introduce a heretofore hidden narrator. Wei asks, "who can know these two hearts?" Unlike rhetorical questions that can be understood as the thoughts of the subject (as in

Niu Qiao's first "Pusa man": "Where is this place 'Liaoyang'?"), this question, by pointedly using "two hearts," is clearly directed outward to the listening or reading audience. The questioner, who has attentively narrated the progress of the encounter, concludes by revealing us to be voyeurs like himself.

The eroticism of the *Huajian ji*'s song lyrics consistently exploits the ironic potential of performed literature: while penetrating private, secluded spaces, the poets stage the desirable woman for our amusement. This exploitation of the performance of song lyrics is spatial. If we were to stop and recall the performance contexts for these lyrics, we would realize that the lines on murky, curtained, smoke-enshrouded chambers were often sung in sunlit gardens and brightly lit court halls, in front of noisy crowds of literate and critical auditors. Like erotic *yuefu* in the "palace style," song lyrics foregrounded the contrast between the private worlds they depicted and the public venues in which they were performed. *Huajian ji* song lyric poets also exploited the temporal ironies of performed literature by frequently drawing attention to the "presentness" of the moment in comparison to the vanished past. In its more complex manifestations, this juxtaposition plays out for the listening or reading audience the poetic subjects' obsessive retelling of past events.

At its simplest, the strategy of highlighting the present moment by sighing over the past is nothing more than the *carpe diem* refrain found in the oldest poetry. Wei Zhuang's fourth "Pusa man" is perhaps the most famous among early song lyrics:

"Pusa man" (4th of 5)
Wei Zhuang

"I urge you, tonight we must drink deeply, while we're in our cups, let's not speak of tomorrow!"	勸君今夜須沉醉 樽前莫話明朝事
"I greatly value your sentiments, my host—the wine is deep in our cups, and my feelings are deep as well!"	珍重主人心 酒深情亦深
"I'm only sorry that the spring night is fleeting—don't complain that the golden cups are too full!	須愁春漏短 莫訴金杯滿

Let's take our wine and laugh away—
how long does life last anyway?"[90]

遇酒且呵呵
人生能幾何

This lyric gives us Wei Zhuang at his most colloquial, in the language of friends at a drinking party. The simple closing line—"how long does life last anyway?"—is perhaps the most conventional statement of Chinese party songs. But Wei Zhuang seems to be playing with style here, as if he were imitating the rough and colloquial language of popular song. The lyric reads like a pose, a role that Wei Zhuang is assuming for a boisterous moment. If so, it was a role that other *Huajian ji* poets could also play.

Niu Qiao puts an erotic twist on the camaraderie of *carpe diem* drinking poems, blending Wen Tingyun's detailed description and Wei Zhuang's colloquial sentiment in the last of his seven "Pusa man" lyrics:

"Pusa man" (7th of 7)
Niu Qiao

In the jade tower, on a cool mat of duck-and-drake brocade,	玉樓冰簟鴛鴦錦
her powder blends with fragrant sweat, flowing on the mountain pillow.	粉融香汗流山枕
Beyond the curtains, the sound of well-pulleys—	簾外轆轤聲
her frowns hide laughing surprise.	斂眉含笑驚
Willow-shadowed mists are thick, obscuring;	柳陰煙漠漠
from her drooping curls cicada hairpins fall.	低鬢蟬釵落
"Even if I'm abandoned forever,	須作一生拌
I'll make your pleasure today complete!"[91]	盡君今日歡

The first stanza of Niu's lyric imitates Wen Tingyun's fragmented, shifting details of the boudoir and the woman inside it. The opening line also teases the reader by setting up one romantic scenario and then quickly shifting to another: at first, we see a "cool mat," an image that first suggests that the woman is alone, but then we see her "fragrant sweat" dissolving onto her pillow, which tells us that she is rather busy. The "sound of well-pulleys" outside, ap-

---

90. Ibid., 75.
91. Ibid., 145.

parently the cause of the woman's "laughing surprise," tells us that we are in an *alba*, a morning lovers' song and, moreover, that we are eavesdropping on the lovers in action.

As Wen Tingyun often does, Niu Qiao uses the change in stanzas to focus on another scene in the second stanza. The descriptive binome *momo* 漠漠, "thick, obscuring," modifying the "willow-shadowed mists," reinforces the sense of early morning from the first stanza. But these "thick, obscuring" mists, like the many screens and curtains in other "Pusa man" lyrics (and throughout the collection), heighten the isolation of the woman in the second line, though the two lines are not syntactically parallel. Just as the willows' shadow hides the boudoir, the woman's hair obscures her face. More importantly, however, her falling curls and hairpins, which were often a sign of a woman's lonely indolence, here indicate the dishevelment from a sexual encounter. The closing lines of the lyric inject a new voice and style in startling contrast to the previous lines. The woman tells her man (whom we now are certain is present): "Even if I'm abandoned forever, / I'll make your pleasure today complete!" Her words are startling in two ways: first, she uses a style of speech that seems rough against the smooth, delicate description that preceded her words. The plain verb *zuo* 作 and the phrase *yisheng* 一生, "a lifetime," as a measure word for abandonment—similar to *yichang chou* ("a sceneful of sorrow"), in his second "Pusa man"—heighten the effect of spoken language. Like Wei Zhuang, Niu Qiao seems to understand the "punch" of vernacular in important moments in lyrics—here, the direct speech placed in the closing lines casts the usually silent, decorative, and decorous female subject in a new light. The woman's promise to her lover, "I'll make your pleasure complete!" is rather different from Wei Zhuang's depiction of a host urging his guest to drink. In Niu's lyric, we have a woman promising to fulfill, or exhaust, *jin* 盡, her lover's pleasure, *huan* 歡, a word that in this context connotes sexual as well as emotional pleasure.[92] In contrast to Wei Zhuang's lyric of

---

92. We should note that Niu Qiao does not escape condemnation by later critics for this use of colloquial (some say vulgar) language and frank invitation: the Qing commentator Wang Shizhen labeled it "excessively familiar and intimate." Ibid.,

carpe diem camaraderie—in which both host and guest can enjoy themselves in the face of the question "how long does life last anyway?"—Niu's female speaker promises her guest pleasure while confronting her own, sadder fate. The eroticism of this lyric's *carpe diem* sentiment also exposes the imbalance of power in the lovers' encounter.

In Niu Qiao's lyric, we can see that he has selectively imitated elements of both Wen Tingyun's and Wei Zhuang's styles, and yet he has exceeded Wen in eroticism and surpassed Wei in frank speaking. As we saw in his other "Pusa man" lyrics, Niu Qiao was a careful student of Wen Tingyun's descriptive technique, and he uses it here to good effect. But the sense of erotic, almost vulgar excess is palpable, and even seems deliberate. It may have been a part of the game of imitation and borrowing the Shu poets seem to have enjoyed: in other words, by emulating (*xue* 學) a predecessor, one could demonstrate one's mastery of the earlier style by pushing it to its extreme. For some poets, this degree of imitation of Wen Tingyun's style borders on fetishization. Niu Qiao's stanza shifts, Li Xun's use of Wen Tingyun's pairs of partridges, and Wei Chengban's narrow focus on the robes and faces of his female subjects all seem alike in this regard: examples of imitating Wen's rhetorical structures (some of which themselves derive from quatrain aesthetics), descriptive techniques, and word choice, elements that are easy to isolate and reproduce. However, themes or motifs can be studied and reiterated to excess as well; the "dream" motif examined in this chapter may be another example of this kind of excessive imitation. The "Pusa man" lyrics offer both showy, self-conscious imitation of Wen and Wei—Niu Qiao being the most skilled in this art—and more integrated, subtler study of other poets' styles, such as we find in Mao Xizhen's work. The fact that both kinds of imitation are found in the anthology suggests that the Shu editors' notion of skillful imitation (*ni* 擬) was broad enough to admit both subtle and more obvious varieties of artifice (*qiao* 巧).

146, n4. Other readers have filiated the closing lines of this lyric to Wei Zhuang, though not to his "Pusa man" lyrics (see *Tang Wudai ci jishi huiping*, 788–89).

The central role of imitation in the *Huajian ji* should also be placed in the larger context of the representation of romance in poetry, and the centrality of craft in that tradition. As I argued earlier, romantic poetry in the Tang and romantic lyrics in Shu were written within the confines of centuries-old conventions and tropes. The plot of the romantic story—boy meets girl, boy leaves girl, girl is sad—rarely changed, but the poets' construction of the scenes or episodes of the romance did. Furthermore, as romance moved from the genre of *shi* to that of song lyrics, it took on a new guise. Ouyang Jiong's proud championing of artifice as the Shu poets' foremost aesthetic interest relocates poetic value from the expression of personal experience (*yan zhi* 言志) to the construction of fictional, anonymous experience. On these grounds, imitation reveals the poets' imaginative formulation of an aesthetics of romantic song lyrics. The *Huajian ji* poets by their practice, and Ouyang Jiong through his preface, valorize imitation as a constitutive element of their genre. The fact that Ouyang's argument was almost indefensible in the terms of the orthodox literary tradition does not diminish his contribution to the genre or to literary history.

In this chapter, we have seen the ways in which the *Huajian ji* poets identified and copied their late Tang predecessors in their lyrics and used selective imitation to build their own romantic vignettes. At various moments, I have called attention to the contrast between Wen Tingyun's more lyric and Wei Zhuang's more narrative song lyrics, and I have suggested that the Shu poets explored a middle ground between the two poles. As I will demonstrate in other tune title sets, the choice for Shu poets was not so much between individual poetic models as between poetic styles and registers. In the next chapter, I continue my study of imitation, particularly thematic imitation, but I argue that the contrast between Wen and Wei is perhaps overread, and that they and the Shu poets who followed them had greater breadth than readers have acknowledged. Through their borrowing and adaptation of Tang models, Shu poets blended modal imagery with varying subjectivities to create an emotional coherence for their song lyrics. In developing their own style, the Shu poets did not abandon the conventions of the tradition or the examples of their masters, but many aimed for a more harmonious blend of the disparate elements. And, as we will see in other lyrics, they explored the possibilities of sequences, responses, and clever imitation not only of their predecessors but of one another.

FIVE

Gender in the Huajian ji *Song Lyrics*

Style, Subject, and Voice

In the "Pusa man" lyrics, we saw the great influence that Wen Tingyun and, to a lesser degree, Wei Zhuang exercised on later *Huajian ji* poets. Imitation and borrowing were an essential component of the Shu poets' art of writing song lyrics; quotation and imitation of styles functioned as both homage and self-promotion. Presumably any popular musician could write a catchy lyric within the broad and well-known conventions of love songs, but probably only a poet would want to write lyrics that imitated various Tang poets' styles or that mixed poetic and vernacular language. In the *Huajian ji*, Shu poets copied their predecessors' styles (*ti* 體)—their techniques, phrases, and vocabulary. Given the conventions of anonymity and fictionality proposed by the *Huajian ji* (writing in a voice or voices patently not one's own), its poets' interest in imitation is unsurprising. Paul Rouzer has called Wen Tingyun's poetic style a "poetry of surfaces," a phrase that suggests not only Wen's love of close description but also his reluctance to probe deeper than the beautiful surfaces he depicted so skillfully. In this poetic style, whether practiced by Wen or one of his imitators, depth was a trompe l'oeil, created by layer on layer (*chong die* 重疊) of alluring objects and simple emotions. The range of imitation and borrowing that we saw in the "Pusa man" lyrics demonstrates the Shu poets' fondness for Wen and Wei and also their technical skills, their grasp of the songwriting craft as they conceived it. And yet, as we saw in a number of the later poets' "Pusa man" lyrics, later poets imitated selectively. Shu poets like Li Xun and Ouyang Jiong, in quite different ways, worked toward greater narrative and modal coherence, generally eschewing Wen's most discontinuous description and Wei's most colloquial speech. This artful imitation by later *Huajian ji* poets reveals the self-conscious literariness of Shu song lyrics and is one important sign of the appearance of a true *genre* sensibility.[1]

The "Pusa man" lyrics of Chapter 4 helped us distinguish imitation from convention; the lyrics to "Jiu quanzi" and "Huanxi sha" in this chapter allow us to broaden our understanding of the collection's poetics by considering the use of voice and point of view. In examining the "Pusa man" lyrics that included first-person speakers, I suggested that the Shu poets were imitating Wei Zhuang's more colloquial style and preference for direct voices. However, as I noted at the beginning of Chapter 4, we cannot ascribe the Shu poets' use of first-person voice solely to imitation of Wei Zhuang. As even a cursory reading of anonymous medieval

---

1. However, we should note that the imitation in the *HJJ* is not the kind of emulation or imitation of Tang poets that poets of the Song and Ming sometimes practiced. Later poets read Tang poetry as the work of identifiable poetic personalities: in later readers' eyes, the Tang poets' aims, or intentions, *zhi*, were manifest in their work. In order to write in Du Fu's voice, therefore, one had to fully comprehend Du Fu's responses to the circumstances he encountered. Northern Song and later "imitation" of Tang poets (there does not seem to be an English word that adequately matches the Chinese conception), like any literary imitation, developed from a specific reading and interpretive practice, but it was not the practice of the *HJJ* song lyric poets. For a discussion of some Northern Song perspectives on this problem, see Sargent, "Can Latecomers Get There First? Sung Poets and T'ang Poetry."

yuefu reveals, the use of direct speech was a longstanding practice in poetry and songs about romance. In the "Pusa man" lyrics, Wei Zhuang's looser syntax and strong voices served as a colloquial counterbalance to Wen Tingyun's denser, more mannered style, and it was apparent that certain Shu poets understood well the useful lightness of Wei's style. In the following analysis of two more tune title sets, lyrics to the tunes "Jiu quanzi" 酒泉子 (Wine springs) and "Huanxi sha" 浣溪沙 (Sands of [silk-]washing streams), I argue that despite some of their obvious differences, Wen and Wei are not as stylistically opposed as others have suggested. Furthermore, for them and for the *Huajian ji* poets that succeeded them, the style of a lyric was determined in great part by the use of point of view. In the "Jiu quanzi" and "Huanxi sha" lyrics by other poets, the distinct stylistic influences of Wen and Wei are still visible, but they are not as prominent as in "Pusa man." We find the later poets working once again in a range between the two poets and exploring areas that Wen and Wei did not. Although I would be hesitant to call the later poets' stylistic synthesis an innovation, their careful use of different voices in romantic song lyrics marks an important step away from the lyrics of the Tang poets that preceded them.

With respect to point of view, the lyrics of the *Huajian ji* fall roughly into two groups: those that use an anonymous third-person observer to describe a female subject (a few of which switch to a first-person female voice for a portion of the lyric), and those that use a male first-person speaker. The former is by far the largest group, but the second group exerts an important and distinctive influence in the anthology. There are, however, also two interesting smaller groups of lyrics: one comprised of lyrics that can be read or translated persuasively from either a third- or a first-person point of view, and another, smaller set of lyrics written in a strong first-person voice of uncertain gender. In these two smaller groups of lyrics, the ambiguity of perspective or voice surely stems from the performance needs of song lyrics; this ambiguity would allow either kind of song to be performed plausibly by either male or female singers. This explanation, however, does not diminish the literary impact of this use of voice, which was the emergence of a gender-neutral voice in which to express romantic desire and sorrow.² In the lyrics of this chapter, we will see a few occasions in which poets seem deliberately to suppress gender cues in order to create such a voice. Throughout, I note the pressures that the reading traditions of medieval poetry place on these lyrics, pushing them toward a male or female voice.

The most useful tools in determining point of view are the conventions of medieval romantic verse and the lexical or syntactic indications of voice. The conventions of Southern Dynasties palace-style poetry and Tang boudoir verse dictate that descriptions of women's faces or clothing are perceived from the vantage point of an anonymous third-person observer, not from a male viewer implicated in the scene. Although the observer is anonymous and thus not explicitly gendered by the language of such poems, these descriptions of the captive boudoir woman are plainly voyeuristic. As Grace Fong has noted of the earlier medieval "palace-style" version of this perspective, "in this poetry, the female figure's surface is valorized while her interiority, when not left opaque, is colonized as the exclusive domain of love and longing." What Fong calls the "poetic paradigm of a female image subordinated to the gaze and the play of desire" stands behind many of the *Huajian ji* lyrics, but it is not the only view of the woman, or representation of desire, available to its poets.³ First-person voices, whether male or female, tend to announce themselves most commonly in word choice and syntax. For example, transitive verbs that refer to emotions or perceptions (such as "remember," *yi* 憶, "imagine," *xiang* 想, or "forget," *wang* 忘), placed at the beginning of a syntactic unit, strongly suggest first-person speakers. Such lines often serve as the frames for descriptive or narrative passages that follow, and they shape the

---

2. Grace Fong's work on gendered voices in song lyrics has been especially useful for this chapter. See "Engendering the Lyric: Her Image in Voice and Song," in Yu, ed., *Voices*; "Inscribing Desire: Zhu Yizun's Love Lyrics in *Jingzhiju qinqu*"; and "Persona and Mask in the Song Lyric." A recent study of voice in early song lyrics also explores the potential of the indeterminate persona in the genre, and considers from different perspectives some of the same issues I discuss in this chapter: see Samei, *Gendered Persona and Poetic Voice: The Abandoned Woman in Early Chinese Song Lyrics*.

3. Fong, "Engendering the Lyric," 114.

perception of what appears within the frame. Just as the reader assumed that the subjectivity of the observed, silent woman was opaque—that her face and appearance were the only avenues to her interior state—the reader's (or listener's) assumption in a poem or song that "remembers" is that the anonymous speaker is voicing an unmediated account of his or her experience.

As we have seen in the "Pusa man" set and will see again in some of the "Jiu quanzi" and "Huanxi sha" lyrics, the *Huajian ji*'s reputation as "richly beautiful" is fully realized in the lyrics that describe female subjects. The "Pusa man" lyrics depict numerous flowers, perfumes, mists, smoke, blankets (both warm and sometimes cool), and dimly lit interiors. Many of these objects along with some of the themes explored in "Pusa man" lyrics—dream-states, liminal moments and spaces, the passage of time—recur in the "Huanxi sha" set also. In the majority of these lyrics, the female subject is silent; her inner state is revealed by her appearance and by the natural and artificial objects that surround her. This dynamic suggests that the poetic value behind this representation of the female subject is that of *hanxu* 含蓄, or "reserve." This term, and others like it, became part of discussions of poetic value in the mid- and late Tang; it refers to the reader's sense of an unstated, perhaps inexpressible meaning that lingered after reading or hearing. Such discussions linked this value to the reader's perception of meaning that was "beyond words," *yanwai* 言外, or "beyond the image," *xiangwai* 象外.[4] In the landscape quatrain, for example, the quality of reserve was the emotional resonance that lingered within a closing line that did not directly express emotion. In song lyrics such as the "Pusa man" set, an equivalent move might be the use of a natural image that resonates modally with the female subject but is not an obvious mirror or symbol for the woman: the image of "flowers filling the branches" that closes Wen Tingyun's third "Pusa man" lyric would be one such example. Wen Tingyun's use of this strategy in both his song lyrics and other kinds of poetry demonstrates the sophistica-

---

4. See Owen, "Ideas of Poetry and Writing in the Early Ninth Century," *End of the Chinese 'Middle Ages,'* 122–29, for a discussion of this poetic value, particularly its problematic relationship to craft.

tion and consistency of his own poetic practice; other *Huajian ji* poets' imitation of this technique shows that they recognized its power.

When the women in the *Huajian ji* lyrics do speak, either they lament their plight in words as evasively brief as those of the third-person observer's rhetorical question ("Where is this place 'Liaoyang'?"), or they offer direct, sometimes colloquial, invitations to their companions ("I'll make your pleasure today complete!"). The latter female voice—long associated with "folk" *yuefu* such as the "Midnight" songs and their literati imitations and found much more commonly in the Dunhuang lyrics—is not heard often in the anthology. When it emerges, it does so in an erotic context (such as a depiction of a sexual encounter) and is often teasing and coquettish. As we saw in Niu Qiao's seventh "Pusa man" lyric, that voice sounds almost jarringly crude against the demure silences of other women. It is not surprising that we hear so little of it in the collection. Even the lyrics that overtly refer to the songs of women— such as the set of "Nan xiangzi" 南鄉子 (Southland [songs]), which portray the "lotus-picking," *cai lian* 采蓮, seasonal rituals of southern women—tend to describe such women rather than letting us hear their voices. Ouyang Jiong clearly had the demure style of these lyrics in mind when he said that the song lyrics of the *Huajian ji* would replace the "songs of the lotus boat."⁵

In a few of the "Jiu quanzi" lyrics and throughout the "Huanxi sha" set, we find a greater number of lyrics marked with a male or indeterminately gendered first-person voice than in the "Pusa man" lyrics, which are more influenced by Wen Tingyun's voyeuristic model. Lyrics with first-person male voices differ from third-person lyrics in significant ways. In lyrics with male voices and in those few lyrics that are not strongly gendered, both syntax and word choice are plainer, including colloquial phrases and "empty" words; their images are simpler and clearly connected; and their subjects usually express their emotions directly. We saw all of these traits in Wei

---

5. Ouyang Jiong himself composed eight lyrics to the tune "Nan xiangzi," and Li Xun, another Shu poet, composed another ten, for the total of eighteen in the collection.

Zhuang's "Pusa man" lyrics, although I suggested then that Wei Zhuang was himself playing a role for that series. Shu poets followed Wei Zhuang's stylistic lead (though they did not imitate him at his most "folksy") in creating their own first-person male voices. The strong first-person male voice we hear in places throughout the *Huajian ji* is certainly a descendant of the bluff, hearty, male voices of medieval frontier and banquet *yuefu*; although they diminished in popularity in the latter half of the dynasty, these voices appeared in verse through the late Tang. Poetic genres such as *yuefu* and subgenres of *shi* such as boudoir poetry (which often overlapped with *yuefu* in content and conventions), which announced their generic codes in their titles, were not to be read as expressions of the poet's personal experiences, but as "fictional," patently invented. The impact of such poems thus depended on their ability to construct a convincing portrait from categorical emotions and conventional imagery.[6] A good Tang poet did not need to be a voyeur to write a competent boudoir quatrain. In the same manner, texts that were identified by their tune titles as being song lyrics would likely have evoked the same reading practice; their voices would be understood as fictional, as the expressions of stock characters in the romantic story.

However, I would argue that the male voice in the *Huajian ji* song lyrics can also be filiated to a different voice in Tang poetry: the self-revelatory voice of occasional *shi*. In this regard, I think the *Huajian ji* poets, and particularly the Shu poets, should be credited with innovation. In Tang occasional *shi*, the poet sought to capture his personal response to a certain situation; he both revealed and was revealed to others. Guided by cues given in the title, those who read such poetry assumed that the experiences and feelings described were authentic and autobiographical. The "authenticity" of this poetry was created both by the poet, who wrote from the tradition

---

6. The great exception to this complex interweaving of conventions would be Li Bai, who was rarely content to remain within either formal or topical restrictions in his *yuefu*. However, his constant disruptions of the subgeneric proprieties of Tang poetry only serve to make those proprieties more evident in other poets' works.

of individual response to circumstances, and by the reader, whose expectations of the poetry were shaped by poetic practice and genre norms. The difficulty in decoding the voices of the *Huajian ji* comes in part from its early moment in the tradition, when the generic expectations for song lyrics were still being shaped. Just as literati *quzi ci* did not have a stable formal or thematic identity vis-à-vis other genres of Tang poetry, the reading practices for Tang song lyrics were sometimes shaped by authorial intention or by context. At one extreme, we have the "Zhu zhi" and "Yangliu zhi" song cycles of Liu Yuxi and Bai Juyi, which are explicitly framed and claimed by the poets themselves as part of their personal histories. But at the other end, we have Wen Tingyun, whose song lyrics—with little corroborative evidence—were used by later readers to reconstruct a portrait of a playboy and political failure.

The lyrics of the *Huajian ji* have not traditionally been read as poems of personal experience, with the exception of some of Wen Tingyun's lyrics and, occasionally, those of Wei Zhuang. The historical resistance to biographical readings of the *Huajian ji* song lyrics surely comes in part from the scarce information we have about its poets, with the exception of Wen and Wei.[7] However, the first-person, male-voiced lyrics of two poets who lived only a few decades after the Shu poets—the Southern Tang ruler Li Yu and the courtier Feng Yansi—are consistently read as works of lived experience, particularly the melancholic lyrics of Li Yu.[8] Given these differences in the reading tradition, I think we should reevaluate the first-person male voices of the *Huajian ji* lyrics in light of the development of the generic identity of *ci* and the history of literati acceptance of *ci*. Throughout the *Huajian ji*, poets often followed Wen Tingyun's model to create a delicate, descriptive, and static

---

7. Wen Tingyun's lyrics were famously subjected to biographical and allegorical analysis by the Qing scholar Zhang Huiyan 張惠言 (1761–1802); many of Zhang's interpretations, along with dismissals of his readings by later commentators, are collected in *Tang Wudai ci jishi huiping*. Ye Jiaying has critiqued Zhang's interpretations in *Jialing lun ci conggao*, 10–17.

8. Daniel Bryant illustrates the circularity of the reading tradition that mines Li Yu's lyrics for biographical detail in his introduction to *Lyric Poets of the Southern T'ang*, xiii–xx.

style for lyrics that portrayed abandoned women. Despite the strategic placement of vernacular phrases in such lyrics, the poets were promoting a style that owed more to Tang poetry, particularly romantic poetry, than to popular song. In the same manner, I suggest that the *Huajian ji* poets' development of the male-voiced lyric represents an effort to rework the song lyric to literati tastes from a different angle: by using a confessional voice of male longing, the poets appropriated *the impression* of emotional sincerity—the authenticity of *shi*—for song lyrics as a literary genre.

Given the lack of evidence other than the song lyrics themselves, we can only speculate about the poets' intentions with respect to song lyrics. But the choices of the Shu compilers of the *Huajian ji* reveal a few patterns. Throughout the anthology, the male-voiced song lyric never appears singly, as the sole lyric to a particular tune, and it rarely appears in small sets of two or three. We find male-voiced lyrics more often in sets with four or more lyrics, and the tune title set "Huanxi sha" is one in which they are quite prominent. Aside from confirming what even the casual reader can discern, that the descriptive lyrics on abandoned women are the norm for the anthology, this tendency to place male-voiced lyrics in sets offers the possibility of reading lyrics in sequence or as dialogue. With respect to the number of male-voiced lyrics in the collection, one scholar recently estimated that "only" 20 percent of the collection's lyrics seem to be written in a male voice (I disagree with this estimate, since I think that number should include lyrics whose voices could be either male or female).[9] Using this count would mean that at least a hundred song lyrics in the collection contain first-person male voices—or, to use a relevant comparison, almost three times the number of extant lyrics by Li Yu, the tenth-century poet most commonly linked to the use of the first-person male voice in song lyrics.[10] In the *Huajian ji* lyrics to "Jiu quanzi" and "Huanxi sha,"

---

9. Wang Zhaopeng, *Tang Song ci shi lun*, 58. Although I argue that the *Huajian ji* use of the male voice is more important than Wang suggests, his discussion of the shifting subjects of *ci* in this volume (57–63) is both new and useful.

10. The argument that Li Yu's male-voiced lyrics represent first-person experience has been made by many scholars of song lyrics, an exception being Bryant,

the male-voiced lyrics often appear to be set against lyrics with female subjects, in a kind of double reflection on the romantic experience. We saw this juxtaposition of different viewpoints in two of Niu Qiao's "Pusa man" lyrics, but I noted there that it was less common in the "Pusa man" lyric set as a whole. In the "Huanxi sha" set, it appears that the Shu editors juxtaposed male-voiced and female-centered lyrics within a set to draw attention to a poet's use of different styles.[11] This juxtaposition of lyrics in different voices occurs in other tune titles, and a few times as two stanzas in a single lyric (Sun Guangxian has three such lyrics), but the "Huanxi sha" set, as the largest in the anthology, gives us a formally consistent body of lyrics in which to observe the contrasts.

The Shu editors' inclusion of male-voiced song lyrics had important consequences for the collection and, I would argue, for the development of the song lyric as a genre. One consequence was to broaden the range of what male voices could say about romantic loss and desire. As I stated above, the male voice in the *Huajian ji* song lyrics can be traced not only to the male voices in medieval *yuefu* but also to the self-revelatory voices of Tang *shi*.[12] The expression of longing and sorrow over separation from friends and family was a common feature in a number of subgenres of High Tang poetry, such as exile poetry, and poems sent back and forth among friends. The experiments by mid-Tang poets with expanding the topical boundaries of poetry—admitting irreducibly personal experiences and emotions—particularized these subgenres even further.[13] In late Tang romantic verse, poets expressed a new eroticism and more directly articulated feelings toward women, and male-voiced song lyr-

---

cited above, n5. For example, Chang, *Evolution of Chinese Tz'u Poetry*: "Most of [Li Yu's] works (except for the narrative *tz'u* produced during his early years) are to be taken as direct lyrical expression, revealing the depth of his most private feelings" (66).

11. It seems likely that the poets meant such lyrics to be performed together; at the very least, the Shu compilers' choices foreground the possibility.

12. See Samei, 175–90, for a discussion of the range of male voices in ninth- and tenth-century song lyrics.

13. On this topic, see Owen, "Singularity and Possession," and "Wit and the Private Life," in *End of the Chinese 'Middle Ages,'* 12–33 and 83–106.

ics made those expressions of desire even more explicit.[14] This development transgressed both literary and social boundaries. The expression of love and longing in *shi* was directed at friends and family, relationships with Confucian approval; but by borrowing that voice to express longing for women represented as sexually available and thus outside sanctioned social relations, song lyric poets implicitly violated the social conventions of *shi* poetry. And yet the impact of this move is lessened in the *Huajian ji* by the greater influence of the conventions of anonymous voices inherited from song traditions and by the continuing preference for descriptive portraits of women over confessions of male desire inherited from medieval romantic verse. To adopt for a moment a strategy I have criticized in traditional readings of the *Huajian ji* (seeking the seeds of what flowered later in the tradition), I suggest that this move toward a male voice is latent in the *Huajian ji* and only afterward becomes a problem for the genre. There are incompatible impulses already in the *Huajian ji*—tensions between the individual and the categorical, between male and female expressions of feeling—that persist from the tenth-century coalescence of the genre into its full realization as Song *ci*. After examining the lyrics of "Jiu quanzi" and "Huanxi sha," I discuss some of the problematic implications of the use of the male voice in the *Huajian ji* at the end of this chapter.

Narrowing the Stylistic Range: Lyrics to the Tune "Jiu quanzi"

The 26 lyrics to the tune "Jiu quanzi" make the tune title set the third largest in the *Huajian ji* (along with the "Lin jiang xian" set, which also has 26 lyrics). The tune title set is important in other ways: there are no fewer than 18 formal variations represented by these lyrics; 11 out of the 18 *Huajian ji* poets have lyrics to the tune, which gives us a range of individual styles; and, outside of 4 lyrics

---

14. Rouzer has examined the boundaries of these kinds of expressions in the late Tang, as well as Li Shangyin's transgressions of those boundaries, in *Articulated Ladies*, 286–309.

Table 4
Huajian ji Poets with Lyrics to "Jiu quanzi"

Poet	Number of lyrics	Poet	Number of lyrics
Wen Tingyun	4	Niu Xiji	1
Wei Zhuang	1	Gu Xiong	7
Niu Qiao	1	Sun Guangxian	3
Zhang Bi	2	Mao Xizhen	2
Mao Wenxi	1	Li Xun	4

from the Dunhuang corpus whose dates are uncertain, these are the first "Jiu quanzi" lyrics extant in the song lyric tradition (see Table 4).[15]

The great formal variation in the *Huajian ji* "Jiu quanzi" lyrics suggests the possibility that, despite the early appearance of the title in the *Jiaofang ji*, the tune and/or the metrical structures used by these poets were still fluid. The variation of metrical structure *within* a single poet's lyrics further supports this speculation: for example, each of Li Xun's four lyrics to "Jiu quanzi" features different metrical, rhyme, and tonal patterns.[16] The most common

---

15. I have used Aoyama Hiroshi's analysis of the metrical and rhyme patterns of the *HJJ* tune titles for this data. (*Tō Sō shi kenkyū*, 240–49.) The tune title "Jiu quanzi" is found in the *Jiaofang ji* (Ren, *Jiaofang ji jianding*, 129). For the four Dunhuang "Jiu quanzi" lyrics, see Ren, *Dunhuang geci zongbian*, 438–44, 489–90 (this lyric is missing a second stanza), and 493–98. Although the metrical structure of the three complete lyrics (4/7/7/5 and 7/7/7/5) is different from any of the *HJJ* "Jiu quanzi" lyrics, the first Dunhuang lyric has a similar rhyming pattern to one in the *Huajian ji*, in which the first *ping* rhyme, announced in the opening line, is alternated with a *ze* rhyme (given scribal errors and some illegibility, Ren cautions against defining the rhyme patterns for the other two complete lyrics, 494). The content of the first lyric (438) refers to the invasion of the "imperial palaces" and people fleeing disaster; the other two complete lyrics (494–98) are to the topics "Horses" and "Swords." In *Dunhuang qu chutan*, Ren dated the first lyric to after the year 895; in *Dunhuang geci zongbian*, arguing on the basis of the manuscript's physical evidence, he suggests that it could be much earlier.

16. Only one other tune title in the *HJJ*, "He zhuan" 河傳, has this degree of metrical, rhyme, and tonal variation. "He zhuan" is found neither in the *Jiaofang ji* nor in the Dunhuang corpus. Among the 77 total tune titles of the collection, 41

metrical structure for the *Huajian ji* lyrics to "Jiu quanzi" is 4/7/3/3/3 for the first stanza, and 7/7/3/3/3 for the second stanza (sometimes substituting five characters for the seven in the second line). However, the final set of three-character phrases at the end of both stanzas is more correctly read as a penultimate line of 3-3 (with a secondary rhyme sometimes occurring in the sixth character) and a final line of three characters (the final character of which returns to the primary rhyme).[17] These three-character phrases are the most striking feature of the "Jiu quanzi" metrical structure. As I noted in the previous chapter, the heterometric rhythms of song lyrics gave rise to experimentation on the part of literati poets. As deployed by the *Huajian ji* poets in this tune title set and other tune titles, the three-character line or line segment contains a single image or narrative element, and is often set in parallel against other three-character units.[18] The use of three-character phrases in series obviously works against the flow of the five- and seven-character lines we saw in "Pusa man," and which we will see again in "Huanxi sha." In place of the discursive continuity often seen in longer lines, poets use the series of threes to pile up discrete details, enhancing the tendency toward fragmentation that we have already observed in the work of Wen Tingyun. With respect to the metrical variation of lyrics to this tune, we should recall that variation in line length does not indicate different tunes or rhythms, but rather the practice of altering line length by adding or deleting a word as the lyricist saw

---

have metrical patterns with more than one variant. Aoyama points to the variability of "Jiu quanzi" as evidence of the transitional period that the *HJJ* represents in the history of song lyrics. (Aoyama, *Tō Sō shi kenkyū*, 257.)

17. Thus: 4/7/3-3/3 in the first stanza and 7/7 (or 5)/3-3/3 in the second.

18. Many other tune titles have metrical patterns with inset 3/3 lines that use parallelism ("Genglouzi" being an important one in the *HJJ*); the use of 3/3/3 sets is much less common. The 3/3 set of lines can be understood as a single heptametric line with a caesura, but adding yet another triplet unbalances that structure with a triplet "coda." There is one lyric to "San zi ling" 三字令 (Three-word tune), by Ouyang Jiong, that is written entirely in lines of three characters. Other lyrics that use 3/3/3 lines are "Xi xizi" 西溪子, "Xian zhongxin" 獻衷心, "Libie nan," and "Xiang jian huan" 相見歡.

fit.[19] In general, the variation of a single line's length within a lyric (replacing a line of seven words with one of five, for example) does not distinguish it strongly from other lyrics to that tune; however, the *repeated* use of an altered line or lines (replacing a 7/7 couplet with a 3/3 couplet) usually makes a substantial difference in the rhetorical structure of a piece.

The "Jiu quanzi" stanza is brief—the longest variation of the lyric has only 45 characters—and the combination of overall brevity and short lines restricts the descriptive and modal range of the lyrics considerably. Wen Tingyun's second and third lyrics of four to "Jiu quanzi" demonstrate the limitations of the form as well as his ability to transcend them by placing his individual stamp on the lyric. In the Chinese text, I have indicated the complex interlocking rhyme scheme that Wen and a few other poets use for lyrics for this tune title. In the following two lyrics, the main rhyme, a *ping* tone rhyme, is introduced in the opening line (marked "R1"); the secondary rhyme, a *ze* tone rhyme, is introduced in the second line of the first stanza ("R2"); and the tertiary rhyme, also a *ze* tone rhyme, occurs in the second stanza ("R3"). Although I will only occasionally comment on the phonological qualities of the lyrics, it is important to recognize the complexity of the rhyme scheme of certain tune titles. This interlocking rhyme scheme is another element of the *Huajian ji* song lyrics that distinguishes them clearly from *shi* poetic forms, and reveals an unexpected internal formal integrity with respect to the Tang song lyrics that preceded them.

"Jiu quanzi" (2nd of 4)
Wen Tingyun

The sun shines in the screened window	日映紗窗 R1
on the gilt duck censer and the little screen's deep mountain green.	金鴨小屏山碧 R2

---

19. Picken uses examples of "Jiu quanzi" to show that Chinese poets could insert or delete words to a line without straying from the fundamental rhythmic or melodic structure of a song. Picken, "The Musical Implications of Chinese Song-Texts," 53–77.

From spring in her homeland, mists and fogs block her— 　　故鄉春、煙靄隔 R2
she puts out the orchid-oil lamp. 　　背蘭釭 R1
Melancholy in last night's makeup, looking from her high chamber: 　　宿妝惆悵倚高閣 R3
a thousand miles of cloud shapes thinning. 　　千里雲影薄 R3
Grasses grow to even height, flowers fall once more, 　　草初齊、花又落 R3
swallows, pair on pair.[20] 　　燕雙雙 R1

(3rd of 4)

The woman of Chu has not gone—[21] 　　楚女不歸 R1
nestled by the tower, a little river of spring water. 　　樓枕小河春水 R2
The moon shines alone, wind rises once more— 　　月孤明、風又起 R2
apricot blossoms thin. 　　杏花稀 R1
Jade pins hanging aslant from clouds of coiled hair, 　　玉釵斜簪雲鬟髻
on her skirts, gilt-stitched phoenixes. 　　裙上金縷鳳 R3
Eight lines of letter,[22] a thousand miles of dream— 　　八行書、千里夢 R3
geese fly southward.[23] 　　雁南飛 R1

Although Wen Tingyun's lyrics do not often show this pattern, these two lyrics form a pair: the first offers a typical portrait of the abandoned woman, but the second lyric, at least in its opening stanza, is recounted from the perspective of the male lover. Set apparently in the same seasonal moment, the end of spring, the lyrics echo each other's images and lines.

The first lyric, which occurs in the morning, presents a familiar collage of decorative objects and unspeaking woman. The action is slight—the woman looks out from her room—and the emphasis

---

20. *HJJZS*, 25–26.

21. The "woman of Chu" is the goddess of the Xiang, from the "Gaotang Rhapsody." I discuss the *HJJ* poets' use of this story in detail in Chapter 6.

22. The "eight lines of letter" allude to a text by the Han literatus Ma Rong, in which a letter is described as having only eight lines of text. In at least one Tang poem the phrase is used to refer to love letters. *HJJZS*, 26, n5.

23. *HJJZS*, 26–27. I take one alternate character in this lyric: in the final line of some texts, *gui* 歸 is given as an alternative for *fei*. I think it unlikely that Wen would have used the same word twice in a single lyric and certainly not as a repeated rhyme word (*gui* being the rhyme introduced in line 1).

is on observing first her and then on what she sees from her "high chamber": spring at its height and swallows in busy pairs. The only word of emotion appears in the unspecific "melancholy," *chouchang* 惆悵, externalized by her slept-in makeup. The absent lover, though not present in the scene, can be seen in the "thousand miles of cloud," whose thinness, *bo* 薄, signals his faithlessness as one who has "made light of his promise," *boming* 薄命. Wen Tingyun's fondness for quick cuts manifests itself here in the three-character lines, which give us a series of images to integrate. In the first stanza, the syntax of the 3-3/3 series seems deliberately discontinuous: although the first two sets of three can be read as a single, inverted sentence ("from spring in her homeland / mists and fogs block her"), the third line of three, "she puts out the orchid-oil lamp," seems to close the scene before we have understood its meaning. Is the "spring in her homeland" the scene depicted on the screen, and the "mists and fogs" those coming from the duck censer and the orchid lamp? The woman's gesture of extinguishing the lamp suggests that she has been awake since dawn, waiting for her lover, who is presumably on the other side of the fogs and mists. In the second stanza, the intent of the three-character phrases is more apparent: "Grasses grow to even height, flowers fall once more, / swallows, pair on pair." Each syntactic unit marks the specific moment in the season (late spring) with a different image that speaks to her plight. The syntactic parallelism of "Grasses grow to even height, flowers fall once more" (草初齊, 花又落) heightens the sense of painful repetition, as does the appearance of Wen Tingyun's trademark "pairs" of birds.

The fourth "Jiu quanzi" lyric opens with what appears to be a male perspective ("The woman of Chu has not gone"), a most unusual phenomenon for Wen.[24] The natural images of the first stanza—moonlight, spring stream, wind, apricot blossoms—and the lack of boudoir decoration differentiate the lyric both from the lyrics preceding it and from others by Wen Tingyun. Although the static image of the woman that abruptly opens the second

---

24. Aoyama singles this lyric out for comment for its use of a male perspective (*Tō Sō shi kenkyū*, 6).

stanza—depicting her tumbling hairpins and gilt-stitched phoenix skirts—seems to shift the scene to the woman's boudoir, it is more plausible to read the lines as a memory or dream-image prompted by the "Eight lines of letter / a thousand miles of dream" that follow. The third "Jiu quanzi" is set in the morning, the fourth at night, but their images complement each other: in the woman's lyric, we see the downward motion of the feminine, *yin* image of "flowers fall once more" (花又落); in the man's lyric, we find the surging, masculine, *yang* image of "wind rises once more" (風又起). In one, the clouds stretch out for thousands of *li*, in the other, the subject travels a thousand *li* in dream. Both lyrics close with images of birds, signifying different contrasts: to the woman, the pairs of swallows mock her solitariness; to the man, the sound and sight of geese flying mock the fact, announced in the opening line, that *she* will not return. Although written from the point of view of the male lover, Wen Tingyun's fourth "Jiu quanzi" is a familiar scene of abandonment.

The late Tang poet Zhang Bi reworks the scene of loneliness in Wen Tingyun's third lyric to "Jiu quanzi" in his first of two lyrics to the tune.

"Jiu quanzi" (1st of 2)
Zhang Bi

Spring rains beat at the window—	春雨打窗 R1
startled from dream, I wake to the sky at dawn.	驚夢覺來天氣曉 R2
The painted halls are deep, the red flame tiny—	畫堂深、紅焰小 R2
I put out the orchid-oil lamp.	背蘭釭 R1
The wine's fragrance strikes my nose, as I lazily open the crock—	酒香噴鼻懶開缸 R1
so sad that there's still no one to get drunk with.	惆悵更無人共醉 R3
In the old nests, new swallows,	舊巢中、新燕子 R3
chattering pair on pair.[25]	語雙雙 R1

Zhang Bi's lyric follows Wen Tingyun's third "Jiu quanzi" on a number of levels. Zhang uses the same metrical structure in all but two lines and three of the same rhyme words (*chuang* 窗, *gang* 釭,

---

25. *HJJZS*, 161.

shuang 雙). A few differences, however, reveal Zhang to be playing with—not just stealing—Wen Tingyun's work. The first stanzas of each lyric are very similar, as the lines in bold indicate:

Wen Tingyun's 1st stanza
  "Jiu quanzi" #2

The sun shines in the screened window,
on the gilt duck censer and little screen's deep mountain green.
From spring in her homeland, mists and fogs block her—
she puts out the orchid-oil lamp.

日上紗窗 R1
金鴨小屏山碧 R2
故鄉春、煙靄隔 R2
背蘭釭 R1

Zhang Bi's 1st stanza
  "Jiu quanzi" #1

Spring rains beat at the window—
startled from dream, I wake to the sky at dawn.
The painted halls are deep, the red flame tiny,
I put out the orchid-oil lamp.

春雨打窗 R1
驚夢覺來天氣曉 R2
畫梁深、紅焰小 R2
背蘭釭 R1

Where Wen opens with a sunny spring morning, Zhang counters with rain that wakens the dreamer; Wen's ornamented interior is replaced in Zhang's lyric with a contrast between the "depth" of the interior and the tiny flame that cannot penetrate the scene's implied dimness, a contrast heightened by the parallelism of the two three-character lines. The verbs of Zhang's second line suggest a first-person speaker: "startled from dream, I wake . . ." (驚夢覺來). The closing image of the first stanza of both lyrics is identical: in Wen's lyric, the observed woman has her back to the lamp; in Zhang's lyric, the speaker is turned away from the lamp.

At the stanza break, however, Zhang Bi takes a different turn. Echoing the "melancholy," *chouchang* 惆悵, of Wen Tingyun's lyric ("Melancholy in last night's makeup . . ." 宿妝惆悵), Zhang's speaker prefers to seek solace in the wine crock, though lamenting that there is no one "to get drunk with." To close, Zhang twists the final lines of Wen Tingyun's spring scene into a play on the nests of lovers and birds:

Wen Tingyun's final lines
  "Jiu quanzi" #2
Grasses grow to even height,

Zhang Bi's final lines
  "Jiu quanzi" #1
In the old nests,

flowers fall once more, swallows, pair on pair.[26]	new swallows, chattering pair on pair.[27]
草初齊 花又落 燕雙雙	舊巢中 新燕子 語雙雙

In these lines, Zhang imitates Wen Tingyun closely enough to show that he is doing so deliberately, and yet he alters enough to create a new scene from the old. Wen's last lines are framed by the woman's moving to look out from her "high chamber"—the grass, flowers, and swallows are what she sees. Zhang, on the other hand, prefaces his final lines with the speaker drinking wine and regretting that "there's no one to get drunk with"—the "nests" and "swallows" in his closing lines are figures for the human lovers. Where Wen Tingyun's lyric clearly presents a boudoir woman but not necessarily a strong first-person voice, in Zhang's lyric we have a first-person speaker whose gender is indeterminate. Reading Zhang's lyric against Wen's, we are perhaps pushed toward seeing Zhang's speaker as the abandoned woman (the "lazily" adds to that impression), but there are no strong internal cues beyond the interior setting. If we hear the speaker as a woman, the morning wine adds a slightly *louche* tone to the scene that is not found in Wen Tingyun's lyric; reading the speaker as a man makes Zhang's play on Wen Tingyun's lyric that much more entertaining, since he has retold the other poet's vignette, in the other poet's words, from a new perspective. Zhang himself becomes the "new swallow" in Wen Tingyun's nest.

Zhang Bi's lyric shows the extent to which poets could imitate Wen Tingyun, from the level of rhetorical structure down to his rhymes, and yet still reject some of his more distinctive stylistic traits. Wen Tingyun shows; Zhang tells and then comments on the telling. In the contrast between Wen and Zhang, the different perspectives establish different moods for the lyrics. Two "Jiu quanzi" lyrics from the Shu poet Li Xun show us that the *Huajian ji* poets

---

26. Ibid., 25–26.
27. Ibid., 161.

could stray even further from Wen Tingyun while still remaining within the narrow limitations of "separation sorrow."

"Jiu quanzi" (2nd of 4)
Li Xun

Rain soaks blossoms to bits:	雨漬花零 R1
red petals scatter, fragrance withering around the pool.	紅散香凋池兩岸 R2
My feelings at parting go far, but spring songs are cut off,	別情遙、春歌斷 R2
enclosed by silver screens.	掩銀屏 R1
Solitary sails at last depart from Chu.	孤帆早晚離三楚 R3
Listlessly I strum the filigreed zither—so much sorrow.	閒理鈿箏愁幾許 R3
The feeling in the tune, the message from the strings—	曲中情、絃上語 R3
I can't bear to listen!²⁸	不堪聽 R1

(3rd of 4)

Autumn rains go on and on,	秋雨聯綿
their sound scattered among dying clusters of lotus.	聲散敗荷叢裏
On my pillow, how can I bear to listen to it through the deep night?	那堪深夜枕前聽 R1
The wine begins to clear from my head.	酒初醒 R1
Entangled by sorrow, disturbed by longing— watches toll without end.	牽愁惹思更無停 R1
The candle has gone out, its fragrance cold— the sky is about to lighten.	燭暗香凝天欲曙
Drizzle and mist, chill and rain	細和煙，冷和雨
pierce the curtain sashes.²⁹	透簾旌 R1

These two lyrics are bound together in many ways: by the same rhyme and a shared rhyme word (*ting* 聽) that announces the shared perception of unbearable sounds (music in the first, rain in the second), by the rains of late spring in the first and of autumn in

---

28. Ibid., 385.
29. Ibid., 386.

the second, and by the images of penetration and continuation throughout both. In both lyrics, the strong expression of emotion linked to perception—in this case listening ("I can't bear to listen!" and "How can I bear to listen . . . ?")—indicates first-person voices, but only in the second "Jiu quanzi" lyric is the speaker's gender made clear.[30] In that lyric, the "feelings at parting," the screens that block the speaker, the "solitary sails" that leave, and the playing of a "filigreed zither" all indicate a female subject. This woman seems almost overburdened with indications of "feeling," *qing* 情: in the two stanzas, we have "*feelings* at parting" *bieqing* 別情, "*solitary* sails" *gufan* 孤帆, "so much *sorrow*" *chou jixu* 愁幾許, "the *feeling* in the tune" *qu zhong qing* 曲中情, and the "*message* in the strings" 絃上語. The trope of unbearable emotion carried in music was an old one, but it became particularly popular in the mid- and late Tang, certainly in part because of the flourishing entertainment culture; Bai Juyi's "Song of the Pipa" is perhaps the best-known example from that era. But Bai Juyi's poem, in which the *poet* is moved by the music and words of the female *pipa* player, reveals Li Xun's alteration of the trope: in Li Xun's lyric, the woman is alone, playing for herself—and even then, she "cannot bear" the sound of her own music. Li Xun has taken the two figures of the player and the listener(s) and combined them into the same subject. By removing the mediating narrator, he creates the immediacy of listening and being overwhelmed by music. This sense would have only been doubled when a singer performed the lyric.

The second lyric opens with an image of spring rains destroying flowers, signaling the abandoned woman's loss of beauty; the third lyric opens with the image of autumn rain that goes "on and on," *lianmian* 聯綿, announcing the theme of the lyric. Unlike the second lyric, in which an excess of *qing* spills over into music, the third

---

30. Even Chinese commentators seem uncertain about the subject of this lyric; for example, in one recent edition (Shen and Fu, eds., *Huajian ji xinzhu*, 449), the editors pointedly do not indicate the gender of the speaker, although they note that the subject is female in the other three of Li Xun's four "Jiu quanzi" lyrics; in another edition (*QTWDCSZ*, 987), the editors mark all four subjects as female. Earlier editions generally do not single out the gender of the lyrics' subjects for comment.

lyric relies on images of continuity to indicate the speaker's emotional distress. The gender of the third lyric's subject is ambiguous, but the contrast between the two is exemplified by the third lines of the first stanzas of each. Where the female subject laments that "my feelings at parting go far, but spring songs are cut off—/ enclosed by silver screens," the subject of the second lyric in the same position emphasizes the endlessness of feeling: "On my pillow, how can I bear to listen to it through the deep night? / The wine begins to clear from my head." The speaker is not blocked by screens or "cut off," but rather "entangled," *qian* 牽, or "bound," and "disturbed," *re* 惹, by endless feeling. (We will see the same metaphors used in a few "Huanxi sha" lyrics below.) Here the third lyric uses visual and tactile perceptions to establish mood: the autumn rains continue endlessly, the candle goes out, and the drizzle, mists, and chilly rain penetrate the speaker's room. This focus on the natural scene, the withholding of emotion, the "sobering up," and the lack of other objects marked as feminine allow the possibility of reading the lyric in either a male or female voice. This is yet another kind of reserve: although the speaker communicates a generalized distress ("How can I bear . . . ?"), the emotions are transferred to the scene rather than being directly articulated by the subject.

Although the autumn scene of Li Xun's third "Jiu quanzi" lyric seems distant from Wen Tingyun's spring boudoirs, they share many of the same poetic concerns: the constant juxtaposition of scene and feeling, whether the scene stands in ironic contrast to the emotional state or mirrors it; the use of liminal moments (seasonal changes, dawn, twilight); and the blurring forces of memory, wine, and dream. Looking back at Zhang Bi's "Jiu quanzi" lyric, we see that he begins with spring rain at a window that wakes a dreamer at dawn ("Spring rains beat at the window / Startled from dream, I wake to the sky at dawn"). Li Xun's rain is autumnal, but it, too, penetrates the speaker's consciousness, keeping him (or her) awake and sobered as "the sky is about to lighten." The emotions of these lyrics are narrow indeed—restricted to "melancholy" (*chouchang* 惆悵), "feelings from parting" (*bieqing* 別情), and "sorrow" (*chou* 愁)—but the lyrics offer a surprising range of perspectives and stylistic choices. Wen Tingyun's preference for static presentations of female subjects is manifest in his second "Jiu quanzi," but he also experiments briefly with a male perspective in the third lyric, only to resume close description in the second stanza. In contrast, the lyrics of Zhang Bi and Li Xun avoid the voyeurism and the stasis of Wen Tingyun's style, choosing instead to write from the perspective of their subjects. This choice pushes the poets toward a different kind of poetic organization, one clearly linked to the poetics of Tang *shi*. Where Wen Tingyun lingers on the surfaces of his female subjects and their boudoirs, relying on the reader's familiarity with romantic conventions to make sense of his fragmented scene, Zhang Bi and Li Xun here create lyrics with a modal coherence that relies upon the poetic subject for intelligibility. Unlike Tang landscape poetry—a subgenre that also foregrounds the perceiving subject, in which the viewer constructs a scene and his response to that scene based on conventions of "viewing" and the demands of parallelism (the gaze moves from top to bottom, or from far distance to foreground, for example)—these romantic lyrics are created out of the perceiving subject's responses to cues in the scene, cues that are usually not parallel or linear in any respect. There may sometimes be a general sense of movement from outer world to inner world, particularly in the first stanza (Li Xun's rain that penetrates flowers and the consciousness of the speakers), but in the second stanza the poet can just as easily cut back to the outer world or remain inside the boudoir.

The discontinuity of sensory perception, and its power as a kind of poetic organization, became a central element of *ci* poetics in the Song, and it is directly linked to the emergence of the first-person speaker as the preferred point of view for song lyrics. As the structure of "Jiu quanzi" makes clear, the heterometric lines of song lyrics prompted poets to experiment with the placement of imagery and emotional response within stanzas; no consistent pattern holds for all of the lyrics, though occasional consistencies appear in certain pairs. The "Jiu quanzi" lyrics did not reveal, however, the possible differences poets might have wanted to establish between the perceptions of male and female subjects. For this question, we turn to a set of lyrics with an even broader range of perspectives: lyrics to the tune "Huanxi sha."

Beyond Wei Zhuang: Lyrics to the Tune "Huanxi sha"

The "Huanxi sha" lyrics are important to the *Huajian ji*. Out of the 77 tune titles in the anthology, "Huanxi sha" has by far the greatest number of lyrics: 57 lyrics by ten poets are collected. The tune title set is also notable for the large number of lyrics collected per poet: five poets have more than 7 "Huanxi sha" lyrics each (Xue Zhaoyun, Zhang Bi, Gu Xiong, Sun Guangxian, and Mao Xizhen). As we will see below, interesting sequence possibilities emerge within these relatively large sets of lyrics. Furthermore, apparently because of the large number of lyrics to the tune, lyrics to "Huanxi sha" are listed first in the poets' individual sections. The effect of this ordering is to present "Huanxi sha" as the most important tune title in the collected work of the poets who wrote lyrics to this tune (see Table 5).

The metrical structure of "Huanxi sha" is one of the most consistent in the anthology: it contains two stanzas of three lines of seven characters each.[31] In other words, the most popular form in the collection is not only isometric, but uses the most common line of late Tang poetry and the most frequent in isometric songforms: the seven-character line.[32] This serves to counterbalance my comments in Chapter 4 on the importance of heterometric verse in the *Huajian ji*; although the *Huajian ji* poets used an unprecedented number of heterometric verse forms, tunes for which poets com-

---

31. There is one title among the 77 that is likely a variant form of "Huanxi sha": it is titled "Huan sha xi," or "Stream of Silk-Washing Sands." Mao Xizhen has one lyric to this tune; its form is only slightly different from that of "Huanxi sha," since it has two stanzas of 7/7/7/3. This form is found in the Dunhuang "Huanxi sha" lyrics, in both the *Yunyao ji* and the miscellaneous *quzi*. The tune title "Huanxi sha" also appears in the *Jiaofang ji* (Ren, *Jiaofang ji jianding*, 78). Ren suggests that the 7/7/7/3 stanza form antedated the 7/7/7 form in *Jiaofang ji jianding*, 78, but does not give his evidence for that conclusion. There are a number of alternate titles for the form. See Wen Ruxian, *Cipai huishi*, 381–82.

32. In *Tang sheng shi*, Ren collects 53 *sheng shi* in the five-character line, 63 that use the seven-character line. However, Ren's selections are intentionally narrow, in accordance with his definition of *sheng shi* as a subgenre.

Table 5
Huajian ji Poets with Lyrics to "Huanxi sha"

Poet	Number of lyrics	Poet	Number of lyrics
Wei Zhuang	5	Gu Xiong	8
Xue Zhaoyun	8	Sun Guangxian	9
Zhang Bi	10	Yan Xuan	1
Mao Wenxi	2	Mao Xizhen	7
Ouyang Jiong	3	Li Xun	4

posed isometric lyrics remained popular, even in the work of poets datable to the Latter Shu.[33] However, I suggest that this points to the enduring popularity of certain songs whose metrical structures were already established in the Tang, rather than a continuing tenth-century preference for composing or preserving lyrics in isometric verse. The lateness of many of the *Huajian ji* tune titles for which we have heterometric lyrics—lateness that is suggested by the tune's first appearance in the *Huajian ji*—points to the Shu poets' increasing use of heterometric forms for new tunes. Although written in the familiar heptametric line, the structure of "Huanxi sha" poses one challenge for poets used to writing in *shi* forms: the two stanzas each contain only three lines, a structure that upsets the balanced couplets of quatrains or other *shi* forms with even numbers of lines.[34] As we will see, parallelism is an important part of these song lyrics, but it appears almost despite the tercet structure.[35]

---

33. The isometric versions (there are lyrics in both forms) of "Yang liu zhi," for which there are twenty examples in the *HJJ*, also support this conclusion.

34. Tang poetry contains songforms in six lines, but only one extant Tang literati song lyric—by Han Wo, to "Huanxi sha"—is found in two stanzas of three lines. Six-line songs are normally constructed as three couplets, with the rhyme falling at the end of lines 2, 4, and 6, and optionally line 1, which is not the rhyme pattern of "Huanxi sha." With respect to the number of lines in each stanza of two-stanza lyrics in the *Huajian ji*, the dominant form by far is the stanza of four lines, a structure that surely reflects the use of even-numbered measures of music per stanza.

35. The rhyme pattern for the majority of the "Huanxi sha" lyrics contains a single *ping* rhyme for both stanzas, placed at the end of lines 2, 3, 5, and 6, and oc-

Following the pattern of the collection as a whole, the majority of the "Huanxi sha" lyrics contain subjects that are clearly marked as female, whether they are observed (as is most common) or speaking. However, there are several exceptions to this pattern: lyrics written in a voice that is either gendered male or left ambiguous. These lyrics are never found as the first lyric of a poet's set, whether due to the poet's design or due to the arrangement of the *Huajian ji*'s editors, but are rather placed within a set and often toward its end.[36] In lyrics by the late Tang poet Zhang Bi and the Shu poet Gu Xiong, the shift from female to male perspective enables a reading of the lyrics as a juxtaposition of different viewpoints on the same affair. The same three components of scene, woman (occasionally man), and emotion found in "Pusa man" and "Jiu quanzi" appear in the "Huanxi sha" lyrics also. The "Huanxi sha" lyrics feature an even greater use of the rhetorical question to express emotion than that seen in "Pusa man," where emotion was more often veiled. As in many *xiaoling* lyrics, the first stanza of a lyric to "Huanxi sha" establishes the setting and the mood of the lyric; statements of emotion or rhetorical questions most often appear in any of the three lines of the second stanza. In the lyrics that show strong parallelism in the first two lines of the second stanza, the emotional expression is frequently reserved for the closing line.

---

casionally line 1. The opening line of the second stanza in some lyrics ends with a *ze* tone-word, often a *rusheng* word, that was clearly meant to serve as a strong contrast to the *ping* rhymes. Aoyama, "*Kakanshū* no shi (4): *Kakanshū* shi no keishiki ni tsuite," 74. Aoyama notes two exceptions to this pattern. Although there is a clear preference for tonal balancing, there is no single tonal pattern followed consistently in the set, which is true for many of the tune title sets in the collection overall. Given this rhyme structure, the rhetorical structure tends to follow one of two patterns: either the first two lines cohere as a couplet (following the pattern of *shi* couplets) and the final line stands alone rhetorically (although it rhymes with the second line), or the opening line introduces the final two lines, which are set in parallel.

36. This pattern of male-voiced lyrics (never as the single lyric or one of two lyrics to a tune, and more commonly later in a set) holds true for the anthology as a whole, with only one exception that I have been able to identify.

The "Huanxi sha" lyrics are notable for yet another reason: unlike the "Pusa man" or "Jiu quanzi" sets, the set of 57 "Huanxi sha" lyrics includes not a single lyric by Wen Tingyun. In the lyrics, selection, and arrangement of the "Pusa man" lyrics, Wen Tingyun's stylistic influence was overtly acknowledged by Shu poets and the *Huajian ji* editors. Such was also the case in the "Jiu quanzi" set. The "Huanxi sha" lyrics, however, provide us an opportunity to look for imitation of Wen Tingyun's style without his immediate textual models as precedent. As I argued in the beginning of this chapter, we discover in the "Huanxi sha" set that the style of a lyric—in which we can now identify imitation and lexical borrowing—depends much more heavily on point of view than it does on individual poetic models. At the same time, the preferences of individual poets—their particular poetic interests *within* the narrow topical and lexical boundaries of the *Huajian ji*—also begin to come into focus.

In Wei Zhuang's "Pusa man" lyrics, we saw the poet at his most colloquial and hearty; in his "Huanxi sha" lyrics, Wei assumes a calmer, more melancholy mood. Although his syntax remains direct and his vocabulary simple, Wei Zhuang's treatment of romantic topics in his five "Huanxi sha" lyrics seems closer to Wen Tingyun than before. Wei Zhuang continues to distinguish himself from Wen by his shifting use of voice. The following three lyrics depict a series of abandoned women from the viewpoints of an anonymous observer, a first-person male voice, and a first-person female voice.

"Huanxi sha" (1st of 5)
Wei Zhuang

In the cool dawn, her makeup done, on Cold Food Day,	清曉妝成寒食天
bracelets of willow twine amid filigreed flowers.	柳毬斜裊間花鈿
She rolls up the shades, goes out in front of the painted hall.	卷簾直出畫堂前
She points out a peony bud beginning to crack open;	指點牡丹初綻朵
when the sun is high, still she leans on the red balustrade.	日高猶自憑朱欄

| Frowning yet not speaking, she regrets spring's waning.[37] | 含顰不語恨春殘 |

Even in translation, the overall simplicity of Wei Zhuang's language and syntax is apparent, but here he avoids the strong colloquial phrases of his "Pusa man" lyrics. This lyric depicts a woman in (and just outside) her boudoir: after finishing her toilette, she goes outside, points out the flowers, leans on a railing (in ruminating melancholy, presumably), and frowns, not speaking, at the passing of spring. Her "regret" comes not only from the passing of flowers but also from the failure of her lover to appear. The seasonal markers of the lyric frame the woman's appearance and feelings: it is Cold Food Day (the end of spring), and peonies are beginning to "crack open." Wei's use of the peony—which blooms in early summer and is known for its showy, lush blooms—marks both the season and the woman. Although the peony was a metaphor for the self-consciously decorative courtesan, Wei's choice of a *budding* peony suggests another liminal moment: the woman stands poised between spring and summer. The lyric's final words, "spring's waning," *chun can* 春殘, have been foreshadowed by everything that preceded them. In the end, we might wonder if this lyric is really a romantic lyric on the abandoned woman in spring or is rather the reverse—a lyric that uses the "abandoned woman" trope to describe "spring's waning." Just as the woman points to the peony, the lyric "points out" (*zhidian* 指點) the woman as springtime object. It is only the final line that offers an indication of her emotional state, as we see her "frowning, yet not speaking," *han pin bu yu* 含顰不語. Here, the petulant or frustrated "frowning" is read as "regret," *hen* 恨, at the passing of spring. But we understand her state better than she does herself, for we see that she, too, is the one who is *can*, "waning," but also "fading,"—losing her beauty and appeal. This is the challenge posed to the song lyric poet by the voyeur's view-

---

37. Elsewhere, I have translated *can* as "remnants" or "fragments," but when it occurs with a word that indicates time, such as "spring," I use a word such as "waning" to give the sense of time's passage. I translate *can* as "fading" when the reference is to colors or fragrance, as in Wen Tingyun's third "Pusa man" lyric, and Niu Qiao's first "Pusa man" lyric. *HJJZS*, 69.

point: to reveal the woman's internal state (which she herself cannot articulate) by constructing a scene that speaks for her.

The focus of Wei's third "Huanxi sha" lyric is quite different: although the lyric begins in the mind and eye of the male speaker, the aim of the lyric is for the male speaker to "secretly imagine" the appearance of the absent woman.

"Huanxi sha" (3rd of 5)
Wei Zhuang

Through melancholy remnants of dream, mountain moonlight shines down—	惆悵夢餘山月斜
a lone lamp shining on the wall, her back to the window screen.	孤燈照壁背窗紗
The small tower's high chamber is Miss Xie's home.[38]	小樓高閣謝娘家
I secretly imagine her face of jade—what does it resemble?	暗想玉容何所似
One branch of spring snow—frozen plum blossoms.	一枝春雪凍梅花
Completely covered in fragrant mists—a cluster of morning auroras.[39]	滿身香霧簇朝霞

As in the "Jiu quanzi" lyrics, the use of the emotion, "melancholy," *chouchang* 惆悵, in the first line fixes the mood of the lyric but does not specify the gender of the "dreamer"; in the opening position of the first line of the lyric, it suggests a first-person speaker. The lines of description that follow seem to switch away from the moonlit chamber to a remembered or dreamed scene. Once again, the woman's back is silhouetted by light from inside her room, blocking her from being fully seen. Unlike other poets, who would move on from that image of the silhouetted back, Wei Zhuang unnecessarily identifies the woman as a courtesan in the closing line of the first stanza: "The small tower's high chamber is Miss Xie's home."

---

38. "Miss Xie" (*Xie niang*) was a name commonly used to refer to a courtesan in romantic poetry and lyrics. It appears nine times, and there are another six references to "[Miss] Xie's house," *Xie jia*, in the *HJJ*. For "Xie niang" as a reference to a courtesan, see the examples in Jin, *Quan Song ci diangu kaoshi cidian*, 989-90.

39. *HJJZS*, 70-71.

The opening of the second stanza returns to a first-person voice, marked by *anxiang* 暗想 (I secretly imagine) as the speaker plunges more deeply into imagination or dream to contemplate the woman's "face of jade," *yurong* 玉容. The closing couplet makes it clear how vividly he envisions her, as he offers us two versions of "what she resembles": "one branch of spring snow—frozen plum blossoms" and "completely covered in fragrant mists—a cluster of morning auroras." Both the language and the syntax of this second stanza are deliberately artful. Rather than revealing the male speaker's emotion (for the emotion has been revealed in the opening line), the rhetorical question "What does it resemble?" comes from the poet. The line and its response play on a famous passage from the *Shishuo xinyu* (A new account of tales of the world), in which Xie An spontaneously composed a poetic line—"White snow fluttering and flying—what is it like?" 白雪紛紛何所似—to which his nephew and niece responded with lines on salt and willow catkins.[40] Wei Zhuang's response to Xie An's question continues the game: "One branch of spring snow—frozen plum blossoms." The closing couplet is nearly syntactically parallel and strictly tonally parallel: "one branch" set against "completely covered," "spring snow" against "fragrant dew," and the metaphorical use of "frozen" for blossoms countered by the "cluster" of auroras. Instead of the melancholy recollection of a separated lover signaled by the opening line, the lyric leaves the impression of being a carefully staged, self-consciously "poetic" vignette.

In closing this lyric with an elegant and allusive couplet rather than a direct emotional statement, Wei Zhuang shows that his song lyric style included more than the hearty male persona of his "Pusa man" series. His "Huanxi sha" lyrics give us even more examples of his range. As we see in his fifth "Huanxi sha" lyric, Wei sometimes allows his female subjects to express their longing and melancholy directly.

---

40. *Shishuo xinyu jiaojian*, 72.

"Huanxi sha" (5th of 5)
Wei Zhuang

Night after night, I long for you as the water clock wears down.	夜夜相思更漏殘
Heartsick, I lean on the balustrade in the bright moonlight.	傷心明月憑欄杆
I imagine you longing for me in the chill of brocade quilts.	想君思我錦衾寒
Though so close, the painted hall seems as deep as the sea.	咫尺畫堂深似海
Since recalling you, I can only take out my old letters to read.	憶來唯把舊書看
How long will it be till we clasp hands to enter Chang'an?[41]	幾時攜手入長安

The topic of the fifth lyric is time and the perception of its passage, as the opening line makes clear: "Night after night, I long for you as the water clock wears down." The repetitiveness of "night after night," *ye ye* 夜夜, echoes the dripping of the water clock. Like any thwarted lover, the speaker goes out to lean on her balustrade; but there she envisions her absent lover differently from in the lover's dream of the previous lyric—she sees him missing her, in the "chill of brocade blankets." (This image is rather hopeful, since she assumes he is alone.) As in the previous lyric, Wei Zhuang uses verbs of perception to establish the first-person speaker: in the first line, "long for [you]," *xiang si* 相思,[42] introduces the possibility of a lover's confessional voice, and the unambiguous "imagine *you* longing for *me*" (*xiang jun si wo* 想君思我) in the third line settles the question. Although the subject of the lyric is certainly speaking directly, in this first stanza the voice is not strongly gendered male or female; the leaning on the balustrade and the sound of the water clock, both of which were associated with boudoir scenes of women, are the only clues that suggest gender.

---

41. *HJJZS*, 72.
42. I read *xiangsi* as "long for you," but it could also be read in other contexts as "long for him/her."

The opening line of the second stanza compounds the speaker's perception of the night's length, as she notes the lover's great distance: "the painted hall seems as deep as the sea"—even though it is actually close. Returning to her obsession with time, in the last two lines the speaker dwells on both the past and the future. In response to the past, she can only read old letters when overwhelmed by memory; as she looks to the future, she can only wonder aloud when they will be together again. Read against the "leaning on the balustrade" of the previous stanza, the letters (which were usually received by the abandoned woman) and the "painted hall" of this stanza push the voice toward the feminine. In the previous chapter, we noted that the theme of the "presentness" of the moment attracted a number of *Huajian ji* poets, Wei Zhuang chief among them. In contrast to the *carpe diem* sensuality we saw in the lyrics studied in Chapter 4, however, this lyric's treatment of time focuses on the pain and "unbearability" of the present moment, emotions that are shared by both men and women. The typical escapes for all lovers are dream (often aided by wine) and memory, but, as we see here, poets often portrayed these escapes as unattainable or else as heartbreaking when attained. Yet unlike the sorrow of abandonment, which was only voiced by women, the sorrow over the passage of time was one that both male and female voices confessed.

The "Huanxi sha" lyrics show Wei Zhuang to be perfectly capable of writing lyrics in different styles, including a style that is self-consciously literary and descriptive; at the same time, however, he seems more comfortable with the direct style allowed him by a first-person voice, whether male or female. We should also recall that the story of Wei's most famous poem, the "Lament of the Lady of Qin," was written as a narrative recounted in a first-person *female* voice. First-person voice was evidently a mode he preferred and in which he excelled.[43] Hypotactic syntax and colloquialism are an integral part of Wei Zhuang's song lyrics, but they are the consequences of the specific poetic choice to use first-person speakers. In

---

43. Wei also uses the first-person female voice in the colloquial style typical of his first-person male voices in his song lyrics, something that the Shu poets did not imitate. See, for example, the second lyric to "Si dixiang," *HJJZS*, 101.

this respect, he and Wen Tingyun still stand as the two extremes on the stylistic spectrum of the anthology. When we look at the lyrics of other *Huajian ji* poets, we see the contrast of these two styles being extended, sometimes amplified, by others.

The "Huanxi sha" lyrics of the late Tang poets Xue Zhaoyun and Zhang Bi reveal the later poets to be conscious of Wen and Wei as models, but they also show both poets to be more concerned than either Wen or Wei with integrating the elements of a lyric smoothly and coherently. In both poets' work, we find a strong awareness of poetic craft, from the use of imagery to the construction of parallel couplets. Xue Zhaoyun, who has only nineteen lyrics in the *Huajian ji*, has no fewer than eight "Huanxi sha" lyrics collected (and no more than three to any other tune title), which suggests that the Shu editors particularly admired the style of his "Huanxi sha" set.[44]

"Huanxi sha" (1st of 8)
Xue Zhaoyun

Red marsh-blossoms at the ferry, just as autumn rains begin—	紅蓼渡頭秋正雨
sand-imprinted tracks of gulls naturally turn into lines.	印沙鷗跡自成行
Tangling her hair and tossing sleeves, wild winds are fragrant.	整鬟飄袖野風香
Not speaking, but frowning, [mirrored] in the depths by the shore—	不語含顰深浦裏
How many times has she bitterly sorrowed over her sailing man?	幾回愁煞棹船郎
Swallows return, the sail disappears—the waters are boundless and deep.[45]	燕歸帆盡水茫茫

Xue's skills of imitation and composition show in every line of this first lyric. In a pattern we have seen often, Xue uses the first stanza to set the stage for the emotions and action of the second; in this case, the parting takes place outdoors, at a river ferry, in autumn

---

44. For a discussion of the critical responses to this lyric, see Zhang, *Huajian ci lunji*, 233–46.

45. *HJJZS*, 110.

rain. (The entire lyric strongly resembles Li Xun's first "Pusa man" lyric, examined in Chapter 4.) The opening line gives us the setting and mood: the appearance of the ferry indicates a journey, and therefore a lovers' parting, and the autumn rain adds another note of melancholy to the traditional season of parting. The "red marsh-blossoms" are certainly real flowers growing by the river, but they also hint at the woman's presence (woman-as-flower) in the scene. Finally, the use of the modifier *zheng* 正 (just at that time) in the final phrase *qiu zheng yu* 秋正雨 (just as autumn rains begin) draws attention to the immediacy of whatever is about to happen.

The subsequent line is even more skillfully crafted. "Imprinted on sand, tracks of gulls turn into lines" needs some explication. The image is one of script: the gulls' tracks are, like graphs, "printed," *yin* 印, on the sands. The tracks "become," or "naturally turn into," lines, *zi cheng hang* 自成行. But the imprinted tracks become lines of text only to the eye of the perceptive poet. This striking image was not Xue's own; it was adapted from other poets' versions of the metaphor, which itself comes from the legend of Cang Jie, the creator of Chinese script. Han Yu, in a *lianju*, linked verse, exchange with his friend Meng Jiao, writes of "sandy seal-script imprinted on turning flats." Li He reworked the same image in a couplet: "Washed sands nicely white and flat, / The standing horse imprints green characters." The later poet Du Mu also tried his hand: "Sandy isles imprinted by hooves of fawns."[46] Xue Zhaoyun reworks the image by making birds the source of the tracks, as they are in the Cang Jie myth, and then heightens the comparison by seeing not only individual graphs but lines of text in the "imprints." Xue's adaptation seems almost gratuitous in context unless we consider how a text in the landscape might speak to a scene of separation: lines of text suggest lines of letters to be sent and received. As we saw in the Shu poets' "Pusa man" lyrics, each natural detail contributes to determine mood, from the sorrow of autumn rain, to "lines" of

---

46. These three instances of the image are discussed by Owen in *End of the Chinese 'Middle Ages,'* 34–35. The translations of the lines by Han Yu, Li He, and Du Mu are Owen's.

letters of separation in the sand, to the turbulent, masculine "wild winds" that send her sleeves and hair flying in the first stanza's last line.

The second stanza turns to the woman, though not to her voice. The phrase "not speaking, but frowning" (*bu yu han pin* 不語含顰) is the reverse of a phrase in Wei Zhuang's first "Huanxi sha" lyric: "Frowning yet not speaking, she regrets spring's waning" (含顰不語恨春殘). In Xue's lyric, however, we find the woman standing on the shore, mirrored in the "depths" of the river, instead of leaning on the balustrade. She is rendered doubly opaque: mute and distorted by reflection. Her presence at the riverside is explained in the next line, in a question that reveals her emotions: "How many times has she bitterly sorrowed over her sailing man?" As in many lyrics that describe the abandoned woman, this question seems to be voiced not by her but by the poet. But as soon as we are told of the woman's "sailing man," we find that he has already left: "Swallows return as the sail disappears—the waters are boundless and deep." The ubiquitous swallows are "returning," in typical contrast to the sailboat carrying her lover, which is almost "extinguished," *jin* 盡, in the obscure distance. As she stares out over the river, the waters appear "boundless and deep," a paraphrase of the reduplicative binome *mang mang* 茫茫. Aside from the "bitter sorrow" of the penultimate line—a feeling that is attributed only tentatively to the woman—this lyric creates an emotional resonance that remains latent rather than being elaborated by the scene.

Xue Zhaoyun's carefully crafted lines reveal him to be interested in writing lyrics that employ the more complex imagery and language of regulated verse. In its focus on the natural contexts for the scene of parting, Xue's first lyric little resembles Wen Tingyun; in his second lyric, however, Xue imitates Wen's descriptive technique for his own purposes.

"Huanxi sha" (2nd of 8)
Xue Zhaoyun

Over caltrop blossoms on the filigreed mirror, a brocade sash hangs;	鈿匣菱花錦帶垂
silently she looks out from the balustrade at the time for taking off her makeup.	靜臨檻欄卸頭時

As bound coils of hair hang down to her earrings, she reckons his return.	約鬟低珥算歸期
In the lush garden, grasses are green—Xiang sandbars are far apart;	茂苑草青湘渚闊
amid remnants of dream pointlessly comes the water clock's faint sound.	夢餘空有漏依依
Two years to this day have crushed the fragrant blossom.[47]	二年終日損芳菲

In this lyric, we can see traces of Wen Tingyun's distinctive style, in the focus on objects in the boudoir, the glimpse of the woman's face or hair, and the absence of direct emotional expression. But, unlike Wen, Xue connects the details of the scene quite clearly in context, rather than allowing the discrete images to stand apart. The image of the first line, in which a brocade sash hangs over a mirrored case, is explained by the second line: it is the end of the day, the "hour of undressing." The erotic detail of the woman's uncoiling hair is also explained by the time of day, and her "reckoning his return" (*suan guiqi* 算歸期) tells us that her lover did not appear. Like Wei Zhuang's fifth "Huanxi sha" lyric, this lyric explores the passage of time and the tension between expectation and reality. At first, the line that opens the second stanza seems simply like decoration—green grasses in an overflowing garden, sandbars separated by the full waters of a wide river—but both the lushness of the garden and the breadth of the river (caused by spring rains) are markers of late spring, when the lover should already have returned. As in Wei Zhuang's third lyric, where moonlight falls through and seems to dissipate the "remnants of dream," *meng yu* 夢餘, in Xue's lyric we have the sound of a water clock distantly and "pointlessly" filtering through the same "remnants of dream." The sound of the clock is pointless because it marks only the disappearance of her memories and dreams of her lover, not the time to his return.[48] As a summation of the lyric's exploration of time, the final line pulls both stanzas together with the result of the woman's "reckoning" at the

---

47. *HJJZS*, 111.
48. The "Genglouzi" lyrics of many poets, particularly those of Wen Tingyun, explore this topic specifically.

close of the first stanza: it has been "two years ago to this day," by her count, that she has been waiting. The passage of time has "crushed the fragrant blossom," destroying both her looks and her spirits.

Xue Zhaoyun integrates the two stanzas both thematically and formally, exploiting the tension between expectations and reality. The thematic elements of the "Pusa man" lyrics are again present here—the liminal moment of twilight, the dream, the perceptions of time's passage—as are the typical objects of description—the woman's face and figure at her toilette, the vibrancy of the natural world set against the emptiness or stillness of the interior world—but in this lyric they are used to indicate the passage of different kinds of time. The juxtaposition of the woman as she silently "looks out from the balustrade" with the phrase "the time for taking off her makeup," *xie tou shi*, suggests that the woman's expectations have been disappointed: she has to undress, having dressed for someone who did not arrive. The twilight scene of undress might indicate the opening of a lovers' encounter, but the image of the woman reckoning her lover's return in the last line denies this possibility. In the two opening lines of the second stanza, the green of the lush grasses and the "breadth" of the river swollen with spring rains—the time of lovers' reuniting—is countered by the "distance" or "indistinctness," *yiyi*, of the waterclock's sound that ticks away the long moments of separation. And the woman's thoughts of the future (reckoning his return) in the last line of the first stanza are disappointed in the second stanza, which ends by looking to the past ("two years to this day"). Not a word is misplaced or thoughtlessly used, nor are there any empty particles or vernacular phrases. In terms of the rhetorical structure of the lyric as a whole, the two stanzas echo each other: both begin with descriptions of the present moment and end by pointing toward another moment in time. The first stanza closes with the woman's reckoning from the present forward in time to her lover's return, and the second stanza closes with the poet's reckoning backward from the present to the time when the lovers parted.

Like Wen Tingyun, Xue Zhaoyun prefers silent female subjects. For both poets, the close description of women in their interior settings replaces their direct speech. Given that the emotional range of female subjects was extremely narrow to begin with (the difference between "sorrow" and "melancholy" being negligible in these lyrics), poets could strip down a boudoir scene to merely a few details and still create a mood. However, as the most fragmented and static of Wen Tingyun's lyrics demonstrate, there were limits to the intelligibility of these sketchy scenes. Most of the *Huajian ji* poets did not imitate Wen Tingyun at his most opaque; Niu Qiao, in his "Pusa man" series, and Zhang Bi were the exceptions among the collection.

"Huanxi sha" (1st of 8)
Zhang Bi

The perfumed carriage with filigreed wheels passes the willow dike;	鈿轂香車過柳堤
amid the smoke from birch-candles, a horse neighs and neighs.[49]	樺煙分處馬頻嘶
For him, she's gotten deeply drunk, but not quite dazed.	爲他沉醉不成泥
Flowers fill the post house pavilion, fragrant dew grows fine.	花滿驛亭香露細
The cuckoo's sound is cut off, as the "jade toad" sets.[50]	杜鵑聲斷玉蟾低
Hiding her feelings, without speaking, she looks from the west of the tower.[51]	含情無語倚樓西

Zhang Bi's lyric consists of quick glimpses and small details of a seemingly incoherent scene. Reconstructing a story here requires attention to the clues in each line. The opening line shows us an ornate carriage crossing a "willow dike." The ornate carriage, as we saw in Niu Qiao's second "Pusa man" lyric, is likely to contain a courtesan; the willow dike was a favorite spot for romantic encounters. But the next line seems to place us elsewhere, outside the carriage, in a room or space filled with birch-candle smoke. The

---

49. The "birches" were candles in birch bark.
50. The toad was believed to be one of the denizens of the moon; the "jade toad" is thus a periphrasis for the moon.
51. *HJJZS*, 152.

horse's neigh is a common sign of the arrival or departure of the male lover, who rides his own horse, as opposed to riding in a carriage. The two lines, though not syntactically parallel, give us parallels on a number of levels: in the first line, we see a carriage, with (we assume) a woman inside, passing, *guo*, the willow dike. In the second, a "clearing," *fen chu* 分處, appears in the smoke, through which the horse's neighs penetrate. The female and male lines are made parallel by the dual images of crossing and penetration into a space marked as private or romantic. The closing line of the first stanza suggests a particular occasion, as well: "For him, she's gotten deeply drunk, but not quite dazed." This line explicitly announces the actors whose presence we have inferred; the line also heightens the eroticism of the lyric, and the simplicity of the syntax makes the woman's expectations clear. In this context, drunkenness is not an escape from the present moment, but a means to intensify it. This is why she is "not quite dazed," *bu cheng ni* 不成泥.

Zhang Bi uses the change in stanzas to signal a change in time: instead of the smoke and drunkenness of the first stanza, we find flowers, dew, and dawn in the second stanza. The opening two lines, though not syntactically parallel, set the new scene. The flowers covered with fine dew suggest that it is early morning, and the setting moon confirms it. We are apparently at the scene of the morning-after separation. Other details hint at an imminent parting: the cuckoo's cry (a reminder of separation), the use of the verb *duan* ("cut through," but also "cut off [from one another]") to describe its sound, and the suggestion that the flowers "filling" the courtyard are fallen to the ground of the pavilion. Zhang's choice of the two verbs *xi* 細, "grows fine," and *di* 低, "sets," as final rhyme-words also heightens the sense of attenuation and ending in both lines. Zhang Bi reworks a phrase used by Wei Zhuang and Xue Zhaoyun in his final line: the woman stands, "hiding her feelings, without speaking" 含情無語 (Wei, "Huanxi sha" #1: 含嚬不語, and Xue, "Huanxi sha" #1: 不語含嚬). In Zhang's lyric, however, her feelings are successfully "hidden" throughout.

Although his first lyric copies Wen Tingyun, Zhang Bi's second and third "Huanxi sha" lyrics demonstrate his mastery of different perspectives on the romantic story.

"Huanxi sha" (2nd of 10)
Zhang Bi

On horseback, my feelings fixed, I recall past revels:	馬上凝情憶舊遊
reflected flowers and sunken bamboo in the small stream's flow,	照花淹竹小溪流
over a filigreed zither, amid gauzy curtains, a jade hair pick.	鈿箏羅幕玉搔頭
I've long since left her gates, traveling beneath the moon—	早是出門長帶月
How can I bear our separation for yet another autumn?	可堪分袂又經秋
In evening winds and setting sun—overwhelming sorrow![52]	晚風斜日不勝愁

(3rd of 10)

I stand alone on the cold steps, gazing at the moon glow;	獨立寒階望月華
dew thickens, and fragrance drifts from courtyard flowers.	露濃香泛小庭花
By the embroidered screen, she sadly puts out the light of a single lamp.	繡屏愁背一燈斜
Ever since the clouds and rain have broken up and scattered,	雲雨自從分散後
in this human realm there's no route to the transcendent's home.	人間無路到仙家
I can only rely on soul-dreams to visit the ends of the earth.[53]	但憑魂夢訪天涯

The two lyrics need to be examined not only against the evocative and opaque lyric that preceded them but also against one another, because their rhetorical structures are almost identical. Both lyrics announce a male speaker in the first line of the first stanza. In the second lyric, the opening, "on horseback," tells us that the subject of the lyric is male, and the use of the verb "recall," *yi* 憶, indicates a first-person voice. The same object is accomplished in the third

---

52. Ibid., 152–53.
53. Ibid., 153.

lyric, with the opening line that tells us the speaker is "standing alone," *du li* 獨立, and gazing, *wang* 望, which together indicate a male speaker.

In both lyrics, the actions of the first line—"remembering" and "gazing," which are placed in the same position in the respective opening lines—serve as the frame for the subsequent couplets, which give us sharp, static images of a space and a person not within the speaker's grasp. The first stanzas of both lyrics open with a male voice that frames the recollection or object of the gaze from a fixed location (ending the line with a rhyme), then moves to a description of the setting (another rhyme), and then concludes with a close-up of part of the woman's body (final rhyme). In the second lyric, the couplet concerns memories of "past revels": a natural setting of spring flowers and flowing water, and suggestive details of the woman's presence, such as her inlaid zither and jade-pinned head. The couplet in the third lyric presents a spring evening scene, and a glimpse of the woman's back. Paradoxically, in the second lyric the couplet's images are bright and well detailed by the clarity of memory, but in the third lyric—even though the speaker is evidently in the street gazing up at the woman's room—his gaze cannot penetrate the layers of concealment created by the dew thickening, *nong* 濃, the drifting fragrance, and the brocade screen.

The second stanzas of both lyrics open abruptly with a shift in time. In the second lyric, the male lover brings himself back to the present moment and his concern for the future, asking himself, "How can I bear our separation for yet another autumn?" Instead of answering this unanswerable question, he closes with a plaint: "In evening winds and setting sun—overwhelming sorrow!" In the third lyric, the speaker expresses his relationship with his lover throughout the second stanza, via the conventional figure of the woman-as-transcendent, *xian* 仙. He opens by recalling the "clouds and rain" (a figure for sexual intercourse) that have since "broken up and scattered," *fensan* 分散, like the two parted lovers. The closing two lines treat separation in terms of space rather than time: the woman's "transcendent home" is at such a distance (at the "ends of the earth," *tianya* 天涯) that it is only attainable through "soul-dreams," the vehicle for the spiritual journeys so common in the *Huajian ji* lyrics.

Zhang's self-conscious use of different styles is evident in both lyrics. He genders and locates the speaker (male, riding a horse) and also announces the topic ("recollection") in the opening line of the second lyric: "On horseback, my feelings fixed, I recall past revels." The recollection that follows in the descriptive couplet, however, is a static scene with few verbs; its reflected flowers and "sunken" (because reflected in water) bamboo are seen in "the small stream's flow," *xiao xi liu* 小溪流, rather than in "the flowing stream" (the inversion needed for the rhyme). The final line of the stanza is even more elliptical, giving us objects associated with boudoirs and the metonym of the "jade hair pick" for the woman. But in the second stanza, Zhang resumes and intensifies the first-person voice, shifting to the more colloquial tone of phrases such as *ke kan* 可堪 ("how can I bear . . . ?") and *bu sheng* 不勝 ("overwhelming," or "inexhaustible") to express the speaker's sorrow. The same movement between poetic registers appears in the third lyric as well, in the direct syntax and strong male voice pervading the opening lines of the stanzas: "I stand alone on the cold steps, gazing at the moon glow," and "Ever since the clouds and rain have broken up and scattered." The subsequent woman-as-transcendent image was a staple of romantic lyrics, and it does not receive particularly original treatment here. The trope extends the vague reference to goddess visits signaled by the "clouds and rain" of the previous line; Zhang then completes the stanza by referring to the "ends of the earth" to which he would need to travel in dream to visit his vanished "transcendent."

Although Zhang Bi deliberately moves back and forth between descriptive and expressive modes in these song lyrics, the voices in his "Huanxi sha" lyrics express a surprising similarity of feeling. In both lyrics, the opening lines gender the first-person voices as male, and yet the sentiments that are articulated echo the terms used elsewhere in the collection by female voices. In the "Jiu quanzi" lyrics, Li Xun's speakers cried, "I can't bear to listen!" and asked, "How can I bear to listen?" In the "Huanxi sha" lyrics, the phrase "how can I bear [a certain plight]?" (*ke kan, na kan* 那堪, and once as *qi kan* 豈堪) occurs six times—three times in lyrics with strong male voices (Zhang Bi's second lyric and two lyrics by Li Xun) and three times in lyrics with female subjects. The same gender-neutrality of feeling is found in Zhang's third lyric, where the male speaker relies on dream-journeys, which are used often by female speakers in "Pusa man" and in other lyrics to travel to the side of male lovers.

And yet there are still a few differences between the expressions allowed female and male subjects in these lyrics, particularly in the more erotic song lyrics: women do not conjure up visions of handsome men, nor do they express desire for sexual intimacy beyond a generalized longing for "good times" or "happiness" with their lovers. At the same time, male desire is rarely articulated or acknowledged in a first-person voice; instead, it is performed as a voyeuristic recollection of the woman. The eroticism of the *Huajian ji*'s song lyrics quite often comes from the staging of a sexual encounter, where glimpses of skin and hints of feeling are enough to set the mood, and the final, most private moment is withheld from the gaze of the audience. Much of the eroticism is descriptive and static, but, as we saw in the flirtatious "Pusa man" lyrics by Wei Chengban, a few poets do narrate the progress of the sexual encounter. The question of voice in erotic song lyrics is an interesting one: in order to stay within the broadest boundaries of literary propriety (insofar as we can reconstruct those boundaries from extant Tang poetry), poets had to take an observing stance, one that allowed them to control the view and maintain distance from the action. Ouyang Jiong's lyrics come closer to the lovers than do those of perhaps any other poet in the anthology, and for that reason, later readers found them excessively salacious.[54]

"Huanxi sha" (3rd of 3)
Ouyang Jiong

When they meet, they cease to speak of having shed tears—	相見休言有淚珠
as the wine wears off, once again they can recount their pleasures.	酒闌重得敘歡娛
By phoenix screen and mandarin duck pillow, they spend the night behind gilded doors.	鳳屏鴛枕宿金鋪

---

54. Noted in *QTWDCSZ*, 911.

Amid orchid musk's thin scent, hear breathing in and out;	蘭麝細香聞喘息
through fancy gauze and fine crochet, see sinew and skin.	綺羅纖縷見肌膚
At this moment, does she still resent her faithless lover or not?[55]	此時還恨薄情無

This lyric provides an excellent example of the clever lyrics poets could write with trite phrases and conventional themes: the trick was to present them in a new—or, in this case, prurient—combination. The lovers' encounter is signaled from the first words of the opening line, "meet each other," after which Ouyang makes sure to include the requisite objects: wine (for relaxation and arousal), screen (to conceal), pillow (drawing attention to the lovers' being in bed), incense (for the correct obscuring and fragrant ambiance), and gauzy, crocheted clothing that reveals as much as it covers.

We should note, however, that Ouyang takes pains to depict these objects in a manner that enhances the mood of the scene. For example, the lovers are not depicted drinking the wine or becoming drunk; instead, it is only after the wine that they have consumed "wears off" that they are able to recount their pleasures. This detail enhances the intimacy of the scene, since it suggests not the public rowdiness of the party but rather the quieter, private moments in which they can speak and do other things. Ouyang is quite clear about the subject under discussion: it is not *wang shi* 往事, "past affairs," which occur often in other romantic lyrics, but "pleasures," *huanyu* 歡娛, a compound that in this context includes past happiness and sexual pleasure. And in the closing line of the stanza, as we might expect, the two lovers spend the night together amid the traditional objects of a courtesan's boudoir.

The second stanza is by far the most explicit and intimate description of a sexual encounter in the anthology, but it is also syntactically well-crafted. A literal translation of the opening parallel couplet demonstrates its calculated ambiguity:

---

55. *HJJZS*, 210.

蘭	麝	細	香 //	聞	喘	息
orchid	musk	thin	fragrance //	hear	breathing	in/out
綺	羅	纖	縷 //	見	肌	膚
ornate	gauze	fine	crochet //	see	sinew	flesh

We have two choices in our reading of the second stanza: we could continue to read it from the point of view of the third-person observer that was introduced in the first stanza, or we could switch to a first-person male voice. The first choice produces the translation I offered, where the poet and his audience truly become voyeurs of the sexual encounter. Yet the two verbs "hear" and "see," since they are verbs of sensation, strongly suggest a first-person male voice, a subject who is experiencing the sound and sight of his lover. Nor does the closing line of the stanza settle the issue. The rhetorical question, "At this moment does she still resent her careless lover or not?" could be read as a comment by the omniscient narrator, but also as a teasing question from the "faithless lover" himself. My interpretation of the line as the comment of a third-person observer comes from comparison with the many other rhetorical questions in the *Huajian ji*'s romantic lyrics. Furthermore, it seems to respond to the question Ouyang Jiong asks at the end of his first "Huanxi sha" lyric of three: "At this moment whom does her heart lie next to?" (*ci shi xin zai A-shei bian* 此時心在阿誰邊), a question that seems to be spoken by the poet with regard to the abandoned woman who has been described in the opening stanza. Therefore, I continue to read the second stanza in the third person, and the line as the observer's final mocking comment on the intimate scene he has so attentively detailed.

In the end, as in many of the lyrics examined in this chapter, the choice between first- and third-person narrators in Ouyang Jiong's lyric is only a problem in English translation, not in Chinese. No matter who is doing the seeing and hearing, the audience is still given an erotic close-up of the sexual encounter. But the significance of the poet's choice of speaker or voice is made explicit in the erotic lyrics of Ouyang Jiong and other Shu. In the case of the "neutral" third-person point of view, the default gender is male—not because the poets were themselves male but because the tradition of romantic poetry, from Southern Dynasties palace-style poetry to

Tang boudoir quatrains, had as its foundation the depiction of female beauty and desirability. Such depictions were, for the most part, written as detailed descriptions of a woman's face, figure, and demeanor, with the occasional expression of sentiment added for a pathetic or coquettish effect. The erotic lyrics of the *Huajian ji* remain firmly within this tradition. The decorum that is violated in this lyric is the decorum of eroticism in poetry—Ouyang exceeded the proprieties of intimate revelation—not the decorum of gender.

As final examples of the *Huajian ji* poets' ability to maneuver between styles by changing voices, let us look at two "Huanxi sha" lyrics by the Shu poet Gu Xiong. In his series of eight lyrics, Gu Xiong offers both male and female perspectives on the experience of separation.[56] His "Huanxi sha" lyrics that focus on the abandoned woman are indeed written in the delicate, highly descriptive style that dominates the collection. Two of the eight lyrics are written in a first-person voice that is clearly gendered male, but the emotions expressed by the male voices are identical to those expressed by the women in the other six lyrics. The last two lyrics in his set of eight show the contrasts in style and the similarities of emotional expressions attributed to male and female subjects.

"Huanxi sha" (7th of 8)
Gu Xiong

Geese echo in the distant skies, the jade water clock [sounds] clearly;	雁響遙天玉漏清
beyond the small screened window, the moon is hazy, then bright.	小紗窗外月朧明
On the kingfisher curtains, golden ducks; incense has burned down.	翠幃金鴨燭香平
Why doesn't he return? News and letters are cut off.	何處不歸音信斷
Fine evenings pointlessly startle my dreaming soul awake.	良宵空使夢魂驚

---

56. Gu Xiong switches back and forth between male and female perspectives in other tune title sets, such as "He ye bei" and "Xian zhong xin."

The mat is cool, the pillow icy—overwhelming feeling![57]	簟涼枕冷不勝情

(8th of 8)

The dew is white, the "toad" bright—autumn arrives again.	露白蟾明又到秋
Happy times and secret meetings—both are far, far away.	佳期幽會兩悠悠
When will this entanglement of dream, this labor of passion be over?	夢牽情役幾時休
I remember the bewitching girl as she faintly frowned:	記得泥人微斂黛
wordlessly, she looked out from the small painted tower.[58]	無言斜倚小畫樓
Secretly thinking on past affairs—overwhelming sorrow![59]	暗思前事不勝愁

Given the way in which the two lyrics echo one another, it is possible that Gu Xiong intended these lyrics to be performed in sequence; the *Huajian ji* editors certainly arranged them so that their juxtaposition would generate the sense of two opposing views of separation. The same setting—an autumn evening—is established in the opening line of each lyric, and, in the closing line, each subject speaks in the same manner of the pain of separation. In the seventh lyric, the opening line's familiar figure of geese (which were seen as bearers of letters and, because of their migration, a symbol of return) sets the season—autumn—and establishes the melancholy tone. The echoes of geese faintly calling in the sky are contrasted against the clarity, *qing*, of the jade water clock's sound as it marks the passage of the evening. The whiteness of the "jade" water clock and

---

57. *HJJZS*, 258.

58. All the editions I have examined have *shu* 書 modifying "tower," with no explanation. However, given the commonness of the phrase *hualou* 畫樓, "painted tower," in the *Huajian ji* (six occurrences, and *hua* occurs frequently in similar compounds such as *huatang* 畫堂, "painted hall," and *hualiang* 畫梁, "painted beams"), it is more likely that the phrase was originally *hualou*. I assume that *shu* was substituted for *hua* very early in the text's history. My translation reflects my emendation.

59. *HJJZS*, 259.

the "moon's brilliance"—all of which are linked by their *yin*, female, and watery associations—suggest a cool, crisp evening. This line tells us that we are in a woman's chamber, as we encounter familiar decorations: in this case, incense and gilt-embroidered ducks on curtains. That the incense has burned down until it is "flat," *ping*, could simply indicate the end of the evening, or it could also suggest that someone who was expected never appeared. In either case, the scene of the first stanza, whether or not it is conveyed in a woman's voice, unfolds within the private space of a woman's boudoir.

The question that opens the second stanza of the seventh lyric confirms the impression of a female subject, since it is usually the female half of the couple, left behind, who wonders of the other, "where is he that he doesn't return?" Her statement that "news" has been cut off has already been foreshadowed by the sound of the geese of the opening line, whose voices echo as they return in migration, but who carry no news to the waiting woman. The final two lines of the lyric could be read plausibly in either a narrative or speaking voice; I have chosen the latter simply to reinforce the similarities to the eighth lyric. When she tells us that fine evenings (such as this one) "pointlessly startle [her] dreaming soul awake," we understand that the scene in the first stanza was in fact one of expectations and desires disappointed. To reinforce this mood, the lyric closes with the melancholy image of a chilly mat and pillow (an "empty bed," in other words), eliciting the emotional response: "overwhelming feeling!" *bu sheng qing* 不勝情. This phrase—a similar version of which we saw in the closing line of Zhang Bi's second "Huanxi sha" lyric (Zhang: "overwhelming sorrow!" *bu sheng chou* 不勝愁)—is the equivalent of "wordlessness" on the part of a female subject. To translate more literally, it is her feelings that are seemingly limitless, overwhelming, *bu sheng*; in that state, she is unable to communicate further.[60]

---

60. The phrase *bu sheng* X, in which X is an emotion or quality that overwhelms the speaker or observer (in either a negative or positive way)—as with "sorrow," "feeling," "grief" *bei* 悲, "regret" *hen* 恨, "charm" *jiao* 嬌, and "spring [beauty]," *chun* 春—occurs no fewer than fifteen times in the collection, five times at the end

The opening line of the next lyric, the last in Gu's series of eight, establishes its mood and scene with the same economy of words: with the phrase "autumn arrives again," *you dao qiu* 又到秋, Gu suggests the wordplay of *you dao chou* 又到愁, "sorrow comes again" (he uses *chou*, "sorrow," as the rhyme-word for the final line). In contrast to the preceding lyric's details, the eighth lyric's images of autumn seem almost deliberately plain—the dew is a stark "white," and the moon, represented by the synecdoche "toad," is just "bright," like the hazy moon of the seventh lyric. The dew and moon of this lyric are less important modally than thematically: they are reminders of the passage of time, proof of his plaint that "autumn comes again." The second line develops this idea further by turning to the memory of the speaker, who describes, with the reduplicative binome *youyou* 悠悠, the "happy times and secret meetings" of his love affair, evoking distance in both time and space. As we have seen in other lyrics, the shift from description to expression of internal states or to the perception of time often indicates the first-person voice, and the third line here demonstrates that this lyric is no exception. The images of dreams acting to "entangle," *qian* 牽, the lover, and of the passion of love requiring "labor," *yi* 役, indicate a first-person speaker who perceives himself entangled by romance. A similar use of this metaphor is also voiced by the speaker in Li Xun's third "Jiu quanzi" lyric: "Entangled by sorrow, disturbed by longing, watches toll without end" (牽愁惹思更無停). And the question "how long has it been . . . ?" concludes the first stanza's reflection on the passage of time by drawing attention to the speaker's obsession with recapturing past events. As we saw in Xue Zhaoyun's second "Huanxi sha" lyric, where the abandoned woman was "calculating" her lover's return, this obsession with time, past and future, is one that both participants in the romance could share.

By the opening of the second stanza, we are secure in reading the eighth lyric in a first-person male voice; there we hear "I remember," *jide* 記得, the marker of first-person memory used by Wei

---

of the closing lines of "Huanxi sha" lyrics. This is a useful example of lexical borrowing that seems to fill formal needs.

Zhuang and others, and see the "faintly frowning" woman imagined by the speaker. The phrase *jide* is used six times in the *Huajian ji*, and in five of the lyrics in which it is found the voice is clearly marked as a male first-person speaker, who frames a recollection of his lover in subsequent lines.[61] The rhetorical structure of the second stanza is identical to the structure of the first stanzas in Zhang Bi's male-voiced "Huanxi sha" lyrics. In Zhang Bi's lyrics, the male speakers were "recalling," *yi*, and "gazing," *wang*. If we read Gu Xiong's lyric as we read Zhang's, then the male lover is watching the woman "wordlessly look out from the small painted tower" and is thereby able to penetrate her heart, seeing that she is "secretly thinking on past affairs." The "wordlessness" that we have seen so often and the "small painted tower" of the second line suggest that the speaker is still describing the woman of his memory. However, the final line offers us two possible readings: either the male subject is expressing his own feelings as he remembers the "past affairs," or, in a continuation of the previous lines, he is imagining his lover's distress over him. Neither the "secret thinking" nor the colloquial phrase "overwhelming sorrow," *bu sheng chou*, which we saw in Gu's seventh lyric, settles the question. As we saw in Wei Zhuang's third and fifth "Huanxi sha" lyrics, the "secret imagining" that lovers did could include envisioning the absent lover's emotions ("I imagine you longing for me in the chill of brocade quilts") as well as her face. This particular sequence of lyrics raises questions about the importance of contexts—performance contexts and textual contexts—for the reception of song lyrics. Read or performed together, the lyrics echo each other's sentiments; neither voice is more wounded or sorrowful than the other. The lyrics tell us that expressions of romantic loss are not just for abandoned women, and that male lovers too can voice their memories and desires—but their expressions are only similar, not identical. In conclusion, I want to

---

61. The five lyrics are: Wei Zhuang's second "Heye bei," Niu Qiao's first "Jiu quanzi," Niu Xiqi's first "Sheng chazi," Gu Xiong's eighth "Huanxi sha," and Gu's fourth "Heye bei." The exception is Xue Zhaoyun's third "Huanxi sha," which also uses the phrase to open the second stanza and frame the last two lines as the *female* speaker's memory.

use this finding to examine some of the differences in male and female subjectivity as they are represented in the *Huajian ji*.

In Chapter 4, I concurred with the majority of scholars who argue that Wen Tingyun's descriptive style had a greater impact on other *Huajian ji* poets than did Wei Zhuang's looser, more colloquial style. In this chapter, however, I have mounted the apparently contradictory argument that Wen Tingyun's influence is perhaps overemphasized. Instead, I have suggested, the *Huajian ji* poets' choices of perspective or voice had a greater impact on their lyrics than did earlier poets' styles. As we saw in "Pusa man," "Jiu quanzi," and "Huanxi sha," lyrics written from the point of view of a third-person observer focus on the scene and the woman in it. Although some lyrics written in this manner shift into a first-person female voice in a second stanza (recalling that three-quarters of the collection was written in the two-stanza form, making this an option for most poets), the majority retain the observing, voyeuristic viewpoint throughout. The audience deduces the woman's emotional state from the clues in the landscape (autumn rain, spring lushness), from details of objects in the boudoir (cool mats, burnt incense), and sometimes from questions presented as the woman's feelings or the observer's comment. This evocative, descriptive style clearly echoes Wen Tingyun; however, in the "Jiu quanzi" and "Huanxi sha" lyrics of the different poets we have examined in this chapter, we have been able to distinguish discrete components of that style, independent of Wen Tingyun's model within the tune title set.

The features of Wen Tingyun's poetic style that later *Huajian ji* poets imitated most often were his use of metonymic detail in describing women and their boudoirs; his preference for static portraits, presented with few verbs and little action; and his attempts to create an atmosphere of emotional latency, transferring a value of Tang *shi* to his song lyrics. But as the "Jiu quanzi" and "Huanxi sha" lyrics demonstrate, Shu poets had other perspectives and voices—and, consequently, other styles—available to them. Among the early poets in the collection, we can certainly trace the use of first-person speakers to Wei Zhuang, who used them more often than any other poet in the *Huajian ji*, but they were also an important part of the medieval song tradition, particularly in *yuefu* and other forms marked as "folk." The shifts—between observed women and speaking men, observed women and speaking women—that occur from lyric to lyric (and occasionally within a single lyric) reveal the poets' self-conscious choices. If the subject of the lyric is marked as male, we hear the story of the romantic encounter told as first-person remembrance, in a straightforward and often colloquial manner— colloquialism, in this context, suggesting sincerity. But if the first-person male voice "recalls" or "imagines" the woman, the style of the lyric usually shifts also, back to the descriptive, static style used in female-centered lyrics. Although I could offer lyrics from many other tune title sets as further proof, I think the evidence of the lyrics from "Jiu quanzi" and "Huanxi sha" alone demonstrates that the *Huajian ji* poets fully realized the consequences of choosing one perspective over another and even exploited the contrasts in sequences of lyrics with different perspectives.[62]

When we strip away the acknowledged stylistic differences between lyrics with male and female subjects, the substance of the respective lyrics' emotional expression appears at first to be fundamentally the same. For both men and women in the *Huajian ji*'s romantic lyrics, the love story never changes, nor do the kinds of feelings that spring from it. The apparent similarity between male and female responses to the romantic story comes from two sources: from the essentially conventional and categorical nature of the emotions in these romantic lyrics ("sorrow" and "melancholy"), and from the imitative practice on which the *Huajian ji* is based.[63] The conventions of romantic poetry, like those of other subgenres of medieval poetry, include fixed emotional responses to particular

---

62. I would also recall the point I made earlier about the relative importance of these two tune titles in the anthology: taken together, the 26 lyrics to "Jiu quanzi" and the 57 lyrics to "Huanxi sha" constitute 17 percent of the entire collection.

63. On this subject, Stephen Owen has noted the following: "Words like 'love,' 'longing,' and 'sadness' are general categories and only crude ways of articulating particular and constantly changing states of feeling. Using categorical language, the song lyric sought ways to speak of states of feeling more particular, more immediate, and more variable than language readily permitted." Owen, "Meaning the Words," in Yu, ed., *Voices*, 46.

cues. Returning swallows evoke thoughts of separation; passing geese remind one of letters not sent or received; spring scenery calls attention to the lover's loneliness and heartbreak at a time when he or she should be happy and carefree. Unlike poets of later generations—who wondered aloud in song lyrics, "how do I express this special feeling?"—late Tang and Shu poets seem to have enjoyed working within the established bounds of "melancholy" and "longing," just as they appreciated the creative recycling of other poets' words and themes. For the *Huajian ji* poets, the issue was not "how do I express *this* feeling?" but rather, an earlier, perhaps more pressing question: "can I communicate at all?" The emotions that they wanted to express, however, were no more particular than "sorrow" or "feeling."

The *Huajian ji* poets' use of imitation and lexical borrowing also contributes to this sameness of emotional response. As we have seen in the three tune title sets, poets quite freely worked three- and four-character phrases from other poets' lyrics into their own lines. Although I have only noted examples that occur within tune title sets, the *Huajian ji* poets were not so restrained, lifting phrases and lines from one tune title to another. Such borrowing was bound to create a similarity of expression in the work of different poets. Nor can we ignore the hand of the Shu editors in creating an anthology-wide sameness of sentiment; their choices may indeed have excluded lyrics written in voices considered too *outré* for a volume meant to represent Shu's refined sensibility and talent. We cannot determine which played the greater part, but the resulting homogeneity is undeniable.

From the viewpoint of performers of song lyrics and their audiences, shifts in style and perspective would offer them a wider performative range. Such a range had distinct advantages for elite performers and those who performed for elite audiences. Even though the traditional literati approach to the romantic vignette—the description of the boudoir woman's response to separation—remained the standard in the *Huajian ji* lyrics, there were also many lyrics that used male and female first-person voices, or were unproblematically neutral. These choices would give performers both flexibility and intelligibility. The intelligibility of the boudoir vignette was already guaranteed by the medieval poetic tradition; the intelligibility of first-person voices was assured by the use of verbs of emotion and action, and by locative phrases situating the speaking subject in space and time, both old tricks from the realm of popular song. Just as importantly, the music—including melody, instrumentation, and tempo—would shape the audience's understanding of the words they heard and would indeed have suggested a mood even before the singer began to perform. As we have seen often in the lyrics, the poets' use of the framing devices of memory and dream allowed them to move back and forth between poetic registers without sacrificing narrative coherence. In the performance context, imitation and quotation of other lyrics would only heighten the audience's sense of familiarity when hearing a new song, and would also add wit to what are otherwise endlessly melancholy refrains.

This dedication to the melancholy side of love raises questions about the desires encoded in the lyrics and the importance of those desires to the genre of song lyrics after the *Huajian ji*. My previous point—that despite stylistic variations, the range of emotional expression appears the same across changing points of view—brings us to the heart of "romance" in these romantic lyrics. The *Huajian ji* song lyrics offer us a series of snapshots of the vagaries of a love affair between a traditionally passive woman, enclosed in her private space, and a traveling man. As we have seen, the poets' interest was fixed on a very few episodes within the romance: with the exception of the occasional erotic encounter or reunion, the great majority of these lyrics dwell on scenes of separation. Although it emerged from the tradition of medieval romantic poetry, the *Huajian ji* poets' obsession with the sorrow of separation was unprecedented in its intensity. As many scholars have noted, the *Huajian ji* is remarkable in the history of medieval genres in that it links a single form with a single topic: romantic love. This achievement should lead us to question the cultural and literary forces that might have shaped such a choice.

Stephen Owen has argued that romantic *chuanqi* from the Tang "do not represent the social facts of the demimonde; they represent the culture of the demimonde embodied in fictions that are motivated by its deepest concerns."⁶⁴ Given that these stories were authored by men, the social and financial inequalities that were of real concern in the institution of marriage are transformed or ignored. Women are represented in romantic fiction as equal actors, whose actions have equally weighty consequences on their male counterparts. Owen argues that this representation was an essential element of the stories, that "the culture of romance depended on a fiction of continuing free choice." In the romantic lyrics of the *Huajian ji*, however, I think we find a slightly different "culture of romance" at work, one that we can discern by scrutinizing the apparent affective continuity between male and female subjects. We should of course acknowledge that some of the lyrics that detail women's appearance and demeanor are erotically appealing, and that many of the *Huajian ji*'s romantic lyrics seem to be no more than that. At the same time, however, lyrics that use female and male first-person voices (which are the minority) use similar terms for their internal emotional states, articulating the feeling of being romantically attached to someone as an admission of powerlessness, regardless of the subject's gender. Although the poet's focus is usually on the helpless female lovers, we also hear the male voice lamenting his inability to act or to change his circumstances. Specific images make this startlingly clear: Li Xun talks of being "entangled by sorrow, disturbed by longing" 牽愁惹思; Gu Xiong speaks of the "entanglement of dream" 夢牽 and the experience of passion or love as "labor" 役.

In the lyrics to "Jiu quanzi" and "Huanxi sha," we find many instances of the loss of control from both male and female points of view. In Wei Zhuang's male-voiced lyrics, for example, we find the speaker trying to compensate for his lover's absence by using his imagination to summon up her face, or, even more hopefully, the thought of her reciprocal longing for him. Imagination, dream, and memory are the three avenues open to the powerless lover, but we know those methods can also fail. In Xue Zhaoyun's second "Huanxi sha," the female subject is left with only the "remnants" of a dream, through which the sound of the water clock, the symbol of time's inevitable passage, "pointlessly" penetrates. The rhetorical

---

64. Owen, *End of the Chinese 'Middle Ages,'* 133.

question that begins "how can I bear . . . ?"—appearing in Li Xun's "Jiu quanzi" lyrics and Zhang Bi's "Huanxi sha" lyric—is fundamentally an admission that the lover is facing something he or she cannot change but nevertheless has to endure. One could perhaps explain this sense of powerlessness simply by referring to the conventions for poetic representation of love and beautiful women, which dictate that the abandoned woman lament her plight. Certainly the influence of convention should not be discounted, but we also have to contend with the male subject who expresses his longing in the exact same terms—a voice that was a negligible part of the tradition.

I argued at the beginning of this chapter that the *Huajian ji* poets' use of the male voice in romantic lyrics was part of an effort to promote the song lyric as an appropriate literati activity (an attempt to appropriate the "authenticity" of *shi*). If that were true, then why would poets writing in the male voice use the same melancholy, helpless voice used by and about female subjects? We might explore different answers to this question. First, we should not ignore the traditional reading of allegorical intent in romantic poetry. This is *not* to say that these romantic lyrics are miniature allegories of the Shu poets' relationships with Wang Jian and other Shu rulers, but merely to suggest that song lyrics written in male voices that express feelings of helplessness and the inability to communicate with a "distant" beloved might occasionally be used, or read, as comments on other kinds of power relationships. The Former and Latter Shu court settings for the performance of song lyrics would certainly have heightened the possibility of such interpretation.

With respect to romantic relations, the realities of interactions between literati men and courtesans were of course defined by social and financial power. Although anecdotes suggest that the most famous and elite courtesans had the freedom to choose their lovers, the majority of such women most likely did not. In that sense, romantic song lyrics reflected social reality: powerlessness with regard to choice of mate was an attribute of the female half of the couple in both society and its representation. The eternal fidelity of the "abandoned woman" was a powerful and persistent romantic ideal. By sometimes marking that powerlessness as male in their song lyrics, the *Huajian ji* poets were not only invoking traditional representations of the dangers of women's power (the image of "woman-as-bewitching-seductress" or as "toppler-of-states") but were also constructing a new romantic ideal—that of the male subject as an emotional, expressive, and committed lover. As Maija Samei has noted, the abandoned woman persona embodies virtues central to the Chinese ethical tradition, such as endurance, submission, and loyalty, and the figure's embodiment of these virtues was one reason for its endurance.[65] In the *Huajian ji* lyrics with voices marked as masculine, poets reclaim those virtues and add to them their taste for romantic love. The secondary version of the romance laid out by the *Huajian ji* is a new take on the old story: helpless in the face of separation, male lovers could also endlessly long for and reenact the affair in memory, drunkenness, and dream.

And yet the confession of helplessness in the face of overwhelming *qing* voiced by male subjects collapses when we listen more closely: unlike women, who are so often "wordless," "silent," "not speaking," and constantly observed, men in these song lyrics recount their experiences in first-person terms. They "remember" and "imagine," and they preserve the experience in verse. The *Huajian ji* poets' preference for decorative but inaccessible women is countered by the colloquial frankness of their male speakers. The song lyrics tell us that both men and women were bound by time and space from repeating their moments of passion; unlike the silenced female subjects, however, the male subjects of the song lyrics were able to use their first-person voices to recount, and thereby relive, those experiences. I would note that the censure directed at the *Huajian ji* by readers in later dynasties stemmed from its ornate style, which we have filiated to Wen Tingyun, and not from its poets' experimentation with male voices. Furthermore, even the apparent particularity of the *Huajian ji*'s first-person voices (whether male or female) is undermined by the constant borrowing and lexical narrowness of the song lyrics themselves. Ouyang Jiong's emphasis on "craft" should be taken seriously, perhaps even

---

65. Samei, 15.

more so when we read lyrics that seem artless. It may also have disguised what was truly an innovation of the anthology.

In the case of song lyrics as a social practice for literati, Ouyang Jiong and his fellow living *Huajian ji* song lyric poets claimed legitimacy in two ways: by marginalizing the frank female voice of popular song, and replacing it with portraits of lovely quiet courtesans, they created a space for song lyrics within elite society. At the same time, by occasionally borrowing a first-person male voice from *yuefu* and *shi*, they projected elite identity onto a suspect genre. In his preface, Ouyang Jiong advertised the collection in these terms, and yet, somewhat surprisingly, he did not mention the realm of the emotions, *qing*, for which poetry and song had a legitimate claim to speak. Perhaps that is because such a claim would have brought unwanted scrutiny of the kinds of *qing* expressed in the collection: feelings that were destabilizing, obsessive, and uncontrollable, whether experienced by men or women. Today, though representations of women and male desire in the *Huajian ji* lyrics fit neatly into a host of contemporary discussions of gender and eroticism, the realm of emotional expression in romantic song lyrics, and particularly the focus on separation sorrow, remains resistant to analysis. Perhaps this is because study of the historical evidence cannot support much speculation about the social or psychological underpinnings of such expression. In the next chapter, however, analysis of a reversed representation of male and female romantic powerlessness will allow us to reexamine the expression of feeling and desire in the collection and the emergent genre.

SIX

Divine Beauties

Apparitions of "Goddesses" in the *Huajian ji*

Beautiful women in the guise of goddesses or goddesses who descend to behave like courtesans appear throughout the *Huajian ji*, as in this lyric to the tune "Lin jiang xian" ("The Transcendent by the River"):

"Lin jiang xian" (2nd of 2)
Sun Guangxian

Twilight rain is cold and desolate, the deep courtyard shut up.	暮雨淒淒深院閉
She sits fixed before the lamp at the first watch.	燈前凝坐初更
Jade hairpins press down her falling clouds of hair;	玉釵低壓鬢雲橫
behind a half-pulled gauzy curtain,	半垂羅幕
she reflects the candlelight glow.	相映燭光明

From the beginning, she gave her Han pendants with all her heart—[1]	終是有心投漢珮
bowing her head, she tuned the Qin zither.	低頭但理秦箏
Swallows in pairs, simurghs mated—overwhelmed by feeling!	燕雙鸞耦不勝情
She only sorrows over the breaking dawn[2]	只愁明發
that will chase away the clouds of Chu.[3]	將逐楚雲行

Sun Guangxian mixes his allusions casually in this lyric: the woman, a captive in her boudoir, whose appearance is all too familiar from the first stanza, is marked "divine" by a few references to the story of the Han river women (transcendents who visited a mortal man), paired simurghs (that pulled transcendent chariots), and the Chu clouds (that signal a visit from the goddess). The use of these allusions in a lyric to "Lin jiang xian" was not, however, accidental: like many other lyrics to this tune and to other tunes associated with divine women, this lyric conflates the secular romance with the long tradition of goddesses' encounters with mortal men.

From the commentary on the *Huajian ji*, we discover that early readers of the anthology noticed the connections between the contents of certain song lyrics and the tune titles to which they were set.[4] In Chapter 1, we heard the Tang poet Xue Neng complaining about the overuse of the "woman-as-willow" trope in lyrics to the

---

1. The reference to "Han pendants" alludes to a story known from different sources; in the *Lie xian zhuan* version, a mortal man, Zheng Jiaofu, meets two goddesses by the Han river who give him their pendants as love tokens. *Lie xian zhuan jiaojian*, 52–57.

2. "Breaking dawn," *ming fa*, alludes to *Odes* 196, in which the phrase signals the end of a lovers' encounter.

3. "Chu clouds" alludes to the story of the goddess who visited King Xiang of Chu in the "Rhapsody on the Gaotang Shrine" and the "Rhapsody on the Divine Woman," in the *Wen xuan*. *HJJZS*, 299–300.

4. In his *Wudai shihua*, the Qing literatus Wang Shizhen cites the Southern Song commentator Huang Sheng, who noted that "many Tang lyrics followed the title in their compositions. 'The Transcendent on the River' thus speaks of transcendent affairs, and the 'Daoist Nun' narrates Daoist feelings.... Overall, they preserve the meaning of the original title, but later, this slowly changed, and [lyrics] went far from their titles." Wang, *Wudai shihua*, 182.

tune "Yangliu zhi" (The willow branch). The practice of matching content to title all but ceased in the Song, when Tang tunes had been lost and lyrics were written to old metric patterns with new tunes rather than the older musical settings. As a consequence, few scholars have pursued the link between tune title and song lyric content in the works of the late Tang and Five Dynasties. But there are numerous examples of such connections in the *Huajian ji*: the lyrics written to "Genglouzi," beginning with those by Wen Tingyun, almost always include a water clock (or, most often, its sound) or a reflection on the passage of time. Lyrics written to the tune "Nan xiangzi" present conventionally "southern" scenes, which include young women gathering tropical or semitropical flowers, riverine excursions, warm weather, and a pleasure-seeking sensibility. The links between topic and tune title might even have been reinforced by the melodic and rhythmic settings of the tunes themselves ("southern" songs might have used recognizably southern modes or typically southern instruments, for example), which are now lost to us. The links between tune title and content in some of the lyrics of the *Huajian ji* reinforce the argument I have presented throughout this discussion: that late Tang and Shu *quzi ci* were primarily a kind of musical entertainment—a vital, contemporary social activity—and secondarily a literary form, one that Tang and Shu poets were altering and promoting.

In this chapter I explore a particularly important subset of lyrics whose content matches their tune titles: lyrics to two of the tune titles that recall divine encounters or Daoist figures, "Lin jiang xian" (The transcendent by the river) and "Nü guanzi" (The Daoist nun).[5] The lyrics to these tunes in the *Huajian ji*, particularly those composed by Shu poets, exploit the legends of transcendence and divinity in a manner not seen before or after the tenth century. This chapter thus explores a unique feature of the collection that was not

---

5. There are other tune titles whose lyrics show "Daoist" associations, such as "Wushan yiduan xia" (A bit of cloud over Shamanka Mountain), and "He zhuan" (River messages), but space does not permit me to examine those here. However, I believe my conclusions regarding the "Lin jiang xian" and "Nü guanzi" lyrics also apply to the other "Daoist" lyrics throughout the anthology.

widely practiced by the *ci* poets of the Song. The *Huajian ji* poets' use of these stories and allusions distinguishes the "Daoist" tune title sets from other lyrics in the collection in two distinct ways. The lyrics that depict encounters with goddesses explicitly draw upon the high literary tradition, transferring the goddess conventions into the genre of song lyrics. This appropriation of literary material is similar in nature to the appropriation of voice that we saw in the male-voiced lyrics of Chapter 5, and it has a similar objective, which was to elevate song lyrics as a genre. The use of goddess and transcendent encounters has a modal function as well. Some of the lyrics that include Daoist accoutrements, or objects associated with the quest for transcendence, establish a solemn mood quite distinct from the delicate melancholy or playful eroticism of other romantic lyrics in the collection. This modal variation extends the expressive range of the *Huajian* lyrics in a new direction. Although it is a minor trend in the anthology as a whole, it is a distinct minority voice. The uniqueness of the *Huajian ji* song lyrics in this respect is confirmed by the relative scarcity of goddess stories or Daoist objects in the song lyrics from Dunhuang, the Southern Tang, or the early Northern Song. The appearance of such conventions in the *Huajian ji* thus also strengthens the impression of the collection's specific regional style, a characteristic highlighted by Ouyang Jiong in his preface.

In recent decades, a few scholars have examined lyrics to tune titles of the *Huajian ji* in order to argue for what they identify as fundamentally Daoist features. Edward Schafer, in articles on the lyrics to "Nü guanzi" and "Wu shan yiduan xia" (which he translated as "The Capeline Cantos" and "A Bit of Cloud on Shamanka Mountain," respectively), and Suzanne Cahill, in her article on lyrics to "Lin jiang xian" ("The Transcendent Who Presides Over the River"), both argue strongly for the centrality of Daoist language and imagery in these sets of lyrics. By carefully identifying the Daoist references in individual lyrics and placing those references within the framework of encounters with goddesses or other transcendent phenomena, Schafer and Cahill (the latter following the former's lead) sought to demonstrate that "the supposed 'erotic' or sentimental similarities fade into a secondary role when the Taoist motifs . . . are taken with the seriousness that they deserve."⁶ More recently, Li Fengmao has explored the connections between medieval transcendent verse (including *yuefu* and Tang romantic *shi*) and Five Dynasties *quzi ci*. His examination of the mid- and late Tang uses of the female transcendent (*nüxian* 女仙 or *xianzi* 仙子) as a figure for the singing girl has been particularly useful for my discussion because he elucidates the multiple meanings of the trope in late medieval poetry.⁷ Another recent study of the evolution of the "wandering immortal" theme, by the scholar Yan Jinxiong, investigates specific Tang poets' use of Daoist material, giving us a considerably more nuanced understanding of the medieval range of poetic approaches to similar themes and imagery.⁸

In this chapter, I want to reintroduce the erotic and romantic elements into the debate over the influence of Daoism on Tang and Five Dynasties literature, challenging some of Schafer's and Cahill's conclusions; I also hope to show the great range of literary uses of transcendence in the *Huajian ji* as a whole. The Tang use of Daoist imagery in romantic poetry is notable, and it is directly connected to the huge presence of Daoism on the Tang cultural scene. As noted in Chapter 2, Daoism exercised an equally powerful influence on Shu culture, particularly on the culture of the Former Shu, when most of the lyrics by Shu poets of the *Huajian ji* would likely have been composed. Although I will argue that the romantic framework of these song lyrics is ultimately far more important than the Daoist influences, the lyrics demonstrate the richness of the medieval stories by revealing the many ways poets could invoke them.

Goddesses and Daoism in the Huajian ji: A Range of Borrowing Practices

The recent work of scholars of medieval Daoism has increased our understanding of Daoism as it was lived by Tang people and promulgated in Daoist religious institutions and canons. The work

---

6. Schafer, "Capeline Cantos," 17.
7. Li, *You yu you: Liu chao Sui Tang you xian shi lunji*.
8. Yan, *Tang dai you xian shi yanjiu*.

of Isabelle Robinet, Catherine Despeux, and Suzanne Cahill has also begun to uncover the place of medieval women in both Daoist texts and contexts.[9] While it is important to integrate this scholarship into our reading of medieval texts that make use of Daoist language and themes, we should also keep in mind other discourses and material realities that may have shaped such texts. In the case of the *Huajian ji*, this means recalling the contexts of the anthology and its Shu culture. "Romantic" readings and "Daoist" readings are not mutually exclusive: one can always see a goddess in a boudoir lady or sexual overtones in an apparently sacred meeting. The Daoist scriptural tradition on hierogamous unions itself blurs those lines continually.[10] What I hope to demonstrate in this chapter is the need for a nuanced reading of texts that exposes a range of cultural meanings and accounts for literary as well as religious precedents.

In trying to gauge a medieval writer's familiarity with Daoist practices or texts, one is frequently frustrated by a lack of supporting evidence. It may be true that "the Tang can be called the most significant period in the history of Daoism, because it was then that the religion showed that it could satisfy the spiritual, cultural, and political needs of the entire society," but Tang literati did not absorb or follow Daoism—or Buddhism, the other great religious influence of the Tang—uniformly across regions, clans, or over the course of the dynasty.[11] Educated Tang men were of course familiar with the *Laozi* and the *Zhuangzi*—an examination in those texts was even instituted during the reign of Tang Xuanzong—but the reticence of standard biographical sources on the subject of religious

---

9. See Cahill, *Transcendence and Divine Passion: The Queen Mother of the West in Medieval China*, and Despeux, *Immortelles de la Chine ancienne: Taoisme et alchimie féminine*. For an earlier work that explored the literary manifestations of Daoist women, see Schafer, *The Divine Woman*. For a discussion of sexuality that includes both male and female, see Robinet, "Sexualité et taoisme," in Bernos, ed., *Sexualité et religion*, 51–71. A useful overview of both Daoism in the Tang and women in Daoism generally can be found in Despeux's essay in Kohn, ed., *Daoism Handbook*, 339–412.

10. This blurring has also been explored by Daoist scholars. See, for example, Schafer, "The Jade Woman of Greatest Mystery," 387–98; and Bokenkamp, "Declarations of the Perfected," in Lopez, Jr., ed., *Religions in China in Practice*, 166–79.

11. Kohn, ed., *Daoism Handbook*, 339.

practice often makes it difficult to perceive individuals' religious practices outside of what they recorded in their own texts. Therefore, aside from assuming Tang literati to have possessed a general "Daoist cultural literacy" (which may not have included familiarity with any of the scriptural traditions), a modern reader must examine a wide variety of sources to argue that a specific poet is using Daoist terms in a consistent, informed manner.[12] Even if a poet's serious interest in Daoism is borne out by sufficient evidence (such as friendships with Daoist divines, a personal or lineage connection to Daoist schools, or lengthy sojourns at significant religious sites such as Mount Mao), the problem of the reading tradition, or how the references were understood by other Tang literati, remains.[13] Could not other literati less versed in Daoism have read specific, even scriptural, allusions merely as generalized references to "divinity" and "magic" or perhaps have attempted to read past the allusions for some allegorical (political, sexual) meaning that is lost to us? There must have been a sizable gray area in Tang China in which scriptural influences, popular Daoist practices, and common legends blended and interacted, influencing a wide range of elite literature. The danger of not distinguishing among types of usage in the Tang—for example, by labeling all references to *xian* as overtly "Daoist" or, conversely, dismissing such references as entirely secularized clichés—is that we may not perceive the diverse contexts in which elite texts circulated and may thereby silence the multiple resonances the texts could have carried.

---

12. Schafer's work on the Tang poet Cao Tang illustrates the kinds of sources that can be brought together to create a convincing portrait of a Daoist literary figure. Schafer, *Mirages on the Sea of Time: The Daoist Poetry of Ts'ao T'ang*. See also Paul W. Kroll's work on Daoism in the poetry of Li Bai, in "Li Po's *Rhapsody on the Great P'eng Bird*," "Li Po's Transcendent Diction," and "Verses From on High: The Ascent of T'ai Shan," in Lin and Owen, ed., *The Vitality of the Lyric Voice*. This research demonstrates the need to go beyond received interpretations of Tang poetry and culture in order to rediscover material that later generations considered heterodox or irrelevant.

13. For a discussion of the varied ways in which ninth-century poets could use such material, see Owen, *Late Tang*, 300-319.

The use of Daoism and the literati reception of Daoist imagery are especially problematic for the *Huajian ji* song lyrics and for romantic poetry of the ninth and tenth centuries generally, due to medieval Daoism's longstanding association with esoteric sexual practices, its literature on hierogamy, and the conflation of other legends of goddesses with those traditions. Cahill has explored the manifestations in medieval art and literature of Xi wangmu, the "Spirit-Mother of the West" (the highest goddess in Chinese belief), arguing that this highest goddess of Daoism bears two messages in Tang texts, those of "eternal life and the communication between the divine and human realms."[14] As Cahill demonstrates, even in Tang romantic poetry the figure of Xi wangmu herself remains largely unsexualized; rather than appearing as a sought-after lover, she is more often the overseer or enabler of romance. The same cannot be said of the stories of other goddesses, as Cahill acknowledges.[15] Among the goddesses who had, by the Tang, long been linked to encounters with mortal men are those of the Luo River, the Xiang river goddesses, and the goddess of Wu shan, or Shamanka Mountain, whose stories I will explore below. As David Hawkes argued several decades ago, in his essay "The Quest for the Goddess," this narrative itself predates the medieval era and likely traces its roots to pre-Qin shamanism.[16]

In the literature of the period of division, we find a wide variety of texts that relate encounters with named goddesses and anonymous transcendent women. With a few exceptions, the legends of the great riverine goddesses were not appropriated per se by me-

---

14. Cahill, *Transcendence and Divine Passion*, 9. For the name Xi wangmu, I give here the translation proposed by Paul R. Goldin in "On the Meaning of the Name Xi wangmu, Spirit-Mother of the West," 83–85. I will retain the Chinese title below.
15. Ibid., 58.
16. Hawkes, "The Quest for the Goddess." Hawkes identified two pieces of the *Chu ci*, the "Xiang jun" (Deity of the Xiang) and the "Xiang furen" (Mistress of the Xiang River), each of which involved a search by a male shaman for contact with a river goddess or goddesses. According to Hawkes, the more famous "Li sao" (Encountering sorrow), which also contains a male persona that seeks a "Fair One," was "unquestionably a secular poem" that showed the influence of shamanistic practices (77).

dieval Daoist schools; however, the issue of hierogamous union (between mortal men and divine women, as a rule) was a pressing concern of medieval Daoists. The practice of seeking spiritual unions between male, mortal practitioners and female transcendents—which developed in opposition to certain Celestial Master practices such as *heqi* 合氣 (uniting of *qi*)—was central to the revelation of the scriptures of both Shangqing and Lingbao Daoism in the fourth century and thereafter.[17] But this move within the Shangqing and Lingbao traditions existed simultaneously with, and surely also encouraged, stories of enticing transcendent maidens; the stories of goddesses in both the authored literati tradition and in the anonymous *zhiguai* 志怪 (accounts of anomalies) of the pre-Tang era testify to their enduring cultural appeal.[18] In short, the literature concerning transcendent women that Tang writers and readers inherited was extremely mixed, ranging from scriptural traditions that contained paeans to beautiful but only spiritually accessible female deities to fantastic and overtly erotic tales of "jade maidens" who led men away to unearthly realms.

The tendency of Tang writers to conflate different influences—so that goddesses from the secular elite or popular tradition appear surrounded by the trappings of Daoist religious practices—is easy to

---

17. The range of sexual practices in the varieties of medieval Daoism is still poorly understood; however, both syncretistic texts and identifiably Celestial Master texts (as well as criticism of Celestial Master practices found in Shangqing, Lingbao, and Buddhist texts) reveal that sexual practices among mortal men and women were an important ritual in some strains of medieval Daoism. Ritual texts of the Shangqing tradition maintained that spiritual union would replace sexual union. Robinet, *Taoism: Growth of a Religion*, 121. One important narrative of this kind of union in Shangqing Daoism is that of Yang Xi and the female transcendent Consort An, a descendant of Xi wangmu. For a translation and commentary from the *Zhen'gao* on their spiritual courtship, betrothal, and union, see Bokenkamp, "Declarations of the Perfected," 166–79. In the same volume, Paul Kroll has translated a series of poems composed by another female Perfected, the Lady Youying, to court the mortal Xu Mi and persuade him to join her in celestial realms; see Kroll, "Seduction Songs of the Perfected," 180–87.

18. Robert Campany notes the prevalence of stories of sexual contact between humans and nonhumans (of which deity-human contact is but one type) in the *zhiguai*, "accounts of anomalies," from the period of division. Campany, *Strange Writing: Anomaly Accounts in Early Medieval China*, 263–64.

understand and equally easy to find in Tang texts. It may be that the secularized versions of such encounters have survived better due to the conservatism of the mainstream Chinese literary tradition, which tended to marginalize texts deemed exclusively religious in nature. We can, however, also find examples of Daoist reabsorption of such stories in the Tang and afterward. One such example can be found in the biographies of female transcendents recorded by Du Guangting, the court Daoist of the late Tang and Former Shu, in the *Yongcheng jixian lu* 墉城集仙錄 (Record of the assembled transcendents of the heavenly city). In this influential Daoist text (dated to 913, or to the reign of Wang Jian in the Former Shu), Du Guangting provides accounts of the great goddesses, including the important Shamanka Mountain goddess, and of women who practiced Daoism.[19] The secularization of such goddesses in the literary arena thus did not mean that they lost their significance within the religious tradition; instead, we should probably understand these female figures as contested, used by both secular and religious traditions for quite different ends. One final feature of Daoism in the Tang that surely affected the sexualization of Daoist themes and imagery was the reputation of Daoist convents as the houses of sexually adventurous or available women, many of whom were from elite families. (I discuss this problem below, in my examination of lyrics to "Nü guanzi.") This reputation must have fed the Tang popularity of the "transcendent-as-singing-girl" trope, in which a *ji* 妓, "female entertainer," was depicted in the trappings of a goddess or a Daoist novice. Li Fengmao argues that this is specifically a mid- and late Tang literary development, and he has even labeled the poetry that works in this range "transcendent singing girl poetry," *xian ji shi* 仙妓詩.[20]

Thus, centuries before the appearance of the *Huajian ji*, we find in Tang literature a wide range of uses of the figures of the goddess, the transcendent maiden, and the Daoist nun. However, the use of this material in the *Huajian ji* differs from either prose texts or *shi* in a few important ways. As I argued in Chapter 1, one of the hall-

---

19. Kohn, ed., *Daoism Handbook*, 394–95.
20. Li Fengmao, *You yu you: Liu chao Sui Tang youxian shi lunji*, 385–89.

marks of *quzi ci* as a genre in the *Huajian ji* is the lyrics' tendency to suppress specific social or historical contexts. I suggested earlier that this reliance on romantic convention over historical specificity stemmed from the need to create repeatable, unmarked songs for circulation. Stories of goddesses and Daoist imagery enabled the *Huajian ji* poets to avoid references to specific contemporary women and to generally eschew the more vulgar uses of the singing-girl-as-transcendent trope. By importing references to goddesses and Daoist religious practices into *quzi ci*, the *Huajian* poets were also demonstrating their familiarity with the elite versions of such stories or practices and their ability to manipulate the images within the language of the high literary tradition. In contrast, we find scant use of goddess stories or specific references to Daoism in the Dunhuang *quzi ci*.[21] In the anonymously compiled collection of lyrics entitled the *Yunyao ji*, there are three tune titles with potentially Daoist associations, "Tian xianzi" 天仙子 (Heavenly transcendent), "Dong xian ge" 洞仙歌 (Song from the transcendent grotto), and "Feng gui yun" 鳳歸雲 (The phoenix returns to the clouds). There are two lyrics to each tune, but none of them contain any reference to legends of goddesses or transcendence. In the remaining anonymous "miscellaneous tunes," there are three tune titles with Daoist associations, "Bie xianzi" 別仙子 (Bidding farewell to the transcendent; one lyric), "Lin jiang xian" (three lyrics), and "Ye jinmen" 謁金門 (Paying court at the golden gates; four lyrics). Only three of these lyrics have any Daoist allusions; however, they refer to the search for transcendence, not to a spiritual or sexual union with a transcendent. The general scarcity of Daoism in the Dunhuang lyrics is remarkable, when compared to the huge influence of Buddhism in those materials, including the titles of the *quzi ci*. The relative influence of the two religious traditions, differing in their importance to elite *quzi ci* and to what are widely regarded as "popular" *quzi ci*, likely reflects the relative cultural weight of the

---

21. Ren, *Dunhuang geci zongbian*, 58–135, 150–66, 324, 350, 394, 406, 463, 517–22. Li (*You yu you*, 376–82) also analyzes the Dunhuang lyrics for their Daoist content and concludes that the influence of Daoism is minimal and that the few Daoist allusions are only used in the service of the singing-girl-as-transcendent trope.

two religious traditions at different social levels. The influence of Daoism on Tang elite literature can be seen throughout the dynasty, and across a range of literary genres. Its presence in the *quzi ci* of the *Huajian ji* only reinforces the anthology's claim to be an elite literary text.

As I noted in Chapter 2, the strong presence of Daoism on the Shu cultural scene is attested by the work of the court Daoist Du Guangting and in the ample evidence for the Wang rulers' financial support of Daoism at court. Two cultural trends seem to converge, therefore, in tenth-century Shu: first, the Tang literary elite's use of Daoism—specifically, the legends of goddesses visiting mortal men and the related trope of the *xianji* ("transcendent singing girl," to borrow Li Fengmao's useful term); second, the Shu regional interest in Daoism and Daoist cultural activities, which produced paintings of transcendents, biographies of Daoist divine women, and, as in the *Huajian ji*, song lyrics on Daoist nuns and riverine goddesses. Sorting out individual *Huajian ji* poets' religious commitments, given the paucity of biographical data on the poets, is impossible. As we shall see in a number of the lyrics by Shu poets, Shu literati were either more familiar with Daoist terminology and practices or more interested in incorporating that discourse into their texts than were most Tang poets.

As a way of distinguishing among uses of Daoism in the *Huajian ji*, I have made use of Erik Zürcher's categories for describing linguistic and conceptual influences in medieval Buddhism and Daoism. Zürcher proposes the terms "formal borrowing" (the simplest and most easily identified kind of linguistic loan, including that of terminology), "conceptual borrowing" (when "a term denoting a well-defined doctrinal concept . . . has retained some of its original value"), and "complex borrowing" ("the absorption of a coherent cluster of ideas").[22] As will become quickly apparent in my analyses, the majority of poets writing lyrics to "Lin jiang xian" and "Nü guanzi" remained safely within the bounds of formal borrowing; that is, they used terms from Daoism that were either already part of the secular poetic vocabulary or were easily understood in a

---

22. Zürcher, "Buddhist Influences on Taoist Scripture," 84–147.

secular, romantic context. This category would include lyrics, for example, that refer to the figure of the woman as a transcendent (*nüxian*) or that surround the female figure with accoutrements that evoke an otherworldly context. I am construing the second category—conceptual borrowing—fairly broadly, to include lyrics that use stories of goddesses or transcendents as well as lyrics that use specific images associated with Daoism to create a mysterious tone for a romantic encounter. In lyrics that employ formal borrowing, Daoist objects serve to "dress up" the familiar conventions; in those that fall into the category of conceptual borrowing, the use of the "encounter-with-the-goddess" framework or the creation of a mysterious, supernatural mood enhances the eroticism and allure of the lovers' drama. None of the *Huajian ji* lyrics employ complex borrowing as Zürcher defines it, a finding that reinforces my argument that romance is the central theme of the collection. The danger in using such a schema of borrowing is that it may suggest the existence of distinct "traditions" that were not in fact clearly defined—in this case, a "tradition" of romantic poetry that existed separately from a "tradition" of Daoist lore—when in fact there was surely a large area of overlap and mutual influence. However, as we will see below, there are a few cases in which Daoist references are not successfully integrated into the lyrics; these may signal the poets' self-conscious use of a language that was not entirely incorporated into elite poetry or song.

The tune title sets of "Lin jiang xian" and "Nü guanzi" offer an excellent test case for the arguments developed in earlier chapters identifying the important styles, themes, and subjectivities explored in the collection. With respect to the basic components of song lyrics, we find the same elements of subject, scene, and feeling. Liminal states are especially important in these lyrics that attempt to add mystery to the mundane; the themes of the passage of time and the difficulty of communication (utterances being suppressed or voiced through gesture) are also common. Though the lyrics to "Lin jiang xian" and "Nü guanzi" are similar to those of "Pusa man," "Jiu quanzi," and "Huanxi sha" in their representations of male and female subjectivity, their representation of the attribute of romantic powerlessness sometimes differs due to their use of the framing goddess story. In the encounter with the goddess, the male lover is the one who seeks the union (or is granted a union), and the goddess departs to a distant, unattainable location when she chooses. This scenario reverses the mortal romantic story in which men leave behind helpless and fixed women, and this may indeed have been one of the fascinations of the story for literati writers. The first-person voice of the male subject in a goddess story had long roots in the mainstream literary tradition: the early texts most important for that voice, the "Rhapsody on Gaotang" and "Rhapsody on the Divine Woman" (both attributed to Song Yu) and Cao Zhi's "Divine Woman of the Luo River," were preserved in the *Wen xuan* and much imitated throughout the Tang. The use of a first-person male voice seeking a mysterious woman in the *Huajian ji* lyrics is thus another example of the poets' self-conscious reference to and appropriation of particular elements of the "high" literary tradition.[23] However, what becomes ever more apparent as we read across these tune title sets is that even when the *Huajian* poets depicted quasi-mystical unions, they chose to use the stock emotional expressions and imagery of the common love story, whether the subject voicing emotion is gendered male or female. Only a few poets of the "Lin jiang xian" and "Nü guanzi" lyrics manage to use Daoist images or themes in a manner that distinguishes them from other lyrics. But since we have seen that originality was not in itself valued by the *Huajian ji* poets, it is not surprising to also find the same imitation, borrowing, and pasting-together of other poets' work that we have seen in other tune titles.

One feature distinctive to these tune titles is the frequent use of exterior settings. In the lyrics of Chapters 4 and 5, the female figure is most often represented as a prisoner of her chamber: she is cap-

---

23. In contrast, there are a number of poems written by female transcendents to male mortals in the corpus of the Shangqing revealed text, *Zhen'gao*, that seem to use the first-person female voice when addressing their recipients. These poems seek to entice the mortal men to spiritual, not fleshly, union in the heavens, and they use rich descriptions of the realms and palaces of the celestial world along with promises of transcendent bliss. For two studies of these poems, see Kroll, "Seduction Songs of the Perfected," and "The Divine Songs of the Lady of Purple Tenuity," 149–211.

tive, hidden, "cut off," or "locked in" behind smoke, screens, curtains, walls, and gates. Her range of motion is limited to looking out from her balcony, going out in a curtained carriage, or wandering in the closed space of a courtyard.[24] The few lyrics in which we saw female figures at large in the outside world represented the woman at the edge of a body of water (we see a correspondence between this image and watery goddesses in this chapter), bidding farewell to a lover departing by boat, as in Li Xun's first lyric to "Pusa man" and Xue Zhaoyun's first lyric to "Huanxi sha." In those two lyrics, although the women were not constrained by curtains or walls, the body of water itself created a boundary between them and the objects of their vision and desire. But when male figures appear in the collection as a whole, they are usually at liberty in the outside world, whether they appear on the street, on horseback, or on those departing boats. (This, of course, excludes the few lyrics that depict sexual encounters with both lovers present.) In the lyrics that suggest goddess encounters or unions with other kinds of transcendents, however, we often find ourselves in an exterior scene. The seeker of transcendence (masculine) confronts the traces of the divine (feminine) in the elements of the natural world. This technique resonates with the use of natural elements to establish the emotional tone of a lyric, but in the divine encounters, nature is less a projection of human emotions than a full player on the scene. The landscape more concretely *becomes* the woman—it forms her scent, her appearance, and sometimes her figure out of the uncontrollable and swiftly changing elements. This technique of creating the divine female from the natural world—in particular, from the watery, *yin*, natural elements such as clouds, rain, dew, and mists—can be traced as far as the texts in the *Chu ci*. But in the *Huajian ji* as a whole, the captive coquettes predominate; some of the divine women who appear in "Linjiang xian," "Nü guanzi," and other tune titles with similar themes thus offer an important alternative female subject, one of mystery and unseen power.

---

24. In *Tang Song ci shi lun*, Wang Zhaopeng (71–72) discusses the interiority of female subjects in Tang and Five Dynasties lyrics; however, he does not talk specifically about lyrics with Daoist themes.

Finally, in quantitative terms, a study of the *Huajian ji* would be incomplete without some analysis of the tune titles "Lin jiang xian" and "Nü guanzi." There are 26 lyrics to the tune "Lin jiang xian" and 19 to "Nü guanzi," which ranks them, respectively, the third- and fourth-largest groups of lyrics per tune title.[25] The lyrics to the two titles make up almost 10 percent of the anthology. The frequent correspondence between the tune title and the content, which we did not find in the other large tune title sets, is another unusual feature of these lyrics. As we shall see, this does not mean that every lyric to "Lin jiang xian" refers to a water goddess or every lyric to "Nü guanzi" invokes a Daoist nun, but the number of references to transcendents and meetings with elusive goddesses is significantly higher in these tune titles. The tune titles were also particularly important to the Shu poets, who were responsible for 20 of the 26 "Lin jiang xian" lyrics (neither Wen nor Wei have lyrics to "Lin jiang xian" in the *Huajian ji* or elsewhere) and 10 of the 19 "Nü guanzi" lyrics. As noted in Chapter 2, the rulers of the Former Shu (the period when the majority of the *Huajian ji* poets were composing) showed a particular interest in supporting Daoist institutions and officials, an interest that likely translated into a strong Daoist influence on the culture as a whole.[26] Interestingly, we find in the "Daoist" tune title sets a tendency to collect pairs of lyrics from individual poets: there are seven pairs of lyrics in "Lin jiang xian," seven pairs in "Nü guanzi," and three pairs (the entire set) in "Wushan yiduan xia." Though occasionally a chronological sequence is implied, more often there seems to be no obvious rela-

---

25. As noted in Chapter 4, the 169 lyrics to five tune titles—"Huanxi sha" (57), "Pusa man" (41), "Jiu quanzi" (26), "Lin jiang xian," and "Nü guanzi"—constitute 34 percent of the total number of lyrics (500) in the anthology. Conversely, the majority of tune titles (83 percent) have fewer than 10 lyrics each. Whether this reflects Tang and Shu literati preferences or the Shu compilers' tastes, we can only speculate; however, these five tune titles are prominent in most of the eighteen poets' collections.

26. This suggestion is supported by the six lyrics to the tunes "Wushan yiduan xia," all of which were composed by Shu poets, and the ten lyrics by Shu poets to "He zhuan" (out of eighteen), which also use the language and themes of goddess-encounters and Daoism.

tionship between the two. The pairs of lyrics may represent a musical setting or performance practice that involved repeats, perhaps with slight variations in mode or rhythm. I will explore further the potential significance of these pairs in the readings that follow.

Seeking the Goddesses in Lyrics to "Lin jiang xian"

The lyrics to "Lin jiang xian" make a useful complement to the lyrics we have examined thus far, since they have a highly heterometric verse form in comparison to other tune title forms and are varied even within the *Huajian ji* itself. The metrical structure of "Lin jiang xian" in the collection tends to be a doubled stanza of 7/6/7/4-5 (with the final line falling into two segments of four and five characters each). Thus "Lin jiang xian" is more heterometric than "Pusa man" (7/7/5/5 for the first stanza, and 5/5/5/5 for the second) or "Huanxi sha" (two stanzas of 7/7/7), and longer than "Jiu quanzi" (4/7/3-3/3 and 7/7/3-3/3). As we will see, the absence of parallel couplets in the "Lin jiang xian" metrical structure strongly influences the rhetorical flow of the lyrics: we find fewer parallel structures and more syntactical continuity from line to line, which is not the case in lyrics with a predominance of pentametric or heptametric lines, and as a consequence, each line tends to be thematically discrete, resonating with, rather than mirroring, elements of preceding or succeeding lines. The rhyme scheme of "Lin jiang xian" is simple—in the five variations noted by Aoyama, all use a single *ping* rhyme for both stanzas, though the occurrence of the rhyme varies according to metrical structure.[27] The tune title "Lin jiang xian" itself is found in the *Jiaofang ji*, in the Dunhuang texts, and in both the *Huajian ji* and the *Zunqian ji*, though of course we do not know if the High Tang metrical structure resembled its tenth-century counterparts. Like "Huanxi sha," the lyrics to "Lin jiang xian" provide us a set without a model by Wen Tingyun (see Table 6). Although the versions composed by Shu poets differ only

---

27. Aoyama, *Tō Sō shi kenkyū*, 248.

Table 6
Huajian ji Poets with Lyrics to "Lin jiang xian"

Poet	Number of lyrics	Poet	Number of lyrics
Zhang Bi	1	Lu Qianyi	2
Mao Wenxi	1	Yan Xuan	2
Niu Xiji	7	Yin E	2
He Ning	2	Mao Xizhen	2
Gu Xiong	3	Li Xun	2
Sun Guangxian	2		

slightly from one another in terms of metrical structure, the lyric by the Five Dynasties official He Ning uses a somewhat different form, which again points to the presence of a Shu regional style.[28]

In her study of the "Lin jiang xian" lyrics, Cahill argues that the Five Dynasties lyrics to this tune title, including some found in the anonymously compiled later anthology *Zunqian ji*, can be read as variations on the theme of the "quest for the goddess." Cahill traces the origin of this allegorical quest story back to the *Odes* and the *Chu ci*, follows it through its medieval variations and the addition of the Daoist element in the Six Dynasties era, and identifies it as the basic framework of the "Lin jiang xian" set. In her analysis of the structure of the "Lin jiang xian" lyrics, Cahill breaks down the "quest for the goddess" into a six-part scenario composed of the following elements: the setting, an epiphany of the goddess, a union of the goddess and king, a parting, an expression of feelings, and the revelation of an observer to the scene. She states that not all of the six

---

28. Ibid. He Ning's version is similar to a doubled quatrain, with identical stanzas of lines 7/6/7/7, and one rhyme for the entire song, falling in the second, third, and fourth lines of each stanza. In contrast, the Shu versions tend to break up the final line of each stanza into two segments of four and five characters, excepting one of the lyrics by Gu Xiong, which uses a different metric structure of 7/6/7/4-3-3 in both stanzas. As I noted in Chapter 5, the more heterometric form of the Shu lyrics may indicate the greater importance of musical settings to Shu poets. The Dunhuang lyrics to "Lin jiang xian" are slightly more irregular than the Shu lyrics, although they also tend to use doubled stanzas that begin 7/6/7 and have closing lines in segments of 4-5 or 5-5.

elements are present in each lyric, but each lyric contains at least some of them.²⁹ We should recognize this scenario immediately from the romantic lyrics we have read so far, where we also find the setting, the revelation of a female figure, an evocation or description of the romantic encounter, the separation, an expression of feelings, and the closing comment of an external observer, often phrased as a rhetorical expression. The structure of "quest" lyrics, as laid out by Cahill, is identical to that of romantic lyrics. Cahill also notes a number of persistent features of the "Lin jiang xian" set whose importance she ascribes to the "quest for the goddess" theme. Among these features are the repetition of certain phrases, the muted or confused state of things such as light, temperature, and season, the silence or "wordlessness" of the female figure, and the prevalence of feelings of sorrow, resentment, and disappointment.³⁰

Although I concur with Cahill's identification of the central elements of these lyrics, I would argue that these features in fact serve to link the "Lin jiang xian" lyrics strongly to the rest of the collection. In Chapter 4, I focused on the importance of liminal states in romantic vignettes, arguing that liminal moments and spaces reflected the emotional condition of the abandoned woman, who is poised between the dreaming and waking world, uncertain of her fate. Repetition, I have argued, is a technical feature of the anthology that stems from the court setting of composition and the poets' fondness for imitation and borrowing. In Chapter 5, we saw that silence or "wordlessness," phrased as *wuyu* 無語, *buyu* 不語, and so on, is essential to both the poetic craft and to the representation of female subjects in the collection. In short, these key images and themes need to be understood in the broader framework of the anthology, not just within the context of Daoism. By reading the "Lin jiang xian" lyrics against one another and against other lyrics in the collection, the novelty—or conventionality—of their tropes becomes apparent. As we will see, there are a few lyrics that use the goddess-encounter story in a distinctive manner.

---

29. Cahill, "Sex and the Supernatural in Medieval China," 200–201.
30. Ibid., 201–2.

First, I would note that ten of the lyrics to "Lin jiang xian" contain no references at all to transcendence or goddesses. These lyrics are iterations of what is by now a familiar scene: the beautiful, sorrowful woman in an appropriately decorated boudoir.

"Lin jiang xian" (1st of 3)
Gu Xiong

Beneath an azure-dyed vast sky, the pool seems like a mirror.	碧染長空池似鏡
Leaning from the tower to idly gaze fixes my feelings.	倚樓閑望凝情
The delicate fragrance of pink lotus-scented clothes is light;	滿衣紅藕細香清
the ivory-inlaid bed and precious mats	象床珍簟
are hidden by the mountain screen,	山障掩
the jade zither set out for playing.	玉琴橫
Secretly, I imagine the pleasure and laughter of old times;	暗想昔時歡笑事
[but] now I only get a surge of sorrow.	如今贏得愁生
The Mount Bo brazier is warm, its thin smoke light—	博山爐暖淡煙輕
cicadas call, people fall silent;	蟬吟人靜
in the fading sunlight, the little window shines.	殘日傍小窗明

(3rd of 3)

The moon's hues penetrate the shades, wind enters bamboo—	月色穿簾風入竹
a pair of brows leaning on the screen in a sorrowful hour.	倚屏雙黛愁時
Two or three branches of flowers on the steps hold dew,	砌花含露兩三枝
as if weeping resentful tears—	如啼恨臉
her broken spirit ruins her face and demeanor.	魂斷損容儀
Incense embers burn away unseen, the gilt duck censer cools.	香爐暗消金鴨冷
How can she bear his forsaking their meeting planned before?	可堪辜負前期

Her embroidered robe in disarray, curls and
  chignon falling,
so much melancholy—
the threads of her feelings reach to the ends of
  the earth.[31]

繡襦不整鬟鬢欹

幾多惆悵
情緒在天涯

The women in these two lyrics could be the same person, observed at sunset and then later in the evening. All the standard trappings are here: the balcony, the expensive baubles, the zither whose sound is too painful to hear, the gilt censer burning out in vain, and the woman delicately crying over her fate. The only notable difference between the two is the option (which I have taken) of reading the first lyric in a first-person female voice. Linguistic cues that we have seen before—such as the use of the verbs *wang*, "gaze," and *xiang*, "imagine"—suggest a first-person speaker, as does the colloquial phrase that is very similar to one of Niu Qiao's "Huanxi sha" lines: "[but] now I only get (*yingde* 贏得) a surge of sorrow."[32] Although the second lyric uses the rhetorical question "How can she bear . . . ?," *ke kan* 可堪, which in some lyrics suggests a first-person speaker, here it seems to be the observing narrator's comment, an impression strengthened by the lines of description of the woman's clothing and face. What we do not find is any reference to transcendence or goddesses in the lyrics' imagery or narrative frame.

The "Lin jiang xian" lyrics that use the themes or language of transcendence do so quite obviously, as in Sun Guangxian's second lyric, with which we began the chapter. In the first stanza of Sun's lyric, an apparently mortal woman is trapped in her chamber, fixed behind a curtain. It is not until the second stanza that the poet inserts references to transcendent maidens or divine encounters.

---

31. *HJJZS*, 272–74.

32. Niu's line, in the second of his seven "Huanxi sha" lyrics, was "I only got a sceneful of sorrow," *ying-de yichang chou* 贏得一場愁, and Gu's line is "I only get a surge of sorrow," *ying-de chou sheng* 贏得愁生.

"Lin jiang xian" (2nd of 2)
Sun Guangxian

Twilight rain is cold and desolate, the deep courtyard shut up.	暮雨淒淒深院閉
She sits fixed before the lamp at the first watch.	燈前凝坐初更
Jade hairpins press down her falling clouds of hair,	玉釵低壓鬢雲橫
behind a half-pulled gauzy curtain,	半垂羅幕
she reflects the candlelight glow.	相映燭光明
From the beginning, she gave her Han pendants with all her heart—	終是有心投漢佩
bowing her head, she tunes the Qin zither.	低頭但理秦箏
Swallows in pairs, simurghs mated—overwhelmed by feeling!	燕雙鸞偶不勝情
She only sorrows over breaking dawn	只愁明發
that will chase away the clouds of Chu.	將逐楚雲行

Drawn from the anonymous early medieval text *Lie xian zhuan* (Biographical accounts of transcendents), the references to the Han river women, along with the simurghs and the "clouds of Chu," seem little more than ornamentation here, particularly since the woman is trapped and abandoned, unlike either the Han women (who enticed a mortal man and then left him) or the Shamanka Mountain goddess (who herself left the King of Chu, a story told in Song Yu's "Rhapsody on the Gaotang [Shrine]"). Sun's lyric shows us the ways poets could insert references to stories of divine women as decoration rather than adopting a specific narrative or point of view. This kind of formal borrowing is simply a jumble of unconnected allusions that does not alter the lyric's basic frame of reference.

More interesting and coherent than Sun's lyric, however, are the "Lin jiang xian" lyrics by the Shu poet Yan Xuan. Yan Xuan's two lyrics use the dream-meeting between King Xiang of Chu and the goddess of Shamanka Mountain as a narrative framework.[33] In Tang

---

33. Song Yu is a somewhat shadowy figure, and the authenticity of pieces attributed to him, including this rhapsody, is suspect. According to Knechtges, "the most reliable accounts say that [he] served at the court of King Qingxiang of Chu,"

poems on travels and landscapes, as well as those written to an old *yuefu* title, "Shamanka Mountain Is High" 巫山高, the Shamanka Mountain setting appears often, and poets who described the scene would be expected to allude to the *Wen xuan* "Rhapsody on Gaotang" 高山賦 and its associated images. In the "Rhapsody on Gaotang," Song Yu describes a meeting of a former king with the goddess, by Shamanka Mountain, near the Yangzi river, and he tells King Xiang how to meet her; in "Rhapsody on the Divine Woman" 神女賦, the king encounters the goddess himself in a dream.[34] In medieval poetry, her attributes are "clouds and rain," which come from the lines she was said to have spoken to the king, "Mornings I am dawn cloud, / Evenings I am pouring rain" 旦爲朝雲, 暮爲行雨.[35] Tang poets made frequent use of the "clouds and rain" trope, but more often as a simple reference to a sexual encounter, not as an appropriation of the Gaotang / Divine Woman story.

"Lin jiang xian" (1st of 2)
Yan Xuan

When the rain ends, heavy fragrance rises from water lilies and caltrops.	雨停荷芰逗濃香
On the river banks, cicadas cry from hanging willows.	岸邊蟬噪垂楊
The old pond stands pointlessly amid the luxuriant growth.	物華空有舊池塘
I don't find the transcendent girl— where is she dreaming of King Xiang?	不逢仙子 何處夢襄王
On the fine mat, resting opposite each other, the mandarin duck pillows are cold.	珍簟對欹鴛枕冷
Recently, all is covered with dust, desolate.[36]	比來塵暗淒涼

---

the same "King Xiang" that figures in the rhapsody. Knechtges, *Wen Xuan*, vol. 1, 388.

34. The "dreamer" of the encounter with the goddess could also be Song Yu; however, in poetry of the Tang, references to the story suggest that poets thought King Xiang was the recipient of the goddess's visit. For one discussion of the identity of the dreamer, see Rouzer, *Articulated Ladies*, 60–61, n40.

35. *WX* 19.876. Translation from Knechtges, *Wen xuan*, vol. 1, 327.

36. Most texts read *cilai* 此來, but *bilai* 比來 exists in at least one edition, according to Li Yi (341). My translation reflects the emendation.

About to lean on the high balustrade, my regret extending everywhere—	欲憑危檻恨偏長
the lotus flowers' pearly strands	藕花珠綴
seem like beads of sweat fixed in powder.[37]	猶似汗凝妝

The lyric uses a Shamanka Mountain reference to frame a scene that clearly takes place long after the union, but the perspective of the poem is somewhat unusual: we seem to see through the eyes of a visitor to the site of the meeting between King Xiang and the goddess. The hint of the goddess's presence comes in the first line: "When the rain ends, heavy fragrance rises from lilies and caltrops." The ending rain signals the end of the encounter; the fragrance that "rises" suggests her former presence. In the first stanza, the speaker "pointlessly" sees the landscape where they met, and tells us, "I don't meet the transcendent girl."[38] The final line of the first stanza is difficult and offers two possible interpretations. It seems to ask, "Where is she dreaming of King Xiang?" This would suggest that the "transcendent girl" is longing for her lover in dream, whereas in the original story, the king dreams of his encounter with her. This may be a case of lover's wishful thinking, as we saw in Wei Zhuang's "Huanxi sha" line, "I imagine her longing for me." Alternatively, the line may mean, "Where is the dreaming King Xiang?" In that case, the speaker offers himself as a visitor to the site of the encounter, rather than taking on the persona of an abandoned King Xiang. In the end, the poet still appears to be appropriating the role

---

37. *HJJZS*, 341.

38. My translation, "transcendent girl," can hardly approximate the familiar, even affectionate, tone suggested by adding the suffix *zi* 子 to the term "transcendent," *xian* 仙. In this context, the suffix not only indicates that the "transcendent" is female but also conveys intimacy. The tone might be clearer if compared to a specifically Daoist designation such as *nüxian*, "transcendent woman," where the use of "woman" imparts both a gender specificity and an emotional neutrality that *xianzi* lacks. In the *Huajian ji*, there is also a tune title "Heavenly Transcendent Girl," "Tian xianzi" 天仙子, whose lyrics use themes similar to those under discussion. The only other use of the term *xianzi* in the *Huajian ji* comes in a lyric by He Ning to the "Tian xianzi" title, where the woman so designated is clearly an abandoned mortal woman. The essential secularity of the term is suggested by the fact that it is not commonly used in Daoist texts. See n65 for the use of *zi* in other tune titles.

of King Xiang, as an interloper who takes on the identity—and desire—of the male lover seeking his goddess.

The speaker surveys the natural scene for the "transcendent girl" in the first stanza but finds no trace of her until the second stanza. He retreats to familiar quarters: the woman's boudoir. In an interesting contrast to most of the boudoirs we have seen, however, this one is completely empty, cold, and filled with dust. The speaker seems to play both roles: he positions himself in the traditional female stance, looking out from the boudoir for the beloved, and yet he is seeking a *woman* who has vanished from the interior scene. The visual field yields clues to the emotional and physical state of the now-vanished lovers. Although the lyric's narrative is grounded in the story of King Xiang and the goddess of Shamanka Mountain, the "regret" found in the landscape is that of everyone and no one in particular, as it extends across the speaker's field of view. In this final look outward, he seems to catch sight of the goddess in a very sensual image: the beads of rain "strung" (*zhui* 綴) on lotus appear to him as pearls of sweat suspended on a powdered face. This image's eroticism evokes a past sexual encounter, and pushes the lyric toward the contemporary, human world, in which the male speaker remembers his own erotic experience.

In both of these lyrics, Yan Xuan blends subgeneric traditions of *shi* poetry: the visit to scenes of ancient legends, the story of the divine encounter of the goddess and King Xiang of Chu, and the story of parted mortal lovers. In his second lyric, he draws even more heavily on the *yuefu* and *shi* tradition of poems on Shamanka Mountain itself.[39] Here, the speaker is both visiting the site of the encounter and reliving the encounter through his imagination or dream.

---

39. The *yuefu* title "Wu shan gao" (Shamanka Mountain is high) is given in the *Yuefu shiji* in the Han *naoge* section. Of the 21 poems to the title, 9 come from the Qi, Liang, or Chen eras, and 12 from the Tang. However, there are many more poems in Tang poets' collections that use the conventions from the Shamanka Mountain story but do not use the exact title "Wu shan gao."

"Lin jiang xian" (2nd of 2)
Yan Xuan

The cold of the twelve high peaks seems to stretch beyond the sky;[40]	十二高峰天外寒
bamboo tips lightly brush the transcendent altar.[41]	竹梢輕拂仙壇
Her precious robes, trailing rain, are at the ends of the clouds.	寶衣行雲在雲端
Behind painted shades in the palace depths,	畫簾深殿
fragrant mists fade away in a chilly wind.	香霧冷風殘
I'd like to ask where the King of Chu has gone—	欲問楚王何處去
the kingfisher screens still conceal a golden simurgh.[42]	翠屏猶掩金鸞
Gibbons call in bright moonlight shining on empty beaches—	猿啼明月照空灘
a traveler in a lone boat	孤舟行客
himself wakens from dream, sad and distressed.	驚夢亦艱難

The traces of the descriptive conventions of Tang poems on Shamanka Mountain are found throughout Yan's lyric. Edward Schafer has summarized them concisely in his article on the "Wushan yi duan xia" lyrics in the *Huajian ji* and the *Zunqian ji*. Schafer identifies the mountains' color, height, and watery environs (including clouds, rain, and mist) as the most important natural elements of the scene; the sound of gibbons, the presence of auroral clouds, and reference to the shrine of the goddess to which the poet is making a

---

40. The "twelve peaks" are the peaks of Shamanka Mountain. The allusion immediately situates the reader in the Shamanka Mountain story of the King Xiang of Chu and the goddess.

41. The "transcendent altar," *xian tan*, was not a term commonly used in Daoist scriptures; this is the only appearance of the world "altar," *tan*, in the collection.

42. The grammar of this line is clear, the meaning not entirely so: simurghs, *luan*, were the mythological creatures believed to pull the carriages of deities (often female deities) through the heavens. In this line, the simurgh may be painted or inlaid on the screen, in which case the line suggests, "although the deity and her lover have gone, there are still traces of them on the objects of the human realm." Alternatively, the "golden simurgh" may refer to the figure of the goddess herself, in which case we would have the common abandoned woman "hidden" (enclosed, captive) behind the screen.

visit or pilgrimage are the most important scenic details.[43] One well-known Tang poem on the topic was Li Duan's version of "Shamanka Mountain Is High," which was collected in both the Tang anthology *Yulan shi* and the Shu anthology *Caidiao ji*. Li Duan's poem begins: "Shamanka Mountain's twelve layers / all stand amid the azure void" 巫山十二重, 皆在碧虛空.[44] Another mid-Tang poet about whom we know little, Li She 李涉, used the same images in a series of lyrics to the tune "Zhu zhi ci." His fourth lyric opens with the line: "Above the tops of the twelve peaks, the moon is about to set" 十二峰頭月欲低.[45] Yan Xuan uses the same "twelve peaks" for his opening lines, but he is in fact not the first *Huajian ji* poet to rework the image: Huangfu Song, a late Tang poet in the *Huajian ji*, also adapts Li Duan. In his lyric "Tian xianzi" (The heavenly transcendent), Huangfu closes with the line: "The twelve evening peaks stand high and clear" 十二晚峰高歷歷.[46] The depiction of the mountain and its legend could vary widely according to the generic and topical framework a poet chose.[47] In the *Huajian* song lyrics that used the story, poets chose to dwell on the encounter more than the setting.

Unlike poets who wrote *shi* or *yuefu* that signaled the Shamanka Mountain site and legend in their titles, Yan Xuan could use as much or as little of the scenic detail as he liked in his *quzi ci*. In this lyric, he assumes the traditional role of a visitor to the site; he sees the "twelve green peaks" and the "transcendent altar" of what is likely the temple of the goddess, located at the base of the mountain. But is this visit real or merely dreamed? The introduction of a "palace" in the final lines of the first stanza confuses the real scene

---

43. Schafer, "One Bit of Cloud at Shamanka Mountain," 103–4.
44. *QTS* 285.3242.
45. *QTWDCSZ*, 135.
46. *HJJZS*, 59.
47. Where Li Duan focuses on the height and breadth of the landscape, Liu Yuxi, in a poem entitled "The Temple of the Goddess of Shamanka Mountain" 巫山神女廟, emphasizes the loveliness of the goddess: "The lush growth of twelve Shamanka peaks is deepest green, / spires of rock are tall and graceful, recalling the Lady. / Dawn mists briefly part like rolling up a shade; / mountain flowers about to fall seem like faded makeup." Qu, *Liu Yuxi ji jianzheng*, 1441–42. *QTS* 361.4083.

with the scene of what may be the celestial palace of a goddess. The second stanza recalls the seeking visitor of the previous lyric, who seems to be searching for traces of the encounter in the interior and exterior scene. The call of the apes on the "empty" beaches creates a transition from the dream of the encounter (or the dream of seeking the traces of the encounter) to the "traveler" who finds himself abruptly wakened from dream, like the King of Chu.[48] Yan Xuan fully exploits the story of the encounter, and even deepens it, by layering the dream of the visitor over the dream of the king. In these lyrics, the persona of the seeking lover narrates all the stories—the king's, the goddess's, and his own.

Yan Xuan's "Lin jiang xian" lyrics exemplify the *Huajian* poets' use of conceptual borrowing, giving us the most coherent use of the Gaotang goddess legend in the tune title set, but the Gaotang goddess is not the only divine beauty represented in "Lin jiang xian." The seven "Lin jiang xian" lyrics written by the Shu poet Niu Xiji, nephew of the high-ranking minister and *Huajian ji* poet Niu Qiao, stand out among others in the tune title set for two reasons: Niu is the only poet to have more than three "Lin jiang xian" lyrics in the anthology, and in his series of seven, each lyric takes a different transcendent union as its subject. As a series, the seven lyrics make up a clever and attention-getting set of stories of romantic encounters with transcendent beings. The poet's self-conscious artistry is evident throughout: Niu does not inhabit the old stories, as Yan Xuan did; rather, he talks *about* them, describing their characters and locations like a tour guide to Famous Goddesses of China. Niu announces the source story for each lyric with an immediately recognizable reference in the opening line. For example, the first lyric opens with the line "Steep uneven layers of deep green in twelve peaks," where the "twelve peaks" are those of Shamanka Mountain. The fourth lyric opens with, "The river winds about the

---

48. A strikingly similar device is used by Li Xun in his first lyric to "Wu shan yi duan xia," in which a visitor recalls the dream of the king, and the poet blurs the distinction between the encounter, the dream, and what the visitor actually sees. *HJJZS*, 376–77. See also Schafer's translation and commentary in "One Bit of Cloud at Shamanka Mountain," 114–15.

Yellow Tumulus—the spring temple lies idle." The "Yellow Tumulus" points us to the temple of the Xiang River goddesses, who were consorts of the legendary emperor Shun; it is they who are sought by the narrators of the "Xiang jun" and the "Xiang furen" in the *Chu ci*. The fifth lyric opens with "On the pure Luo River's spring radiance, gentle ripples smooth out," which tells us Niu will use the story of the goddess of the Luo River (first told by the poet Cao Zhi). Each lyric states its source story in the first line and goes on to present its version of the legend. The cumulative effect of these seven variations on the encounter with the goddess is to show Niu not as an especially Daoist poet but rather as a highly skilled poet who is well versed in the *literary* uses of this material. We also have to credit the taste of the *Huajian ji* editors in selecting and preserving this set of seven. Clearly, they thought the "Lin jiang xian" series to be Niu Xiji's best work: his remaining eleven lyrics in the anthology are all single lyrics to separate tune titles.

The opening lines of Niu's first lyric, like the opening of Yan Xuan's first lyric, evoke the landscape of the Shamanka Mountain story.

"Lin jiang xian" (1st of 7)
Niu Xiji

Azure precipices scattered across twelve peaks—	峭碧參差十二峰
layer on layer of chilly mists and bitter cold trees.	冷煙寒樹重重
The Turquoise Lady's palace compounds and basilicas are the traces of transcendence.[49]	瑤姬宮殿是仙蹤
In golden braziers behind pearly curtains,	金爐珠帳
fragrant fogs thicken in the daylight.	香靄晝偏濃
Ever since the King of Chu's dream was startled and broken off,	一自楚王驚夢斷
there's no path to meet her in the human realm.	人間無路相逢
Even today, the clouds and rain bear a sorrowful visage.[50]	至今雲雨帶愁容

---

49. The Turquoise Lady is another term for the Shamanka Mountain goddess.
50. Li Yi notes that Niu is borrowing the Tang poet Wang Xisheng's line here. *HJJZS*, 200.

As the moon sets over the river, 月斜江上
a traveling sailboat rings its dawn bells.[51]   征棹動晨鐘

To understand the rhetorical and conventional limits within which Niu and Yan are working, it is useful to compare the images of their lyrics. Although there are few instances of borrowing exact phrases, the similarity of description and rhetorical structure is striking; I have italicized the images that are found in both lyrics, though the two poets do not use the same words or phrases in each case.

Yan Xuan' 1st stanza
  "Lin jiang xian"
cold *twelve peaks* (十二峰)

transcendent altar (仙壇)
precious robes and passing rain at end of clouds (寶衣行雨, 雲)
painted shades, *palace* (宮) depths
fragrant *mists* (霧), *chilly* (冷) wind

Niu Xiji's 1st stanza
  "Lin jiang xian"
steep, uneven *twelve green peaks* (十二峰)
chilly mists (冷煙), cold trees
palaces (宮) & basilicas of Turquoise Lady; *traces of transcendence* (仙蹤)
golden braziers, pearly curtains

thickening *fogs* (靄) of incense

2nd stanza
King of Chu gone (楚王)

kingfisher screens show her golden simurgh
call of gibbon on *moonlit beaches* (明月照空灘)
lone traveler in a boat (孤舟行客)

startled from *dream* (夢) distressed

2nd stanza
King of Chu's dream broken off (楚王, 夢)
no way to meet the goddess in this realm
clouds & rain (雲雨) show her face

moon setting over the river (月斜江上)
traveling (oars of a) boat (征棹) that rings dawn bells

This display not only shows the two poets to be plumbing the same conventions for the Shamanka Mountain story, but it also demonstrates the two poets' similar narrative approaches. In both lyrics,

---

51. Ibid.

the scene of the opening stanza contains no one, whether human or divine, only "traces," *zong* 蹤, of their presence. The second stanza then jumps in time to the early morning following the night encounter. All the images appropriate to the story are in place: the "twelve peaks," the traces of the goddess, the King of Chu, and the clouds and mist that both entice and cloak. In Niu's lyric, the first stanza appears to be describing a celestial scene similar to the icy palaces of Chang E, the moon goddess. Like Chang E, the Turquoise Lady here dwells in an extensive and jeweled estate that identifies her as a celestial being. Deep in one of her palaces, we find the thick incense smoke that so often in the terrestrial realm indicates a lovers' tryst. Yan Xuan similarly suggests a boudoir setting in his lyric, describing the mists being caught "behind painted shades in the palace depths." In the first stanzas of both lyrics, we have an apparently magical scene with no figures, created by the poet out of objects in the imagined exotic and highly eroticized landscape.

Although he uses similar images, Niu Xiji pulls back from the scene and its frame story in his second stanza. He shifts from describing the scene as if he were a participant to recounting the legend: "Ever since the King of Chu's dream was startled and broken off." In the second line, he grounds the narrator in the mortal world: "in the human realm, there's no path to meet up with her" (*renjian wu lu xiang feng* 人間無路相逢).[52] The use of the time-phrases "ever since," *yi zi* 一自, and "even today," *zhi jin* 至今, combined with the syntactic continuity of the two first lines, gives the second stanza a more narrative flow, in contrast to Yan Xuan's use of syntactically discontinuous images ("I'd like to ask where the King of Chu is gone—/ the kingfisher screens still hide a golden simurgh. / Gibbons call in bright moonlight shining on empty beaches"). Unlike Yan Xuan's use of the legend—where the speaker seems to be reenacting the King of Chu's quest—Niu's lyric presents the Shamanka Mountain story *as* a story. The closing image of a traveling sailboat signals the end of Niu's reflections and brings the reader back into the

---

52. This line seems to be imitating a line in the third "Huanxi sha" lyric by Zhang Bi, which states: "In this human realm, there's no path to the transcendent's home" 人間無路到仙家. *HJJZS*, 153.

mortal, temporal realm. Yan Xuan's lyric merges the scene of the dream with that of the narrating *dreamer* who is wakened by the sound of apes; the bells in Niu's lyric sound in the dawn air and dissolve the fantasy entirely, returning the ethereal scene to a river landscape. As in most of his seven "Lin jiang xian" lyrics, Niu creates an observer's distance here. His narrative approach, particularly the critical "summing-up" in the second stanza, underscores his role as the poetic interpreter of the ancient story.

Niu Xiji's fifth lyric retells a goddess story in an even more self-conscious manner, depicting the Luo River goddess and referring explicitly to the Wei poet Cao Zhi's rhapsody about her. The Luo River goddess was traditionally believed to be Fufei, the legendary Fu Xi's daughter, who drowned in the Luo river. Cao Zhi's "Rhapsody on the Luo River Goddess" is notable in the early rhapsody tradition for its sensual, detailed description of the goddess's appearance; Niu Xiji seems to be working along similar lines in his own treatment.[53]

"Lin jiang xian" (5th of 7)
Niu Xiji

On the pure Luo's spring radiance, gentle ripples smooth out:	素洛春光瀲灩平
a thousand layers of seductive face begin to appear.	千重媚臉初生
Riding above the waves in gauze stockings, her movements are delicate and gentle.	凌波羅襪勢輕輕
Mists enshroud the sun—	煙籠日照
her pearl and kingfisher [ornaments] glinting, half-seen.[54]	珠翠半分明
The wind tugs at her precious robes, as if she were about to dance—	風引寶衣疑欲舞

---

53. Knechtges, *Wen xuan*, vol. 3, 357.

54. The description of the goddess here invokes her appearance in Cao Zhi's rhapsody: "She drapes herself in the shimmering glitter of a gossamer gown. . . . Bedecks her hair with head ornaments of gold and kingfisher plumes, / Adorns herself with shining pearls that illumine her body." Knechtges, *Wen xuan*, vol. 3, 359.

the simurgh turns, the phoenix soars, startling her away.[55]	鷟回鳳騫堪驚
And though we know their secret consent went unfulfilled,	也知心許恐無成
the rhapsody of the Prince of Chen has had renown for a thousand years.[56]	陳王辭賦 千載有聲

Niu uses the same third-person observer to describe the appearance and departure of the Luo River Goddess. In the tradition of deities associated with natural sites, the goddess literally emerges from the physical landscape—in this case, from dispersed sunlight and the waves of the river. She moves lightly and daintily, and like many seductive women, both divine and mortal, her appearance is enhanced by being partly obscured. The second stanza's opening lines show her clothes being blown aside—the *yang* force of the wind is shown to be encroaching on the female figure's robes. But the encounter described here, like the one in Cao Zhi's rhapsody, will go unconsummated: Niu tells us of the parting of the simurgh and the phoenix (two mythical animals associated with, respectively, the masculine and feminine principles) as the phoenix is "startled," perhaps by the encroaching wind.

In the lyric's final lines, Niu the poet steps in to give us the moral of his retold story of the Luo River Goddess. Although the hearts of the goddess and her suitor were indeed true, their desires went unrealized; yet the poet can rest assured that his words, like Cao Zhi's, will live on—this last line hinting that such "renown" is more desirable than any ephemeral union. Niu's repetition of the word "thousand" seems telling here: in the first stanza, ripples form "a thousand layers of seductive face," and in the second, we find the promise of fame lasting "a thousand years." The beauty of the goddess is ultimately no match for the immortality promised by writing; satisfied desire may bring ecstasy, but frustrated desire can bring fame. It is a curious ending to a lyric that opened with a tan-

---

55. Li Yi notes that Niu is reworking a line from Lu Ji's "Rhapsody on the Floating Clouds" that was cited in the Tang encyclopedia and reference manual *Chu xue ji* and reworked by other poets such as Han Yu. *HJJZS*, 204.

56. The Prince of Chen is the poet Cao Zhi. *HJJZS*, 203-4.

talizing prelude to a divine meeting. The poets of the collection often use the final line to "return" to the mortal world after a divine experience, but Niu's eagerness to insert himself as *poet* into the scene is unusual.

We see a similarly self-conscious approach to a story of transcendence in Niu's third lyric, where Niu focuses on the female, mortal lover of a pair.

"Lin jiang xian" (3rd of 7)
Niu Xiji

Inside the palace walls by the Wei River, Qin trees wither.	渭闕宮城秦樹凋
Climbing the Jade Tower alone—so wearisome.[57]	玉樓獨上無聊
Full of feeling and yet not speaking, she begins to play the flute.	含情不語自吹簫
The melody's purity matches her regret—	調清和恨
following the wind, it floats up on heaven's paths.	天路逐風飄
Why did that dragon rider suddenly descend?	何事乘龍人忽降
As if he had been summoned by her deepest wish,	似知深意相招
hand in hand, their path to the Three Clarities was not long.[58]	三清攜手路非遙
On the screens and panels of the human world,	世間屏障
colorful brushes have painted her charming grace.[59]	彩筆畫嬌嬈

As in the other lyrics, the story here—that of Xiao Shi, the flutist, who ascended to the heavens with his wife, Long Yu, daughter of

---

57. The Wei River, the Qin trees, and the Jade Tower are all allusions to the story of Xiao Shi. Lord Mu of Qin brought the talented flutist Xiao Shi to his court, married him to his daughter Long Yu, and built the Jade Tower for them. Later, they ascended to the heavens riding phoenixes. Niu is tweaking the story a bit, using the point of view of Long Yu and having Xiao Shi descend, riding a dragon (like the simurgh, associated with the male, especially when paired with the phoenix), to whisk her away to the heavens. Even though Xiao Shi is traditionally understood as the flutist, other versions of the story document Long Yu's talent for playing the flute. (Li Yi cites, as an example of such variations, the *Taiping guangji* version of the story, which also portrays Long Yu as a flutist who calls down phoenixes with her flute and ultimately ascends with her husband to the heavens, she on a phoenix and he on a dragon; *HJJZS*, 202.)
58. The "Three Clarities" refers to the three Daoist heavens.
59. *HJJZS*, 202.

the King of Qin—is announced in the first line with the references to the Wei River and the "Qin trees." Two elements make a third-person voice more natural for the piece as a whole: the first is the use of the phrase "hiding her feelings yet not speaking" (*han qing bu yu* 含情不語), the description of the female demeanor we saw often in the "Huanxi sha" lyrics.[60] It seems more likely that this is an observer's comment on Long Yu's actions rather than her own statement about herself. The description of the sound of her flute as it ascends toward heaven also suggests an external narrator and observer. The entire second stanza, which again shows us Niu commenting on the story, strongly indicates a third-person reading, since Niu asks a question about the story ("Why did that dragon rider suddenly descend?"), ascribes intentions to the characters ("as if he was summoned by her deepest desire"), and closes by describing all the paintings of Long Yu, the woman whose story he has just retold, in the human world. Each line of this second stanza pulls further back from the immediate scene of the encounter.

The narrative structure of this lyric is linear: the first stanza depicts a lonely woman longing for someone, and the second stanza moves to their magical encounter and journey. The first stanza closes with the regretful sounds of Long Yu's flute following "heaven's paths," and the second stanza opens with the dragon rider (the male lover, Xiao Shi) descending, presumably because her passionate playing caught his attention. Once united, they depart for the "Three Clarities," a phrase that, despite its importance in Daoist texts, appears simply to mean "the heavens" here.[61] As he did in the Luo River goddess lyric, Niu shifts perspective in the final line, framing his own storytelling with the reference to paintings of Long

---

60. Consistent with the usage of similar phrases in the anthology, we find "full of feeling, without speaking" 含情無語 and "full of feeling, pointing far away" 含情遙指 in two other "Lin jiang xian" lyrics, by Sun Guangxian and He Ning, respectively; both are found in third-person descriptions of female subjects.

61. This use of "Three Clarities" is an excellent example of the need for case-by-case analysis of a poet's use of terms. For a similar problem in other Tang poems, see Stephen Bokenkamp's analysis of the use of the term *bi luo* 碧落, "Taoism and Literature: The *Pi-lo* Question," 57–72. Bokenkamp's use in this article of Zürcher's conceptualization of linguistic borrowing has served as a model here.

Yu and her story in the "human world." Although he does not allude to his own literary skills in this closure, he is once again pointing to the importance of artistry in preserving, and retelling, such legends. Furthermore, he may also be proffering a different explanation of Long Yu's surprise at her lover's sudden appearance: instead of being drawn by her emotional flute-playing, Xiao Shi, too, may have been "summoned" by her great beauty.

Taken by itself, the reference to the paintings of beautiful women on screens is not particularly original, but as part of a series that celebrates the representation of female divinities in art and literature, Niu's closure is striking and logical. By distancing his audience from the intimate scenes of his lyrics, Niu artfully points to his own appreciation of the "charming grace" of the story and asserts his own authority to comment and reinterpret the tale. As he did in the previous lyric, referring to Cao Zhi's rendition of the Luo river goddess, Niu suggests that his works, like those painted screens, will live on in this world for their own charming grace. In a more speculative vein, given the evidence of a flourishing painting culture in Shu and the stories of ekphrases (poems on paintings) by Ouyang Jiong and others at the Shu court, we could easily imagine Niu's set of seven lyrics as a poetic accompaniment to a series of paintings on the theme of "encounters with the goddesses." Such matching may never have occurred, but Niu's self-conscious artistry surely appealed to the Shu connoisseurs of both literature and the visual arts.

The lyrics to "Lin jiang xian" by Yan Xuan and Niu Xiji reveal these two poets to be not only well versed in the linguistic and descriptive conventions of goddess encounters but also able to create coherent scenarios from those conventions. In contrast, the "Lin jiang xian" lyrics by Sun Guangxian and Gu Xiong show them to be content with superficial references—or no references at all—to transcendent affairs. However, throughout the "Lin jiang xian" lyrics, references to objects and places in the human world predominate. Just as the lyrics to "Pusa man" and "Huanxi sha" focused on the pathos of the abandoned woman, the "Lin jiang xian" lyrics dwell on the fate of the human lover left behind. This may seem a minor point—why wouldn't poets be interested in the human angle?—and yet it underscores the essential continuity of the *Hua-*

jian ji lyrics with the secular medieval tradition. Unlike Daoist hymns or poems about goddesses of the celestial realm, in which the traits of the goddess are reverently enumerated, these song lyrics are firmly planted in the dusty world of human affairs.

However, as we saw in Yan Xuan's two lyrics and Niu Xiji's first and fifth lyrics, one critical difference between more overtly secular romantic lyrics and those given over to divine encounters is that the relationship of the male and female characters is often reversed—the goddess is the one who decides whether or not she will bestow her love. Exteriorizing the female figure further underscores her identity as an independent, even capricious being, one who can move about in the celestial and terrestrial realms as she pleases. Along the same lines, the use of a male subject for the abandoned lover alters the balance of power in the romance. Even if they are ultimately only coquettes in transcendent clothing, the "divine" women are represented as being able to come and go at their own will, while their male lovers can only express feelings of regret and despair. Within the medieval literary tradition, the use of the goddess motif seems to have been the only way to conceptualize this power reversal. The representation of the roles of the male and female participants in the "Lin jiang xian" lyrics is completely consistent with the tradition of encounters with goddesses, but it seems striking when read against the "helpless woman" convention that informs the majority of the *Huajian ji*'s romantic lyrics. And yet, as Niu Xiji takes such care to tell us, it is the male poets (or painters) who have the last word. After we examine lyrics from "Nü guanzi," I will consider the effect that the range of gender roles in these tune title sets has on our reading of romance in the *Huajian ji* as a whole.

"Get thee to a nunnery"? A Reading of "Nü guanzi"

The tune title "Nü guanzi," like "Lin jiang xian," appears in the *Jiaofang ji* and in the *Zunqian ji*, but not in the Dunhuang lyrics or in the lyrics by Southern Tang poets.[62] However, the use of Daoist

---

62. The three lyrics to "Nü guanzi" in the *Zunqian ji* are by the Shu poets Ouyang Jiong (2) and Yin E (1).

allusions in lyrics to "Nü guanzi" is by no means exclusive to Shu: Tang poets also experiment with Daoist language in "Nü guanzi." Edward Schafer, in his article on Five Dynasties lyrics to this title, "The Capeline Cantos: Verses on the Divine Loves of Taoist Priestesses," discussed the development of terms for Daoist religious women in the medieval period. There, he translated *nü guanzi* as "capeline," a "fairly informal equivalent" of the more formal *nü Daoshi* 女道士 (gentlewoman of the Dao).[63] In the Shangqing school of Daoism dominant during the Tang, they were called both *nü daoshi* 女道士 and *nüguan* 女冠, for their distinctive headdress.[64] The informality of the tune title, however, is signaled by the suffix *zi*, which we saw above in the familiar term *xianzi*.[65] In keeping with what I think is the informal quality of the title in these lyrics, I translate it more loosely, as "The Daoist Nun," a general term for a female Daoist religious that may have other connotations. Just as many of the "Lin jiang xian" lyrics retell stories of famous female transcendents, some of whom were associated with water, many of the "Nü guanzi" lyrics make explicit comparisons of women with Daoist novices, whether or not they behave as such.

The formal features of "Nü guanzi" are stable in the *Huajian ji*; there is only one rhyme pattern and one metrical structure, in two different stanzas, as follows: 4/6/3/5/5 and 5/5/5/3. The rhyme

---

63. Schafer, "Cantos," 14. He also notes that the term seems to have become the normal title of a Daoist priestess by Song times. His translation "capeline" comes from the word *guan* 冠, cap, which refers to the woman's headgear. Daoist faithful were distinguished by their particular caps, which were often yellow and/or lotus-shaped, with "petals."

64. Kohn, ed., *Daoism Handbook*, 384.

65. It is difficult to date the appearance of this suffix in Chinese texts, but it appears with increasing frequency in the Tang and Song periods. The *Han yu da cidian*, for example, gives a usage in the Tang-era text *You xian ku* as the earliest of its citations (vol. 4, 163). According to Ren Bantang, its occurrence in so many *quzi* titles in the *Jiaofang ji* (69 titles of 343 total) indicates that it was used for tunes that were brief, *xiao qu* 小曲, and that the suffix was used to distinguish the brief tunes from the tune suites, *da qu* 大曲. Although Ren does not address the history of the suffix in other contexts, he points out that no medieval song tunes before the Tang contained it. His speculation thus assumes that the use of *zi* as a diminutive suffix predated the High Tang. Ren, *Jiaofang ji jianding*, 123.

pattern is somewhat unusual: the first two lines of the first stanza rhyme with a *ze* tone word, but the rhyme of the rest of the lyric is consistently a single *ping* rhyme, falling in the third and fifth lines of the first stanza and in the second and fourth (final) lines of the second stanza. As in the "Lin jiang xian" set, the lyrics to "Nü guanzi" tend to be preserved in pairs, although only a few of these pairs seem to have an internal temporal or narrative logic that draws together the two lyrics. The pairing may represent a musical practice that is lost to us.

Unlike the "Lin jiang xian" set, the lyrics to "Nü guanzi" contain two by Wen Tingyun (see Table 7). As in lyrics to "Pusa man," Wen sets the model that other poets follow. In both of his lyrics, Wen Tingyun presents a beautiful woman who goes off to "seek transcendence," but, as we shall see, the difference between his would-be Daoist nuns and his courtesans is very slight.

In her book on the importance of Xi wangmu in medieval literature, Suzanne Cahill discusses the role of Daoist nuns in the Tang and their relationship to the Spirit-Mother. She summarizes the reasons a Tang woman might have chosen to become a Daoist nun:

> She might take holy orders for various reasons: as a means of refuge or retreat at the death of a husband, as a purifying intermission between husbands, . . . as a survival tactic for members of the imperial harem dismissed during anti-luxury campaigns, as a means of escaping palace intrigue and danger, as a method of avoiding marriage and living an independent life outside the family, and as a way of obtaining an education. Some parents sent sick daughters to a convent in the hopes of curing them; in times of famine, parents might hand over starving daughters so they might survive. These motives exist in addition, of course, to genuine religious vocation, which is hard to measure.[66]

Cahill is quick to acknowledge one significant problem in the study of Tang Daoist nuns: literary and historical sources either are too focused on elite Daoist women's lives or else are too generalized to provide much solid evidence about their practices or daily routine.

---

66. Cahill, *Transcendence and Divine Passion*, 216.

Table 7
Huajian ji Poets with Lyrics to "Nü guanzi"

Poet	Number of lyrics	Poet	Number of lyrics
Wen Tingyun	2	Sun Guangxian	2
Wei Zhuang	2	Lu Qianyi	2
Xue Zhaoyun	2	Mao Xizhen	2
Niu Qiao	4	Li Xun	2
Zhang Bi	1		

What is clear from Cahill's summary of women's motives, however, is that women who became nuns were entering a life outside the sanctioned Confucian family relationships of daughter, wife, and mother and that in these Daoist convents they acquired skills and freedoms that distinguished them from other Tang women.

Daoist nunneries, like medieval European convents, were built on family lines, with "mothers" and "sisters" who recreated a family hierarchy and the "terms of fictive kinship."[67] As was also true in Europe, the structure of the Daoist nunnery was mirrored by the brothel hierarchy, with its "madam" and "sister" prostitutes, a fact that did not go unnoticed by Tang society. The parallels of sexual freedom between the nunnery and the brothel went further in China, however, since former courtesans and imperial harem women—women with a history of sexual experience outside of marriage—often entered Daoist convents, sometimes only briefly, before remarrying. Again, medieval and Renaissance European literature gives us numerous parallels in jokes about promiscuous nuns, stories of prostitutes masquerading as nuns, and comparisons of convents to brothels. As noted above, Tang poets frequently used references to Daoist female religious or, alternatively, "female transcendents," *nüxian*, as codes for entertainment girls and prostitutes. But there also exists a subset of Tang poems on women's entry into Daoist convents—describing in particular the transit of "palace women" from one kind of institution to another—that Li

---

67. Ibid., 227.

Fengmao titles "poems on 'sending off the palace woman as she enters the Dao'" (*song gongren ru Dao* 送宮人入道).[68] Most famous among women who followed this path were some nine Tang princesses, including two daughters of Ruizong who became ordained, Tang Xuanzong's famous Prized Consort Yang, as well as many "retired" courtesans.[69] Catherine Despeux points out the possible advantages for imperial women who chose this path:

> Separated from society through their religious conversion, the women could yet exert a political influence, while at the same time taking refuge from the ubiquitous palace intrigues. They benefited from the economic privileges of their new status and had a great deal of personal freedom. Records show they often led a licentious life, undertook extensive travels, and devoted themselves to art and literature.[70]

In short, Daoist convents were notable institutions on the Tang cultural scene, and women who entered them were often prominent in Tang society. And the reputation of Daoist convents as havens for women who had once been married, in concubinage, or in socially questionable sexual relationships surely encouraged the popularity of the nun-as-prostitute trope in the popular imagination and in elite literature.

Furthermore, the nun-as-prostitute trope obviously shared common ground in Tang literature with the transcendent-as-prostitute trope. It is useful to look at an example of the latter trope in order to see the continuities with the "Daoist" women in the "Nü guanzi" tune title set. Sun Qi, the late Tang author of the *Beili zhi*, wrote a piece to the courtesan Wang Funiang that portrays a "transcendent" who is clearly not in a religious order.

---

68. Li, *You yu you*, 293–94.

69. One of these princesses, who became known as the "Princess of Jade Perfection," *yuzhen gongzhu* 玉眞公主, is discussed in Schafer, "The Princess Realized in Jade," 1–23. For a detailed study of the ordination of the princesses, see Benn, *The Cavern-Mystery Transmission: A Taoist Ordination Rite of A.D. 711*. Benn notes that "between 618 and 906 seventeen T'ang princesses (including Princesses T'ai-p'ing, Gold-Immortal, and Jade-Perfected) out of two hundred and twelve were inducted into Taoist orders" (104). For a discussion of the meanings of and mechanisms for Tang princesses entering Daoist convents, see Li, *You yu you*, 294–300.

70. Kohn, ed., *Daoism Handbook*, 389.

Sent to the Entertainment Girl (*jiren* 妓人) Wang Funiang
Sun Qi

In rainbow-colored and kingfisher transcendent clothes, and rosy skin,	綵翠仙衣紅玉膚
in her delicate grace, her age approaches the year of "splitting the gourd."[71]	輕盈年在破瓜初
In her auroral cups, she drunkenly urges Master Liu to gamble;[72]	霞盃醉喚劉郎賭
her clouds of chignon, falling indolently, invite "Amah"'s comb.[73]	雲髻慵邀阿母梳
She doesn't fear the chill invading the precious ornaments on her belt,	不怕寒侵緣帶寶
but fusses each time the wind lifts her skirt, and clasps it tight around her.	每憂風舉倩持裾
In vain you might imagine "Little Xi" doing her morning makeup—[74]	謾圖西子爲妝樣
but Little Xi could never quite compare to her.[75]	西子元來未得如

Typical allusions to transcendence are here—such as those to "transcendent clothes" and "Master Liu"—as well as the reference to "Amah," the madam of the house, a reference that Cahill suggests alludes to Xi wangmu. However, the poem could not be clearer on the woman's occupation. The markers of sexual availability, such as

---

71. "Splitting the gourd," *po-gua* 破瓜, plays on the character *gua*, which, when split, makes two "eight" characters, for a total of sixteen, the age of a girl's sexual maturity. It is thus a euphemism for the first sexual experience. Its usage as a trope for sexual ripeness can be dated at least to the Eastern Jin, to a poem by Sun Cho; it also occurs in He Ning's "He manzi," collected in the *Huajian ji*.

72. "Master Liu" refers to Liu Zhen, one of two men (the other being Ruan Zhao) who followed a stream in search of transcendent maidens, in the *You ming lu*.

73. "Amah" here refers to the madam of the singing house or brothel. Cahill, who also examines this poem in her work on the Spirit-Mother of the West, thinks that the phrase also points to the figure of Xi wangmu. *Amu* 阿母 was a familiar term for her. Cahill, *Transcendence and Divine Passion*, 237–38.

74. "Little Xi," *Xizi* 西子, is an informal reference to Xi Shi, the famous beauty of Yue, given to the king of Wu to distract him and make him lose his kingdom.

75. *QTS* 727.8328. This poem was also selected by Wei Hu for the *Caidiao ji*, where it appeared under the title "Sent to an Entertainment Girl." (Fu, *Tang ren xuan Tang shi*, 803–4.) The poem first appears in the *Beili zhi*, as a poem sent to Wang Funiang from Sun Qi himself. See Rouzer, *Articulated Ladies*, 275–76.

drunkenness, tumbling hair, and partially opened clothes would prove her to be a courtesan of some sort, but the reference to "splitting the gourd" settles the matter almost too bluntly. Although he is being complimentary after a fashion (according to the *Beili zhi* story in which this appears, Sun composed the poem for the courtesan, whom he admired), Sun Qi sketches this woman with all the accoutrements of her métier. We will not see this level of frankness in the "Nü guanzi" set, but some of the "nuns" certainly resemble Sun Qi's singing girl in appearance and demeanor. The poem provides an excellent example of the ways in which late Tang poets deployed "Daoist" images in order to dress up courtesans. Sun Qi employs the language of Daoism to flatter his subject, and yet his use of that language does not conceal her true identity.

The range of uses of Daoist imagery in the "Nü guanzi" set is even broader than that of "Lin jiang xian." In "Lin jiang xian," poets borrowed the narrative framework of meeting the goddess for some of their lyrics; however, in "Nü guanzi," there is no single narrative, only a more miscellaneous use of objects and scenes that might indicate the presence of a transcendent or religious aspirant. A few lyrics evoke a generalized scenario by referring to a "Master Liu" who seeks, or has left, a "transcendent" woman. "Master Liu" refers to the story of two men recorded in the medieval "accounts of anomalies" text *You ming lu* 幽明錄 (Record of the hidden and illuminated). Liu Zhen and Ruan Zhao went seeking medicinal herbs on Mount Tiantai; they lost their way, but suddenly discovered peaches in a tree and cakes that floated on a stream from the mountain. Tracing the stream back to its source, the men encountered two "jade maidens"; they all went off happily together into the mountain realm, but when the men decided to return home, they discovered that seven generations had passed. Some time afterward, the two men disappeared, perhaps to find their divine mates again. By the Tang, "Master Liu" and "Master Ruan" were clichéd figures for male lovers, similar to "Miss Xie," who appears as a generic courtesan in romantic poetry. Unlike the long medieval literary tradition of goddess encounters, however, the story of Masters Liu and Ruan had a simple plot and few related images for poets to draw on. It is thus not surprising to find that poets who refer to "Master

Liu" (such references were more common than to "Master Ruan," though the two are sometimes paired) do so in a way that does not seem to engage other elements of the story.[76] But as in the "Lin jiang xian" set, there are also six "Nü guanzi" lyrics that have no references to Daoist figures or objects whatsoever.

Many of Edward Schafer's remarks on the "Nü guanzi" lyrics enrich our understanding of the texts, but because he did not see that the interpretive framework for the tune title set might extend beyond the Daoist associations of "Nü guanzi," his readings ultimately underestimate the importance of the romantic and erotic conventions in the lyrics. An example of the limitations of his framework can be found below, in an introductory passage to his translations:

> The supposed "erotic" or sentimental similarities fade into a secondary role when the Taoist motifs ... are taken with the seriousness they deserve.... The most obvious feature of the *nü kuan tzu* stanzas is the constant repetition of words and phrases—it is also a feature of other *tz'u* forms—which inevitably directs the reader's thoughts to "formulaic" poetry.... In short, it may be that a kind of urban oral tradition underlies the sophisticated lyrics set to popular songs by the masters of the *tz'u* form. But if such is indeed the case, we must still beware of the naive assumption that the exploitation of these lexical items is "mere" in any sense: the undeniable splendors of Homer are studded with such common currency, given inimitable luster by the craft of the true poet.[77]

---

76. There are twelve references to "Master Liu" in the *Huajian ji*, five of which are found in "Nü guanzi" lyrics, two in "Tian xianzi" lyrics, two in "Huanxi sha," and three others in three different tune titles. Four of the twelve references are to Masters Liu and Ruan. Thus, seven of the twelve references appear in tune title sets that are nominally concerned with divinities, supporting the argument that poets paid some attention to the meanings of tune titles when composing lyrics. We should also note the possible influence of the *you xian* poems by the late Tang poet Cao Tang, which concerned the "wanderings" of various immortals, and included the adventures of Liu and Ruan in the Tiantai mountains. Fourteen of Cao Tang's poems on this topic were preserved in the *Caidiao ji* (Fu, *Tang ren xuan Tang shi*, 795–99). For a discussion of the relationship of these poems to Daoist tales and to one another, see Owen, *Late Tang*. See also Yan, *Tang dai youxian shi yanjiu*, 389–92.

77. Schafer, "Capeline Cantos," 17.

As noted in Chapters 4 and 5, the "constant repetition of words and phrases" is a formal feature of the anthology as a whole, to such a degree that I have defined it as a constitutive element of the song lyric genre in Shu. Schafer's suggestion that "a kind of urban oral tradition" informs these lyrics is not too dissimilar to my own argument for a Shu court practice of skillful imitation. However, his argument that the Daoist imagery of the tune title set is nowhere "mere" or formal is unsustainable when the "Daoist" lyrics are compared to others in their respective tune title sets or to other lyrics in the larger collection.

Evidence of Schafer's sensitivity to the particulars of the "Nü guanzi" lyrics can be found in the list of features he singles out for comment: the prevalence of descriptions of women's clothing, the use of fragrance, the many mists and clouds, the predominance of blue-green colors, makeup on women's faces, "muted or suppressed speech," and words that suggest "lightness, restraint, inhibition, fading, and other concepts that have to do with subdued or partly concealed qualities, actions, and feelings."[78] As I have argued in Chapters 4 and 5, these features are typical of the romantic tradition and are not specific to this one tune title or even to the set of "transcendent" tune titles. Schafer also discusses two further features that I agree are particular to this set: these are the poets' references to the "libation platform," *jiaotan* 醮壇 (Schafer translates this as "sacred platform"), a cleared and raised space for performing ritual, and the two allusions to the ritual "Pacing the Void," *bu xu* 步虛, in which a celebrant traced the paths of celestial bodies in a pattern on the ground.[79] We shall see in lyrics examined below that these elements certainly change the tone of a lyric, but they do not necessarily make the lyric's story an exclusively sacred event.

Like the "Lin jiang xian" lyrics, the "Nü guanzi" lyrics fall along a very broad spectrum, ranging from lyrics with almost no Daoist

---

78. Ibid., 20–22.

79. On the practice, its history, and its implications for medieval literature, see Bokenkamp, "The 'Pacing the Void' Stanzas of the Ling-pao Scriptures." See also Schafer, *Pacing the Void*.

imagery to those whose use of Daoist stories and references is quite prominent. Of the nineteen "Nü guanzi" lyrics, six have no currently identifiable references to transcendent objects or figures; these six are the two lyrics by Wei Zhuang, three of Niu Qiao's four lyrics, and one of Mao Xizhen's pair. We find mere formal borrowing in a few lyrics, as in Wen Tingyun's two lyrics and the fourth of Niu Qiao's four (since we have noted before that Wen and his imitator Niu were very dedicated to secular and erotic depictions of women, their common lack of interest in Daoist imagery should come as no surprise). On the level of conceptual borrowing, we find a few lyrics that use the goddess-encounter. Like the "Lin jiang xian" lyrics by Yan Xuan and Niu Xiji, these "Nü guanzi" lyrics (including those by Li Xun and Lu Qianyi) set the story in an exterior, natural scene but follow the traditional romantic plot. At the most religious end of our range of Daoist usage, two lyrics by Xue Zhaoyun clearly describe a ritual centering on a Daoist nun's quest for transcendence. These lyrics avoid any suggestion of romance and are by far the most serious of the tune title set.

We recognize the abandoned courtesan in a few of the most secular of the "Nü guanzi" lyrics, exemplified in the following, by Niu Qiao and Mao Xizhen:

"Nü guanzi" (4th of 4)
Niu Qiao

Flying in pairs, dancing in pairs—	雙飛雙舞
on a spring day, orioles warble in the rear garden.	春晝後園鶯語
She rolls up her gauze shades.	卷羅帷
The letter in brocade has long been sealed,	錦字書封過了
but geese up in the Silver River pass slowly.[80]	銀河雁過遲
Mandarin duck and drake arrayed on the precious bed curtains—	鴛鴦排寶帳
nutmeg embroidered along linked branches.	荳蔻繡連枝

---

80. The letter in brocade refers to a story from the *Jin shu* "biographies of exemplary women" (*Jin shu* 96.2523) in which a wife sent poems to her husband in brocade on fabric; it came to mean a letter sent from a woman to her lover. Geese, traditionally seen as bearers of letters, are here up in the sky by the "Silver River," or Milky Way.

Not speaking through her even lines of pearly tears— 不語勻珠淚
at the time when flowers fall.[81] 落花時

<blockquote>

"Nü guanzi" (2nd of 2)
Mao Xizhen
</blockquote>

With her delicate moth-brows and lovely face:[82]	修蛾慢臉
not speaking, she makes a little "sandalwood heart,"	不語檀心一點
and does her "little mountain" hair.[83]	小山妝
Her cicada temple-curls fall, hiding lustrous tints.	蟬鬢低含綠
Gauzy robes are lightly brushed with yellow.	羅衣淡拂黃
Depressed, she comes to the deep courtyard;	悶來深院裏
she paces idly, fallen flowers on all sides.	閑步落花傍
Her fragile hands ever-so-gently adjust	纖手輕輕整
the jade brazier's incense.[84]	玉爐香

The two lyrics present familiar close-ups of the abandoned woman: the first shows us her boudoir, the second her face and figure. Where Niu Qiao uses the conventional "pairs" of objects—a letter, tears, and the signs of passing spring—to signal the abandonment, Mao Xizhen suppresses even these cues, hinting only at her "depression," *men* 悶, and idleness.

Further into the world of transcendence, we find hints of the Daoist nun in the lyrics by Wen Tingyun, but Wen's manner of depicting such women suggests that they are merely dressing up in borrowed clothing.

---

81. *HJJZS*, 134.

82. This *man* 慢 is interpreted as *man* 曼 (lovely in appearance). *Man* 慢 in this sense also occurs in Yan Xuan's "Yu meiren" ("Her face so lovely, her smiles so fair—/ When they see one another, boundless passion" 臉慢笑盈盈, 相看無限情).

83. The "sandalwood heart" refers to the color (red) and shape (a tight bow, or heart shape) of the woman's lipsticked mouth; the "little mountain" hair refers either to her hair, which is coiled into a "hill" on her head, or perhaps to the shape of her brows. I follow Li Yi here in reading this as a hairstyle.

84. *HJJZS*, 357.

"Nü guanzi" (1st of 2)
Wen Tingyun

Suppressing her charm, with a hint of smile,	含嬌含笑
in her slept-in kingfisher brows and faded rouge, she's demure, alluring.	宿翠殘紅窈窕
Temple-curls like cicadas,	鬢如蟬
cold jade hairpins above the autumn waters [of her eyes]—	寒玉簪秋水
light silks envelop her in emerald mist.	輕紗卷碧煙
Snowy breast in the simurgh mirror,[85]	雪胸鸞鏡裏
nandinas before the phoenix tower.[86]	棋樹鳳樓前
She entrusts a word to her Blue Beauty companion:[87]	寄語青娥伴
"[We should] soon seek transcendence."[88]	早求仙

In Wen Tingyun's voyeuristic style, the first stanza reveals the woman in her morning attire, flirtatiously "suppressing" her charms. The scene exhibits a light eroticism in its description of her slept-in makeup, the partial concealment of her figure, and the glimpse of breast in the next stanza. The second stanza introduces things associated with a transcendent's dwelling: the simurgh mirror, the nandinas, the "phoenix tower" itself, and the "Blue Beauty companion." But when juxtaposed against the conventionally erotic tone of the first stanza, these objects seem less a part of a transcendent's world and more the poet's flattery of his female subject. Even the closing, "[We should] soon seek transcendence," does not seem

---

85. The "simurgh mirror" is likely a hand mirror with a simurgh design on its back. The association of simurghs with mirrors comes from an Eastern Jin story of a simurgh that was shocked by its reflection. The allusion invokes female vanity. For a discussion of the uses of the simurgh in medieval literature, see James M. Hargett, "Playing Second Fiddle: The *Luan*-Bird in Early and Medieval Chinese Literature," 249–52.

86. Nandinas (*qi shu* 棋樹) were said (in the *Shanhai jing* and later sources) to grow in the Spirit-Mother of the West's realm and on Mount Tiantai and so became associated with transcendents. Schafer, "Capeline Cantos," 37–38. The "phoenix tower" is a generic term to indicate the dwelling of a transcendent.

87. The woman's "Blue Beauty companion" is dressed in the color for a young maidservant, but Wen probably also intends a reference to other *qing* 青-hued messengers, such as birds, who carried messages for Xiwang mu.

88. *HJJZS*, 41.

to be an exhortation to become a Daoist novice, but rather a promise to seek the "transcendence" of a meeting with her lover.[89] If we believe her statement, we would at least have to wonder what kinds of behavior Wen Tingyun thought appropriate to a nun. But Wen does not, in fact, give us enough clues to determine the woman's identity or career conclusively—this could perhaps be the scene of a courtesan vowing to leave her former life for the career of a *nü guan*.[90]

Wen Tingyun's second lyric describes the woman in her boudoir and includes similar references to transcendents. But the scene also includes a male lover, who is figured as the transcendent visitor.

"Nü guanzi" (2nd of 2)
Wen Tingyun

Above her auroral cape, clouds of hair—	霞帔雲髮
in the filigreed mirror, her transcendent visage seems like snow.	鈿鏡仙容似雪
Painting her sorrowful brows,	畫愁眉
covering her words, she retreats behind a light fan,	遮語回輕扇
suppressing her shyness, she lowers the embroidered bed curtains.	含羞下繡帷
In the jade tower, they gaze at each other long;	玉樓相望久
in her flowery bedchamber, she regrets his coming late.	花洞恨來遲
Soon, he must ride off on his simurgh—	早晚乘鸞去
"Don't leave me behind!"[91]	莫相遺

Although the identity of the male lover who rides away on the simurgh is unstated, the opening stanza once again focuses on the

---

89. In his discussion of this lyric, Aoyama refers to the trope of the transcendent grotto as the site of sexual encounter to which men could escape, as in the Tang story *You xian ku*, "Roaming in the Cavern of Transcendence." *Tō Sō shi kenkyū*, 21–22.

90. See Zhang Yiren's analysis of the different readings of this lyric found in modern editions of *HJJ*, in *Huajian ci lunji*, 174–81.

91. My translation of this final line parallels the final line of the first lyric, a line that also appears to be direct speech. The use of the negative imperative particle *mo* 莫 suggests that the woman is speaking to her departing beloved. The editors of *Quan Tang Wudai ci shizhu* also indicate this reading, glossing *yi* 遺 as "abandon" (*QTWDCSZ*, 366–7). *HJJZS*, 42.

half-exposed, half-concealed allure of the woman in the "flowery bedchamber" where the lovers meet. The repeated use of images of concealment and revelation in these two lyrics is striking: the word *han*, "suppressed" or "hidden," is used three times in the two lyrics, and in the second lyric, the woman even uses a fan to block her speech, as she then shyly lowers the curtains to conceal them both. As in so many lyrics by Wen Tingyun, a coherent narrative is sacrificed for descriptive detail. In the end, the traces of transcendent imagery are also subordinated to the erotic details of the lovers' tryst.

A similar sprinkling of Daoist references marks the portrait of a lovely maiden by Wen Tingyun's best imitator, the Shu poet Niu Qiao. Of his four lyrics to the "Nü guanzi" tune, only the third refers to transcendents in any fashion.

"Nü guanzi" (3rd of 4)
Niu Qiao

In starry cap and auroral cloak,[92]	星冠霞帔
she dwells in Stamen-Pearl Palace.[93]	住在蕊珠宮裏
Pendants tinkling,	佩叮璫
brilliant kingfisher [hair] fluttering its cicada wings,	明翠搖蟬翼
her fragile jade fingers tend her slept-in makeup.	纖珪理宿妝
At the libation platform, spring grasses are green;	醮壇春草綠
in the courtyard of herbs, apricot flowers are fragrant.[94]	藥院杏花香

---

92. The "starry cap" and "auroral cloak" refer to the garments of a Daoist religious, although "lotus crowns," often yellow in color, were more common. Schafer notes a few occurrences of "star crowns" in canonical texts ("Capeline Cantos," 29–30). Goddesses clothed in "auroras" (pink morning mists) were common in literature from the "Rhapsody on the Gaotang Shrine" and after. Daoist texts write of transcendents being clothed in "cloaks," *pei* 帔, which were often said to be made of feathers (suggesting the possibility of flying away to the heavens) in shades of yellow and pink.

93. According to Daoist texts, among them the *Huangting neijing jing*, the Stamen-Pearl Palace was located in a specific Daoist Heaven. Its use here seems similar to Wen's use of "phoenix tower" to describe the woman's dwelling.

94. The "libation platform," discussed above, and the "courtyard of herbs" are parallel references to Daoist spaces. Herbs were grown and consumed by Daoists to achieve longevity and transcendence.

| The blue bird carries her heart's affairs[95] | 青鳥傳心事 |
| and sends them to Master Liu.[96] | 寄劉郎 |

Niu's lyric presents us with an interesting reading challenge. On the one hand, this poem abounds with references to transcendent beings, from the woman's "starry cap and auroral cloak" to her dwelling in "Stamen-Pearl Palace." Read alone, this lyric offers us a "Daoist" reading: she is a nun or a female transcendent who lives in a typically unearthly paradise, sending messages to her mortal lover. But read against other *Huajian ji* lyrics and against Wen Tingyun's two "Nü guanzi" lyrics, Niu's woman seems less clearly divine.

The structure of Niu's lyric is identical to that of Wen Tingyun's first lyric: the first stanza describes the woman's appearance in intimate detail (Niu even echoes Wen's "cicada temple-curls," and Wen's "slept-in kingfisher [hair]" shows up as Niu's "slept-in makeup"), and the second stanza relates her actions or feelings. The first stanza of each lyric describes the woman's external surroundings; the second stanza features a "blue" messenger carrying word to an absent lover. Where Wen Tingyun remains in the woman's boudoir for the second stanza, Niu Qiao moves outside, to a specific spring scene. The "libation platform" points to a specific Daoist offering rite; Niu's borrowing of the phrase here suggests a romantic interlude of wine drinking.[97] Although Niu Qiao's imagery pushes his vignette closer to the realm of transcendent encounters, the lyric's rhetorical structure, when compared to that of Wen Tingyun's first lyric, indicates his intention of portraying the romance of the scene, not its numinous qualities. Focusing too narrowly on the lyric's Daoist references might mean neglecting Niu Qiao's clever engagement with the thematic tradition—including the secular literary use of Daoist imagery—and the romantic conventions. In Niu Qiao's lyric, we discover once again his great talent for imitating—and perhaps outdoing—Wen Tingyun, the master of the erotic vignette.

---

95. The "blue bird" was traditionally the messenger of Xiwang mu.

96. *HJJZS*, 133.

97. This usage itself may be a borrowing from the Tang poet Li Shangyin, who, in a witty poem, depicted a scene of monks and officials observing the beauty of a singing girl at a *jiaotan*. *QTS* 541.6226–27.

In contrast to Wen Tingyun's and Niu Qiao's borrowing of terms, the lyrics of Zhang Bi, Lu Qianyi, and Li Xun more skillfully blend Daoist images and the romantic tradition. Both Lu and Li present their "Nü guanzi" lyrics as thwarted romances and use the "Master Liu" story for their narrative framework. As we saw in the "Lin jiang xian" lyrics, the shift from description to narrative can substantially alter the mood of a romantic vignette, though it does not necessarily signal a more serious or thoroughgoing use of Daoist allusions. In the following two lyrics by Zhang Bi and Lu Qianyi, we see Daoist images integrated with the rhetorical structure, narrative conventions, and female subjectivity familiar from "Pusa man" and "Huanxi sha." Lu Qianyi imitates Zhang Bi very closely: not only does Lu follow Zhang's structure and images, he also uses Zhang Bi's second rhyme (the *ping* rhyme of lines 3 and 5 of the first stanza and lines 2 and 4 of the second stanza), including two of the same rhyme words (*shen* 深 and *yin* 陰).[98] In my translation, I have highlighted images that are repeated, or only slightly modified, from one poet's lyric to the other.

Zhang Bi, "Nü guanzi" #1
  First stanza
Dewy flowers and misty grass—
silent and lonely in the Five
  Clouds and Three Isles.[99]
Spring just at its height.
Her looks are failing—
  dissipating jade—
her perfume fades where it
  lingers on her collar.

Lu Qianyi, "Nü guanzi" #1
  First stanza
By the phoenix tower are nandinas—
melancholy since **Master Liu went
  away.**
Just at the height of spring,
in her grotto, vainly filling
  with sorrow.
Letters in the human realm can't
  be found.[100]

---

98. The similarity of these two lyrics was first noted by Schafer, who also explored them in his discussion of lexical repetition (in "Capeline Cantos," 17–18). See also Zhang Yiren's discussion of the relationship of Lu's lyric to other lyrics in the collection, *Huajian ci lunji*, 269–74.

99. The "Five Clouds" are those of the five auroral colors; the "Three Isles" are the three magical islands of the eastern sea: Penglai, Fangzhang, and Yingzhou.

100. As Li Yi notes (159), the word *xin* in both lyrics could be read plausibly either as the adverb "truly" or as "letters." Given the use of *xin* and also *xin chen* in two other *HJJ* lyrics, I translate both uses as "letters."

Second stanza	Second stanza
Where bamboos are sparse, the empty balustrade is silent;[101] where pines are dense, the libation platform is shadowed. Why did **Master Liu go away?** His **letters** are vanished and lost.[103]	Where bamboos are sparse, the hall of fasting seems remote;[102] where pines are dense, the libation platform is shadowed. Falling clouds of hair as she lowers her head to gaze— "Can he know my heart?"[104]
露花煙草 寂寞五雲三島 春正深 貌減潛消玉 香殘尚惹襟 竹疏處檻靜 松密醮壇陰 何事劉郎去 信沉沉	鳳樓棋樹 惆悵劉郎一去 正春深 洞裏愁空結 人間信莫尋 竹疏齋殿迥 松密醮壇陰 倚雲低首望 可知心

The rhetorical structure of the lyrics is identical: the first stanza establishes the location and season of the abandoned woman, and the second stanza moves to an exterior setting, where each woman laments her loss. In both, we see the woman in a location associated with a transcendent—in Lu, the "phoenix tower," and in Zhang, the "Five Clouds and Three Isles." Spring is at its height in each—Lu Qianyi simply switches two words in his line (Lu: *zheng chun shen* 正春深; Zhang: *chun zheng shen* 春正深). Nevertheless, both women's melancholy persists, knotting up in Lu's woman and ruining the appearance of Zhang's. Lu has obviously taken Zhang's

---

101. "Empty balustrade" is a direct translation of *xu jian* 虛檻. It may refer to a fence or some kind of enclosure that marks off a spot for ritual, making it both syntactically and semantically parallel to "libation platform," or it may simply mean the place where the lovers had once met.

102. The "hall of fasting," *zhai dian* 齋殿, seems to refer to a building used for ritual fasting and feasts, similar to *zhaitang* 齋堂 or *zhaigong* 齋宮.

103. *HJJZS*, 159.

104. *HJJZS*, 335–36.

couplet from the opening of his second stanza and changed two words: "empty balustrade" becomes "hall of fasting." Where Zhang closes with a lament for Master Liu's departure, Lu places the same information earlier, in the first stanza, and closes with a rhetorical question voiced by the abandoned woman. Lu Qianyi's rewriting of Zhang Bi's lyric demonstrates once again the Shu poets' fondness for creative borrowing, and the appreciation for skillful imitation of the *Huajian ji* compilers.[105]

Daoist ritual paraphernalia is prominent in both lyrics, though it is not clear to what end it is being put. Do the Daoist elements in fact alter the fundamental dynamic of the romance? In the second stanzas of both lyrics, the female subject appears to visit the empty space where, presumably, she encountered her "Master Liu"; although the location is described clearly, we do not see the woman performing specific rituals, nor does she engage the sacred space in any meaningful way. She is as detached from the natural setting as women in other lyrics are from the ornaments of their chambers. The phrases used to describe the settings—"the libation platform," the "hall of fasting"—are unusually specific but the rhetorical questions—"Why did Master Liu go away?" and "Can he know my [or her] heart?"—seem, in contrast, almost too familiar. Furthermore, the relationship of the lyrics' male and female lovers reverses the original story of the mortal Masters Liu and Ruan, who, like King Xiang and Cao Zhi in their encounters with goddesses, were found by the female transcendents. These lyrics present their female subjects as women abandoned by their lovers; they are thus figured as the maidens who guided Liu and Ruan to their mysterious realm. Zhang Bi suggests this point of view in his line "Silent and lonely in the Five Clouds and Three Isles" (*jimo wuyun sandao* 寂寞五雲三島), implying that the female subject is in a celestial realm, an implication that Lu Qianyi makes even more clearly in the line

---

105. We find more creative variation on some of the elements of these lyrics in Sun Guangxian's third lyric to "Nü guanzi." The last two lines of his first stanza are "As spring grows late, letters are vanished, lost; / to the ends of the earth, where might I find him?" 春晚信沉沉, 天涯何處尋. *HJJZS*, 290.

"Letters in the human realm can't be found." But unlike the narrative framework of the goddess encounters in "Lin jiang xian," which reversed the romantic obligations of the male and female participants, this version of the story of Liu and Ruan merely reiterates the familiar tale of roaming men and fixed women. This is indeed a Daoist treatment of romance, but its plaintive refrain is still voiced by a lonely female subject: "Where is he?"

Lu Qianyi's second "Nü guanzi" lyric succeeds in creating a more otherworldly (and original) atmosphere by its emphasizing the setting of the encounter rather than the conventionalized emotions of its participants. The same is true of Li Xun's two "Nü guanzi" lyrics. In these lyrics, the poets avoid describing the physical appearance or the emotions of the female character and instead emphasize the scene and the events that occur there.

"Nü guanzi" (2nd of 2)
Lu Qianyi

Upon the platform for Pacing the Void,[106]	步虛壇上
scarlet pennants and rainbow banners lean toward each other,[107]	絳節霓旌相向
drawing the perfected transcendent.	引眞仙
Jade pendants shake in mooncast shadows—[108]	玉珮搖蟾影
musky smoke curls up from the golden brazier.	金爐裊麝煙
As dew grows heavy, the frosty writing slips grow wet.	露濃霜簡濕
The wind strengthens, blowing aside the feather robes.[109]	風緊羽衣偏

---

106. For the ritual of "Pacing the Void," see n79, above.

107. These pennants and banners appear to be the insignia for the ritual that is "drawing the transcendent." Li Yi notes that this line is taken from a poem by Han Wo, "Three poems in six-character meter," in which Han writes: "Carmine pennants and rainbow banners linger long" (*jiang jie ni jing jiu liu* 絳節霓旌久留). Li Yi, *HJJZS*, 336.

108. The jade pendants are probably on the belt of the transcendent. They would shake as she walked or if she took off her robes. The "mooncast shadows," *chan ying* 蟾影, use the periphrasis of "toad," *chan*, for the moon.

109. The "feather robes" are transcendent clothing; see n92, above.

She wants to linger, but it's so hard to stay— 欲留難得住
so she returns to the heavens.¹¹⁰ 卻歸天

This lyric exhibits a greater commitment to explicitly Daoist imagery and contexts than any we have seen so far, and it is at the same time noticeably erotic. The last two lines of the first stanza hint at a sexual encounter in terms familiar from romantic lyrics—the movement of the jade pendants in response to bodily movements and the rising smoke from musk incense that masks the scene are easily understood. The coming dawn, signaled by the heaviness of dew that melts bits of frost, reveals the encounter to be almost at its warmest moment. The feather robes that are blown aside by an increasingly urgent wind are meant to titillate both the lover in the poem and the reading or listening audience. By avoiding direct description of the participants and focusing on the modal qualities of the scene, Lu heightens the linked religious and erotic tensions of the potentially divine encounter far more successfully than did other *Huajian ji* poets.

The ritual of "Pacing the Void" that opens the lyric signals the divine nature of the desired encounter, and the pennants and banners are explicitly present to "draw," *yin* 引, or attract, the "perfected transcendent," *zhenxian* 眞仙. The use of the "Pacing the Void" ritual links this song lyric to another important tune title of the Tang and the earlier medieval period, the "Bu xu ci" (Lyrics for Pacing the Void), a Daoist hymn to which a number of Tang poets composed lyrics. This title long antedates the development of *quzi ci* in the Tang.¹¹¹ In most of the Tang lyrics, poets referred to some Daoist material, most often the encounter with the goddess.¹¹² Lu Qianyi surely knew this tradition well, and he engages it here; the

---

110. *HJJZS*, 336.
111. For example, the *Yuefu shiji* collects a total of 47 poems to the title "Bu xu ci" and another to "Bu xu yin." Twelve of these date from before the Tang. *Yuefu shiji*, 1099–106. For a study of these lyrics with respect to the Lingbao tradition, see Bokenkamp, "The 'Pacing the Void' Lyrics."
112. There are ten Tang lyrics composed to this title collected in the *Quan Tang Wudai ci shizhu*, but others exist in the *Quan Tang shi*. *QTWDCSZ*, 126–27, 175–76, 212, 258–59, 404, 428.

ritual is noted only twice in the collection, in this lyric and in one below, by Li Xun. Furthermore, Lu's use of the term *zhenxian* is unique in the *Huajian ji*, and even the word *zhen*, meaning "perfected," only occurs four other times in the anthology—three times in "Nü guanzi" lyrics and once in a "Lin jiang xian" lyric. "Perfected transcendent" is a formal term for a Daoist divinity; in its tone, it is very far from "transcendent girl," *xianzi*. Jade pendants are worn by mortals as well as divinities, but the reference to the "feather robes" distinguishes the visitor as divine. Unlike other lyrics that seem to have magical objects scattered around for effect, everything in Lu's lyric contributes to the atmosphere: a specific ritual sets the scene, which is decorated in an appropriate ritual manner, and the participants are hidden from direct sight, befitting an encounter with a supernatural being. As we have seen in other lyrics, direct description of the female face and form is an easy way to mark her as an object of sexual desire (and not a particularly valuable object at that). Lu's glimpses of the figure's robes and pendants in motion are no less erotic than direct description, but the erotic focus is on all that is *not* seen rather than on the revealed figure.

Even more provocative in this lyric is the lack of gender cues for the "perfected transcendent." In the last stanza, there are no indicators of gender to clarify the ambiguity created by the usual absence of pronouns. The tradition of the encounter with the goddess (as well as the feather robes being blown open by the *yang* wind) leads me to read the visitor as female, but the secular romantic tradition would dictate that the one who visits and then leaves be male. The transcendent's apparel does not help us: both male and female divinities could wear jade pendants and feathered robes, and both male and female religious could "pace the void." The gender ambiguity of Lu's lyric contrasts with the more clearly gendered male and female roles found in purely romantic lyrics, or in lyrics of encountering the goddess. It seems that a sexual union, whether actual or dreamed, takes place in this lyric; however, the use of Daoist images and the avoidance of direct description of the female subject make the lyric a welcome and original change from other lyrics that depict divine encounters, such as those we saw in Niu Xiji's "Lin jiang xian" set.

Li Xun's first "Nü guanzi" lyric presents a similar divine encounter with the same gender ambiguity. The similarities to Lu's second lyric are so obvious that we should assume they are not accidental, but since both poets lived and wrote during the Former Shu, we cannot determine who might have imitated whom.

"Nü guanzi" (1st of 2)
Li Xun

The stars are high, the moon at zenith—	星高月午
at the deepest place among cinnabar cassias and green pines,[113]	丹桂青松深處
the libation platform lies open.	醮壇開
From gilded chimes is struck a light dew;[114]	金磬敲清露
pearly streamers stand in the kingfisher moss.	珠幢立翠苔
The sounds of Pacing the Void are dim and distant.	步虛聲縹緲
As he visualizes her image, his thoughts stray back and forth.[115]	想象思徘徊
In the dawn sky, the path of return	曉天歸去路
points to Penglai.[116]	指蓬萊

Li Xun sets his scene with some of the same ornaments found in Lu Qianyi's lyric: the "libation platform" is prepared, with "pearly streamers" (instead of pennants) decorating the space in preparation for a deity's arrival. And it seems the moment is ripe: it is the

---

113. "Cinnabar cassia" was a cassia with red bark. The connection between cinnabar, used in Daoist longevity elixirs, is clearly intended here; though, as Schafer suggests, the contrast of red and green trees is also important in the visual scene ("Capeline Cantos," 53).

114. The chimes, *qing* 磬, were made of stone; here, they are decorated in gilt. They were common in both Buddhist and Daoist temples. In the *Huajian ji*, they appear only in Li's two "Nü guanzi" lyrics.

115. The phrase *xiang xiang* 想象 is one that may resonate on different levels. Schafer ("Cantos," 53) translates it as "actualizes her image" and explains it as "fixing, or 'actualizing,' of astral deities in parts of one's body." Bokenkamp describes the practice in detail: "Known as 'retentive contemplation' or 'retentive visualization,' the method involves the creation and manipulation of images to achieve desired goals." *Early Daoist Scriptures*, 288. Presumably, the "desired goal" of the lover here would be to bring back the departed beloved. However, the phrase can be found in many Tang poems to mean simply "imagining."

116. *HJJZS*, 383.

deepest, most mysterious time of night, when the stars are at their height and the moon is at the peak of its transit. The striking chimes announce the beginning of the event—perhaps heralding the goddess's arrival—but in Li's lyric, even references to her clothing are suppressed. The second stanza, like many second stanzas we have seen, occurs after the meeting; the opening line—"The sounds of Pacing the Void are dim and distant"—indicates either that she has now left the place where they met, or perhaps that in his memory, the sounds of the ritual are already fading. Just as the abandoned women of "Pusa man" and "Huanxi sha" try to contact the beloved through the medium of dream, the lover here longingly "visualizes [his lover's] image," in an attempt to recreate her presence. But the only trace of her is the "path of return" in the dawn sky, like the sun-tinged contrail of a jet, that "points toward Penglai," or her celestial home.

Like Lu Qianyi, Li Xun intimates a meeting between mortal and divine being in a sacred space, but Li's lyric has even fewer indications of what happened or who participated in the event. The temporal structure resembles that of romantic lyrics—Li focuses on the moments before and after the meeting, deepest night and the following dawn—but the ritual setting and Daoist allusions create a far more otherworldly atmosphere than we find enveloping the mortal trysts of other lyrics. And, as in Lu's lyric, the gender roles are unspecified, though I have again read them to involve a goddess visiting a mortal male. The effect of these features is cumulative: the further away a poet moves from the conventions of romantic lyrics, the more convincing is his evocation of the supernatural quality of a divine encounter. Li's lyric is one of the few—but certainly one of the best—examples of the consistent and serious use of Daoist imagery in the *Huajian ji*.

Despite the meaning of the tune title "The Daoist Nun," only two lyrics in the "Nü guanzi" set, those by Xue Zhaoyun, appear to refer directly to a Daoist nun rather than to a specific legendary goddess or a generic female dressed as a transcendent. Xue's first lyric describes a young woman's departure from the world of men and her search for transcendence, and the second lyric appears to depict the subsequent career of the same woman, now transformed into a divinity. Of course, Xue's transcendent is, like the *xianzi* we have seen, engaged in romantic dalliance with a "Master Liu," but his lyric is the only one in the tune title set that gives us the female divinity's point of view. In reading these two lyrics, I follow Schafer's interpretations without argument; the scenes the two lyrics depict are quite clearly Daoist in nature and show little connection to the scenes of boudoir longing.

"Nü guanzi" (1st of 2)
Xue Zhaoyun

Departed to seek transcendence—	求仙去也
kingfisher-inlaid golden combs are all put aside.	翠鈿金篦舍
She enters the craggy peaks.	入崖巒
Fogs envelop her yellow gauze cloak,	霧卷黃羅帔
clouds carve her white jade crown.[117]	雲雕白玉冠
Amid wilderness mists, the stream-threaded cave is chilly.	野煙溪洞冷
In forest moonlight, the stone bridge is bitter cold.	林月石橋寒
In the still night, beneath pines blown by wind,	靜夜松風下
she pays obeisance at the Altar of Heaven.[118]	禮天壇

The lyric begins abruptly but clearly: "Departed to seek transcendence" not only tells us where the woman has gone but also adds finality to her gesture with the prosaic particle *ye* 也, which ends the line. This opening line gives us an excellent opportunity for intratextual reading in the "Nü guanzi" set. If we recall Wen Tingyun's elegant coquette, who declares to her "Blue Beauty companion" that they should give up their frivolous life, we should also recall that we have no way of judging, from Wen's description, the seriousness of the female subject's intent. But we could easily read Xue's opening line, and the subsequent narrative, as the continuation of Wen's story—in the closing line of his second lyric, Wen's

---

117. Here, the woman is clad in the yellow cloak and white crown of a Daoist religious.

118. The "Altar of Heaven" would seem to refer to the space where sacrifices to Heaven were made, but since these were performed by the emperor, this altar is likely dedicated to celestial rituals of another sort. Schafer suggests "Sky Altar" ("Capeline Cantos," 46). *HJJZS*, 123.

courtesan declares, "[We should] soon seek transcendence," *zao qiu xian* 早求仙; Xue's lyric opens with the blunt statement that someone has "Gone to seek transcendence," *qiu xian qu ye* 求仙去也. We cannot determine if Xue intended his lyric to respond to Wen's, but the cool solemnity of the woman in Xue's lyric stands in stark contrast to the decorated enchantress of Wen's lyric, who has by no means discarded her finery. In Xue's lyric, the female subject not only casts aside her feminine ornaments—and by extension, her allures and desires—but she escapes the boudoir, making her way into a chilly natural world littered with feminine symbolism (mists, caves, streams, moonlight) to perform ritual obeisance at the Altar of Heaven (a specifically masculine shrine). We could not be further from the rouged and powdered "transcendent girls" of other lyrics.

Xue's second lyric could plausibly be read as the subsequent step in this woman's career: life in a celestial realm as a female transcendent.

"Nü guanzi" (2nd of 2)
Xue Zhaoyun

In cloudy gauze and misty chiffon,	雲羅霧縠
newly presented with the ordination register of covenantal authority[119]	新授明威法籙
and letters from the descended Perfected.	降真函
Her chignon threaded with blue silk,	髻綰青絲髮
and through her crown, azure jade hairpins are drawn.	冠抽碧玉簪
As she comes and goes, she crosses the Five [Clouds];	往來雲過五
when she leaves or stays, she passes the Three [Islands].[120]	去住島經三

---

119. Li Yi suggests that the phrase *mingwei* in this line refers to a generalized "brilliant majesty" that inhered in sacred rites (*HJJZS*, 124). However, Stephen Bokenkamp (personal communication) suggests that the *ming* of this phrase may instead be a substitution for *meng*, in which case the line would refer to a type of ordination register, entitled *mengwei* 盟威 (register of covenantal authority). For *mengwei*, see Benn, *Cavern-Mystery Transmission*, 79–80. My translation reflects the emendation.

120. The "Five Clouds" were said to be in the realm of the transcendents. The "Three Isles" of the transcendents were Penglai, Fangzhang, and Yingzhou.

| As soon as she meets Master Liu's messenger, | 正遇劉郎使 |
| she opens the turquoise-sealed letters.[121] | 啓瑤緘 |

Here, we see the female divinity in action, but first we are assured of her authenticity and readiness for her role as a transcendent. She has received the official records of transcendence, the registers of ordination that identify her as a new ordinand.[122] She is still richly decorated, but now we see her in blue and azure (*bi* 碧), colors common in the cool atmosphere of the transcendent realms.[123] Whereas the hapless "Master Liu" can only wait for her appearance in the mortal world, the goddess comes and goes at will, traversing the Five Clouds and Three Isles in her travels between the worlds. When she is not visiting, she eagerly awaits messages from her earthbound lover. By taking the title "The Daoist Nun" at face value in these two lyrics, Xue Zhaoyun highlights the artifice and repetitiveness of the many lyrics that borrow references and stories to dress up their mortal romances in divine robes. And yet, in the final lines of his second lyric, even Xue returns to the overriding concern that motivates the women portrayed in the anthology: their relationships with all-too-mortal men. Strangely enough, this final lyric that tells the story of the mortal-transcendent romance from the point of view of the goddess greatly resembles lyrics that describe courtesans in their boudoirs. Xue's goddess is depicted in the first stanza wearing diaphanous clothing, her hair pinned up with elegant silk and hairpins; in the second stanza, this divinity seems just as quick to open new letters from her "Master Liu" ("*as soon as* she meets Master Liu's messenger") as the mortal women in other lyrics. Although her ordination may have elevated her to a place in the celestial hierarchy, this by no means puts her out of romantic cir-

---

121. *HJJZS*, 124.

122. Benn discusses the role of such registers in ordination and notes the slightly different weight they were given in different texts. Zhang Wanfu, a witness to the 711 ordination of two Tang princesses, states that "wearing talismanic registers enables the recipient to control and impede the demonic influences and protect the gods and energies of the center [that is, the inner gods of the human body]." Benn, *Cavern-Mystery Transmission*, 76–77.

123. Schafer, "Capeline Cantos," 47.

culation. In short, we must conclude that in this lyric, as in most of the "Nü guanzi" set, the Daoist ritual paraphernalia do not fundamentally alter the romantic focus of the lyrics.

I argued earlier that the tune title sets of "Lin jiang xian" and "Nü guanzi" are critical to our understanding of the *Huajian ji* for two reasons: the lyrics to the two tunes constitute almost 10 percent of the anthology, and they demonstrate a song lyric composition practice—that of closely matching the content of a lyric to its tune title—that was lost in the Song. In this examination of the *Huajian ji* poets' use of Daoist imagery, however, I have concluded that, in general, the lyrics of these tune titles are variations on the conventional romantic theme. The variations can be as simple as the use of one or two Daoist terms or as complex as the exploration of a divine encounter, complete with appropriate ritual clothing and appurtenances; but ultimately these stories remain within the boundaries of the romantic conventions explored in Chapters 4 and 5. Schafer and Cahill accomplished much by pointing out to readers the frequency of Daoist images in these tune title sets, but their argument for the greater importance of Daoist ideals throughout all these lyrics cannot be sustained.

While working within the romantic tradition examined in previous chapters, the lyrics of these tune title sets reveal provocative new twists on motifs and techniques employed in other lyrics. Particularly interesting is the poets' exploration of the relationship of male and female lovers in divine encounters. As we saw in lyrics by Niu Xiji and Li Xun, when the female lover is a divinity, the gender roles appear reversed: the woman instigates meetings and can end them at her whim. This reversal of gender roles resembles to some degree the overlap of emotional expression we saw in Chapter 5, where both male and female subjects are overheard expressing the same feelings of regret and despair. But in the goddess-encounter lyrics, the female role is further strengthened as the scene is exteriorized, and the goddess is made part of the uncontrollable natural environment. Both "Pusa man" and "Huanxi sha" demonstrate how the *Huajian ji* poets consistently used the natural setting to establish the mood of a lyric; in the lyrics depicting unions with goddesses, the female character is not so much affected by her environment as she is an integral part of it. Like nature itself, she is ultimately unknowable and uncontrollable. Although the literary and religious precedents for such female divinities were ancient, they were explicitly articulated within medieval Daoism; perhaps most notable in this connection is the story of the courtship of Yang Xi and Consort An, in the revealed fourth-century text *Zhen gao*. In that narrative, the male protagonist "is gendered 'feminine' in his relationship to the goddess," a gendering that includes the reversal of wedding ritual roles and conduct.[124] The secularized versions of encounters with jade maidens also often imputed powerlessness (or at least a very great willingness to please) to the male character.

In the stories, poems, and songs that invest the female lover with such awesome powers, writers raise the stakes of the romantic encounters considerably. If the male, mortal lover succeeds in winning the goddess—even if only for one night—it shows him to be a powerful figure in his own right; if he fails, and only catches a glimpse of her, he is still participating in the truly ancient tradition of seeking the goddess. Within the framework of the romantic story, the sexual union brings different consequences for the male and female characters: as a suitor to the goddess, the male character implicitly claims high status for himself, and the female's erotic appeal is considerably enhanced. Yet in the song lyrics of the *Huajian ji*, even if we do encounter this reversed relationship, the male lover is always the one to tell his story of encountering the goddess. Niu Xiji reminds us cleverly and repeatedly that artistic renderings—poems, lyrics, paintings—of these encounters live on even when memory or legend has faded away. We do not find, in the *Huajian ji*, encounter-with-the-goddess lyrics from the point of view of the goddess. This voice was not a part of the secular literary tradition; moreover, the *Huajian ji* poets were much more interested in portraying the heartache of the person left behind, whether that person is the abandoned boudoir woman or the luckless male suitor. Furthermore, as the sexiest "Huanxi sha" lyrics have shown us, the eroticism of the *Huajian ji* is fundamentally voyeuristic, and the female subject, whether listless or active, is what poets wanted to see and expose.

---

124. Bokenkamp, "Declarations of the Perfected," 170.

The fact that her exposure was both physical and emotional was certainly part of the pleasure of such song lyrics.

The Shu poets' use of Daoist imagery has important implications for our understanding of the anthologists' broader project. Experimenting with a marginal literary genre within the context of the reading tradition, the poets of the *Huajian ji* deliberately lay claim to the extensive literary precedents for poetry about encounters with goddesses. Wen Tingyun, like many other late Tang poets, casually used the tropes of transcendence in his lyrics; the Shu poets' extension of Daoism in their song lyrics should be seen as part of their effort to legitimize the song lyric as a literati practice. If we accept Ouyang Jiong's defense of artifice as the hallmark of skillful song, we must see the deployment of Daoist imagery in "Lin jiang xian" and "Nü guanzi" as yet another example of the Shu poets' craft. These tune titles demonstrate that their originality lies not so much in the prevalence of Daoist paraphernalia or goddess stories as in the unique blending of transcendent and secular romantic stories—in effect, the appropriation of divine imagery for the practice of writing romantic song lyrics. The presence in the *Huajian ji* of a large number of these lyrics proves that this poetic taste was certainly appreciated by the Shu connoisseurs who compiled the work. The fact that neither contemporary popular songwriters—as evidenced by Dunhuang lyrics—nor very many Song poets continued this trend further highlights the regional uniqueness of Shu. This conclusion is further supported by the lyrics of Shu poets to other tune titles not discussed here—such as "Wu shan yiduan xia," "Tian xianzi," and "He zhuan"—that also refer to transcendents.

Finally, I think that the lyrics to "Lin jiang xian" and "Nü guanzi," despite their use of Daoist imagery and narratives, reveal essential thematic connections to other tune title sets in the collection and thus demonstrate the importance of reading within the anthology as a whole. Whether we look at the use of dream as a vehicle for erotic transport, memory as the means to recreate the romantic encounter, despair over the passage of time, or the inability to communicate suppressed feeling, all these lyrics share common concerns. Adopting a reading strategy, as I have done in these chapters, that moves away from specific allusions and individual poets (about whom we know so little) and toward the collection's contextual backdrop in tenth-century Shu enables us to discern more clearly the interaction of culture and literature across time. This group of Shu poets looked to their Tang predecessors and the elite literary tradition for inspiration and material, but they cultivated the song lyric as their own craft.

Conclusion

The story of the *Huajian ji* in succeeding dynasties is in many ways linked to the reputation of the kingdom of Shu and its fate in the chaotic tenth century. One lyric by Lu Qianyi attracted attention over the centuries because many readers believed it commemorated the fall of Shu and its court of music and beauty.

"Lin jiang xian" (1st of 2)
Lu Qianyi

Behind the gilt locks of countless doors, the desolate garden is still:	金鎖重門荒苑靜
The screened windows face the autumn air in sorrow.	綺窗愁對秋空
Since the kingfisher beauties left, all is empty, without a trace.	翠華一去寂無蹤
The sounds of singing and piping from the jade towers,	玉樓歌吹
cut off, have long since followed the wind.	聲斷已隨風
The misty moon doesn't know that the human world has changed—	煙月不知人事改
as night grows late, it comes to shine again on deep palaces.	夜闌還照深宮
Lotus blossoms crowd against one another in wild ponds:	藕花相向野塘中

unseen they grieve for the fallen kingdom,　　暗傷亡國
clear dew weeping on their fragrant red.¹　　清露泣香紅

As the scholar Zhang Yiren has shown, it is extremely unlikely that this lyric concerns the demise of the Former Shu and, since the lyric was collected in the *Huajian ji* in 940, impossible for it to commemorate the fall of the Latter Shu in 965.² It seems much more probable that Lu Qianyi was merely using the conventions of poems on "tones of the fallen states" (*wang guo yin* 亡國音) to transform the scene of boudoir sorrow so common in the collection into a scene of melancholy emptiness. As in Tang poems depicting the sites of now-vanished kingdoms, in this lyric the physical objects of the landscape do more than just mirror the emotions of human subjects; they are the only remnants of feeling left, after the inhabitants of the palaces have disappeared. We can understand the temptation for later readers to see the lyric as a lament for Shu, given its praise of the "singing and piping from jade towers" for which Shu was famous. Readers from the Song and later dynasties were quick to find a parallel between the perspective of this lyric and that found in a few lyrics by Li Yu (the last ruler of the Southern Tang) that apparently lament the loss of his kingdom.³ Similar in appeal to the many stories of decadent, doomed kingdoms in Chinese history, the idea that the *Huajian ji* contained a self-conscious comment on its own culture was alluring, even if it was not true. Rather than looking forward to a historical moment its author likely did not see, the lyric, like the collection itself, reaches back into ancient literary tradition for its inspiration.

In this book, I have explored the relationship between the culture of Shu and its song lyric practice, arguing that the perspectives of literary and cultural history give us new ways of understanding the *Huajian ji* as both a cultural artifact and a collection of poetic texts.

---

1. *HJJZS*, 334.
2. Zhang, *Huajian ci lunji*, 263–69.
3. See Zhang, 264–65, for examples of readers who noted a parallel between Li Yu and Lu Qianyi. On the link between Li Yu's life and his poems lamenting his kingdom, see Bryant, *Lyric Poets of the Southern T'ang*, xxix–xxx.

The political and social changes under way in the late Tang and in tenth-century Shu fostered the making of the anthology; at the same time, the new cultural independence enjoyed by Shu literati gave them the freedom to propose a new kind of *wen* for inclusion in elite culture. Although this independent Shu culture of connoisseurship was attacked after the Song conquest, its traces are evident in the *Huajian ji* and other cultural products of the two Shu kingdoms. The *Huajian ji* offered its collection of *quzi ci* as both a practice—what certain courtiers were doing in a specific place and time—and, through the lyrics it collected, as a fully conceptualized genre. The link between court culture as historical context and court composition as a literary force can be seen in the poetics of the *Huajian ji* song lyrics, which feature a narrow range of voices and share techniques of imitation and thematic repetition and variation. Although we cannot know how much the selections of the *Huajian ji* ignored alternative styles or voices from Shu, two possibilities emerge from the evidence, which comprises stylistically similar lyrics from the same group of poets found in the Song-period anthology *Zunqian ji*. Either the *Huajian ji* compilers selected lyrics that manifested the range of Shu tastes, or the *Huajian* style was popular enough to provoke the anonymous compiler of the *Zunqian ji* to collect more of the same from the *Huajian* poets' extant works.[4] If the former is true, the coherence of the *Huajian ji* may be not simply a product of selection and compilation but a fair representation of Shu song lyrics. If the latter is true, then we have good evidence for Song readers' admiration of the *Huajian ji* style, which in turn sheds light on the reception history of the collection.

My study of the *Huajian ji* cannot fully consider the history of its later influence, though there are many indications that poets of *ci* through the Qing continued to read and assess the collection as a literary work. The publication evidence for the *Huajian ji* shows that it circulated widely throughout the Northern and Southern

---

4. The *Zunqian ji* presents the *HJJ* poets in the identical order, which led the scholar Shizukuishi Kōichi to conclude that it was deliberately patterned on the *HJJ* model. Noted in Bryant, "Messages of Uncertain Origin," 306.

Song.⁵ The repeated mentions of the *Huajian ji* in the *cihua* of Qing literati also suggest that the collection continued to be read, though its particular style was not widely imitated by late imperial poets.⁶ We know that later poets of *ci* included the *Huajian ji* in their understanding of the *ci* genre, even if they chose not to follow its formal or stylistic models. My argument for the influence of Shu culture on the *Huajian ji* differs in some significant ways from traditional readings of tenth-century history and of the collection itself. The main lines of argument about the anthology are manifest in the *cihua* of the Song, Ming, and Qing, which provide insights into the history of its reception and influence. As we saw in the first Song emperor's criticism of Ouyang Jiong and the Latter Shu kingdom, many people thought early Song culture to be negatively influenced by the political climate of Shu, and some Song readers of the *Huajian ji* categorized it among the "corrupt" products of a decadent time. However, the linking of the anthology to its historical moment fades over the course of centuries of *ci* composition, collection, and theorization. Late imperial readers instead considered the history of the genre in literary terms, often as part of the larger project of defining first the formal rules and next the fundamental nature of the genre of *ci*. In later critiques, therefore, issues of form and style are often subsumed into a discourse on generic propriety.⁷

As the *quzi ci* of the *Huajian ji* became the genre of *ci* in the Song, poets and readers of *ci* began to create histories and typologies for the genre. Literati who were fond of writing *ci* had good reason to make arguments about its history: in the Chinese literary tradition, constructing a persuasive model of development was one of the

---

5. Chao Qianzhi, the literatus who composed the colophon for the 1148 edition, states that there were numerous other editions at that time (*HJJZS*, 395). There are extant copies of three Song editions of the text, four copies from Ming editions, and many more from the Qing and the twentieth century. It seems likely that the work circulated continuously after Tang Xianzu's edition.

6. The frequency of *cihua* comments on the *HJJ* can be matched to the popularity of the *ci* genre itself in late imperial times.

7. For a useful survey of the history of *ci* reception and theorization, see Xie, *Zhongguo ci xue shi*.

most common methods of establishing a hierarchy of value. The modern *ci* scholar Yang Haiming, in his *Tang Song ci lun gao* (Discussions on Tang and Song lyrics), has summarized the three most prevalent approaches to the history of *ci* as a genre as follows: the "tenor of the age" argument, in which poetic lyrics reveal the moral "tones" of an era; a biological model of rise, maturation, and decline, borrowed from historiography but applicable to literature as well; and the "progressive" theory, in which the genre was understood to be constantly evolving toward fulfilling certain expressive needs.[8] Although I would generally agree with his categorization as it pertains to commentary on the *Huajian ji*, I would call the first two theories historicist and organic, respectively, and the third, a theory of generic economy; I would furthermore suggest that there is often overlap among such approaches. The first theory is Confucian in origin and can be traced to the "Great Preface" of the *Odes*, but the second and third are products of the Song rereading and conceptualization of the literary canon and literary history.

We find representatives of each of these approaches in remarks on the *Huajian ji* from the Song to the Qing. From the Song period, the effort to integrate *ci* into the elite canon in part demanded a defense of *ci*, or at least the *ci* of certain poets. One strategy in the legitimization of *ci*, as Pauline Yu notes, was to appropriate the hermeneutics of the *Odes* to construct a path of development and a hierarchy for song lyrics.[9] As might be expected, many such arguments are fundamentally historicist in nature. By the late Ming and early Qing, poets who lived in a world in which song lyrics had long lost their contextual associations with the entertainment quarters (though not their identity as the literature of *qing*) chose to reinvent the genre according to their perception of correct poetic praxis, a praxis that could embrace both *shi* and *ci*. However, late imperial poets' efforts to filiate the genre to the *Odes* and the *Chu ci* required them to shift the grounds of debate away from style and toward function; as an example, the rereading of Wen Tingyun's *ci* as

---

8. Yang, *Tang Song ci lun gao*, 1–3.
9. Yu, "Song Lyrics and the Canon," 81–87.

allegory by the Qing literatus Zhang Huiyan 張惠言 (1761–1802) was a radical version of this interpretive move.[10] In the same manner, their rejection of the use of vernacular—a critical element of Five Dynasties and Song *ci* poetics, whether in the *haofang* or the *wanyue* style—reveals the extent to which their appropriation of the genre also mandated its reinvention. Therefore, the comments on the *Huajian ji* found in late imperial *cihua* texts should generally be understood as part of a wider discussion among literati who were deeply invested in the song lyric tradition.

The initial comment on Shu song lyrics can be found in the earliest extant *cihua* text, Wang Zhuo's 王灼 *Biji manzhi* 碧雞漫志 (Random jottings from Biji [a quarter of Chengdu]).

> At the end of the Tang and during the Five Dynasties, literary compositions were at their most degraded. Only with [the era's] musical compositions can one be happy. Although they lacked great rhymes and concentrated only on clever technique (*qi qiao* 奇巧), each [school of song lyrics] established its own style and did not copy others. . . . Among the usurping rulers of the various states, Li Chongguang [Yu], Wang Yan, Meng Chang, and the hegemon Qian Shu were all accustomed to wealth and noble status, and pleasured themselves with wine and song.[11]

Wang Zhuo's faint praise of the individual styles of the tenth-century "musical compositions," *yuezhang* 樂章, is overshadowed by his criticism of the climate of the "usurping rulers" and, implicitly, the courts where such songs were performed. The link between the rulers' extravagance and the inadequacy of the mere "clever technique" of tenth-century song lyrics is implicit here. In a colophon to a Southern Song edition of the *Huajian ji*, the poet Lu You 陸游 (1125–1210) connects historical circumstance and literary products explicitly:

---

10. Rouzer, in *Writing Another's Dream*, notes that Zhang's reading of Wen Tingyun was an important rediscovery of Wen Tingyun's song lyrics; before the Qing, Wen was principally known as a *shi* poet (61–62 and n38). See Zhang Yiren's discussion of Zhang Huiyan's critique in *Huajian ci lunji*, 107–20.

11. Wang Zhuo, *Biji manzhi*, in Tang, *Cihua congbian*, 82.

The *Huajian ji* is made of texts composed by people of the Tang and Five Dynasties. It was just during this period, when the world was in upheaval and people ceaselessly fought for survival, that literati officials degenerated to this. It is indeed worth sighing about![12]

In a second colophon to the anthology, Lu You tempers his criticism only slightly, arguing that the Tang poets who lived after the Dazhong era (847–60) simply did not have the talents of their High Tang forebears. Lu You describes these late Tang poets as "those who wrote lyrics to follow the notes" (*yisheng zuo ci zhe* 倚聲作詞者), whose literary inadequacies stemmed from their own lack of talent, and who desired that their lyrics be "easily understood while drinking."[13] Lu You's two colophons demonstrate that the traditional belief that "degenerate" historical moments produced only corrupt literary works was always available to readers of the Song and later dynasties. They also prefigure one emerging narrative of the evolution of *ci* as a genre, in which lyrics arose out of the creative exhaustion of *shi* at the end of the Tang.

Some decades later, the Southern Song bibliophile Chen Zhensun 陳震孫 balances Lu You's criticism by defending the *Huajian ji* in its entry in his bibliography, *Zhizhai shulu jieti* 直齋書錄解題:

Huajian ji, 10 *juan*

Ouyang Jiong of Shu wrote the preface; it was compiled by the "Vice Minister for the Court of Imperial Regalia, Zhao Chongzuo," of whom we know nothing. The collection's lyrics begin with Wen Tingyun and include eighteen poets in all, for a total of 500 lyrics. This work is the ancestor of the recent practice of filling in words according to the music. In the late Tang and Five Seasons [Dynasties], the spirit and forms of poetry (*shi* 詩) became mean and vulgar, like countless people all singing the same note. But the "long-and-short-line" [of song lyrics] alone had refined artistic technique (*jing qiao* 精巧) and great beauty that later generations could not match. As for anyone who does not understand this matter, he can see what "Fang-weng," Lu Wuguan [You] had to say.[14]

---

12. In *HJJZS*, 400.
13. Ibid. These colophons and others to the extant editions of the *HJJ* are also collected in Jin, *Tang Song ciji xuba huibian*, 339–48.
14. Chen, *Zhizhai shulu jieti* 21.614.

Chen Zhensun's comments are the earliest extant indication of the *Huajian ji*'s status as the founding collection of the genre. Not only does Chen place the collection first in the "song lyric category" (*geci lei* 歌詞類) of his bibliography, but he refers to it explicitly as the "ancestor" of the genre, a phrase that others, such as the twentieth-century critic Wang Guowei, would echo. Here, Chen Zhensun takes a more literary approach, defending the collection on the basis of its artistic merit. In his summation of the origin of song lyrics, Chen deploys the organic metaphor of birth, maturation. In his view, new genres could not emerge until old ones had sputtered out, becoming "mean and vulgar." In the case of the Tang, the genre that had to be played out before song lyrics arose was the genre of *shi* poetry; thus, the *Huajian ji* song lyrics were refined and beautiful because they appeared in the tenth-century "youth" of the song lyric genre. In turn, some later readers who used this organic figure would argue that the *Huajian ji* was too early in the genre's history—that it was "immature" compared to the lyrics of the Song that followed.

To some late imperial readers and composers of song lyrics, the *Huajian ji* became less interesting as a literary model and more of a problem for the genre. One strategy for defending *ci* against its critics was to borrow the hermeneutics of *shi* in order to valorize certain schools of *ci*; adopting the language of orthodox poetic practice to defend a heterodox form engendered new problems, however. Different readers created different hierarchies of value within the growing corpus of song lyrics. For example, we see the hermeneutics of *shi* used against the *Huajian ji* in the Ming literatus Wang Shizhen's 王世貞 (1526–90) assessment of it and another anthology, the *Caotang shiyu* 草堂詩餘 (Remnants of poems from the Thatched Hall).[15]

The *Huajian ji* perfects its little phrases with great artifice (*qiao*), [like] the extravagance of the *Shishuo xinyu*; the *Caotang shiyu* extracts the charm of its lovely words, [like] the excess of the Six Dynasties. Therefore such song lyrics are called "remnants of poems" (*shiyu* 詩餘), and poets (*shiren*) do not make them. Why is this? Because due to their lovely beauty and intimate

---

15. From Wang's *Yiyuan zhiyan*, in *Cihua congbian*, 385.

passion, they suffice only to arouse the feelings and seize upon one's sensual pleasure.... This is the deviant style (*bian ti* 變體) of the song lyric.

In the hermeneutics of *shi*—or more specifically, of the *Odes*—there are norms, *zheng* 正, and deviations, *bian* 變, the latter of which are morally corrupt developments. When one examines the history of *shi* according to this hermeneutical construct, the "deviations" lay out a clear path of degeneration within a single genre; the framework can, however, be applied to the history of all literary genres. Elsewhere in this discussion, Wang argues that *ci* itself was a "deviation" from *yuefu* poetry. Here, the eroticism of the *Huajian ji* makes it deviant even within the tradition of song lyrics. Wang's critique of the collection is not simply that it uses artifice to create superficially beautiful lyrics, but that it uses beauty to arouse the senses exclusively. Or, to reverse Ouyang Jiong's Confucian defense of the collection, Wang Shizhen effectively argues that the *Huajian ji* is indeed "blossoming without bearing fruit."

The late Ming interest in and revival of *ci* as a literary genre has been filiated to the broader interest in *qing*—feeling or passion—found in late sixteenth- and early seventeenth-century culture.[16] The *Huajian ji* was materially affected by this cultural trend when the late Ming dramatist Tang Xianzu 湯顯祖 (1550–1616), the most famous Ming advocate of *qing* and himself a writer of *ci*, sponsored a new edition of the *Huajian ji* in 1575, for which he also wrote brief comments. The text itself had apparently been lost for some centuries but had been rediscovered earlier in the sixteenth century in a Buddhist temple on the grounds of what had been Wang Yan's Xuanhua Park in Chengdu.[17] In a break from his writing of *Mudan*

---

16. For this movement in *ci*, see Chang, *The Late-Ming Poet Ch'en Tzu-lung: Crises of Love and Loyalty*, and Chang, "Liu Shih and Hsü Ts'an: Feminine or Feminist?" in Yu, ed., *Voices*, 169–87. See also Lee, *Enchantment and Disenchantment: Love and Illusion in Chinese Literature*, esp. 50–64.

17. The history of editions of *HJJ* is traced in Glen Baxter, *Huachien chi*, 80–91, although in 1952 he was not able to see some of the editions that are currently held in China. The colophons to the extant editions are collected in *Tang Song ciji xuba huibian*, 339–48. The rediscovery of the text in Chengdu was noted both by Tang Xianzu in his colophon and separately by the Ming literatus Yang Shen, whom Tang credits for the discovery, in Yang's *Ci pin* (*Cihua congbian*, 457). For Tang's

ting 牡丹亭 (The peony pavilion), Tang Xianzu sponsored the edition in order to preserve its contents and to encourage others to appreciate it. Unlike the kinds of evaluative discussions found in *cihua*, Tang's comments on the *Huajian ji* lyrics are casually appreciative and personal. His brief remarks on the evolution of genres—to be expected from a preface or colophon to a collection of a single genre—do not respond to the more polemical claims of Wang Shizhen or other Ming readers of lyrics. However, Tang Xianzu's new edition of the *Huajian ji* may have influenced its future more than any individual *cihua*: from the evidence of extant editions in the Qing, the *Huajian ji* seems to have been regularly reissued from the sixteenth century onward, and the consistent references to the collection in Qing *cihua* indicate that it was also being read.

Other readers of the *Huajian ji* in the late Ming and Qing did not agree with Wang Shizhen's dismissal of the collection. We find an explicit rebuttal of the Ming critic's attack on the *Huajian ji* in the *cihua* of the Qing literatus and *ci* poet Wang Shizhen 王士禎 (1634-1711). In his *cihua* work *Hua Cao mengshi* 花草蒙拾, whose title was taken from the titles of the *Huajian ji* and the *Caotang shiyu*, Wang Shizhen opens with a section polemically entitled "Wen [Tingyun] and Wei [Zhuang] are not the 'deviant style.'" Defending Wen and Wei, Wang Shizhen reverses the hierarchy of "norm" and "deviation" proposed by the Ming critic. Using a standard genealogy of *shi* styles, Wang argues that Wen and Wei represent the worthy pioneers of the song lyric, just as the poets of the Han paved the way for the later poetry of the period of division and the Tang. In addition to defending Wen and Wei as ancestors, he also argues that the *Huajian ji* "method of using words," *zifa* 字法, made the collection's lyrics "distinctively patterned and finely sensuous" to a degree that later poets simply could not match.[18] Wang Shizhen's praise of the

---

colophon, see *Tang Song ciji xuba huibian*, 341–42. Tang's edition, with his commentary, has been reprinted, and his *pingdian* can also be found in *Quan Tang Wudai ci jishi huiping*, under each lyric on which he commented.

18. Wang Shizhen, *Hua Cao mengshi*, in *Cihua congbian*, 673. The defense of the refined style of *HJJ* is part of Wang's argument about the relative positions of the *wanyue* and *haofang* styles, which emerged as stylistic opposites in the Song. In his

Huajian ji as a collection was not widely echoed by other Qing readers; judging from other passages that discuss the collection in Qing *cihua*, the *Huajian ji* as a whole became less interesting to readers over the course of generations, and the commentaries focus instead on individual poets' lines and styles, particularly those of Wen Tingyun and Wei Zhuang. The Qing poets of *ci*, in their literary revival of a practice that had long lost its music, sought poetic models in the lyrics of the Five Dynasties and the Song, and, in that quest, they seem to have found the narrowness of the *Huajian ji* constraining.

The pivotal figure in the twentieth-century history of the reception of the *Huajian ji* was the scholar Wang Guowei 王國維 (1877–1927), whose idiosyncratic and influential *Renjian cihua* 人間詞話 (Comments on lyrics in the human realm) established Wen Tingyun and Wei Zhuang as the forefathers not only of the collection but of the song lyric genre itself. Wang Guowei's few brief comments on the collection focus on its aesthetic features, ignoring the problem of historical context and downplaying the hierarchies implicit in the hermeneutics of *shi*. Here, the history of *ci* is located in an affective model of generic economy, in which genres emerge to fulfill specific expressive needs.

> I much prefer [the Qing critic Chen Zilong]'s explanation [of why poets composed song lyrics]: "Poets of the Song did not understand *shi* and yet they strove to write *shi*.... Therefore in the end, the Song era had no real *shi*.... However, all the feelings of pleasure and joy, sorrow and pain which stirred within their hearts and could not be repressed found expression in *ci*. Therefore what they created was of singular workmanship...." This is also the reason why the *ci* of the Five Dynasties were of such singular excellence.[19]

Although Chen Zilong was defending only the *ci* of the Song dynasty, we note that Wang Guowei extends the argument for *ci* as the appropriate vehicle for *qing* back into the earliest days of the genre,

---

eyes, the *haofang* style developed by Su Shi and Huang Tingjian was the "deviation" from the genre's true nature.

19. Translation from Rickett, *Wang Kuo-wei's Jen-chien tz'u-hua: A Study in Chinese Literary Criticism*, 62–63.

to the time of the *Huajian ji*. In comparison to the contentious tone of some earlier commentators, Wang Guowei's approach to the question of value in song lyrics seems generous. Although many twentieth-century scholars of *ci* followed lines of thought laid down by Qing literati, Wang Guowei's work stands at the end of the traditional literary reception of the *Huajian ji*. It is no coincidence that Wang Guowei is also regarded as the last great poet of the *ci* genre. In the absence of a broad literary community of *ci* writers and connoisseurs in the twentieth century, questions of genre history became the stuff of scholarship, rather than part of the quest for contemporary poetic models.

To conclude, I would like to comment on some avenues of research that might be suggested by this study. With respect to the forms of the genre that came to be known as *ci*, the *Huajian ji* achieved a number of firsts. It offered new forms for older tune titles (whether or not these had new tunes also), it collected new tunes and metric structures, and it promoted the use of heterometric verse for song lyrics. Perhaps the most significant formal development in Song *ci* was the emergence of the longer song-form, the *manci*, which poets used for a fuller exploration of the emotional realms that became the purview of the genre. However, certain features of the shorter, two-stanza *xiaoling* of the *Huajian ji* continued to influence the rhetorical structures of two-stanza forms, including two-stanza *manci*. The *Huajian ji* poets' experimentation with using the *huantou* (stanza break) to mark both changes in subject or voice and temporal and spatial shifts only increased in the work of later poets. Although *xiaoling* and *manci* are often treated separately by scholars of song lyrics, it might be useful to reexamine the kinds of rhetorical strategies that the two forms share. Finally, the *Huajian ji* lyrics reveal an intense consciousness of the lyrics of other poets within the collection and from the Tang *shi* tradition. I hope that my focus on the use of imitation and dialogue in the lyrics of individual *Huajian ji* poets and on the importance of intratextuality in the collection as a whole might prompt similar examinations of other poets' textual techniques; such research could clarify the generic codes of *ci* that operate across the works of different poets in different eras and allow us to read beyond the categories of style and poet.

Although the themes and conventions of the *Huajian ji* were inherited from the romantic poetry of the Tang and early medieval period, the *Huajian ji* poets exploited them with an unprecedented intensity, whether compared to other extant collections or to the works of individual poets from the Tang and earlier. It is clear that the most important of these themes in the *Huajian ji*—the exploration of liminality, the passage of time, the intertwined states of dream, drunkenness, and memory, the unattainability of the beloved—also concerned *ci* poets of the Song. However, as the genre matured and these themes grew even more commonplace within it, poets questioned and commented on such themes explicitly in their lyrics. The problematization of conventions and the emergence of a discourse concerning a genre's fundamental nature (*bense* 本色) are common to the development of literary genres in many cultures; these shifts reveal the community of readers and writers of the genre to be actively engaging and reformulating the genre's constituent elements. The distance between the *Huajian ji* lyrics' constant repetition of "sorrow," *chou* 愁—a word that appears no fewer than 109 times in the collection—and Li Qingzhao's question, "How can the one word 'sorrow' (*chou*) grasp it?" at the end of her famous lyric to "Shengsheng man" 聲聲慢 (Note after note), is but one example of this change. From a broader perspective, Song poets' sense of *ci* as a vehicle to explore the problem of *qing* itself can be seen at least as a logical outgrowth (if we do not wish to say "maturation") of the *Huajian ji* poets' exploration of the difficulty of communication.

As the lyrics of Chapter 5 demonstrated, in spite of the collection's reputation for voyeuristic lyrics in the style of Wen Tingyun, the voices of the *Huajian ji* go beyond the overheard boudoir lament. Ouyang Jiong's claim that the *Huajian ji* lyrics will "replace the songs of the lotus boat" bespeaks a clear desire to displace the "vulgar" female voice of popular song; the lyrics manifest this by speaking from a variety of perspectives. Our view of the female figures of the collection shifts from lyric to lyric, and sometimes from stanza to stanza, as we occasionally find a change from observed object to speaking subject. The minority first-person male voice of the collection, which I argue has been largely ignored by generations of readers, is an essential counterperspective on romance. The Shu poets' juxtaposition of male and female voices in dialogue is the surest sign of the poets' consciousness of the two as alternative positions. In Chapters 5 and 6, I argued that the *Huajian ji* poets' use of a range of poetic perspectives was a critical component of their legitimization of the genre, because they overtly drew upon the medieval traditions of voice found in *shi* poetry and even in the rhapsodies of the early medieval period. Here, I would pose another question: to what extent might this appropriation of elements of the elite literary tradition represent a *masculinization* of song lyrics?

In Chapter 5, I suggested that the use of a strong first-person male voice that remembered and imagined was intended to counter the more helpless, "wordless," feminine subject that was so ruthlessly observed. The use of goddesses in the "Daoist" lyrics of Chapter 6 adds another dimension to that argument. In lyrics that portray encounters with goddesses, the male figures are represented as the seeking and abandoned lovers, and yet they are not themselves wordless or immobilized. By taking on the voice of the mortal man seeking the goddess, *Huajian ji* poets drew upon an ancient mode of representing male powerlessness and brought its literary and spiritual resonances to song lyrics. This is the advantage of reading across the collection as a whole: when we read across different groups of lyrics, we discover that the gendered voice is one key feature of the song lyrics that influences poets' representation of romance. It is true that encounters with goddesses are the topic of only a minority of the lyrics, but their presence complicates the dominant representation of romantic situations, in which women appear as the powerless figures.

The gendered subjectivities of the *Huajian ji* should also be set in the larger context of the development of *ci* in later eras. In the literary field of the Song dynasty, the genre of *ci* itself began to occupy the position of the conceptual feminine, in opposition to the dominant and masculine tradition of *shi*; at the same time there emerged within the genre of *ci* an opposite stylistic hierarchy, in which the masculine, *haofang*, style was perceived as the lesser song lyric style, while the feminine, *wanyue*, style "came to be privileged as orthodox."[20] It might be useful to compare the dialectic definition of the Song-period *ci* styles with the juxtapositions of male and female voices found in the *Huajian ji*, particularly since the *Huajian ji* compilers so clearly saw them as complementary. Comparing male- and female-voiced lyrics within the formal boundary of a single tune title, as I have done here, eliminates the variable of differing rhetorical strategies found in different metrical forms and more clearly exposes the linguistic techniques poets used to establish voice and gender. Examining the lyrics of poets who worked with a variety of perspectives, such as the Northern Song poet Liu Yong 柳永, could help us historicize the construction of voice in the genre. A better understanding of the generic codes used to construct voice in song lyrics could also shed light on the problem of the "feminine" in song lyrics composed by women and the efforts of women poets to create an authentic voice of their own in a genre profoundly affected by the literary conventions of gender.[21]

Finally, I hope that this study will contribute to the research on the representation of romantic love in Chinese literature; in particular, I hope it will underscore the importance of genre in such representations and will suggest possibilities for comparative research across generic boundaries. The development of the theme of liminality in the *Huajian ji* is one revealing example of the ways in which genre and culture shape the representation of romance. The lyrics of the collection demarcate the locations and times of romantic encounters and romantic longing with longstanding conventions from the poetic tradition; the stock boudoirs, balconies, courtyards, and riversides of the collection are made even more familiar through their recurrence. At the same time, these spaces are constantly marked as liminal—through the use of seasonal and diurnal boundaries, the depiction of subjects poised on thresholds or windows, and the reliance on dreams and drunkenness as means to

---

20. Fong, "Engendering the Lyric," 108.
21. For an exploration of this problem in the genre of *shi* and in prefaces to collections, see Robertson, "Changing the Subject: Gender and Self-Inscription in Authors' Prefaces and 'Shi' Poetry," in Widmer and Chang, eds., *Writing Women in Late Imperial China*, 171–217.

confuse the real with the longed-for—with the result that the poetic subjects are almost always depicted between states of consciousness. Although the literary devices controlling the theme of liminality in song lyrics can be traced to earlier medieval poetry, the coterie environment of Shu may have led its poets to imitate and elaborate on this theme as part of their competitive poetics. As Xue Neng's criticism of other poets' "willow" figures reminds us, the conventions of romantic verse could sound hackneyed in the hands of hack poets; in contrast, a poet's exploration of a single theme across a range of senses, affects, and modes would reveal his literary skills, even in such a slight practice as *quzi ci*.

But the *Huajian ji*'s exploration of liminality also reveals the intersection of culture and literature in tenth-century Shu. The liminality of the song lyrics' romantic encounters reflects to the need to locate the destabilizing force of romantic love outside of the present space and time of the court setting.[22] The world of song lyrics, in which male and female subjects are powerless and out of control, is always safely framed as fictional and controlled by the poet, as the musical performance of the song lyrics would have made even more clear. When performed, the voices that so desperately "recalled" and "imagined" would have been replaced by other voices and followed by other versions of the romance in the next lyrics to be sung, thereby dissolving the illusion of immediacy and urgency. The provocation of romantic, even erotic vignettes could be both heightened and controlled in the performance context.

The representation of romantic love in the song lyrics of the *Huajian ji* was thus affected by specific social, cultural, and literary forces, some of which are only faintly perceptible today. As the song lyric genre became a more textual practice from the Song into late imperial times, this representation also changed in response to the altered venues of composition and reception. The increasing literariness of *ci* over time and its concomitant loss of vernacular elements moved the genre closer to *shi*; at the same time, the expression of *qing*, particularly romantic feeling, became relegated to *ci*. In Ming and Qing literature, drama, stories, and novels became

---

22. On this point, see Fong, "Inscribing Desire," 446–47.

more influential forms for the representation of romantic love, and writers working in these genres created new versions of romance. Although the *Huajian ji* was the starting point for the genre of *ci* in elite literature, it is but one piece in the older and longer history of Chinese romantic literature; within this history, its romantic vignettes subvert neat typologies, models of organic maturation, or standard trajectories of rise and fall. The *Huajian ji*'s lyrics of desire and longing instead survive as echoes of a courtly world where poets could "artfully tell the affairs of the heart."

Reference Matter

Bibliography

Amthor, Brigitte. *Meng Chih-hsiang (874–935), der Erste Kaiser von Hou-Shu*. Frankfurt: Verlag Peter Lang, 1984.

Aoyama Hiroshi 青山宏. *Kakanshū sakuin* 花間集索引. Tokyo: Tokyo daigaku Tōyō bunka kenkyūjō, Tōyōgaku bunken sentā, 1974.

———. *Tō Sō shi kenkyū* 唐宋詞研究. Tokyo: Kyūko shoin, 1991.

Aoyama Sadao. "The Newly Risen Bureaucrats in Fujian at the Five Dynasties–Sung Period, with Special Reference to Their Genealogies." *Memoirs of the Tōyō Bunka* 21 (1962): 1–48.

Backus, Charles. *The Nan-chao Kingdom and T'ang China's Southwestern Frontier*. Cambridge and New York: Cambridge University Press, 1981.

Baldrian-Hussein, Farzeen. "Lü Tung-pin in Northern Sung Literature." *Cahiers d'Extrême-Asie* 2 (1986): 133–69.

Bao Gendi 包根弟. "Tan *Huajian ji* zhong di 'yue' yu 'liu'" 談花間集中的 '月'與'柳.' *Furen xuezhi* 13 (1984): 543–60.

Benn, Charles D. *The Cavern-Mystery Transmission: A Taoist Ordination Rite of A.D. 711*. Honolulu: University of Hawai'i Press, 1991.

Birrell, Anne. *New Songs from a Jade Terrace*. London: George Allen and Unwin, 1982.

Bokenkamp, Stephen R. "The Declarations of the Perfected." In *Religions in Practice*, ed. Donald Lopez, Jr., 166–79. Princeton: Princeton University Press, 1996.

———. *Early Daoist Scriptures*. Berkeley: University of California Press, 1997.

———. "The 'Pacing the Void' Stanzas of the Ling-bao Scriptures." Master's thesis, University of California, Berkeley, 1981.

———. "Taoism and Literature: The *Pi-lo* Question." *Taoist Resources* 3.1 (1991): 57–72.

Bol, Peter. *"This Culture of Ours": Intellectual Transitions in T'ang and Sung China*. Stanford: Stanford University Press, 1992.

Bourdieu, Pierre. *The Field of Cultural Production*. Ed. Randal Johnson. New York: Columbia University Press, 1993.

Bryant, Daniel. *Lyric Poets of the Southern T'ang: Feng Yen-ssu, 903–960, and Li Yü, 937–978*. Vancouver: University of British Columbia Press, 1982.

———. "Messages of Uncertain Origin: The Textual Tradition of the *Nan-T'ang erh-chu tz'u*." In *Voices of the Song Lyric in China*, ed. Pauline Yu, 298–348. Berkeley: University of California Press, 1994.

———. "On the Authenticity of the Tz'u Attributed to Li Po." *T'ang Studies* 7 (1989): 105–36.

———. "The Rhyming Categories of Tenth-Century Chinese Poetry." *Monumenta Serica* 34 (1979–80): 319–47.

Cahill, Suzanne E. "Sex and the Supernatural in Medieval China: Cantos on the Transcendent Who Presides over the River." *Journal of the American Oriental Society* 105 (1985): 197–220.

———. *Transcendence and Divine Passion: The Queen Mother of the West in Medieval China*. Stanford: Stanford University Press, 1993.

Campany, Robert Ford. *Strange Writing: Anomaly Accounts in Early Medieval China*. Albany: State University of New York Press, 1996.

Cao Yin 曹寅, ed. *Quan Tang shi* 全唐詩. Beijing: Zhonghua shuju, 1979.

Chang, Kang-i Sun. *The Evolution of Chinese Tz'u Poetry, from Late T'ang to Northern Sung*. Princeton: Princeton University Press, 1980.

———. *The Late Ming Poet Ch'en Tzu-lung: Crises of Love and Loyalism*. New Haven: Yale University Press, 1991.

———. "Liu Shih and Hsü Ts'an: Feminine or Feminist?" In *Voices of the Song Lyric in China*, ed. Pauline Yu, 169–87. Berkeley: University of California Press, 1994.

Chao Gongwu 晁公武. *Junzhai dushu zhi* 郡齋讀書志. Shanghai: Commercial Press, 1933.

Chaves, Jonathan. *Mei Yao-ch'en and the Development of Early Sung Poetry*. New York: Columbia University Press, 1976.

———. "The *Tz'u* Poetry of Wen T'ing-yun." Master's thesis, Columbia University, n.d.

Chen Qiyun 陳啓雲, ed. *Lü shi chunqiu jiaoshi* 呂氏春秋校釋. Shanghai: Xuelin chubanshe, 1984.

Chen Shangjun 陳尚君. *Tang dai wenxue congkao* 唐代文學叢考. Beijing: Zhongguo shehui kexue chubanshe, 1997.

Chen Shih-chuan. "The Rise of the *Tz'u*, Reconsidered." *Journal of the American Oriental Society* 90.2 (1970): 232–42.

Cheng Te-k'un. "The Royal Tomb of Wang Chien." *Harvard Journal of Asiatic Studies* 8 (1944–45): 234–40.

Chow Tse-tsung and Wayne Schlepp. "Ten *P'u-sa-man* Poems from Tun-huang." In *Interpreting Culture Through Translation: A Festschrift for D. C. Lau*, ed. Roger T. Ames, with Chan Sin-wai and Mau-sang Ng. Hong Kong: Chinese University Press, 1991.

Demiéville, Paul, and Jao Tsong-yi, eds. *Airs de Touen-houang: Textes à chanter des VIIIe–Xe siècles*. Paris: Editions du centre national de la recherche scientifique, 1971.

Despeux, Catherine. *Immortelles de la Chine ancienne*. Paris: Pardès, 1990.

Des Rotours, Robert. *Courtisans chinoises à la fin des T'ang entre circa 789 et le 8 janvier 881: Pei-li tche (Anecdotes du quartier du Nord) par Souen K'i*. Paris: Bibliothèque de l'Institut des hautes études chinoises, 1968.

Dong Gao 董誥 et al., eds. *Quan Tang wen* 全唐文. Beijing: Zhonghua shuju, 1983.

Duan Anjie 段安節. *Yuefu zalu* 樂府雜錄. In *Jie gu lu, Yuefu zalu, Biji manzhi*, 18–46. Shanghai: Shanghai guji chubanshe, 1988.

Duan Chengshi 段成式. *Youyang zazu* 酉陽雜俎. Beijing: Zhonghua shuju, 1981.

Dubrow, Heather. *Genre*. London: Methuen Press, 1982.

Egan, Ronald. "The Problem of the Repute of *Tz'u* During the Northern Sung." In *Voices of the Song Lyric in China*, ed. Pauline Yu, 191–225. Berkeley: University of California Press, 1994.

———. *Word, Image, and Deed in the Life of Su Shi*. Cambridge, MA: Council on East Asian Studies, Harvard University, 1994.

Fan Ye 范曄. *Hou Han shu* 後漢書. Beijing: Zhonghua shuju, 1973.

Fang Xuanling 房玄齡 et al. *Jin shu* 晉書. Beijing: Zhonghua shuju, 1974.

Feng Han-i. "The Tomb of Wang Chien." *Archives of the Chinese Art Society of America* (1955): 11–20.

Fong, Grace S. "Contextualization and Generic Codes in the Allegorical Reading of *Tz'u* Poetry." *Tamkang Review* 19 (1988–89): 663–79.

———. "Engendering the Lyric: Her Image and Voice in Song." In *Voices of the Song Lyric in China*, ed. Pauline Yu, 107–44. Berkeley: University of California Press, 1994.

———. "Inscribing Desire: Zhu Yizun's Love Lyrics in *Jingzhiju qinqu*." *Harvard Journal of Asiatic Studies* 54 (1994): 437–60.

———. "Persona and Mask in the Song Lyric." *Harvard Journal of Asiatic Studies* 50 (1990): 459–84.
———. *Wu Wenying and the Art of Southern Song Ci Poetry*. Princeton: Princeton University Press, 1987.
Fowler, Alistair. *Kinds of Literature: An Introduction to the Theory of Genres and Modes*. Cambridge, MA: Harvard University Press, 1982.
Fraistat, Neil, ed. *Poems in Their Place: The Intertextuality and Order of Poetic Collections*. Chapel Hill: University of North Carolina Press, 1986.
Frankel, Hans. "T'ang Literati: A Composite Biography." In *Confucian Personalities*, ed. Arthur Wright, 65–83. Stanford: Stanford University Press, 1962.
———. "*Yueh-fu* poetry." In *Studies in Chinese Literary Genres*, ed. Cyril Birch, 69–107. Berkeley: University of California Press, 1974.
Fu Chongju 傅崇矩, ed. *Chengdu tonglan* 成都通覽. Chengdu: Ba Shu shushe, 1987.
Fu Xuanzong 傅璇琮, ed. *Tang ren xuan Tang shi xinbian* 唐人選唐詩新編. Xi'an: Shaanxi renmin chubanshe, 1996.
Fusek, Lois, trans. *Among the Flowers: The Hua-chien chi*. New York: Columbia University Press, 1982.
Gao Buying 高步瀛. *Tang Song wen juyao* 唐宋文舉要. Beijing: Zhonghua shuju, 1982.
Gao Shiyu 高世瑜. *Tangdai funü* 唐代婦女. Xi'an: San Qin chubanshe, 1988.
Geng Xiangyuan 耿湘沅. "*Huajian* ciren Wen Tingyun yu Wei Zhuang" 花間詞人溫庭筠與韋莊. *Zhonghua xueyuan* 37 (1988): 121–35.
Gimm, Martin. *Das Yueh-fu Tsa-lu des Tuan An-chieh: Studien zur Geschichte von Musik, Schauspiel und Tanz in der T'ang-Dynastie*. Wiesbaden: Otto Harrassowitz, 1966.
Gou Yanqing 勾延慶. *Jinli qijiu zhuan* 錦里耆舊傳. In *Duhua zhai congshu*, in *Baibu congshu jicheng* 39.
Gu Nong 顧農 and Xu Xia 徐俠, eds. *Huajian pai ci zhuan* 花間派詞傳. Changchun: Jilin renmin chubanshe, 1999.
Guillén, Claudio. *The Challenge of Comparative Literature*. Trans. Cola Franzen. Cambridge: Harvard University Press, 1993.
Guo Maoqian 郭茂倩. *Yuefu shiji* 樂府詩集. 4 vols. Beijing: Zhonghua shuju, 1979.
Guo Yuntao 郭允滔. *Shu jian* 蜀鑒. In *Shoushan ge congshu*, in *Baibu congshu jicheng* 52.
Hanabusa Hideki 花房英樹 and Maegawa Yukio 前川幸雄. *Gen Shin kenkyū* 元稹研究. Kyoto: Ibundō shokan, 1977.

Hargett, James M. "Playing Second Fiddle: The *Luan*-bird in Early and Medieval Chinese Literature." *T'oung Pao* 75 (1989): 232-62.

Hawkes, David. "The Quest for the Goddess." *Asia Major* 13 (1967): 71-94.

He Guangyuan 何光遠. *Jianjie lu* 鑒誡錄. In *Xuejin shi yuan*, in *Baibu congshu jicheng*, series 46.

He Ruquan 何汝泉 and Zhong Daqun 鍾大群. "Wei Zhuang yu Qian Shu zhengquan" 韋莊與前蜀政權. *Xi'nan shifan daxue xuebao*, no. 2 (1990): 32-38.

Hiraoka Takeo 平岡武夫 et al. *Tōdai no shijin* 唐代の詩人. Vol. 4 of *Tōdai kenkyū no shiori*. Kyōto daigaku, Jinbun kagaku kenkyūjo, 1960.

Hong Mai 洪邁. *Rongzhai suibi wuji* 容齋隨筆五集. Taibei: Taiwan Commercial Press, 1956.

Hsieh, Daniel. *The Evolution of Jueju Verse*. New York: Peter Lang, 1996.

Hu Kexian 胡可先. "*Beimeng suoyan zhi yi*" 北夢瑣言質疑. *Xuzhou shifan xueyuan xuebao* (March 1987): 6-11, 29.

Hu Shi 胡適. "Ci di qiyuan" 詞的起源. In *Ci xue lunhui* 詞學論薈, ed. Zhao Weimin 趙爲民 and Cheng Yuzhui 程郁綴. Taibei: Wunan tushu chubanshe, 1989.

Hu-Sterk, Florence. "Les 'poèmes de lamentation du palais' sous les Tang: La vie recluse des dames de la Cour." *Études chinoises* 11.2 (1992): 7-33.

Hua Lianpu 華連圃, ed. *Huajian ji zhu* 花間集注. Changsha: Shangwu yinshu guan, 1937.

Hua Zhongyan 華鍾彥, ed. *Huajian ji zhu* 花間集注. Zhengzhou: Zhengzhou shuhua she, 1983.

Hucker, Charles O. *A Dictionary of Official Titles in Imperial China*. Stanford: Stanford University Press, 1985.

Ishida Mikinosuke 石田幹之助. *Zōtei Chōan no haru* 增訂長安の春. Tokyo: Heibonsha, 1967.

Iwama Keiji 岩間啓二. *On Teiin kashi sakuin* 溫庭筠歌詩索引. Kyoto, 1977.

Jauss, Hans Robert. "Littérature médiévale et théorie des genres." In *Théorie des genres*, ed. Gérard Genette and Tzvetan Todorov. Paris: Éditions du Seuil, 1986.

Ji Yougong 計有功. *Tang shi ji shi jiaojian* 唐詩紀事校箋. Ed. Wang Zhongyong 王仲鏞. Chengdu: Ba Shu shushe, 1989.

Jia Jinhua 賈晉華. *Tangdai jihui zongji yu shiren qun yanjiu* 唐代集會總集與詩人群研究. Beijing: Beijing daxue chubanshe, 2001.

Jiang Jianyun 姜劍雲. "Linghu Chu zuopin chuanliu ji sanshi kaoshu" 令狐處作品傳流及散失考述. *Jinyang xuekan*, no. 2 (1992): 91-94, 60.

Jiang Zhelun 蔣哲倫. "*Zunqian ji* he zaoqi wenren ci" 樽前集和早期文人詞. *Shanghai shifan xueyuan xuebao* 4 (1983): 39–41.

Jin Qihua 金啓華, ed. *Quan Song ci diangu kaoshi cidian* 全宋詞典故考釋辭典. Changchun: Jilin wen shi chubanshe, 1991.

Jin Qihua 金啓華 et al., eds. *Tang Song ciji xu ba huibian* 唐宋詞集序跋匯編. Nanjing: Jiangsu jiaoyu chubanshe, 1990.

Johnson, David G. "The Last Years of a Great Clan: The Li Family of Chao-chün in Late T'ang and Early Sung." *Harvard Journal of Asiatic Studies* 37.1 (1977): 5–103.

———. *The Medieval Chinese Oligarchy*. Boulder: Westview Press, 1977.

Katz, Paul. *Images of the Immortal: The Cult of Lü Dongbin at the Palace of Eternal Joy*. Honolulu: University of Hawai'i Press, 1999.

Kishibe Shigeo 岸邊成雄. *Tōdai ongaku no rekishiteki kenkyū—gakusei hen* 唐代歷史的研究. Tokyo: Tokyo daigaku shuppankai, 1960–61.

Kohn, Livia, ed. *Daoism Handbook*. Leiden: Brill, 2000.

Kondō Mitsuo 近藤光男. "*Kakanshū* no teiyō o megutte" 花間集の提要をめぐって. *Tōkyō Shinagaku hō* 5 (1959): 77–93.

Kong Fanjin 孔范今, ed. *Quan Tang Wudai ci shizhu* 全唐五代詞釋注. 3 vols. Xi'an: Shaanxi renmin chubanshe, 1998.

Kroll, Paul W. "The Divine Songs of the Lady of Purple Tenuity." In *Studies in Early Medieval Chinese Literature and Cultural History: In Honor of Richard B. Mather and Donald Holzman*, ed. Paul W. Kroll and David R. Knechtges, 149–211. Boulder: T'ang Studies Society, 2003.

———. "Li Po's Transcendent Diction." *Journal of the American Oriental Society* 106 (1986): 99–117.

———. "Seduction Songs of One of the Perfected." In *Religions of China in Practice*, ed. Donald S. Lopez, Jr., 180–87. Princeton: Princeton University Press, 1996.

———. "Verses from on High: The Ascent of T'ai Shan." In *The Vitality of the Lyric Voice: Shih Poetry from the Late Han to the T'ang*, ed. Shuen-fu Lin and Stephen Owen, 167–216. Princeton: Princeton University Press, 1987.

Kurz, Johannes. "The Politics of Collecting Knowledge: Song Taizong's Compilations Project." *T'oung Pao* 87 (2001): 289–316.

———. "Sources for the History of the Southern Tang (937–975)." *Journal of Sung-Yuan Studies* 24 (1994): 217–35.

———. "A Survey of the Historical Sources for the Five Dynasties and Ten States in Song Times." *Journal of Sung-Yuan Studies* 33 (2003): 187–224.

Laozi Zhouyi Wang Bi jiaoshi 老子周易王弼校釋. Ed. Lou Yulie 樓宇烈. Taibei: Huaxin shuju, 1981.

Lewalski, Barbara Kiefer, ed. *Renaissance Genres: Essays on Theory, History, and Interpretation*. Cambridge: Harvard University Press, 1986.

Li Fang 李昉. *Taiping guangji* 太平廣記. Beijing: Renmin wenxue chubanshe, 1959.

Li Fengmao 李豐楙. *You yu you: Liuchao Sui Tang youxian shi lunji* 憂與遊：六朝隋唐遊仙詩論集. Taibei: Xuesheng shuju, 1996.

Li Guosheng 李國勝, ed. *Wang Changling shi jiaozhu* 王昌齡詩校注. Taibei: Wenshizhe, 1973.

Li Jianliang 李劍亮. *Tang Song ci yu Tang Song geji zhidu* 唐宋詞與唐宋歌妓制度. Hangzhou: Zhejiang daxue chubanshe, 1999.

Li Jing 李璟 and Li Yu 李煜. *Nan Tang erzhu ci jiaoding* 南唐二主詞校訂. Ed. Wang Zhongwen 王仲聞. Beijing: Renmin chubanshe, 1957.

Li Tiaoyuan 李調元, ed. *Quan Wudai shi* 全五代詩. Annot. He Guangqing 何光清. Chengdu: Ba Shu shushe, 1991.

Li, Wai-yee. *Enchantment and Disenchantment: Love and Illusion in Chinese Literature*. Princeton: Princeton University Press, 1993.

Li Yanshou 李延壽 et al. *Nan shi* 南史. Beijing: Zhonghua shuju, 1974.

Li Yi 李誼, ed. *Huajian ji zhushi* 花間集注釋. Chengdu: Sichuan wenyi chubanshe, 1986.

———. *Lidai Shu ci quanji xubian* 歷代蜀詞全輯續編. Chongqing: Chongqing chubanshe, 1992.

———. *Wei Zhuang ji jiaozhu* 韋莊集校注. Chengdu: Sichuan sheng shehui kexueyuan chubanshe, 1986.

Li Zhizhong 李致忠. *Lidai keshu kaoshu* 歷代刻書考述. Chengdu: Ba Shu shushe, 1989.

Lie xian zhuan jiaojian 列仙傳校箋. Ed. Wang Shumin 王叔岷. Taibei: Zhongyang yanjiu yuan, Wenzhe suo, 1995.

Lin, Shuen-fu. "The Formation of a Distinct Generic Identity for Tz'u." In *Voices of the Song Lyric in China*, ed. Pauline Yu, 3–29. Berkeley: University of California Press, 1994.

———. *The Transformation of the Chinese Lyrical Tradition: Chiang K'uei and Southern Sung Tz'u Poetry*. Princeton: Princeton University Press, 1978.

Liu, James J. Y. *Major Lyricists of the Northern Sung, A.D. 960–1126*. Princeton: Princeton University Press, 1974.

Liu Qingyun 劉慶雲. *Cihua shi lun* 詞話十論. Changsha: Yuelu shushe, 1990.

Liu Xun 劉昫 et al. *Jiu Tang shu* 舊唐書. Beijing: Zhonghua shuju, 1975.

Liu Yaomin 劉堯民. *Ci yu yinyue* 詞與音樂. Kunming: Yunnan renmin chubanshe, 1982.

Liu Yiqing 劉義慶. *Shishuo xinyu (A New Account of the Tales of the World)*. Trans. Richard Mather. 2d ed. Ann Arbor: Center for Chinese Studies, University of Michigan, 2002.

———. *Shishuo xinyu jiaojian* 世說新語校箋. Ed. Xu Zhen'e 徐震堮. Beijing: Zhonghua shuju, 1987.

Liu Yongji 劉永濟. *Ci lun* 詞論. Shanghai: Guji chubanshe, 1981.

Liu Zunming 劉尊明. *Tang Wudai ci di wenhua guanzhao* 唐五代詞的文化觀照. Taibei: Wenjin chubanshe, 1994.

———. "Yu 'Huajian' xiangfeng zhongxing 'jiaohua zhi dao': Lun 'Huajian ciren' Niu Xiji de sanwen chuangzuo" 于"花間"香風中行"教化之道"—論"花間詞人"牛稀濟的散文創作. *Nanjing shifan daxuebao* 2 (1992): 60–64.

Lo, Winston Wan. *Szechwan in Sung China: A Case Study in the Political Integration of the Chinese Empire*. Yangmingshan, Taibei: University of Chinese Culture Press, 1982.

Long Yusheng 龍榆生. *Tang Song ci gelü* 唐宋詞歌律. Shanghai: Guji chubanshe, 1980.

Lu Xinyuan 陸心源, ed. *Tang wen shiyi* 唐文拾遺. Taibei: Wenhai chubanshe, 1962.

Lu Zhen 路振. *Jiu guo zhi* 九國志. Annot. Zhang Tangying. In *Shoushan ge congshu*, in *Baibu congshu jicheng* 52.

Luo Kaiyu 羅開玉. "Wang Jian shi zenyang zoushang geju daolu di?" 王建是怎樣走上割據道路的. *Sichuan shifan daxue xuebao* (December 1984): 95–101.

Luo Liantian 羅聯天. *Liang Han Wei Jin Nan Bei chao wenxue piping cailiao huibian* 兩漢魏晉南北朝文學批評材料匯編. Taibei: Chengwen, 1978.

———. *Sui Tang Wudai wenxue piping cailiao huibian* 隋唐五代文學批評材料匯編. Taibei: Chengwen, 1978.

McCullough, Helen Craig. *Brocade by Night: Kokin Wakashū and the Court Style in Japanese Classical Poetry*. Stanford: Stanford University Press, 1985.

McMullen, David. *State and Scholars in T'ang China*. Cambridge: Cambridge University Press, 1988.

Meng Qi 孟棨. *Ben shi shi* 本事詩. Beijing: Zhonghua shuju, 1959.

Miao, Ronald C. "Palace-Style Poetry: The Courtly Treatment of Glamour and Love." In *Studies in Chinese Poetry and Poetics*, vol. 1, ed. Ronald C. Miao, 1–42. San Francisco: Chinese Materials Center, 1978.

Miao Yue 繆鉞 and Ye Jiaying 葉嘉瑩. *Cixue gujin tan* 詞學古今談. Taibei: Wanjuan lou tushu, 1992.

———. *Lingxi cishuo* 靈溪詞說. Shanghai: Shanghai guji chubanshe, 1987.

Murakami Tetsumi 村上哲見. *Sōshi kenkyū: Tō Godai Hoku Sō hen* 宋詞研究：唐五代北宋篇. Tōkyō: Sobunsha, 1976.

———. "Yōryūji shikō" 楊柳枝詞考. *Kaga hakase taikan kinen Chūgoku bunshō tetsugaku ronshū*. Tōkyō: Kodansha, 1979.

Nakata Yūjirō 中田勇次郎. "Tō Godai shiin kō" 唐五代詞韻考. *Shinagaku* 8.4 (1936): 65–102.

Needham, Joseph, et al. *Science and Civilisation in China*. 6 vols. to date. Cambridge: Cambridge University Press, 1954–96.

Okamura Shigeru 岡村繁. "Tōmatsu ni okeru kyokushishi bungaku no seiretsu" 唐末における曲子詞文學の成立. *Bungaku kenkyū* 65 (1968): 85–126.

Owen, Stephen. *An Anthology of Chinese Literature: Beginnings to 1911*. New York: W. W. Norton, 1996.

———. *The End of the Chinese Middle Ages: Essays on the Mid-Tang*. Stanford: Stanford University Press, 1996.

———. *The Great Age of Chinese Poetry: The High T'ang*. New Haven: Yale University Press, 1981.

———. *The Late Tang: Chinese Poetry of the Mid-Ninth Century (827–860)*. Cambridge: Harvard University Asia Center Publications, 2006.

———. "Meaning the Words: The Genuine as a Value in the Tradition of the Song Lyric." In *Voices of the Song Lyric in China*, ed. Pauline Yu, 30–69. Berkeley: University of California Press, 1994.

———. *The Poetry of the Early T'ang*. New Haven: Yale University Press, 1977.

———. *Readings in Chinese Literary Thought*. Cambridge: Council on East Asian Studies, Harvard University Press, 1992.

Ouyang Xiu 歐陽修 et al. *Wudai shi ji* 五代史記. Trans., with an introduction by, Richard L. Davis as *Historical Records of the Five Dynasties*. New York: Columbia University Press, 2004.

———. *Xin Tang shu* 新唐書. Beijing: Zhonghua shuju, 1975.

———. *Xin Wudai shi* 新五代史. Beijing: Zhonghua shuju, 1974.

Palandri, Angela. *Yuan Zhen*. Boston: Twayne, 1977.

Picken, L. E. R. "The Musical Implications of Chinese Song-Texts with Unequal Lines, and the Significance of Nonsense-Syllables, with Special Reference to Art-Songs of the Song Dynasty." *Musica Asiatica* 3 (1981): 53–77.

———. "Secular Chinese Songs of the Twelfth Century." *Studia musicologica Academiae scientarum hungaricae* 8 (1966): 125–72.

———. "T'ang Music and Musical Instruments." *T'oung Pao* 50 (1969): 74–122.

Picken, L. E. R., ed. *Music from the T'ang Court*. 5 vols. to date. Oxford: Oxford University Press, 1981–90.

Pulleyblank, Edwin. *Lexicon of Reconstructed Pronunciation in Early Middle Chinese, Late Middle Chinese, and Early Mandarin*. Vancouver: University of British Columbia Press, 1991.

——. *Middle Chinese: A Study in Historical Phonology*. Vancouver: University of British Columbia Press, 1984.

Qi Huaimei. "*Huajian ji* zhi yanjiu" 花間集之研究. *Taiwan shengli shifan daxue yanjiu qikan* 4 (1960): 507–604.

Qin Fangyu 秦方瑜. *Wang Jian mu zhi mi* 王建墓之謎. Chengdu: Sichuan daxue chubanshe, 1995.

Qiu Qiongsun 丘瓊蓀. *Yanyue tanwei* 燕樂探微. Ed. Wei Fei 隗芾. Shanghai: Shanghai guji chubanshe, 1989.

Qu Tuiyuan 瞿蛻園, ed. *Liu Yuxi ji jianzheng* 劉禹錫集箋證. 3 vols. Shanghai: Shanghai guji chubanshe, 1989.

Rao Zongyi 饒宗頤. *Ciji kao* 詞籍考. Hong Kong: Hong Kong University Press, 1963.

Rao Zongyi, *see also under* Demiéville, Paul

Ren Bantang [Erbei] 任半塘 [二北]. *Dunhuang geci zongbian* 敦煌歌辭總編. Shanghai: Shanghai guji chubanshe, 1987.

——. *Dunhuang qu chutan* 敦煌曲初探. Shanghai: Wenyi lianhe chubanshe, 1954.

——. *Dunhuang qu jiaolu* 敦煌曲校錄. Shanghai: Wenyi lianhe chubanshe, 1955.

——. *Jiaofang ji jianding* 教坊記箋定. Beijing: Zhonghua shuju, 1962.

——. *Tang sheng shi* 唐聲詩. Shanghai: Zhonghua shuju, 1982.

Rickett, Adele. *Wang Kuo-wei's Jen-chien tz'u-hua: A Study in Chinese Literary Criticism*. Hong Kong: Hong Kong University Press, 1977.

Robertson, Maureen. "Changing the Subject: Gender and Self-inscription in Authors' Prefaces and *Shi* Poetry." In *Writing Women in Late Imperial China*, ed. Ellen Widmer and Kang-i Sun Chang, 171–217. Stanford: Stanford University Press, 1997.

Robinet, Isabelle. *Daoism: Growth of a Religion*. Trans. Phyllis Brooks. Stanford: Stanford University Press, 1997.

——. "Sexualité et taoisme." In *Sexualité et religion*, ed. Marcel Bernos, 51–71. Paris: Cerf, 1988.

Rouzer, Paul. *Articulated Ladies: Gender and the Male Community in Early Chinese Texts*. Cambridge: Harvard University Asia Center, 2001.

——. "Watching the Voyeurs: Palace Poetry and the *Yuefu* of Wen Tingyun." *Chinese Literature: Essays, Articles, and Reviews* 11 (1989): 13–34.

———. *Writing Another's Dream: The Poetry of Wen Tingyun*. Stanford: Stanford University Press, 1994.

Sage, Steven F. *Ancient Sichuan and the Unification of China*. Albany: State University of New York Press, 1992.

Samei, Maija Bell. *Gendered Persona and Poetic Voice: The Abandoned Woman in Early Chinese Song Lyrics*. Lanham, MD: Lexington Books, 2004.

Sanders, Graham. "Poetry in Narrative: Meng Ch'i (fl. 841–866) and *True Stories of Poems (Pen-shih shih)*." Ph.D. diss., Harvard University, 1996.

———. *Words Well Put: Visions of Poetic Competence in the Chinese Tradition*. Cambridge: Harvard University Asia Center, 2006.

Sargent, Stuart. "Can Latecomers Get There First? Sung Poets and T'ang Poetry." *Chinese Literature: Essays, Articles, and Reviews* 4 (1982): 165–212.

———. "Contexts of the Song Lyric in Sung Times: Communication Technology, Social Change, Morality." In *Voices of the Song Lyric in China*, ed. Pauline Yu, 226–56. Berkeley: University of California Press, 1994.

Sawazaki Hisayoshi 澤崎久和. "*Huajian ji* di yanxi" 花間集的沿襲. *Cixue* 9 (1992): 90–120.

Schafer, Edward H. "Cantos on 'One Bit of Cloud at Shamanka Mountain.'" *Asiatische Studien* 36 (1982): 102–24.

———. "The Capeline Cantos: Verses on the Divine Loves of Taoist Priestesses." *Asiatische Studien* 32 (1978): 5–65.

———. *The Divine Woman: Dragon Ladies and Rain Maidens in T'ang Literature*. San Francisco: North Point Press, 1980.

———. *The Empire of Min*. Rutland, VT: C. E. Tuttle, 1954.

———. "The Jade Woman of Greatest Mystery." *History of Religions* 17 (1978): 387–98.

———. *Mirages on the Sea of Time: The Taoist Poetry of Ts'ao T'ang*. Berkeley: University of California Press, 1985.

———. *Pacing the Void: T'ang Approaches to the Stars*. Berkeley: University of California Press, 1977.

———. "Passionate Peonies." *Schafer Sinological Papers* 30 (1985).

———. *The Vermilion Bird: T'ang Images of the South*. Berkeley: University of California Press, 1967.

Shen Xiangyuan 沈祥源 and Fu Shengwen 傅生文, eds. *Huajian ji xinzhu* 花間集新注. Nanchang: Jiangxi renmin chubanshe, 1997.

Shen Yue 沈約. *Song shu* 宋書. Beijing: Zhonghua shuju, 1974.

Shi Shuangyuan 史雙元. *Tang Wudai ci jishi huiping* 唐五代詞紀事會評. Hefei: Huangshan shushe, 1995.

Shi Yidui 施議對. *Ci yu yinyue guanxi yanjiu* 詞與音樂關係研究. Beijing: Zhongguo shehui kexue chubanshe, 1989.

Shields, Anna M. "Defining Experience: The 'Poems of Seductive Allure' (*yanshi*) of the Mid-Tang Poet Yuan Zhen (779–831)." *Journal of the American Oriental Society* 122.1 (2002): 61–78.

Sima Guang 司馬光 et al. *Zizhi tongjian* 資治通鑒. Beijing: Zhonghua, 1963.

Sima Qian 司馬遷. *Shi ji* 史記. Beijing: Zhonghua shuju, 1972.

Soper, Alexander Coburn, trans. *Kuo Jo-hsu's Experiences in Painting (T'u-hua chien-wen chih): An Eleventh Century History of Chinese Painting*. Washington, DC: American Council of Learned Societies, 1951.

Sun Guangxian 孫光憲. *Beimeng suoyan* 北夢鎖言. Shanghai: Guji chubanshe, 1981.

Tang Guizhang 唐珪璋. "Nan Tang yiwen zhi" 南唐藝文志. *Zhonghua wenshi luncong*, no. 3 (1979): 337–56.

Tang Guizhang, ed. *Cihua congbian* 詞話叢編. Beijing: Zhonghua shuju, 1986.

Tang Guizhang and Pan Junzhao 潘君昭. "Lun ci di qiyuan" 論詞的起源. In *Cixue yanjiu lunwenji* 詞學研究論文集. Shanghai: Guji chubanshe, 1982.

Tang Song ci yanjiu lunwenji 唐宋詞研究論文集. Zhongguo yuwenxue shebian, 1969.

Tang Wudai biji xiaoshuo xuanyi 唐五代筆記小說選譯. Chengdu: Ba Shu shushe, 1990.

Todorov, Tzvetan. *Genres du discours*. Paris: Éditions du Seuil, 1978.

———. *La notion de littérature et autres essais*. Paris: Éditions du Seuil, 1987.

Tuotuo 脫脫. *Song shi* 宋史. Shanghai: Hanyu da cidian chubanshe, 2004.

Turner, Victor. *The Anthropology of Performance*. New York: Performing Arts Publications, 1986.

———. *From Ritual to Theatre: The Human Seriousness of Play*. New York: Performing Arts Publications, 1982.

Twitchett, Denis. *Printing and Publishing in Medieval China*. London: The Wynkyn de Worde Society, 1983.

———. *The Writing of Official History Under the T'ang*. Cambridge and New York: Cambridge University Press, 1992.

Twitchett, Denis, and John K. Fairbank, eds. *The Cambridge History of China*, vol. 3, *Sui and T'ang China, 589–906*, pt. 1. Cambridge and New York: Cambridge University Press, 1979.

Upton, Beth Ann. "The Poetry of Han Wo (844–923)." Ph.D. diss., University of California, 1980.

van Gennep, Arnold. *The Rites of Passage*. Trans. Monika B. Vizedom and Gabrielle L. Caffee. Chicago: University of Chicago Press, 1960.

Verellen, Franciscus. *Du Guangting (850–933): Taoiste de cour à la fin de la Chine médiévale*. Mémoires de l'Institut des hautes études chinoises, 30. Paris: Collège de France, Institut des hautes études chinoises, 1989.

——. "Liturgy and Sovereignty: The Role of Taoist Ritual in the Foundation of the Shu Kingdom (907–925)." *Asia Major*, 3d ser. 2.1 (1989): 59–78.

von Glahn, Richard. *The Country of Streams and Grottoes: Expansion, Settlement, and the Civilizing of the Sichuan Frontier in Song Times*. Cambridge: Council on East Asian Studies, Harvard University, 1987.

Wagner, Marsha. *The Lotus Boat: The Origins of Chinese Tz'u Poetry in T'ang Popular Culture*. New York: Columbia University Press, 1984.

Wan Yunjun 萬雲駿 and Zhao Shanlin 趙山林. "Zenyang du youguan Tang Song ci di shuji" 怎樣讀有關唐宋詞的書籍. *Wen xian* (July 1987): 231–36.

Wang Dang 王讜. *Tang yu lin* 唐語林. Shanghai: Gudian wenxue chubanshe, 1957.

Wang Dingbao 王定保. *Tang zhiyan* 唐摭言. Shanghai: Guji chubanshe, 1978.

Wang Gungwu. "The *Chiu Wu-tai shi* and History-Writing During the Five Dynasties." *Asia Major* 6.1 (1957): 1–22.

——. *The Structure of Power in North China During the Five Dynasties*. Kuala Lumpur: University of Malaya Press, 1963.

Wang Kunwu 王昆吾. *Sui Tang Wudai yanyue zayan geci yanjiu* 隋唐五代燕樂雜言歌詞研究. Beijing: Zhonghua shuju, 1996.

Wang Li 王力. *Hanyu shi lü xue* 漢語詩律學. Shanghai: Jiaoyu chubanshe, 1962.

Wang Meng'ou 王夢鷗. *Tang ren xiaoshuo yanjiu* 唐人小説研究. 2 vols. Taibei: Yiwen yinshu guan, 1973.

Wang Qi 王琦, ed. *Li Taibai quanji* 李太白全集. 4 vols. Annot. Wang Qi. Beijing: Zhonghua shuju, 1957.

Wang Shizhen 王士禎. *Wudai shihua* 五代詩話. Shanghai: Commercial Press, 1937.

Wang Wencai 王文才. *Chengdu chengfang kao* 成都城坊考. Chengdu: Ba Shu shushe, 1986.

Wang Yanping 王炎平. "Lue lun Qian Hou Shu di guoqing he guoyun" 略論前後蜀的國情和國運. *Sichuan daxue xuebao* (January 1991): 88–93.

Wang Yao 王瑤. "Zhongguo wenxue piping yu zongji" 中國文學批評與總集. In *Guanyu Zhongguo gudian wenxue wenti* 關於中國古典文學問題. Shanghai: Gudian wenxue chubanshe, 1956.

———. *Zhongguo wenxue sixiang* 中國文學思想. Shanghai: Tangdi chubanshe, 1951.
Wang Zhaopeng 王兆鵬. *Tang Song ci shi lun* 唐宋詞史論. Beijing: Renmin wenxue chubanshe, 2000.
Wang Zhongmin 王重民, ed. *Dunhuang quzi ci ji* 敦煌曲子詞集. Shanghai: Commercial Press, 1956.
Wei Hu 韋縠. *Caidiao ji* 才調集. In *Tangren xuan Tangshi xinbian*, ed. Fu Xuancong. Xi'an: Shaanxi renmin chubanshe, 1996.
Wei Zhuang 韋莊. *Youxuan ji* 又玄集. In *Tangren xuan Tangshi xinbian*, ed. Fu Xuancong. Xi'an: Shaanxi renmin chubanshe, 1996.
Wen Ruxian 聞汝賢. *Cipai huishi* 詞牌彙釋. Taibei, 1963.
Wen xuan 文選. Comp. and prefaced by Xiao Tong 蕭統. 6 vols. Shanghai: Shanghai guji chubanshe, 1986.
———. Trans. David R. Knechtges as *Wen xuan, or Selections of Refined Literature*. 4 vols. Princeton: Princeton University Press, 1982–97.
Wixted, John Timothy. *The Song-Poetry of Wei Chuang (836–910 A.D.)*. Occasional Paper no. 12. Tempe: Center for Asian Studies, Arizona State University, 1979.
Wong, Tak-wai. "Baroque clements in Wen T'ing-yun's *Tz'u* Poetry." In *Proceedings of the Tenth Congress of the International Comparative Literature Association, New York, 1982*, vol. 2, *Comparative Poetics/Poetiques comparées*, ed. Anna Balakian et al. New York: Garland, 1985.
———. "Toward Defining Chinese Baroque Poetry." *Tamkang Review* 8.1 (April 1977): 25–72.
Workman, Michael E. "The Bedchamber Topic in the *Tz'u* Songs of Three Medieval Chinese Poets: Wen Tingyun, Wei Chuang, and Li Yü." In *Critical Essays on Chinese Literature*, ed. William H. Nienhauser, Jr. Hong Kong: Chinese University of Hong Kong, 1976.
Wu guo gushi 五國故事. In *Zhibuzu zhai congshu*, in *Baibu congshu jicheng* 29.
Wu Hung. *The Double Screen: Medium and Representation in Chinese Painting*. Chicago: University of Chicago Press, 1996.
Wu Qiming 吳企明. *Tang yin zhiyi lu* 唐音質疑錄. Shanghai: Shanghai guji chubanshe, 1986.
Wu Renchen 吳任臣. *Shiguo chunqiu* 十國春秋. Beijing: Zhonghua shuju, 1983.
Wu Xionghe 吳熊和. *Tang Song ci tonglun* 唐宋詞通論. Hangzhou: Zhejiang guji chubanshe, 1985.
Xia Chengtao 夏承燾. *Tang Song ci luncong* 唐宋詞論叢. Shanghai: Shanghai gudian wenxue chubanshe, 1956.

———. *Tang Song ciren nianpu* 唐宋詞人年譜. Shanghai: Guji chubanshe, 1979.
Xiao Zixian 蕭子顯. *Nan Qi shu* 南齊書. Beijing: Zhonghua shuju, 1972.
Xu Jian 徐堅 et al. *Chuxue ji* 初學集. Beijing: Zhonghua shuju, 1962.
Xu Ling 徐陵, comp. *Yutai xinyong jianzhu* 玉臺新詠箋注. Ed. and annot. Mu Kehong 穆克宏. Beijing: Zhonghua shuju, 1985.
Xue Juzheng 薛居正 et al. *Jiu Wudai shi* 舊五代史. Beijing: Zhonghua shuju, 1976.
Yan Jinxiong 顏進雄. *Tangdai youxian shi yanjiu* 唐代遊仙詩研究. Taibei: Wenjin chubanshe, 1996.
Yang Bojun 楊伯峻, ed. *Chunqiu Zuo zhuan zhu* 春秋左傳注. Beijing: Zhonghua shuju, 1985.
Yang Haiming 楊海明. *Tang Song ci fengge lun* 唐宋詞風格論. Shanghai: Shanghai shehui kexueyuan chubanshe, 1986.
———. *Tang Song ci lun gao* 唐宋詞論稿. Hangzhou: Zhejiang guji chubanshe, 1988.
———. *Tang Wudai ci shi* 唐五代詞史. Shanghai: Jiangsu chubanshe, 1987.
Yang Jun 楊軍, ed. *Yuan Zhen ji biannian jianzhu* 元稹集編年箋注. Xi'an: San Qin chubanshe, 2002.
Yang Weili 楊偉立. *Qian Shu Hou Shu shi* 前蜀後蜀史. Chengdu: Sichuan sheng shehui kexueyuan chubanshe, 1986.
Yao Silian 姚思廉 et al. *Chen shu* 陳書. Beijing: Zhonghua shuju, 1973.
———. *Liang shu* 梁書. Beijing: Zhonghua shuju, 1973.
Yates, Robin D. S. *Washing Silk: The Life and Selected Poetry of Wei Chuang (834?–910)*. Cambridge: Council on East Asian Studies, Harvard University, 1988.
Ye Jiaying 葉嘉瑩. *Jialing lunci conggao* 迦陵論詞論稿. Shanghai: Guji chubanshe, 1985.
———. *Tang Song ci shiqi jiang* 唐宋詞十七講. Changsha: Yue lu shushe, 1989.
———. *Wen Tingyun, Wei Zhuang, Feng Yansi, Li Yu* 溫庭筠, 韋莊, 馮延巳, 李煜. Taibei: Da'an chubanshe, 1988.
———. *Zhongguo cixue ti xiandai guan* 中國詞學體現代觀. Taibei: Da'an chubanshe, 1988.
Yoshikawa, Kōjirō. *An Introduction to Sung Poetry*. Trans. Burton Watson. Cambridge: Harvard University Press, 1967.
Yu, Pauline. "Poems for the Emperor: Imperial Tastes in the Early Ninth Century." In *Rhetoric and the Discourses of Power in Court Culture*, ed. David R. Knechtges and Eugene Vance. Seattle: University of Washington Press, 2005.

———. "Poems in Their Place: Collections and Canons in Early Chinese Literature." *Harvard Journal of Asiatic Studies* 50.1 (1990): 163–96.

———. "Song Lyrics in the Canon: A Look at Anthologies of *Tz'u*." In *Voices of the Song Lyric in China*, ed. Pauline Yu, 70–103. Berkeley: University of California Press, 1994.

Yu, Pauline, ed. *Voices of the Song Lyric in China*. Berkeley: University of California Press, 1994.

Yuan Xingpei 袁行霈. "Wen ci yishu yanjiu: jianlun Wen, Wei cifeng di chayi" 溫詞藝術研究: 兼論溫韋詞風的差異. *Xueshu yuekan* 2 (1986): 48–54.

Zeng Zhaomin 曾昭岷. *Wen, Wei, Feng ci xinjiao* 溫韋馮詞新校. Shanghai: Guji chubanshe, 1988.

Zha Jizhao 查繼超. *Cixue quanshu* 詞學全書. Guizhou renmin chubanshe, 1990.

Zhang Shiming 張式銘. "Lun *Huajian ji* ci di chuangzao qingxiang" 論花間集詞的創造傾向. *Wenxue yichan* 1 (1984): 52–63.

Zhang Tangying 張唐英. *Shu Taowu* 蜀檮杌. In *Yihai zhuchen*, in *Baibu congshu jicheng* 35.

Zhang Yiren 張以仁. *Huajian ci lunji* 花間詞論集. Taibei: Academia Sinica, 1996.

Zhang Zhang 張璋 and Huang Yu 黃畬, eds. *Quan Tang Wudai ci* 全唐五代詞. Shanghai: Shanghai guji chubanshe, 1986.

Zheng Chenghai 鄭成海, ed. *Laozi Heshang gong zhushu zheng* 老子河上公注疏證. Taibei: Huaxin shuju, 1978.

Zheng Huada 鄭華達. *Tangdai gongyuan shi yanjiu* 唐代宮怨詩研究. Taibei: Wenjin chubanshe, 2000.

Zheng Xuemeng 鄭學檬. *Wudai Shiguo shi yanjiu* 五代十國史研究. Shanghai: Renmin chubanshe, 1991.

Zhou Fan 周汎 and Gao Chunming 高春明, eds. *Zhongguo lidai funü zhuangshi* 中國歷代婦女裝飾. Hong Kong: Sanlian shudian youxian gongsi; Shanghai: Shanghai xuelin chubanshe, 1988.

Zhou Zumuo 周祖謨. *Tang Wudai yunshu jicun* 唐五代韻書集存. Beijing: Zhonghua shuju, 1983.

Zhu Hengfu 朱恒夫. *Xinyi Huajian ji* 新譯花間集. Taibei: Sanmin shuju, 1998.

Zhu Xiaozang 朱孝臧, ed. *Qiangcun congshu* 彊村叢書. Shanghai: Guji chubanshe, 1989.

Zunqian ji 樽前集. In *Qiangcun congshu*. Shanghai: Guji chubanshe, 1989.

Zürcher, Erik. "Buddhist Influences on Taoist Scripture." *T'oung Pao* 66 (1980): 84–147.

Index

abandoned women, 30–32, 33–34n37, 37–41, 43, 228, 240–41; in "Huanxi sha," 246, 247, 265, 267; in "Jiu quanzi," 234–35, 238; liminality of, 190–92, 296; in "Nü guanzi," 323, 330–31; in "Pusa man," 175, 202, 207–8, 211, 213, 216. See also separation of lovers
aesthetics, 102, 161–62
ambiguity: of gender, 334, 335–36; of voice, 194, 222–24
An Lushan rebellion, 27, 123, 124, 125
anonymous subjects, 31–32, 39, 40–41, 42, 164, 180, 190, 230. See also voice
"Answering Student Zhang" (anonymous), 42
anthologies: anonymous, 110, 347; categories of, 122–23n5; Confucian, 133; content of, 55, 56–57; creation of, 9, 156. See also Tang anthologies; specific anthologies by name
Aoyama, Hiroshi, 174, 187n46, 188, 294, 326n89
artifice (*qiao*), 3, 10, 161–62, 217–18, 249, 342; *Huajian ji* preface and, 154–55, 157
audience, 7, 154, 272–73
authenticity, 12, 226–28

Bai Juyi, 41, 46, 47, 48, 56, 60–61, 128, 227; *Baishi liutie*, 101; biography of, 64; exchange poems of, 140; lyrics preservation and, 62; "Song of the Pipa," 240; "Yangliu zhi," 17–20; "Yi Jiangnan," 44–47; *yuefu* and, 53
"Bai xinyue," 45
Ban Jieyu, 37
bedchamber, *see* boudoir
Beili zhi (Sun Qi), 34–35, 318–20
Bei Meng suoyan (Sun Guangxian), 74

Ben shi shi (Meng Qi), 19*n*5, 35
bibliographies, 129
Biji manzhi (Wang Zhuo), 101, 350
biographies, 86*n*38, 103, 115, 145, 170; of *Huajian ji* poets, 63–64, 77, 79; of transcendent women, 129, 315. See also *Jiuguo zhi*
Bol, Peter, 80–81
borrowing, 220, 272, 276, 289–93, 296, 323; in "Lin jiang xian," 289, 299, 307; in "Nü guanzi," 289, 329; within tune sets, 173. See also imitation
boudoir, 30–31, 37–41, 223, 226, 297, 302; in "Huanxi sha," 255, 263–67; natural world contrasted with, 207–8; in "Pusa man," 190, 192–94, 199, 202, 206–8, 211. See also setting/scene
Bourdieu, Pierre, 6
brothels, see courtesans; prostitutes
Bryant, Daniel, 174
"Bu xu ci" (Pacing the Void), 45, 322, 333, 336
Buddhism, 283, 288–89. See also monk poets

Cahill, Suzanne, 13, 281–83, 285, 295–96; on Daoist nuns, 316–17, 319, 340
Caidiao ji, 42, 141, 185, 304; exclusions from, 147–48; preface to, 9–10, 120–22, 133, 144, 146, 148. See also Wei Hu
Cang Jie myth, 253
Cao Pi, 117
Cao Tang, 146
Cao Zhi, 136, 309–10, 313, 331; "Rhapsody on the Luo River Goddess," 309, 310, 313

carpe diem sentiments, 196, 214–15, 217
Chang, Kang-i Sun: *The Evolution of Chinese Tz'u Poetry*, 181
Chang E, 308
Chang'an, 26, 27, 32, 70, 81, 98*n*72; Pingkang quarter, 34
changduan ju, 29, 50
"Chang xiang si," 38, 52
Chen, rulers of, 77–78
Chen Shangjun, 108
Chen Zhensun: *Zhizhai shulu jieti*, 93, 351–52
Chen Zilong, 355
Chengdu, 8, 71, 78*n*19, 79, 115, 142; as "Brocade City," 96, 117; Chang'an compared, 84; as cultural center, 9, 13, 116, 142; musical district of, 90. See also Shu, kingdom of
Cheng Han state of Shu, 69
Chongwen zongmu, 55
Chu ci, 292, 295, 306, 349
Chu xue ji, 101
chuanqi, 33–34, 35–36, 41, 273–74
ci, 20–21, 188, 227, 348–50, 352–53, 356; coalescence of, 230; *qing* in, 353, 355; of Song dynasty, 3, 119, 163, 242, 350, 355; structure of, 49, 58; stylistic hierarchy in, 358; of Tang dynasty, 48; *yuefu* and, 353. See also *quzi ci*
cihua, 110*n*106, 176, 348, 355
Classic of Odes, 129–30*n*29, 136–37, 154, 295, 353; Great Preface to, 349; as model anthology, 9, 126
Collection of the Tunes of the Talents, see *Caidiao ji*

collections, 53, 120–21, 130–31. *See also* anthologies; compilation; *specific collections by name*
colloquial language, 163, 171, 177, 216, 350, 360; in "Huanxi sha," 251, 261, 269, 271; in "Pusa man," 196, 201, 215, 220–21, 222, 276
competition, literary, 35, 36–37, 70, 169, 170
compilation, 5, 128–33, 137, 144–45, 347; of *Huajian ji*, 119–20, 150, 176–77, 210. *See also* anthologies
composition, 48–49, 58, 60–61, 96, 174; Ouyang and, 150, 154; as social practice, 157, 162–63. *See also* metrical structures; syntax
conceptual borrowing, *see* borrowing; imitation
concubines, 95–96. *See also* palace women
Confucian history and criticism, 71–72, 95n62, 125–26
Confucius, 9, 138, 152n84, 154, 155. *See also Classic of Odes*
connoisseurship, 36, 120, 347, 356
conventions, thematic, *see* thematic conventions
convents, *see* Daoist nuns
court culture, *see* Shu court
courtesans, 7, 32, 68, 170, 248, 323; as Daoist nuns, 317–18, 320, 326; goddesses and, 278; literati and, 34–35; in Northern Ward, 41–42
craft (*gong*), 10, 36–37, 161–62, 197, 218, 342; in "Huanxi sha," 252–53; in "Pusa man," 221. *See also* artifice
criticism, 124–26, 144, 350–53
Cui Lingqin, 27. *See also Jiaofang ji*
Cui Yingying, 41–42

culture of romance, *see* romance; Tang

Daoism, 13–14, 45, 175–76, 295, 320; "Lin jiang xian" and, 299, 307, 312; rituals of, 83; Shangqing school of, 315; Tang poetry and, 281, 283–87, 314–15; Wei Hu and, 146
Daoism and goddesses, 278–94, 323, 339–40. *See also* goddess encounters
Daoist nuns, 287, 289, 315, 316, 340; courtesans as, 317–18, 320, 326. *See also* "Nü guanzi"
Daoist tune titles: "Bie xianzi," 288; "Dong xian ge," 105n99, 288; "Feng gui yun," 288; "Tian xianzi," 288, 304; "Ye jinmen," 288. *See also* "Lin jiang xian"; "Nü guanzi"
dating, of Dunhuang lyrics, 28–30, 57, 230–31
decadence, *see* "palace-style" poetry; Shu court
Despeux, Catherine, 282–83, 318
deviations, poetic (*bian*), 353, 354
dialogue, intratextual, 11, 228, 249, 356
divine encounters, *see* goddess encounters
dreams, 175, 276, 301, 342, 357, 359–60; goddess encounters as, 304–5, 308–9; in "Huanxi sha," 248–49, 255, 268, 274; in "Jiu quanzi," 236, 241; in "Pusa man," 195, 198, 202, 204–5, 208, 224; as vehicle for spiritual journey, 260–62. *See also* liminality

drunkenness, 62–63, 202, 213, 276, 320, 357; in "Huanxi sha," 258; as liminal state, 207–8, 359–60
Du Fu, 46n64, 132, 146, 221n1; "thatched hut" of, 88, 140–41
Du Guangting, 78n19, 83, 289; *Yongcheng jixian lu*, 287
Du He: Duling Du clan and, 84
Du Mu, 94n61, 140, 145, 253
Duan Chengshi, 43
Dunhuang lyrics, 39, 49, 281, 288, 294, 314, 342; content of, 25n16, 39, 44, 46, 225; dating of, 28–30, 57, 230–31; structure of, 166; Tang culture and, 24

echo, 203, 266, 269. *See also* repetition
ekphrases, 103, 313
elites, *see* literati
emotions, 188, 218, 240–41, 274, 291; categorical, 226; in "Huanxi sha," 245, 254, 265, 267; in "Pusa man," 193, 199, 210; romantic conventions and, 271–72, 273, 340. *See also* feeling (*qing*)
entertainment districts, 25–26, 32–33, 34–35, 46, 169–70. *See also* female entertainers; musical entertainment; popular entertainment
eroticism, 117, 175, 183–84, 211–17, 262, 353; in goddess encounters, 290, 302, 308; in "Huanxi sha," 342; male voice and, 229–30, 264–65; in "Pusa man," 175, 188, 190, 193–94, 208, 225; social convention and, 230, 265; transcendence and, 321, 333, 334; Wen Tingyun and, 63, 65. *See also* sexual encounters
examination system, 5, 9, 86–87, 101
exclusions, from anthologies, 132, 138, 147

feeling (*qing*), 240, 276, 277, 290, 357, 360; "Boudoir Feelings" (*gui qing*), 38; *ci* and, 353, 355. *See also* emotions
female entertainers, 25–26, 32, 35; singing girls, 19n5, 64, 68, 287, 288, 289. *See also* courtesans
female subjects, 11, 124, 341–42; anonymity of, 31–32, 39, 40–41, 164, 180, 190; boundaries of, 291–92; clothing of, 208, 209; as flowers, 116, 240, 253, 256; passivity of, 273, 274; silence of, 224, 234, 256–57, 296, 312. *See also* courtesans; voyeurism
female transcendents, *see* transcendent women
female voice, 12, 171, 188, 222, 225, 275; first-person, 298; in "Huanxi sha," 249–51; male voice juxtaposed with, 228–29, 236, 242, 245, 358; in popular song, 277, 357–58
Feng Yansi, 25, 227
fengliu, 64, 170
first-person voice, 221–23, 225, 240, 242, 273, 291; female, 298; in "Huanxi sha," 249, 250, 251, 259, 264, 270–71; male, 12, 222, 226–27, 264, 268–69, 276–77
"Five Devils" coterie, 107
Five Dynasties, 8, 70n51, 84, 121, 315, 351; histories of, 74, 80. *See also* Ten Kingdoms

flower imagery, 119, 195, 199; peonies, 191*n*52, 247; as symbol of female beauty, 116, 240, 253, 256
Fong, Grace, 223, 359
forms, *see* heterometric verse forms; isometric verse forms; metrical structures
four-line form, 60, 96. *See also* quatrains
fragmentation, syntactic, 167–68, 179, 202, 232
freedom, 33–34*n*37, 190; gender and, 292, 317, 318

Gao Shi, 140; "Song of Yan," 140
Gaotang goddess legend, 305; "Rhapsody on Gaotang," 230, 300
gaze, the, 193, 210, 260. *See also* voyeurism
"Gazing at Spring" (Du Fu), 140
gender, 12, 33, 175, 180, 276, 358–59; ambiguity, 334, 335–36; coding, 171; roles, 13, 340, 341
gender-neutral voice, 180, 222–23, 228, 238, 240, 250; in "Huanxi sha," 225, 245, 248, 261–62, 265
"Genglouzi," 31, 280, 292
genre: classification of, 4, 5; development of, 6, 20–21, 22, 50, 54, 119–20; elevation of, 281; elitism and, 67, 277; establishment of, 119, 121, 163, 275, 277, 342; history of, 48, 153, 167. *See also ci; quzi ci*
goddess encounters, 12–13, 45, 176, 278–94, 332–33, 341; Daoism and, 278–94, 323, 339–40; hierogamous unions in, 176, 258, 283, 285, 286, 290–91. *See also* "Lin jiang xian"; "Nü guanzi"; *specific goddesses by name*
gong, see craft
gong ci, 38, 92–93, 104–5
gongti, see "palace-style" poetry
gong yuan, 37–41
Gou Yanqing, 73
Gu Xiong, 107, 108, 113, 274; "Huanxi sha," 244, 245, 265–69; "Lin jiang xian," 295, 297–98, 313
Guan Xiu, 103, 103*n*89, 107*n*100
Gujin yunhui, 101
Guo Maoqian, 19*n*5, 51
Guo Ruoxu, 102
Guo xiu ji (Rui Tingzhang), 125

Han dynasty, 51; poetry of, 138, 354
Han Yu, 128, 253
Hanlin Academy, 9, 85, 99*n*76, 101, 103
haofang style, 350, 358
"Hao shi guang," 44
Hawkes, David, 285
He Guangyan, 92*n*53, 96*n*64; *Jianjie lu*, 73, 74*n*11, 92*n*53, 95–96; "Tones of the Fallen Kingdoms," 94–96
He Ning, 77*n*18, 113, 186, 187, 295
heptametric form, 60, 96, 127, 167, 244, 294; quatrains, 44, 52, 59*n*87
hereditary houses (*shijia*), 74–75
hermeneutics, 352–53, 355
heterogeneity, of Shu court, 85–86, 115
heterometric verse forms, 11, 18*n*4, 23, 44, 48, 49–50, 51, 55, 58, 59, 70*n*51, 157, 164–65, 243–44; as norm in *quzi ci*, 60; rhythms of, 232, 242; shift from isometric forms to, 58–59*n*86, 165, 167;

syntactic fragmentation and, 167–68; in Tang vs. Shu, 165
He yue yingling ji (Yin Fan), 125, 126
hierogamous unions, 176, 258, 283, 285, 286, 290–91, 358
histories, 71–75, 77, 80, 89, 100; Confucian, 71–72, 95n62; Song, 67–68, 72, 74, 76, 111; of Southern Dynasties, 8, 78–79, 90, 93. See also literary history; *Shiguo chunqiu*
historiography, 71–72, 90, 110
Hu Shi, 29
Huajian ji, 79–80, 288, 361; compilation of, 119–20, 150, 176–77, 210; editors of, 23, 201, 217, 272, 347; exclusions from, 58, 117; as founding collection of genre, 1, 23, 119, 352; influence in Song, 13, 62, 164, 347–48; Lu You's colophon to, 350–51; organization of, 201; political context of, 8, 9, 71, 78, 111, 347; reception of, 77, 347–49; Song editions of, 111; Tang Xianzu's edition of, 353–54. See also specific tune titles; specific lyricists by name
—preface (Ouyang Jiong), 1–2, 77, 80, 183, 218, 281; artifice and, 154, 155, 157; evocation of established genres in, 149, 150, 153, 155; literati and, 112, 143; rhetoric of, 110–11, 148; taste and, 149–56
Huang Quan, 102–3, 103
Huang Yu, 53–54
Huangfu Song, 49, 56, 59, 113, 304; *Zuixiang riyue*, 63
"Huanxi sha," 175, 224, 242–69, 312, 342; colloquial language in, 251, 261, 269, 271; emotions in, 245,

254, 265, 267; gender-neutral voice in, 225, 245, 248, 261–62, 265; importance of, in *Huajian ji*, 12; liminality in, 248, 249, 255, 258, 268, 274; lovers' separation in, 253–54, 256, 258, 265, 266, 267; male voice in, 228–30, 245, 248, 259–61, 268–69, 274; poets with lyrics to, 244; range of perspectives in, 242, 271; setting of, 245, 255, 261, 263, 266–67, 268; sexual encounters in, 262–65; time in, 251, 255–56, 268; voyeurism in, 211, 247–48, 262, 264, 341–42. See also specific poets by name
Hucker, Charles, 82
huyue, 25

imagery, see flower imagery; natural imagery; seasonal imagery; stock imagery
imitation (*ni*), 11–12, 162, 291, 296, 347, 356; in *Huajian ji*, 23, 217–18; in "Huanxi sha," 246, 254; in "Nü guanzi," 327–29, 333, 335; performance and, 272, 273; in "Pusa man," 220–21; quotation and, 220, 273; vs. innovation, 173–74; by Wei Zhuang, 249; of Wen Tingyun, 227–28, 254–55, 257, 270; by Xue Zhaoyun, 252–53, 254. See also borrowing
innovation, 13–14, 63–64, 118, 164–76, 356; formal, 164–69, 171, 173; stylistic, 164, 169–76
"insect-carving," 144
instrumental music, 8, 46, 90, 105n96, 168, 273. See also musical entertainment
intratextuality, 11, 249, 320, 356

isometric verse forms, 23, 49, 165, 167, 243–44; quatrains, 58, 60, 147–48

Jauss, Hans Robert, 6
Jia Dao, 140
Jian'an era, 117
Jiangling, 71
Jianjie lu (He Guangyan), 73, 74*n*11, 92*n*53, 95–96
"Jian qi ci," 45
jiaofang (imperial music instruction quarter), 27, 97–98*n*70
Jiaofang ji (Cui Lingqin), 27, 52, 294, 314
Jiaoran, 140, 218
Jinli qijiu zhuan (Gou Yanqing), 73, 74*n*11
Jinquan ji (Wen Tingyun), 183, 185, 186
Jiuguo zhi, 74, 112
"Jiu quanzi," 12, 175, 221, 222, 230–42, 274; gender-neutral voice in, 225, 240; poets with lyrics to, 231; rhyme in, 232–33, 236, 239; structure in, 231–33; voice in, 228–29, 234, 235–36, 340, 342. *See also specific poets by name*
Jiu Tang shu, 24, 63
Jiu Wudai shi, 74
Jixuan ji (Yao He), 126–27, 128, 131, 133, 138, 140; exclusions from, 132
Johnson, David, 84, 86*n*37
Junzhai dushu houzhi, 55

King Xiang of Chu, *see* Xiang, King of Chu
Knechtges, David R., 36–37

Lady Huarui, 92, 101, 104–5
landscape poetry, 242. *See also* natural imagery
language. *See* colloquial language; vernacular language
Laozi, 132, 283
Li Bai, 21, 55–56, 132, 140, 176, 186*n*45; heterometric verse and, 59; "Jade Steps Plaint," 38; "Road to Shu Is Hard," 140; "Spring Plaint," 40–41
Li Duan, 128, 304
Li Fengmao, 282, 317–18
Li Hao, 73*n*10, 99*n*76, 101
Li He, 168, 253
Li Jian, 55
Li Jing, 25
Li Kangcheng, 125
Li Qingzhao, 357
Li Shangyin, 41, 145, 164, 168
Li She, 304
Li Xun, 115, 142, 221, 274; "Huanxi sha," 244, 335–36; "Jiu quanzi," 231, 238–42, 275; "Lin jiang xian," 295; "Nü guanzi," 317, 329, 335–36; official title of, 108, 109, 113; "Pusa man," 186, 187, 209–10, 292
Li Yan, 96
Li Yi, 31*n*30
Li Yu, 12, 25, 104*n*92, 227
Li Yuxiao, 93
Liang dynasty, 4, 82, 114, 121, 125; poetry of, 36–37, 124
Liaoyang, 199
"Libie nan," 37, 43
Lie xian zhuan, 299
liminality, 175, 241, 290, 296, 357, 359–60; in "Pusa man," 189–91, 202–5, 208, 210, 211, 224

Linghu Chu, 127
"Lin jiang xian," 288, 289, 291, 294–314, 332; abandoned male in, 313–14; Daoism and, 299, 307, 312; goddess encounters in, 302, 304–5, 308–9, 312; mystery in, 290, 292–93; "Nü guanzi" compared, 320, 322–23, 334, 342; poets with lyrics to, 295; structure in, 294–96; transcendent women in, 298, 301–2; voice in, 301, 304–5. *See also specific poets by name*
linked sets, 167, 169
linked verse (*lianju*), 129, 253
literary convention, 36, 38–41, 281, 287, 342. *See also* thematic convention
literary history, 22, 119, 218, 346–55, 359, 361; court culture and, 346–49; criticism and, 350–55; in Qing, 349–50, 360–61. *See also* histories
literary taste, 122, 146
literati, 1, 34, 68, 80–81, 119, 163; competition among, 35, 36–37; courtesans and, 275–76; lifestyles of, 62–63, 68; of Ming, 352; of Northern Ward, 41–42; of Shu, 8, 85, 115; of Song, 29, 51, 176; as sponsors of texts, 106. *See also* poetry and poets
Liu Fangping, 40–41
Liu Wensou, 67
Liu Xie: *Wenxin dialong*, 4
Liu Yong, 201*n*74, 359
Liu Yuxi, 46, 47, 48, 56, 62, 64, 227; exchange poems of, 140; "Yangliu zhi," 17–20
Liu Zan: *Shu guo wenying*, 142

Liu Zhen (Master Liu), 320–21, 329, 331–32, 337, 338
"Liu zhi," 147–48
Liu Zunming, 183
Long Yu, 311–13
long-and-short lines (*changduan ju*), 50
lovers, separation of, *see* separation of lovers
Lu Ji: "Wen fu," 4
Lu Lun, 140
Lu Qianyi: "Lin jiang xian," 295, 345–46; "Nü guanzi," 317, 329–32, 335–36; official title of, 108, 109, 113
Lü Yan, 55, 59
Lu You, 111*n*108, 350–51
Luo River goddess, 285, 306, 309–10, 312, 313
Luo Yin, 88*n*43, 146
Luoyang, 26, 27, 32, 96, 179–80
lyrics, *see quzi ci*

male lover, 313–14, 326–27, 358
male voice, 171, 196, 200, 226–30, 276; authenticity of, 227–28; colloquial language of, 271, 276; eroticism and, 229–30, 264–65; female voice juxtaposed with, 228–29, 234, 236, 242, 245, 358; first-person, 222, 264–65, 268–69, 276, 277; in "Huanxi sha," 228–29, 245, 248, 259–61, 268–69, 275; in "Jiu quanzi," 235–36, 242; as minority voice, 12, 357–58; self-revelatory, 226–27; in *yuefu*, 229, 271, 277
manci (long songs), 166, 168, 356
Mandate of Heaven, 69, 78

Mao Wenxi, 91–92*n*52, 106, 110, 115; "Huanxi sha," 244; "Jiu quanzi," 231; "Lin jiang xian," 295; official title of, 107, 108, 109, 113

Mao Xizhen, 108, 109, 113, 317, 323–24; "Huanxi sha," 244; "Jiu quanzi," 231; "Lin jiang xian," 295; "Pusa man," 186, 187, 204–9, 217

Master Liu, *see* Liu Zhen (Master Liu)

medieval literature, 4, 22, 36–37, 50, 189, 358. *See also* poetry and poets; Tang poetry

melancholy, 46, 47, 171, 190, 235, 346; in "Huanxi sha," 246, 248, 249, 266; in "Jiu quanzi," 241

melody, 105, 273

memory (*yi*), 205, 274, 276, 342, 357; in "Huanxi sha," 251, 260, 269; in Wen Tingyun's lyrics, 195, 202. *See also* liminality; time

Meng Chang, 73, 76, 79, 85–86*nn*37–38, 112, 142; Cao Pi compared, 117; court of, 9, 89, 92, 101–6; regime of, 69, 99*n*76, 103, 111; Wang Yan compared, 100–101

Meng Haoran, 146

Meng Jiao, 253

Meng Zhixiang, 69, 79, 98–100, 112, 142

metrical structures, 10, 11, 48, 51, 167, 359; borrowing and, 173; in "Huanxi sha," 243–44; innovation and, 164–65; in "Jiu quanzi," 231–33, 236; in "Lin jiang xian," 294–95; in "Nü guanzi," 315–16; pentametric verse forms, 127, 167, 294. *See also* hetero- metric verse forms; isometric verse forms

"Midnight" poems (*Ziye*), 41, 225

Ming dynasty, 3, 74, 349, 352, 354, 360–61; *ci* of, 353; *cihua* of, 348; *quzi ci* classification in, 49

monk poets, 97, 128, 132, 140, 147

mood, 38–39, 47*n*66, 163, 195, 281; coherence of, 221, 242; continuity of, 168; in "Huanxi sha," 245, 246, 248, 268; music and, 273; natural imagery and, 253–54, 340; performance and, 46; shifts in, 169; in Wen Tingyun's lyrics, 11, 203, 209. *See also specific moods*

Mu, King of Zhou, 154

Mudan ting, 353–54

Murakami Tetsumi, 20*n*10, 24*n*15, 57*n*82, 181–82

music manuals, 50

musical entertainment, 61, 104, 156, 280; instrumental music, 8, 46, 90, 105*n*96, 168, 273; of Shu, 90–91, 97, 118; of Tang, 21–22, 23–30, 32. *See also* performance

Nakata, Yujiro, 174

"Nan xiangzi," 225, 280

narrative/narrator, 200, 264; absence of, 178, 179, 191, 240, 327; in goddess encounters, 298, 306, 308–9, 312, 332, 341. *See also* voice

natural imagery, 224–25, 241, 253–54, 256, 303–4, 340–41; birds, 235, 236, 254, 266; clouds, 206, 260, 279, 300, 322; mountains, 208; in "Pusa man," 188, 207–10; transcendent female and, 292, 302, 310; water, 209, 292, 315; willow

trees, 19, 43, 44. *See also* flower imagery; seasonal imagery
Nine Classics, printing of, 101
Niu Qiao, 110, 115, 186, 187, 298, 317; career of, 106, 107, 108, 109; "Jiu quanzi," 231; "Nü guanzi," 323–24, 327–29; "Pusa man," 197–202, 206, 215–17, 225, 229, 257
Niu Xiji, 96–97, 106, 108, 109, 115; artistry of, 311, 312–13, 341; "Jiu quanzi," 231; "Lin jiang xian," 295, 305–14, 334
norms (*zheng*), 353, 354
Northern Ward, poetry of, 41–42
"Nü guanzi," 12–13, 280, 281, 289, 314–40; Daoist imagery in, 320, 322, 328–29, 332–36; "Lin jiang xian" compared with, 320, 322–23, 334, 342; mystery in, 290, 292–93; Schafer and, 321–22; setting of, 291–92, 330–32; structure in, 315–16; transcendent women in, 324, 325–29, 334, 336–37. *See also specific poets by name*
nuns, *see* Daoist nuns; "Nü guanzi"

Odes, *see Classic of Odes*
Ouyang Jiong, 66, 103, 119, 120–21, 225, 313; artifice and, 3, 10, 155, 161–62, 218, 342; concern of with rank, 112–15; as court official, 89–90, 106–7, 109, 113; craft and, 162–63, 276–77; criticism of, 348; "He ming chao," 2; "Huanxi sha," 262–65; official title of, 113; as poet, 103*n*89, 148, 150, 221; valorization and, 14, 21, 114, 116–17, 155, 185; Wei Hu and, 143. *See also Huajian ji* preface

Ouyang Xiu, 75, 82–83
Owen, Stephen, 32, 33–34*n*37, 38*n*46, 127, 273–74

painting, 8, 102–4, 313
pairs: of birds, 235, 236; of lyrics, 293–94, 316; of objects, 324; in "Pusa man," 199
"palace lyrics" (*gong ci*), 38, 92–93, 104–5
palace plaints (*gong yuan*), 37–41
"palace-style" poetry, 11, 36–42, 124, 156, 214, 223; male voice in, 264–65
palace women, 92–93, 101–2, 124, 156, 317–18
parallelism: in "Huanxi sha," 244, 245, 258; in "Jiu quanzi," 235, 237, 242; in "Pusa man," 187, 192, 203, 205, 208
parallel prose, 145, 149
parataxis, 164, 181
party songs, 215
patterning (*wen*), 161–62
Pei Zije, 144
pentametric verse forms, 127, 167, 294
performance, 3, 11, 166, 189, 214; artifice and, 154; in court settings, 90–91, 269, 275; demands of, 174; lyric pairs and, 294; mood and, 46; of *quzi ci*, 7, 21, 25–28, 54, 164, 272–73
perspective, *see* voice
Picken, Lawrence, 28, 58–59*n*86
poetry and poets, 29, 67, 115, 168, 187, 349; capital, 140; conventions of, 223; as currency, 170; dialogues between, 11, 249, 320, 356; elite *vs.* folk, 162; herme-

neutics of, 352–53, 355; liminality in, 360; manuals, 4; monks as, 97, 128, 132, 140, 147; as predecessors of *Huajian ji*, 357; separation theme in, 189, 273; structure of, 49, 167, 174, 356; women as, 92, 101–2, 104–5, 132, 140, 147. *See also* Shu poetry; Tang poetry; *specific poets by name*

point of view, 194, 221, 223, 246. *See also* voice

popular entertainment, 7, 44, 57, 64, 177, 244; *quzi ci* in, 23, 25–26, 60–61

popular song, 1, 39, 46, 68, 162, 342; voice in, 277, 357–58

power balance, in love affairs, 176, 217, 275–76; goddess encounters and, 176, 258, 283, 285, 286, 290–91

prefaces, 8, 9–10, 14, 58, 119, 120; to *Caidiao ji*, 120–21, 133, 143–46, 148, 154; to *Odes*, 349; of Tang anthologies, 121–22, 127, 131, 133–39, 153–54; to *Youxuan ji*, 120–21, 132, 133–39, 141; to *Yutai xinyong*, 154. *See also Huajian ji* preface

preservation, of literature, 57, 61–62, 64, 102, 110

privacy, 194, 211, 262. *See also* boudoir

prostitutes, 317–18. *See also* courtesans; female entertainers

"Pusa man," 11, 186–218, 256; abandoned women in, 175, 190, 192, 202, 213, 216; boudoir setting in, 190, 192–94, 199, 202, 206–8, 211; *carpe diem* sentiments in, 196, 214–15; colloquial language in, 196, 201, 215, 220–21, 222; concealment in, 189, 202, 213; dreams in, 195, 198, 204, 205, 224; emotions in, 193, 199, 210; eroticism of, 183, 184*n*40, 188, 208, 211–17, 225; "Huanxi sha" compared, 245–46, 247; liminality in, 189–91, 202–5, 208, 210, 211, 224; natural imagery in, 188, 189, 190, 204, 207–10; parallelism in, 187, 192, 203, 205; poets with lyrics to (list), 187; separation theme in, 189–90, 199–200, 202–3, 206, 211; style in, 178–79, 181–82; voyeurism in, 12, 178, 211, 213–14, 216, 225. *See also specific poets by name*

Qian Qi, 128, 140
Qian Shu shi, 73
qiao, see artifice
Qin Luofu, 37
Qin Qing, 154
qing, see emotions; feeling
Qing dynasty, 3, 49, 75, 176, 347–50, 354–55; literary history in, 349–50, 360–61
"Qingping yue," 45
"Qin Huai" (Du Mu), 140
Qiong yao ji (Li Xun), 142
Quan Tang wen, 102
Quan Tang Wudai ci, 53–57
Quan Wudai shi, 102, 146*n*71
quatrains, 37–42, 95, 127–28, 170, 187, 244; heptametric, 44, 52, 59*n*87; isometric, 58, 60, 147–48; palace, 41–42; regulated, 147–48; series, 169

quotation, 220, 273. *See also* borrowing; imitation

quzi ci (song lyrics), 18, 24*n*15, 51, 96, 282, 304; characteristics of, 163; classification of, 49; definition of, 47–48, 53; as genre, 4, 62, 157, 163, 280, 347; origins of, 28–30, 50; preservation of, 47, 62, 110; Tang poetry as predecessor of, 3, 39, 118, 163–64, 228, 357; *yuefu* and, 51–53, 167–68. *See also ci;* composition; *specific tune titles*

rank of *Huajian ji* poets, 112–15
regional distinctiveness, 69, 281
regulated verse, 127–28, 135*n*45, 140, 147–48, 202; characteristics of, 187, 196–97
religious practice, 283–84. *See also* Daoism
Ren Bantang, 50–51, 57, 95
Renjian cihua (Wang Guowei), 181, 355
repetition, 208–9, 296, 322, 347; echo, 203, 266, 269
reserve (*hanxu*), 224, 241
rhapsodies (*fu*), 67, 300, 309, 310, 313, 358
rhetorical structures, 10–11, 163, 174, 356; in "Nü guanzi," 328, 329–30; questions, 274–75, 298, 331; of Wen Tingyun, 217, 233
rhyme, 163, 174–75, 187, 258, 294, 315–16; in "Jiu quanzi," 232, 233, 236, 239
riverine goddesses, 279, 285–86, 289, 299; Luo River, 285, 306, 309–10, 312–13. *See also* goddess encounters
"River Tune of the Silver Han," 95

Robinet, Isabelle, 282–83
romance, 35–37, 41, 124–25, 175–76, 218; thematic conventions and, 10, 23, 32–33, 146, 164, 189
Rouzer, Paul, 33, 34–35, 36–37, 47; on Wen Tingyun, 182–84, 188, 193, 220–21
Ruan Zhao, 320–21, 331–32
Rui Tingzhang, 125
rulers, 77*n*18, 98–100, 117–18, 123–25, 127, 151*n*82; as audience, 154; of Chen, 77–78; of Shu, 9, 69, 81–82, 100–106, 117; of Song, 67, 89–90, 102, 106; of Tang, 27, 37, 82, 129, 156, 318. *See also specific rulers by name*

Samei, Maija, 276
Sanjiao zhuying, 123
scene, *see* setting/scene
Schafer, Edward, 13, 172, 281–82, 303, 315, 340; "Nü guanzi" and, 321–22
seasonal imagery, 128, 175; autumn, 266, 268; in "Huanxi sha," 247, 266, 268; in "Pusa man," 188, 189, 190, 204; spring, 204, 235. *See also* natural imagery
separation of lovers, 43, 239, 241, 273, 277; abandoned male and, 313–14, 336, 358; in "Huanxi sha," 253–54, 256, 258, 266; in "Pusa man," 189–90, 199–200, 202–3, 206, 211. *See also* abandoned women
separatism, 72, 75, 76
sequence, within tune titles, 228, 243, 266
setting/scene (*jing*), 11, 12, 188, 203, 241, 290; in "Huanxi sha," 245,

261, 268; in "Nü guanzi," 330–32; shifts in, 169; in Tang poetry, 190. *See also* boudoir; natural imagery
sexual encounters, 300; in "Huanxi sha," 262–65; in "Pusa man," 211–13, 215–17. *See also* eroticism; goddess encounters
Shafer, Edward, 13, 172, 181–82, 303, 321–22, 340; "The Capeline Cantos," 315
Shamanka Mountain goddess, 281, 285, 287, 305–9; King Xiang of Chu and, 299–300, 302
"Shamanka Mountain Is High," 300, 304
Shang Yang, 145
Shen Gua, 61
"Shengsheng man," 357
sheng shi, 50–51, 59
shi, *see* literati
Shiguo chunqiu, 75–76, 83–84, 93, 103, 111, 142
shi poetry, *see* poetry and poets
Shishuo xinyu, 249
Shu, kingdom of, 117–18, 275, 345–46, 347, 348, 360; beginning of, 78, 81–83; fall of, 67, 73, 78, 92n53, 96, 111; Former, 13, 77–78, 90–96, 117; Latter, 8–9, 69, 71, 101–6; rulers of, 89–90, 100–106, 112, 117, 293. *See also* Chengdu
—court, 77–90, 88, 117–18, 141; corruption of, 93–95; culture of, 7–8, 10, 22, 69, 87, 177; decadence of, 8–9, 68, 77–78, 117, 157, 176; heterogeneity of, 85–86, 115; literati in, 8, 70, 71, 85, 102, 115; performance in, 90–91, 100, 106;

tastes of, 9, 67, 120, 146. *See also* Chengdu; courtesans
—poetry, 106, 165, 177, 205, 335, 342–43; craft of, 197; as departure from Tang poetry, 173–74; political context of, 8, 9, 71, 78, 79, 111; popular song and, 177; rulers of, 9, 69, 81–82, 100–106, 117; in Tang court, 96–99; Wen Tingyun and, 153, 162, 184–85, 186, 218, 270. *See also* poetry and poets
shuangdie, 167
Shuguo wenying (Liu Zan), 142
Shu jian, 73–74, 74n11
Shun (emperor), 306
Shu Taowu, 73–74, 87–88, 93, 95, 100n78
Sichuan province, 81, 87, 115, 140–41; Shannan circuit, 184–85; Song conquest of, 69, 71
Sikong Tu, 20n8, 56, 58
Siku quanshu zongmu tiyao, 114, 146n70
Sima Guang, 89n47; *Zizhi tongjian*, 75, 83, 89, 93, 95, 97
simurghs, 279, 299
singing and singers, 46, 90, 93, 100, 106; of Ying, 116. *See also* performance
singing girls, 19n5, 64, 68, 287, 288, 289. *See also* courtesans; female entertainers
single-stanza forms, 23, 167
Six Dynasties era, Daoism in, 295
Song dynasty, 20–21, 49, 74, 111, 174; *cihua* of, 348; conquest of Sichuan province, 69, 71; historians, 67–68, 72, 74, 76, 79, 101; influence of *Huajian ji* in, 13, 62, 164, 347–48; invasion of Shu by,

111; literati, 29, 51, 176; poetry, 58, 139, 281; rulers of, 67, 89–90, 102, 106. *See also ci*
song lyrics, *see quzi ci*
Song shi, 73n10, 74
Song Yu, 116, 150–51n77, 154; "Rhapsody on Gaotang," 300
sorrow (*chou*), 34n37, 241, 357
Southern Dynasties, 77–78, 223, 264–65; evoked in *Huajian ji* preface, 149, 150, 153; history of, 8, 78–79, 90, 93; lyrics of, 14, 151n79; poetry of, 36–37, 124, 188. *See also* "palace-style" poetry
"Spring Feelings" (*chun qing*), 38
spring imagery, 204, 235. *See also* seasonal imagery
"Spring Plaint" (*chun yuan*), 38, 40–41
stanzas, 60n88; *huantou*, 169, 356; in "Jiu quanzi," 232, 233; parallelism in, 187, 192; shifts in, 164, 169, 174, 194–95, 217
stock imagery, 195, 206, 226, 291, 359
stock themes, 42–43, 146
structures, metrical, *see* metrical structures
subjectivity, *see* voice
Sun Guangxian, 74, 113, 115, 186, 187, 317; "Huanxi sha," 244; "Jiu quanzi," 231; "Lin jiang xian," 278–79, 295, 298–99, 313
Sun Qi, 34–35, 41, 318–20; "Sent to the Entertainment Girl," 319–20
suyue, 25
synesthetical parallels, 205. *See also* parallelism
syntax, 171, 174–75, 200, 223–24, 246, 261; continuity of, 294, 308;

fragmentation of, 167–68, 179, 202, 232; hypotactic (open) style, 181, 182, 196

"Ta ge ci," 45
"Tale of Yingying" (Yuan Zhen), 41–42
Tang anthologies, 53, 119, 121–41, 148; bibliographies of, 129; exclusions from, 138; prefaces of, 121–22, 127, 131, 133–39, 153–54
Tang dynasty, 68, 110, 115, 119, 183; conquest of Shu, 96; court of, 96–99; cultural trends of, 4, 50, 56, 61, 64, 69; Dali period, 128; decline of, 83; executions of Shu officials in, 99; fall of, 141, 346; Kaiyuan period, 126, 127; literati, 8, 23–24, 44, 46, 82–85; Mingzong, 69; performance in, 7, 21–22, 25–30; popular culture of, 28, 29, 33, 119; *quzi ci* of, 23–25, 29–30, 42, 44–47, 48–51, 54–58; rulers of, 27, 37, 82, 129, 156, 318; Southern, 25, 71, 79, 227, 281; Taizong, 124–25; Tianbao period, 126, 127; Wu (empress), 105n96, 123, 129; Xianzong, 127; Xuanzong, 27, 37, 156, 318; Yuanhe period, 26n18, 128; Zhuangzong, 99. *See also* medieval period
—poetry, 3, 10, 12, 140, 218, 223; *chuanqi*, 273–74; Daoism and, 281, 283–87, 314–15; High, 37–41, 140, 147; Mid and Late, 41, 142; as precedent for Shu lyrics, 21, 39, 157, 163, 228, 357; *quzi ci* and, 227, 280, 289; self-revelation in, 229–30; settings of, 190; Shu

departure from, 173–74; structure in, 294; themes of, 357. *See also* poetry and poets

Tang sheng shi (Ren Bantang), 18*n*4, 26*n*19, 50, 70*n*51

Tang Xianzu, 353–54

"Taohua qu," 43

Ten Kingdoms, 8, 70*n*51, 72, 75, 101*n*81, 121; *quzi ci* in, 50, 53, 62. *See also* Five Dynasties

thematic convention, 172, 340; in "Nü guanzi," 328; of "Pusa man," 188–89, 256. *See also* literary convention; romance

third-person observer, 12, 264, 270, 310, 312. *See also* narrative/narrator

three-character phrases, 232, 235, 237

ti, see forms; genre

Tian Lingci, 81

tianci, 95

time, 164, 175, 189, 197, 205, 357; anachronism, 199; in "Genglouzi," 280; in "Huanxi sha," 251, 255–56, 258, 268, 274; shifts in, 169, 193

titles of *Huajian ji* poets, official, 107–9, 112–15

Todorov, Tzetan, 6

tonal patterns, 163, 174–75, 187

transcendent women, 260, 261, 280, 282, 285, 316; biographies of, 315; in "Lin jiang xian," 298, 301–2; male seeker and, 291, 292; natural imagery and, 292, 302, 310; in "Nü guanzi," 324–26, 328, 334, 336–37; as prostitutes, 317–18; secular contrasted with, 325–26, 328, 342; as singing girls (*xianji*), 287, 288, 289. *See also* Daoist nuns; goddess encounters

transcription, 165

Tuhua jianwen zhi (Guo Ruoxu), 102

tune titles: borrowing within, 173; difference within, 176; lyrics preservation and, 61–62; sequence within, 228, 243, 266. *See also specific titles*

Turner, Victor, 189

Turquoise Lady, 305, 308

two-stanza form, 23, 49, 164–67, 356

van Gennep, Arnold, 189

Verellen, Franciscus, 71*n*7, 78*n*19, 83

Veritable Records (*shilu*), 73, 74*n*11, 101

vernacular language, 163, 171, 177, 216, 350, 360. *See also* colloquial language

voice, 12, 175, 221–24, 242, 270–71, 357–58; ambiguity of, 194, 222–24; anonymous, 42, 221–23, 230; gender-neutral, 180, 238, 245, 248, 250, 261–62; in "Huanxi sha," 258; in "Jiu quanzi," 234, 236, 240, 242; juxtaposition of male and female, 228–29, 236, 242, 245; in "Lin jiang xian," 301, 304–5; in literary history, 359; performance and, 272–73; in *shi* poetry, 170, 226, 229, 270, 277; shifts in, 164, 169, 181, 203, 246, 270–71; subjectivity and, 11, 12, 270, 290; syntax and, 223–24; time and, 251. *See also* female voice; first-person voice; male voice voyeurism, 193–94, 213–14, 223; in "Huanxi sha," 247–48, 262, 264, 341–42; in "Pusa man," 12, 175, 178, 211, 216, 225; Wen Tingyun and, 242, 270, 325, 357, 358

Wang Changling, 38*n*46, 40*n*51; "Plaint of the Blue Tower," 39–41
Wang Gungwu, 73*n*10, 80
Wang Guowei, 352, 355–56; *Renjian cihua*, 181, 355
Wang Jian, 73, 79, 115, 141, 177, 184; Daoism and, 289; rule of, 69–70, 81–84, 87–89, 88–89, 98; tomb of, 90–91
Wang Shizhen (Ming), 352; *Caotang shiyu*, 354
Wang Shizhen (Qing): *Hua Cao mengshi*, 354–55
Wang Wei, 128, 140, 146
Wang Xianzhi, 81
Wang Ya: *Hanlin geci*, 61
Wang Yan, 61, 79, 89, 90, 142, 353; decadence and, 91–92, 94, 96; Meng Chang compared, 100–101; poetry of, 93, 95; rule of, 69, 98; *Yanhua ji*, 93, 142
Wang Zhuo, 350
wanyue style, 350, 358
Warring States, 116, 138
Wei Chengban, 107–8, 109*n*103, 113, 115; "Pusa man," 186, 187, 211–14, 262
Wei Hu, 42, 121, 133, 145–48, 154; as Shu official, 9, 142–43. *See also Caidiao ji*
Wei poets, 117, 309
Wei Zhuang, 9–10, 110, 115, 122, 142, 146, 227; as compiler, 133, 137, 144–45, 147; criticism and, 354–55; "Huanxi sha," 244, 246–52, 254, 255, 268–71, 274; "Jiu quanzi," 231; "Lament of the Lady of Qin," 251; in literary history, 120–21, 122, 185, 186, 187; "Nü guanzi," 317, 323; "Pusa man," 176–77, 179–82, 200–201, 211, 218, 220; as Shu official, 84, 87–88, 90, 108, 113, 141; structure of, 49, 171, 181, 182, 196, 251; style of, 179–80, 196–97, 214–15, 216–17, 218, 221–22; versatility of, 249, 251. *See also Youxuan ji*
Wen Tingyun, 56, 145, 146, 195, 203, 209; biography of, 113–14, 184, 227; criticism and, 354–55; descriptive technique of, 183, 188, 193, 195, 217, 327; "Genglouzi," 30–32; *Huajian ji* and, 11, 164, 168, 171, 176–77; "Huanxi sha," 246; imagery of, 224–25; imitators of, 220–21, 227–28, 254–55, 257, 270; "Jiu quanzi," 231, 233–39, 241–42; in literary history, 349–50; "Nü guanzi," 316, 317, 323, 325–29; structure and, 49, 59, 179, 202, 232; style of, 12, 183, 226, 235, 276, 327; transcendence tropes and, 342; voyeurism and, 63, 65, 242, 270, 325, 357, 358; Wen Xian, son of, 184; Wen Yi, grandson of, 184–85; *yuefu* and, 185*n*44, 188, 214. *See also* "Pusa man"
Wensi boyao, 123, 129
Wenxin diaolong (Liu Xie), 4
Wen xuan (Xiao Tong), 5, 9, 36, 114, 138, 300; as model anthology, 123–24

wine, 213, 238. *See also* drunkenness
wit, 169, 171, 273
Wolan ji (Han Wo), 184
woman's chamber, *see* boudoir
women, *see* abandoned women; *under* female; palace women
women, as goddesses, *see* goddess encounters
women, transcendent, *see* transcendent women
women poets, 92, 101–2, 104–5, 132, 140, 147
Wu Renchen: *Shiguo chunqiu*, 75–76, 83–84, 93, 103, 111, 142
Wu Zhaoyi, 101
Wudai shi shi (Ouyang Xiu), 75
Wuguo gushi, 74
Wu shan, goddess of, 285
"Wushan yiduan xia," 281, 293, 303

Xiang, King of Chu, 299–302, 305, 308, 331
Xiang River goddess, 285, 306
Xiao Shi, 311–13
Xiao Tong, 138
xiaoling lyrics, 165–66, 168–69, 245, 356
Xie An, 249
Xie Tiao, 136
"Xihe jianqi," 45
Xikun chouchang ji, 182
Xin Tang shu, 24, 129
Xin Wudai shi, 75, 78n19, 82–83, 100n79
Xiwang Mu (goddess), 150n76, 154, 285
Xizong (Tang emperor), 81
Xu Hun, 146
Xu Ling, 36, 124, 153, 154, 156
Xuanhua Park (Chengdu), 91, 353

Xue Neng, 19–20, 33, 48, 56, 58, 360; willow trope and, 19, 43; "Yangliu zhi," 279–80
Xue Tao, 140
Xue Zhaoyun, 113; "Huanxi sha," 244, 252–57, 268, 274, 292; "Nü guanzi," 317, 323, 336–40

Yan Jinxiong, 282
Yan Xuan, 107, 108, 113, 303–4; "Huanxi sha," 244; "Lin jiang xian," 295, 299–309
Yang (Sui emperor), 78
Yang Haiming: *Tang Song ci lun gao*, 349
Yang Xiong, 144
"Yangliu zhi," 17–20, 43–46, 58–60, 95–96, 147–48, 227; of Xue Neng, 279–80
Yangzhou, 26
Yanhua ji (Wang Yan), 93, 142
yanyue, 25
Yao He: *Jixuan ji*, 126–27, 128, 131, 132, 133, 138, 140
Yates, Robin, 87n40, 88
Ye Jiaying, 181, 184, 193
Yellow Tumulus, 305–6
"Yi Chang'an," 44
"Yi Jiangnan," 44–47, 59
Yi Jing, 20n8, 55; "Wang Jiangnan," 55
"Yi qi ling," 45, 59
Yin E, 107, 108, 109, 113, 186, 187; "Lin jiang xian," 295
Yin Fan, 125, 126
"Yin Qin E," 43
Ying, singers of, 116
yisheng tianci, 58
Yongcheng jixian lu (Du Guangting), 287

yongwu shi, 37
You ming lu, 320
Youxuan ji, 9–10, 120, 122, 140, 142, 145; compilation of, 131–32; exclusions from, 132; as model anthology, 141, 148; preface to, 133–39
Yu, Pauline, 4–5, 68*n*6, 119, 125, 132–33, 349
Yu Xuanji, 140
Yuan Gong, 97; "Grieving over the Fall of the Kingdom," 97
Yuan Jie: *Qiezhong ji*, 125, 126, 127, 128
Yuan Weide, 103
Yuan Zhen, 26*n*18, 58, 128, 145–47; "Lianchang Palace Lyric," 140; "Tale of Yingying," 41–42
yuefu, 14, 26, 225, 226, 300, 302; anonymous, 169, 221–22; in *Caidiao ji*, 147; *ci* as deviation from, 353; heterometric verse and, 50; male voice in, 229, 271, 277; *quzi ci* and, 46, 51–53, 167–68; themes in, 36, 41, 44, 124; Wen Tingyun and, 185*n*44, 188, 214
Yuefu shiji (Guo Maoqian), 51, 151*n*79–80
Yuefu zalu, 24
Yulan shi, 21*n*12, 126–28, 131, 133
Yunyao ji, 288

Yutai houji, 125
Yutai xinyong (Xu Ling), 5, 36–37, 121, 123, 150, 156; criticism in, 124–25; preface to, 154

Zhang Bi, 108, 113, 147, 275; "Huanxi sha," 244, 245, 252, 257–62, 267, 269, 275; "Jiu quanzi," 231, 236–38, 242; "Lin jiang xian," 295; "Nü guanzi," 317, 329–32
Zhang Bin, 147
Zhang Huiyan, 227*n*7, 350
Zhang Tangying, 73–74*n*11, 95*n*62
Zhang Yiren, 346
Zhang Zhang, 53, 54
Zhao Chongzuo, 66*n*1, 67, 112, 117
Zhao Tingyun, 112
Zhen gao, 341
"Zhe yangliu," 52
Zhongxing jian qi ji, 126–27
Zhu Wen, 82
"Zhu zhi" song cycle, 59–60, 227, 304
Zhuangzi, 283
Zhuying xueshi ji, 123
Zizhi tongjian (Sima Guang), 75, 83, 89, 93, 95, 97
Zunqian ji, 110, 177, 294, 295, 303, 314–15; compilers of, 347
Zuo zhuan, 155
Zürcher, Erik, 289–90

Harvard East Asian Monographs
(* out-of-print)

*1. Liang Fang-chung, *The Single-Whip Method of Taxation in China*
*2. Harold C. Hinton, *The Grain Tribute System of China, 1845–1911*
 3. Ellsworth C. Carlson, *The Kaiping Mines, 1877–1912*
*4. Chao Kuo-chün, *Agrarian Policies of Mainland China: A Documentary Study, 1949–1956*
*5. Edgar Snow, *Random Notes on Red China, 1936–1945*
*6. Edwin George Beal, Jr., *The Origin of Likin, 1835–1864*
 7. Chao Kuo-chün, *Economic Planning and Organization in Mainland China: A Documentary Study, 1949–1957*
*8. John K. Fairbank, *Ching Documents: An Introductory Syllabus*
*9. Helen Yin and Yi-chang Yin, *Economic Statistics of Mainland China, 1949–1957*
 10. Wolfgang Franke, *The Reform and Abolition of the Traditional Chinese Examination System*
 11. Albert Feuerwerker and S. Cheng, *Chinese Communist Studies of Modern Chinese History*
 12. C. John Stanley, *Late Ching Finance: Hu Kuang-yung as an Innovator*
 13. S. M. Meng, *The Tsungli Yamen: Its Organization and Functions*
*14. Ssu-yü Teng, *Historiography of the Taiping Rebellion*
 15. Chun-Jo Liu, *Controversies in Modern Chinese Intellectual History: An Analytic Bibliography of Periodical Articles, Mainly of the May Fourth and Post-May Fourth Era*
*16. Edward J. M. Rhoads, *The Chinese Red Army, 1927–1963: An Annotated Bibliography*
*17. Andrew J. Nathan, *A History of the China International Famine Relief Commission*

Harvard East Asian Monographs

*18. Frank H. H. King (ed.) and Prescott Clarke, *A Research Guide to China-Coast Newspapers, 1822–1911*

*19. Ellis Joffe, *Party and Army: Professionalism and Political Control in the Chinese Officer Corps, 1949–1964*

*20. Toshio G. Tsukahira, *Feudal Control in Tokugawa Japan: The Sankin Kōtai System*

*21. Kwang-Ching Liu, ed., *American Missionaries in China: Papers from Harvard Seminars*

*22. George Moseley, *A Sino-Soviet Cultural Frontier: The Ili Kazakh Autonomous Chou*

23. Carl F. Nathan, *Plague Prevention and Politics in Manchuria, 1910–1931*

*24. Adrian Arthur Bennett, *John Fryer: The Introduction of Western Science and Technology into Nineteenth-Century China*

*25. Donald J. Friedman, *The Road from Isolation: The Campaign of the American Committee for Non-Participation in Japanese Aggression, 1938–1941*

*26. Edward LeFevour, *Western Enterprise in Late Ching China: A Selective Survey of Jardine, Matheson and Company's Operations, 1842–1895*

27. Charles Neuhauser, *Third World Politics: China and the Afro-Asian People's Solidarity Organization, 1957–1967*

*28. Kungtu C. Sun, assisted by Ralph W. Huenemann, *The Economic Development of Manchuria in the First Half of the Twentieth Century*

*29. Shahid Javed Burki, *A Study of Chinese Communes, 1965*

30. John Carter Vincent, *The Extraterritorial System in China: Final Phase*

31. Madeleine Chi, *China Diplomacy, 1914–1918*

*32. Clifton Jackson Phillips, *Protestant America and the Pagan World: The First Half Century of the American Board of Commissioners for Foreign Missions, 1810–1860*

*33. James Pusey, *Wu Han: Attacking the Present Through the Past*

*34. Ying-wan Cheng, *Postal Communication in China and Its Modernization, 1860–1896*

35. Tuvia Blumenthal, *Saving in Postwar Japan*

36. Peter Frost, *The Bakumatsu Currency Crisis*

37. Stephen C. Lockwood, *Augustine Heard and Company, 1858–1862*

38. Robert R. Campbell, *James Duncan Campbell: A Memoir by His Son*

39. Jerome Alan Cohen, ed., *The Dynamics of China's Foreign Relations*

40. V. V. Vishnyakova-Akimova, *Two Years in Revolutionary China, 1925–1927*, tr. Steven L. Levine

41. Meron Medzini, *French Policy in Japan During the Closing Years of the Tokugawa Regime*

Harvard East Asian Monographs

42. Ezra Vogel, Margie Sargent, Vivienne B. Shue, Thomas Jay Mathews, and Deborah S. Davis, *The Cultural Revolution in the Provinces*
43. Sidney A. Forsythe, *An American Missionary Community in China, 1895–1905*
*44. Benjamin I. Schwartz, ed., *Reflections on the May Fourth Movement.: A Symposium*
*45. Ching Young Choe, *The Rule of the Taewŏngun, 1864–1873: Restoration in Yi Korea*
46. W. P. J. Hall, *A Bibliographical Guide to Japanese Research on the Chinese Economy, 1958–1970*
47. Jack J. Gerson, *Horatio Nelson Lay and Sino-British Relations, 1854–1864*
48. Paul Richard Bohr, *Famine and the Missionary: Timothy Richard as Relief Administrator and Advocate of National Reform*
49. Endymion Wilkinson, *The History of Imperial China: A Research Guide*
50. Britten Dean, *China and Great Britain: The Diplomacy of Commercial Relations, 1860–1864*
51. Ellsworth C. Carlson, *The Foochow Missionaries, 1847–1880*
52. Yeh-chien Wang, *An Estimate of the Land-Tax Collection in China, 1753 and 1908*
53. Richard M. Pfeffer, *Understanding Business Contracts in China, 1949–1963*
*54. Han-sheng Chuan and Richard Kraus, *Mid-Ching Rice Markets and Trade: An Essay in Price History*
55. Ranbir Vohra, *Lao She and the Chinese Revolution*
56. Liang-lin Hsiao, *China's Foreign Trade Statistics, 1864–1949*
*57. Lee-hsia Hsu Ting, *Government Control of the Press in Modern China, 1900–1949*
*58. Edward W. Wagner, *The Literati Purges: Political Conflict in Early Yi Korea*
*59. Joungwon A. Kim, *Divided Korea: The Politics of Development, 1945–1972*
60. Noriko Kamachi, John K. Fairbank, and Chūzō Ichiko, *Japanese Studies of Modern China Since 1953: A Bibliographical Guide to Historical and Social-Science Research on the Nineteenth and Twentieth Centuries, Supplementary Volume for 1953–1969*
61. Donald A. Gibbs and Yun-chen Li, *A Bibliography of Studies and Translations of Modern Chinese Literature, 1918–1942*
62. Robert H. Silin, *Leadership and Values: The Organization of Large-Scale Taiwanese Enterprises*
63. David Pong, *A Critical Guide to the Kwangtung Provincial Archives Deposited at the Public Record Office of London*
*64. Fred W. Drake, *China Charts the World: Hsu Chi-yü and His Geography of 1848*

Harvard East Asian Monographs

- *65. William A. Brown and Urgrunge Onon, translators and annotators, *History of the Mongolian People's Republic*
- 66. Edward L. Farmer, *Early Ming Government: The Evolution of Dual Capitals*
- *67. Ralph C. Croizier, *Koxinga and Chinese Nationalism: History, Myth, and the Hero*
- *68. William J. Tyler, tr., *The Psychological World of Natsume Sōseki*, by Doi Takeo
- 69. Eric Widmer, *The Russian Ecclesiastical Mission in Peking During the Eighteenth Century*
- *70. Charlton M. Lewis, *Prologue to the Chinese Revolution: The Transformation of Ideas and Institutions in Hunan Province, 1891–1907*
- 71. Preston Torbert, *The Ching Imperial Household Department: A Study of Its Organization and Principal Functions, 1662–1796*
- 72. Paul A. Cohen and John E. Schrecker, eds., *Reform in Nineteenth-Century China*
- 73. Jon Sigurdson, *Rural Industrialism in China*
- 74. Kang Chao, *The Development of Cotton Textile Production in China*
- 75. Valentin Rabe, *The Home Base of American China Missions, 1880–1920*
- *76. Sarasin Viraphol, *Tribute and Profit: Sino-Siamese Trade, 1652–1853*
- 77. Ch'i-ch'ing Hsiao, *The Military Establishment of the Yuan Dynasty*
- 78. Meishi Tsai, *Contemporary Chinese Novels and Short Stories, 1949–1974: An Annotated Bibliography*
- *79. Wellington K. K. Chan, *Merchants, Mandarins and Modern Enterprise in Late Ching China*
- 80. Endymion Wilkinson, *Landlord and Labor in Late Imperial China: Case Studies from Shandong by Jing Su and Luo Lun*
- *81. Barry Keenan, *The Dewey Experiment in China: Educational Reform and Political Power in the Early Republic*
- *82. George A. Hayden, *Crime and Punishment in Medieval Chinese Drama: Three Judge Pao Plays*
- *83. Sang-Chul Suh, *Growth and Structural Changes in the Korean Economy, 1910–1940*
- 84. J. W. Dower, *Empire and Aftermath: Yoshida Shigeru and the Japanese Experience, 1878–1954*
- 85. Martin Collcutt, *Five Mountains: The Rinzai Zen Monastic Institution in Medieval Japan*
- 86. Kwang Suk Kim and Michael Roemer, *Growth and Structural Transformation*
- 87. Anne O. Krueger, *The Developmental Role of the Foreign Sector and Aid*
- *88. Edwin S. Mills and Byung-Nak Song, *Urbanization and Urban Problems*

Harvard East Asian Monographs

89. Sung Hwan Ban, Pal Yong Moon, and Dwight H. Perkins, *Rural Development*
*90. Noel F. McGinn, Donald R. Snodgrass, Yung Bong Kim, Shin-Bok Kim, and Quee-Young Kim, *Education and Development in Korea*
*91. Leroy P. Jones and Il SaKong, *Government, Business, and Entrepreneurship in Economic Development: The Korean Case*
92. Edward S. Mason, Dwight H. Perkins, Kwang Suk Kim, David C. Cole, Mahn Je Kim et al., *The Economic and Social Modernization of the Republic of Korea*
93. Robert Repetto, Tai Hwan Kwon, Son-Ung Kim, Dae Young Kim, John E. Sloboda, and Peter J. Donaldson, *Economic Development, Population Policy, and Demographic Transition in the Republic of Korea*
94. Parks M. Coble, Jr., *The Shanghai Capitalists and the Nationalist Government, 1927–1937*
95. Noriko Kamachi, *Reform in China: Huang Tsun-hsien and the Japanese Model*
96. Richard Wich, *Sino-Soviet Crisis Politics: A Study of Political Change and Communication*
97. Lillian M. Li, *China's Silk Trade: Traditional Industry in the Modern World, 1842–1937*
98. R. David Arkush, *Fei Xiaotong and Sociology in Revolutionary China*
*99. Kenneth Alan Grossberg, *Japan's Renaissance: The Politics of the Muromachi Bakufu*
100. James Reeve Pusey, *China and Charles Darwin*
101. Hoyt Cleveland Tillman, *Utilitarian Confucianism: Chen Liang's Challenge to Chu Hsi*
102. Thomas A. Stanley, *Ōsugi Sakae, Anarchist in Taishō Japan: The Creativity of the Ego*
103. Jonathan K. Ocko, *Bureaucratic Reform in Provincial China: Ting Jih-ch'ang in Restoration Kiangsu, 1867–1870*
104. James Reed, *The Missionary Mind and American East Asia Policy, 1911–1915*
105. Neil L. Waters, *Japan's Local Pragmatists: The Transition from Bakumatsu to Meiji in the Kawasaki Region*
106. David C. Cole and Yung Chul Park, *Financial Development in Korea, 1945–1978*
107. Roy Bahl, Chuk Kyo Kim, and Chong Kee Park, *Public Finances During the Korean Modernization Process*
108. William D. Wray, *Mitsubishi and the N.Y.K, 1870–1914: Business Strategy in the Japanese Shipping Industry*

Harvard East Asian Monographs

109. Ralph William Huenemann, *The Dragon and the Iron Horse: The Economics of Railroads in China, 1876–1937*
*110. Benjamin A. Elman, *From Philosophy to Philology: Intellectual and Social Aspects of Change in Late Imperial China*
111. Jane Kate Leonard, *Wei Yüan and China's Rediscovery of the Maritime World*
112. Luke S. K. Kwong, *A Mosaic of the Hundred Days:. Personalities, Politics, and Ideas of 1898*
*113. John E. Wills, Jr., *Embassies and Illusions: Dutch and Portuguese Envoys to K'ang-hsi, 1666–1687*
114. Joshua A. Fogel, *Politics and Sinology: The Case of Naitō Konan (1866–1934)*
*115. Jeffrey C. Kinkley, ed., *After Mao: Chinese Literature and Society, 1978–1981*
116. C. Andrew Gerstle, *Circles of Fantasy: Convention in the Plays of Chikamatsu*
117. Andrew Gordon, *The Evolution of Labor Relations in Japan: Heavy Industry, 1853–1955*
*118. Daniel K. Gardner, *Chu Hsi and the "Ta Hsueh": Neo-Confucian Reflection on the Confucian Canon*
119. Christine Guth Kanda, *Shinzō: Hachiman Imagery and Its Development*
*120. Robert Borgen, *Sugawara no Michizane and the Early Heian Court*
121. Chang-tai Hung, *Going to the People: Chinese Intellectual and Folk Literature, 1918–1937*
*122. Michael A. Cusumano, *The Japanese Automobile Industry: Technology and Management at Nissan and Toyota*
123. Richard von Glahn, *The Country of Streams and Grottoes: Expansion, Settlement, and the Civilizing of the Sichuan Frontier in Song Times*
124. Steven D. Carter, *The Road to Komatsubara: A Classical Reading of the Renga Hyakuin*
125. Katherine F. Bruner, John K. Fairbank, and Richard T. Smith, *Entering China's Service: Robert Hart's Journals, 1854–1863*
126. Bob Tadashi Wakabayashi, *Anti-Foreignism and Western Learning in Early-Modern Japan: The "New Theses" of 1825*
127. Atsuko Hirai, *Individualism and Socialism: The Life and Thought of Kawai Eijirō (1891–1944)*
128. Ellen Widmer, *The Margins of Utopia: "Shui-hu hou-chuan" and the Literature of Ming Loyalism*
129. R. Kent Guy, *The Emperor's Four Treasuries: Scholars and the State in the Late Chien-lung Era*
130. Peter C. Perdue, *Exhausting the Earth: State and Peasant in Hunan, 1500–1850*

Harvard East Asian Monographs

131. Susan Chan Egan, *A Latterday Confucian: Reminiscences of William Hung (1893–1980)*
132. James T. C. Liu, *China Turning Inward: Intellectual-Political Changes in the Early Twelfth Century*
*133. Paul A. Cohen, *Between Tradition and Modernity: Wang T'ao and Reform in Late Ching China*
134. Kate Wildman Nakai, *Shogunal Politics: Arai Hakuseki and the Premises of Tokugawa Rule*
*135. Parks M. Coble, *Facing Japan: Chinese Politics and Japanese Imperialism, 1931–1937*
136. Jon L. Saari, *Legacies of Childhood: Growing Up Chinese in a Time of Crisis, 1890–1920*
137. Susan Downing Videen, *Tales of Heichū*
138. Heinz Morioka and Miyoko Sasaki, *Rakugo: The Popular Narrative Art of Japan*
139. Joshua A. Fogel, *Nakae Ushikichi in China: The Mourning of Spirit*
140. Alexander Barton Woodside, *Vietnam and the Chinese Model.: A Comparative Study of Vietnamese and Chinese Government in the First Half of the Nineteenth Century*
*141. George Elison, *Deus Destroyed: The Image of Christianity in Early Modern Japan*
142. William D. Wray, ed., *Managing Industrial Enterprise: Cases from Japan's Prewar Experience*
*143. T'ung-tsu Ch'ü, *Local Government in China Under the Ching*
144. Marie Anchordoguy, *Computers, Inc.: Japan's Challenge to IBM*
145. Barbara Molony, *Technology and Investment: The Prewar Japanese Chemical Industry*
146. Mary Elizabeth Berry, *Hideyoshi*
147. Laura E. Hein, *Fueling Growth: The Energy Revolution and Economic Policy in Postwar Japan*
148. Wen-hsin Yeh, *The Alienated Academy: Culture and Politics in Republican China, 1919–1937*
149. Dru C. Gladney, *Muslim Chinese: Ethnic Nationalism in the People's Republic*
150. Merle Goldman and Paul A. Cohen, eds., *Ideas Across Cultures: Essays on Chinese Thought in Honor of Benjamin L Schwartz*
151. James M. Polachek, *The Inner Opium War*
152. Gail Lee Bernstein, *Japanese Marxist: A Portrait of Kawakami Hajime, 1879–1946*
*153. Lloyd E. Eastman, *The Abortive Revolution: China Under Nationalist Rule, 1927–1937*

Harvard East Asian Monographs

154. Mark Mason, *American Multinationals and Japan: The Political Economy of Japanese Capital Controls, 1899–1980*
155. Richard J. Smith, John K. Fairbank, and Katherine F. Bruner, *Robert Hart and China's Early Modernization: His Journals, 1863–1866*
156. George J. Tanabe, Jr., *Myōe the Dreamkeeper: Fantasy and Knowledge in Kamakura Buddhism*
157. William Wayne Farris, *Heavenly Warriors: The Evolution of Japan's Military, 500–1300*
158. Yu-ming Shaw, *An American Missionary in China: John Leighton Stuart and Chinese-American Relations*
159. James B. Palais, *Politics and Policy in Traditional Korea*
*160. Douglas Reynolds, *China, 1898–1912: The Xinzheng Revolution and Japan*
161. Roger R. Thompson, *China's Local Councils in the Age of Constitutional Reform, 1898–1911*
162. William Johnston, *The Modern Epidemic: History of Tuberculosis in Japan*
163. Constantine Nomikos Vaporis, *Breaking Barriers: Travel and the State in Early Modern Japan*
164. Irmela Hijiya-Kirschnereit, *Rituals of Self-Revelation: Shishōsetsu as Literary Genre and Socio-Cultural Phenomenon*
165. James C. Baxter, *The Meiji Unification Through the Lens of Ishikawa Prefecture*
166. Thomas R. H. Havens, *Architects of Affluence: The Tsutsumi Family and the Seibu-Saison Enterprises in Twentieth-Century Japan*
167. Anthony Hood Chambers, *The Secret Window: Ideal Worlds in Tanizaki's Fiction*
168. Steven J. Ericson, *The Sound of the Whistle: Railroads and the State in Meiji Japan*
169. Andrew Edmund Goble, *Kenmu: Go-Daigo's Revolution*
170. Denise Potrzeba Lett, *In Pursuit of Status: The Making of South Korea's "New" Urban Middle Class*
171. Mimi Hall Yiengpruksawan, *Hiraizumi: Buddhist Art and Regional Politics in Twelfth-Century Japan*
172. Charles Shirō Inouye, *The Similitude of Blossoms: A Critical Biography of Izumi Kyōka (1873–1939), Japanese Novelist and Playwright*
173. Aviad E. Raz, *Riding the Black Ship: Japan and Tokyo Disneyland*
174. Deborah J. Milly, *Poverty, Equality, and Growth: The Politics of Economic Need in Postwar Japan*
175. See Heng Teow, *Japan's Cultural Policy Toward China, 1918–1931: A Comparative Perspective*
176. Michael A. Fuller, *An Introduction to Literary Chinese*

Harvard East Asian Monographs

177. Frederick R. Dickinson, *War and National Reinvention: Japan in the Great War, 1914–1919*
178. John Solt, *Shredding the Tapestry of Meaning: The Poetry and Poetics of Kitasono Katue (1902–1978)*
179. Edward Pratt, *Japan's Protoindustrial Elite: The Economic Foundations of the Gōnō*
180. Atsuko Sakaki, *Recontextualizing Texts: Narrative Performance in Modern Japanese Fiction*
181. Soon-Won Park, *Colonial Industrialization and Labor in Korea: The Onoda Cement Factory*
182. JaHyun Kim Haboush and Martina Deuchler, *Culture and the State in Late Chosŏn Korea*
183. John W. Chaffee, *Branches of Heaven: A History of the Imperial Clan of Sung China*
184. Gi-Wook Shin and Michael Robinson, eds., *Colonial Modernity in Korea*
185. Nam-lin Hur, *Prayer and Play in Late Tokugawa Japan: Asakusa Sensōji and Edo Society*
186. Kristin Stapleton, *Civilizing Chengdu: Chinese Urban Reform, 1895–1937*
187. Hyung Il Pai, *Constructing "Korean" Origins: A Critical Review of Archaeology, Historiography, and Racial Myth in Korean State-Formation Theories*
188. Brian D. Ruppert, *Jewel in the Ashes: Buddha Relics and Power in Early Medieval Japan*
189. Susan Daruvala, *Zhou Zuoren and an Alternative Chinese Response to Modernity*
*190. James Z. Lee, *The Political Economy of a Frontier: Southwest China, 1250–1850*
191. Kerry Smith, *A Time of Crisis: Japan, the Great Depression, and Rural Revitalization*
192. Michael Lewis, *Becoming Apart: National Power and Local Politics in Toyama, 1868–1945*
193. William C. Kirby, Man-houng Lin, James Chin Shih, and David A. Pietz, eds., *State and Economy in Republican China: A Handbook for Scholars*
194. Timothy S. George, *Minamata: Pollution and the Struggle for Democracy in Postwar Japan*
195. Billy K. L. So, *Prosperity, Region, and Institutions in Maritime China: The South Fukien Pattern, 946–1368*
196. Yoshihisa Tak Matsusaka, *The Making of Japanese Manchuria, 1904–1932*
197. Maram Epstein, *Competing Discourses: Orthodoxy, Authenticity, and Engendered Meanings in Late Imperial Chinese Fiction*

Harvard East Asian Monographs

198. Curtis J. Milhaupt, J. Mark Ramseyer, and Michael K. Young, eds. and comps., *Japanese Law in Context: Readings in Society, the Economy, and Politics*
199. Haruo Iguchi, *Unfinished Business: Ayukawa Yoshisuke and U.S.-Japan Relations, 1937–1952*
200. Scott Pearce, Audrey Spiro, and Patricia Ebrey, *Culture and Power in the Reconstitution of the Chinese Realm, 200–600*
201. Terry Kawashima, *Writing Margins: The Textual Construction of Gender in Heian and Kamakura Japan*
202. Martin W. Huang, *Desire and Fictional Narrative in Late Imperial China*
203. Robert S. Ross and Jiang Changbin, eds., *Re-examining the Cold War: U.S.-China Diplomacy, 1954–1973*
204. Guanhua Wang, *In Search of Justice: The 1905–1906 Chinese Anti-American Boycott*
205. David Schaberg, *A Patterned Past: Form and Thought in Early Chinese Historiography*
206. Christine Yano, *Tears of Longing: Nostalgia and the Nation in Japanese Popular Song*
207. Milena Doleželová-Velingerová and Oldřich Král, with Graham Sanders, eds., *The Appropriation of Cultural Capital: China's May Fourth Project*
208. Robert N. Huey, *The Making of 'Shinkokinshū'*
209. Lee Butler, *Emperor and Aristocracy in Japan, 1467–1680: Resilience and Renewal*
210. Suzanne Ogden, *Inklings of Democracy in China*
211. Kenneth J. Ruoff, *The People's Emperor: Democracy and the Japanese Monarchy, 1945–1995*
212. Haun Saussy, *Great Walls of Discourse and Other Adventures in Cultural China*
213. Aviad E. Raz, *Emotions at Work: Normative Control, Organizations, and Culture in Japan and America*
214. Rebecca E. Karl and Peter Zarrow, eds., *Rethinking the 1898 Reform Period: Political and Cultural Change in Late Qing China*
215. Kevin O'Rourke, *The Book of Korean Shijo*
216. Ezra F. Vogel, ed., *The Golden Age of the U.S.-China-Japan Triangle, 1972–1989*
217. Thomas A Wilson, ed., *On Sacred Grounds: Culture, Society, Politics, and the Formation of the Cult of Confucius*
218. Donald S. Sutton, *Steps of Perfection: Exorcistic Performers and Chinese Religion in Twentieth-Century Taiwan*

Harvard East Asian Monographs

219. Daqing Yang, *Technology of Empire: Telecommunications and Japanese Expansionism, 1895–1945*
220. Qianshen Bai, *Fu Shan's World: The Transformation of Chinese Calligraphy in the Seventeenth Century*
221. Paul Jakov Smith and Richard von Glahn, eds., *The Song-Yuan-Ming Transition in Chinese History*
222. Rania Huntington, *Alien Kind: Foxes and Late Imperial Chinese Narrative*
223. Jordan Sand, *House and Home in Modern Japan: Architecture, Domestic Space, and Bourgeois Culture, 1880–1930*
224. Karl Gerth, *China Made: Consumer Culture and the Creation of the Nation*
225. Xiaoshan Yang, *Metamorphosis of the Private Sphere: Gardens and Objects in Tang-Song Poetry*
226. Barbara Mittler, *A Newspaper for China? Power, Identity, and Change in Shanghai's News Media, 1872–1912*
227. Joyce A. Madancy, *The Troublesome Legacy of Commissioner Lin: The Opium Trade and Opium Suppression in Fujian Province, 1820s to 1920s*
228. John Makeham, *Transmitters and Creators: Chinese Commentators and Commentaries on the Analects*
229. Elisabeth Köll, *From Cotton Mill to Business Empire: The Emergence of Regional Enterprises in Modern China*
230. Emma Teng, *Taiwan's Imagined Geography: Chinese Colonial Travel Writing and Pictures, 1683–1895*
231. Wilt Idema and Beata Grant, *The Red Brush: Writing Women of Imperial China*
232. Eric C. Rath, *The Ethos of Noh: Actors and Their Art*
233. Elizabeth Remick, *Building Local States: China During the Republican and Post-Mao Eras*
234. Lynn Struve, ed., *The Qing Formation in World-Historical Time*
235. D. Max Moerman, *Localizing Paradise: Kumano Pilgrimage and the Religious Landscape of Premodern Japan*
236. Antonia Finnane, *Speaking of Yangzhou: A Chinese City, 1550–1850*
237. Brian Platt, *Burning and Building: Schooling and State Formation in Japan, 1750–1890*
238. Gail Bernstein, Andrew Gordon, and Kate Wildman Nakai, eds., *Public Spheres, Private Lives in Modern Japan, 1600–1950: Essays in Honor of Albert Craig*
239. Wu Hung and Katherine R. Tsiang, *Body and Face in Chinese Visual Culture*
240. Stephen Dodd, *Writing Home: Representations of the Native Place in Modern Japanese Literature*

Harvard East Asian Monographs

241. David Anthony Bello, *Opium and the Limits of Empire: Drug Prohibition in the Chinese Interior, 1729–1850*
242. Hosea Hirata, *Discourses of Seduction: History, Evil, Desire, and Modern Japanese Literature*
243. Kyung Moon Hwang, *Beyond Birth: Social Status in the Emergence of Modern Korea*
244. Brian R. Dott, *Identity Reflections: Pilgrimages to Mount Tai in Late Imperial China*
245. Mark McNally, *Proving the Way: Conflict and Practice in the History of Japanese Nativism*
246. Yongping Wu, *A Political Explanation of Economic Growth: State Survival, Bureaucratic Politics, and Private Enterprises in the Making of Taiwan's Economy, 1950–1985*
247. Kyu Hyun Kim, *The Age of Visions and Arguments: Parliamentarianism and the National Public Sphere in Early Meiji Japan*
248. Zvi Ben-Dor Benite, *The Dao of Muhammad: A Cultural History of Muslims in Late Imperial China*
249. David Der-wei Wang and Shang Wei, eds., *Dynastic Crisis and Cultural Innovation: From the Late Ming to the Late Qing and Beyond*
250. Wilt L. Idema, Wai-yee Li, and Ellen Widmer, eds., *Trauma and Transcendence in Early Qing Literature*
251. Barbara Molony and Kathleen Uno, eds., *Gendering Modern Japanese History*
252. Hiroshi Aoyagi, *Islands of Eight Million Smiles: Idol Performance and Symbolic Production in Contemporary Japan*
253. Wai-yee Li, *The Readability of the Past in Early Chinese Historiography*
254. William C. Kirby, Robert S. Ross, and Gong Li, eds., *Normalization of U.S.-China Relations: An International History*
255. Ellen Gardner Nakamura, *Practical Pursuits: Takano Chōei, Takahashi Keisaku, and Western Medicine in Nineteenth-Century Japan*
256. Jonathan W. Best, *A History of the Early Korean Kingdom of Paekche, together with an annotated translation of* The Paekche Annals *of the* Samguk sagi
257. Liang Pan, *The United Nations in Japan's Foreign and Security Policymaking, 1945–1992: National Security, Party Politics, and International Status*
258. Richard Belsky, *Localities at the Center: Native Place, Space, and Power in Late Imperial Beijing*
259. Zwia Lipkin, *"Useless to the State": "Social Problems" and Social Engineering in Nationalist Nanjing, 1927–1937*
260. William O. Gardner, *Advertising Tower: Japanese Modernism and Modernity in the 1920s*

Harvard East Asian Monographs

261. Stephen Owen, *The Making of Early Chinese Classical Poetry*
262. Martin J. Powers, *Pattern and Person: Ornament, Society, and Self in Classical China*
263. Anna M. Shields, *Crafting a Collection: The Cultural Contexts and Poetic Practice of the* Huajian ji 花間集 (*Collection from among the flowers*)